NEW MEXICO IN MAPS

NEW MEXICO IN MAPS

EDITED BY
JERRY L. WILLIAMS
AND
PAUL E. MCALLISTER

UNIVERSITY OF NEW MEXICO PRESS
ALBUQUERQUE

Library of Congress Cataloging in Publication Data
Main entry under title:

New Mexico in maps.

Bibliography: p.
Includes index.
1. New Mexico—Maps. 2. New Mexico—Economic conditions—Maps. 3. New Mexico—Historical geography—Maps. 4. New Mexico—Social conditions—Maps. I. Williams, Jerry L. II. McAllister, Paul E.

G1505.N4 1981 912′.789 81-675344
ISBN 0-8263-0601-2 AACR2

 International Standard Book Number 0-82
0601-2. Library of Congress Catalog Card Num
81-675344.

*This book is dedicated to
the wives and children
who sacrificed time and
patience while we prepared
this book.*

*To Shirley with Amy and Brian
and
To Carol with Andy*

acknowledgments

Thanks are due to the staff of the Technology Application Center, University of New Mexico, for their work in producing the original edition of this book. Michael Inglis, production coordinator, Elaine Faust, cartographer, and Amelia Budge, text editor, deserve special appreciation. The cartographic staff—Denise Glore, Lisa Turano, Bruce Kofron, and John Cochran—and the editorial staff—Ellen Seusy, Lynn Price, and Shirley Williams—also did fine work, as did the clerical staff—Julie Trollinger, Viola Baca, and Chris Poor.

We would like to express our appreciation to Ron Berg, Jim Cheek, Willie McKenzie, Tom Payne, Rudy A. Rodriguez, Bob Rollins, and Dave Spear of the University of New Mexico Printing Plant, for their patience and guidance during this project.

table of contents

contributors

Don Anderson
Engineer
Environmental Health Agency
City of Albuquerque

Thomas K. Budge
Remote Sensing Specialist
Technology Application Center
University of New Mexico

Michael T. Byrnes
Director, Program Administration
National Energy Information Center Affiliate
University of New Mexico

J. F. Callender
Associate Professor
Department of Geology
University of New Mexico

Leo Carbajal
Economist
Bureau of Business and Economic Research
University of New Mexico

Linda Cordell
Associate Professor
Department of Anthropology
University of New Mexico

Donald Cutter
Professor
Department of History
University of New Mexico

Bill Eisenhood
Meteorologist
KOB-TV
Albuquerque, New Mexico

Denise Glore
Graduate Student
Department of Biology
University of New Mexico

Jerome Hall
Associate Professor
Civil Engineering
University of New Mexico

Michael Inglis
Division Manager
Technology Application Center
University of New Mexico

Byron B. King
Counselor
Southwest Community Mental Health Center
Las Cruces, New Mexico

Barry Kues
Assistant Professor
Department of Geology
University of New Mexico

Paul McAllister
Analyst
Department of the Air Force
Albert F. Simpson Historical Research Center
Montgomery, Alabama

Stan Morain
Associate Professor
Department of Geography
University of New Mexico

Howard Morgan
Weatherman
KOAT-TV
Albuquerque, New Mexico

Glen Robertson
Assistant Professor
Department of History
Fort Lewis College
Durango, Colorado

Richard G. Rogers
Statistician
New Mexico Tumor Registry
University of New Mexico

Stephen Sayles
Assistant Professor
Department of History and Social Sciences
New Mexico Military Institute
Roswell, New Mexico

Kim Seidler
Graduate Student
Department of Geography
University of New Mexico

Karleene Smith
Teaching Assistant
Department of Geography
University of New Mexico

Rodman E. Snead
Professor
Department of Geography
University of New Mexico

Gordon Venable
Graduate Student
Department of Biology
Law Student, Law School
University of New Mexico

Jerry L. Williams
Assistant Professor
Department of Geography
University of New Mexico

Lynn Wombold
Demographer
Bureau of Business and Economic Research
University of New Mexico

Leo Yates
Family Life Specialist
Cooperative Extension Service
New Mexico State University
Las Cruces, New Mexico

preface

New Mexico presents a varied and colorful picture to all of us. Some of us are spellbound by its scenery while others strive to touch base with the vestiges of history that cover the landscape. The many cultures within one setting have long been a major attraction to New Mexico, and the twentieth century national demand for resources has provided the continuing economic incentives for assuring a steady flow of immigrants. *New Mexico in Maps* is intended for all of those who use the state. For the new arrivals with a curiosity about what is located in their environment, the book provides the first comprehensive overview of New Mexico. For the old timers with their own mental atlas of New Mexico, these maps recall the way things were and update the way things are.

New Mexico in Maps is the product of several years of research about this land of enchantment. The frustrations of touring the countryside without a guide motivated such a general text. Much reference material did exist throughout New Mexico, but little of it had been mapped or presented in a general multitopical format. The preliminary assumption that we made when the atlas was in its formative stages was that most of the maps we would use for the book had already been compiled. Our task would simply involve collecting and editing the loose assortment of maps and texts so that they would be suitable for a general audience. However, outside of the *Historical Atlas of New Mexico* by Beck and Haase, there were few general maps of the state. Most were of a highly technical nature that would provide sound data but would require remapping. This left us with the realization that although we would have to start from scratch, we would also have the flexibility to include a number of topics of more specific interest to New Mexicans.

We selected two state atlases as quality models for mapping and topic presentation: The *Atlas of Oregon* and *Atlas of Kentucky*. The black and white shelf-sized format is similar to *Zambia in Maps* from the Independent African nation series produced by the University of London. The *New Mexico Statistical Abstract* of the Bureau of Business and Economic Research provided much of the summary information used in the maps of this book, and also guided the selection of subjects in the population and economic sections. The *Historical Atlas of New Mexico* and T. M. Pearce's *New Mexico Place Names* were also useful in mapping historical and governmental data. But the bulk of information for this book comes from an endless search for data through libraries, government offices, and interviews with people in every corner of the state. The Research Allocation Committee of the University of New Mexico funded some of this data collection in the summer of 1978. With this support Geographer Williams was able to travel to each county in New Mexico and interview people.

Although the names of all those who contributed to the book would be impossible to list here, we would like to recognize the ones who made a special effort. Robert U. Anderson, Director of the Government Research Unit, University of New Mexico, provided access to significant data bases and much appreciated support at critical times during our research efforts. In the southwestern quarter of New Mexico we express our appreciation to Bob Atwood of Reserve; John Fleming of Silver City; Leah Jones and Bill Lane of Deming; and Nate Broadhead and Loring Spitler of Las Cruces. Recognition in the northwest quarter goes to Octavia Felin of Gallup; Eleanor MacDonald of Farmington; Bob Bright of Aztec; Don Graham of Chama; David Chaves of Tierra Amarilla; and Ruth Armstrong of Corrales. Much of the information on local areas of the southeast was collected from Ralph Dunlap and Leslie Olson of Carrizozo; Ginger Yearly, G. L. Tucker, Bill Gage, and Wyatt Atkins of Alamogordo; Ned Tandy of Roswell; Bill Beauchamp of Lovington; and Mrs. J. V. Sterns of Fort Sumner. The main sources in the northeast were Alan Vigil of Taos; Jim Purdy and Ramon Mares of Santa Fe; John Gavahan of Las Vegas; Doug Murray of Raton; Bill Wheatly and Roy Pogue of Clayton; Wyman Madole of Roy; and Napolean Martinez of Santa Rosa. Without the information provided by innumerable people along the routes we travelled and the data supplied by the Councils of Government, county officials, and Office of the Secretary of State, the formidable task of editing the material that passed by us for two years would have been impossible.

More than thirty professionals in government and academic positions contributed their expertise to sections of the book. Collecting the drafts, editing, forwarding to proofreaders, reediting the texts, along with map compilation, map editing, and coordinating maps to texts required great effort. Amelia Budge and Mike Inglis volunteered much time to this task and are responsible for reducing the number of errors that inevitably occur in this type of compilation. All of the maps in the atlas are originals that required many hours of planning and drafting. The high quality of the graphics is primarily the result of the patience and perseverance of Elaine Faust. She joined the project in midstream, following the departure of Denise Glore, who drafted several of the maps used in the book. Lastly, but most importantly, The Technology Application Center provided the facilities and seconded many of their full-time staff to part-time work on the atlas project.

The book is intended for a broad audience. It has been written to serve the general public as a touring guide or reference book of the state. It has been designed for possible adoption as a textbook for either secondary school or college level classes. We are aware that the book is not all- inclusive, and a short list of excluded topics has already been established for later addition. We hope you enjoy our first effort. It has been a labor of love.

Jerry L. Williams
Paul E. McAllister

a note on the second printing, 1981

This book was conceived in the mid 1970s and first published in 1979. In 1980 the New Mexico Board of Education authorized a new school district—Zuni Pueblo School District, in western New Mexico. In 1981 the state legislature created a new county—Cibola County. Cibola County comprises much of what was formerly western Valencia County; its county seat is Grants. The existence of these new entities is not reflected in this book. We plan to prepare a revised edition as soon as time permits, and we will, of course, include this kind of new information in that edition. We will also correct errors in this edition. We urge our readers to let the publisher know of any errors in this edition and to share with us their ideas for additional maps.

Jerry L. Williams
June 1981

general reference map of new mexico

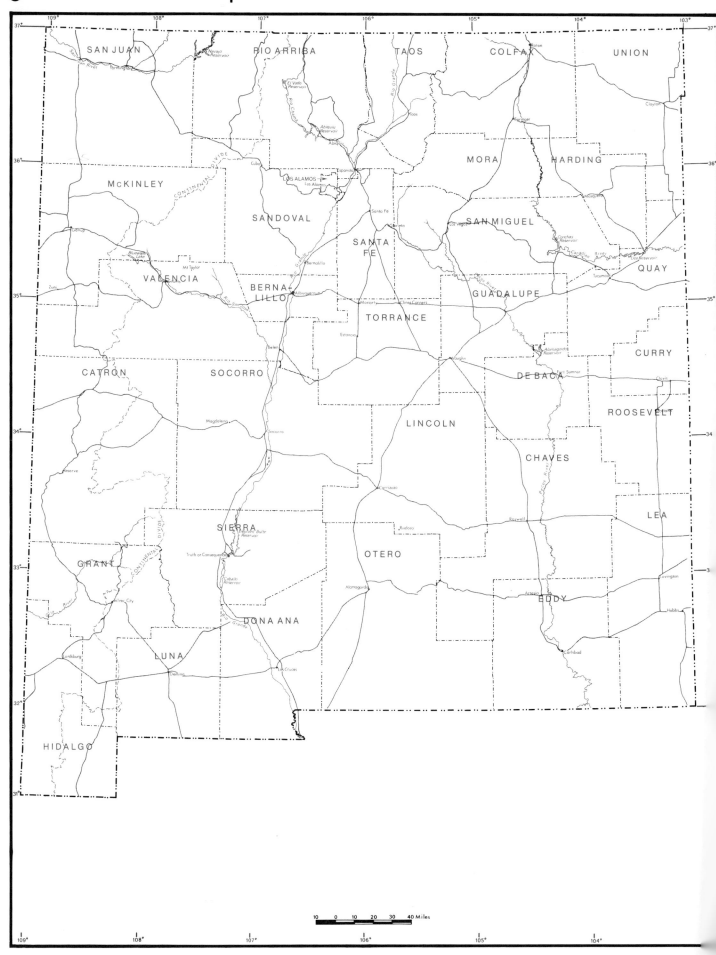

natural environment

geologic structure

The geology of New Mexico has undergone vast changes since its original formation. The state has experienced vast oceans and land-locked evaporative basins, large volcanic eruptions, and witnessed huge mountain ranges being formed and eroded away to rolling plains. The landscape we live on today has existed for only a brief time in history and has undergone many striking and violent changes. This discussion will analyze four time periods, or eras, in New Mexico's geologic history: the Precambrian (more than 600 million years ago), the Paleozoic (230 to 600 million years ago), the Mesozoic (70 to 230 million years ago), and the Cenozoic (70 million years ago to the present).

Precambrian Era

The cores of many of New Mexico's major mountain ranges are comprised of Precambrian rock. These mountain ranges include the Sandias, Sangre de Cristos, Pedernal Hills, Burro, Brazos, Zuni, and the San Andreas Mountains. Relatively little is known of the Precambrian Era since most of the rocks from this time are either buried or have been eroded away. It is known that large masses of quartz and feldspar sandstones were covered by thick flows of rhyolite and andesite lava which covered almost all of the state during this period of violent activity. Enormous intrusions of hot granite then formed mountains over a mile high which were subsequently eroded down to rolling plains. The bases of these eroded mountains were later elevated to form the mountains we see today.

Paleozoic Era

Although some primitive lifeforms were known to have existed during the Precambrian in other areas, the first known fossils to appear in New Mexico occurred during the Cambrian Period, the beginning of the Paleozoic Era. The major Cambrian deposits in the state occur in the Bliss Sandstone of the San Andreas Mountains. During the Ordovician Period southern New Mexico was covered by warm, shallow seas and the number and variety of invertebrate lifeforms increased tremendously. Although the fossiliferous Ordovician deposits covered many areas of the state, erosion has removed many of the beds, leaving the remaining deposits south of the San Andreas Mountains. The Silurian and Devonian Periods are noted as being moist and muddy and were times of heavy erosion. An important event during the Devonian was the appearance of the first land plants.

During the Mississippian Period much of southern New Mexico was covered by oceans and many thick, fossiliferous limestone beds were deposited, such as the Escabrosa, Lake Valley, and Rancheria Limestones. In northern New Mexico during the late Mississippian many caves were eroded in the porous limestones causing the region to have a karst topography with many sinkholes and underground rivers.

The emergence of the Pennsylvanian Period brought great changes in the landscape and laid the foundation of the mineral wealth the state enjoys today. North of present day Albuquerque the giant Uncompahgre Mountains rose and shed rock debris into nearby oceans. The Pedernal Mountains stretched from the present day Pedernal Hills to Ruidoso. Erosional debris also filled the Delaware Basin in the southeastern corner of the state; debris such as limestones, shales, and sandstones. These sediments later became the rich oil and gas deposits now being tapped in the region. Oil and gas-forming deposits also eroded off the western flanks of the Uncompahgre Mountains and formed petroleum strata in the Four Corners area. The Pennsylvanian was also a great coal-forming period in North America due to the vast marshes and swamps created during this time across the continent. New Mexico, however, had few of these marshes and swamps, causing the state's coal deposits to occur in thin lenses scattered across the area.

The Permian Period in New Mexico can be best noted for events occurring in the southeastern Delaware Basin. This period saw the creation of the Capitan and Goat Seep Reefs and, ultimately, the Carlsbad Caverns. Additional oil-bearing limestones were deposited in the area. The late Permian in the southeast saw the deposition of the Salado Salt, which achieved depths of almost 2000 feet. In the Carlsbad area this potassium-rich formation is now host to an extensive potash mining industry.

Mesozoic Era

The early Mesozoic found dry land over much of New Mexico. Rolling hills dominated the landscape and dinosaurs were the principal lifeform. The Cretaceous Period in the late Mesozoic was a time of intense volcanic activity in the Lordsburg area and there was a transition in the northwest from swamps to beach and marine deposits. During this time the Mesa Verde Group of formations were laid down in the north including the coal-bearing Fruitland Formation that rims the San Juan Basin.

The end of the Mesozoic saw the beginning of the Laramide Uplift which formed the Rocky Mountains. New Mexico emerged from the oceans and mountains formed in southern Colorado and northern New Mexico where the Sangre de Cristo now stand. Erosion deposited sediments in the Raton Basin creating coal formations near Raton. The Laramide Uplift also saw the decline of the dinosaurs and the rise of the mammals.

Cenozoic Era

The beginning of the Cenozoic saw the end of the Laramide Uplift and left the New Mexican landscape much as it appears today, although the climate was more humid. Great swamps filled the Raton Basin and contributed to the coal beds already there. In the southwestern part of the state intense volcanic activity occurred. Hot vapors and solutions were extruded which most likely formed the rich ore deposits currently being mined there. The Datil-Mogollon region was rocked with volcanic explosions and Mt. Taylor, a high volcanic pile, and the Jemez Caldera, one of the largest calderas in the world, were formed.

The latter part of the Cenozoic saw the uplift of mountain blocks along great fault lines; mountains such as the Sandias, Manzanos, San Andreas, and the Sacramentos. At the same time as the mountain uplift, many valleys were formed by downfaulting, the most significant of which is the Rio Grande Rift now occupied by the Rio Grande River. The final touches were placed on the landscape with the extrusion of the Carrizozo and Grants lava flows and the formation of the White Sands gypsum dunes by wind deposition.

Thomas K. Budge

Scale of geologic time in millions of years	Era	Geologic age		Rocks	Dominant life
70	CENOZOIC	Neogene	Pleistocene	Bandelier volcanic ash, basalts, sand dunes, river gravels, glacial & lake beds.	Man
			—1 my—		
			Pliocene	Volcanic rocks of Mt. Taylor, early Valle Grande & Gila region; Santa Fe, Gila, and Ogallala Fms.	Mammals
			—11 my—		
			Miocene		
			—25 my—		
160		Paleogene	Oligocene	Datil, Espinaso, and other volcanic rocks.	
			—40 my—		
			Eocene	Baca, Animas, Nacimiento, San Jose, Raton, Poison Canyon, Galisteo, El Rito, Blanco Basin, & Cub Mountain Fms.	
			—60 my—		
			Paleocene		
370	MESOZOIC	Cretaceous		Upper sandstone, shale, & coal. Mesaverde, Pierre, & Niobrara. Dakota Ss. and Mancos Sh. Volcanic rocks, limestone, sandstone, and conglomerate.	Dinosaurs
			—135 my—		
		Jurassic		Morrison Fm., Summerville Fm., Zuni Ss., Todilto Ls. & gypsum, Entrada Ss.	
			—180 my—		
		Triassic		Wingate Ss., Dockum Fm., Chinle Fm., Santa Rosa Ss., Moenkopi Fm.	
1500 +	PALEOZOIC	Permian		Rustler Dolomite; redbeds Castile gypsum, Salado Salt. Artesia Grp.—Capitan reef San Andres Ls.—Goat Seep reef Glorieta Sandstone Yeso Fm.—Bone Spring Fm. Abo Redbeds—Hueco Ls.	Amphibians
			—280 my—		
		Pennsylvanian		Mostly limestone; beds of shale & sandstone; lenses of gypsum, salt, and coal.	
			—310 my—		
		Mississippian		Helms & Paradise Fms. Rancheria Ls. Lake Valley & Escabrosa Lss. Arroyo Penasco & Tererro Fms.	Fish
			—345 my—		
		Devonian		Percha Shale, Ouray Ls. northern dol., ss, and sh.	
			—400 my—	erosion	
		Silurian		Fusselman Dolomite	
			—425 my—	erosion	
		Ordovician		Montoya Dolomite El Paso Limestone Bliss	Invertebrates
			—500 my—		
		Cambrian		Sandstone	
				erosion	
	PRECAMBRIAN			quartzite, gneiss, andesite, granite, pegmatite, schist, greenstone.	Simple primitive forms

TABLE OF GEOLOGIC TIME

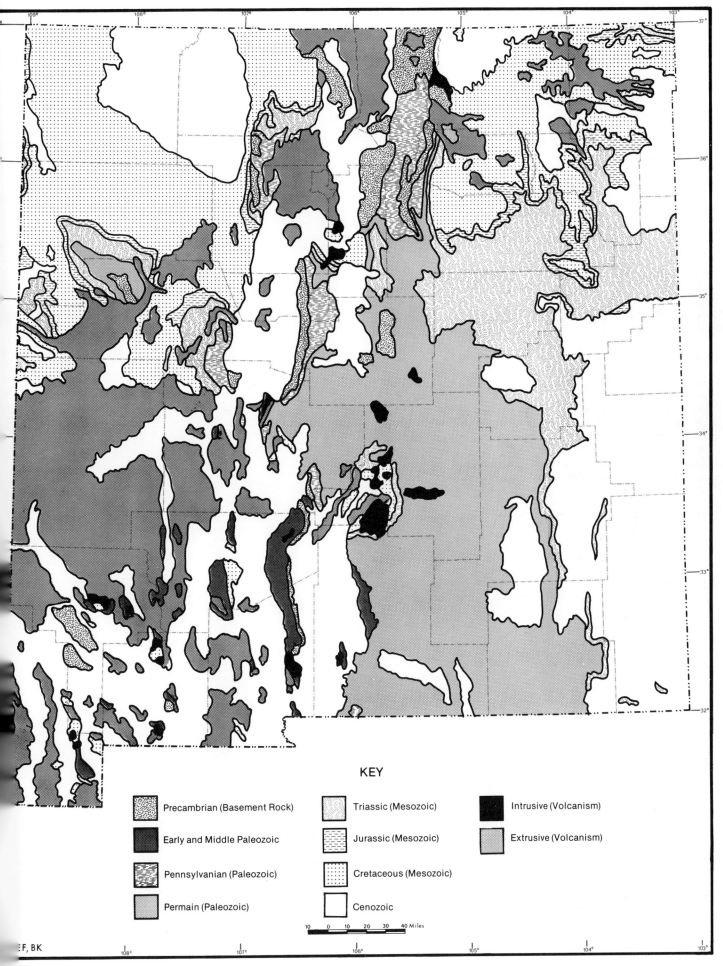

KEY

Precambrian (Basement Rock)

Early and Middle Paleozoic

Pennsylvanian (Paleozoic)

Permain (Paleozoic)

Triassic (Mesozoic)

Jurassic (Mesozoic)

Cretaceous (Mesozoic)

Cenozoic

Intrusive (Volcanism)

Extrusive (Volcanism)

10   0   10   20   30   40 Miles

EF, BK

young faults and geothermal areas

New Mexico straddles a major boundary between two distinct geologic zones. The region to the east, called the High Plains is characterized by geologic stability, where earthquake activity, volcanoes, and high mountains are rare. The western zone, which extends from central New Mexico to the Pacific Ocean, is active. Mountains, volcanoes, earthquakes and large topographic relief are common. The two zones are separated along a north-south line of high relief which bisects New Mexico. This boundary is formed by the Rio Grande rift, a major fracture in the earth's surface that extends from Mexico to northern Colorado. The rift is an elongate trough resulting from downward movement of a large block of the earth's crust along large fractures, or faults. The faulted block forms a low spot in the topography of the state, along which the Rio Grande flows. The mountains on either side of the Rio Grande valley have been upthrown many thousands of feet along the bounding faults. They mark the edges of the Rio Grande rift.

The Rio Grande rift was formed by crustal extension, the pulling apart of the earth's crust. This extension is caused by a large-scale motion of crustal plates of continental dimensions. West of the Rio Grande rift, the crust is intensely broken by extension associated with plate motion, while to the east it has not yet been affected. The map illustrates the distribution of faults and volcanic activity related to the formation of the Rio Grande rift. All of these features have formed in the last 20 million years; many are much younger. Volcanic activity less than 1000 years old has been documented at the Valley of Fires State Park near Carrizozo and at McCartys near Grants. Earthquakes along many faults indicate that vertical movement is still occurring along the rift.

In the northern half of the state, the Rio Grande rift is very distinct, appearing as a series of faults that trend generally north-northeastward from Socorro to the Taos area. The fault patterns in southern New Mexico are more complex as a result of increased crustal extension affecting a larger region. In this region it is more difficult to identify the rift, but the northerly trending faults in the south-central part of the state mark a broad zone along which the rift continues southward. The crust of the southwestern corner of the state has also been extended in a wide region. This area is part of the Basin and Range Province, which continues through southern Arizona into southeastern California. Instead of a single rift, the Basin and Range Province contains many "mini-rifts" with complicated fault patterns.

When the earth's crust is pulled apart, it becomes thin. This thinner crust is a less efficient insulator of heat, and so heat from the earth's hot interior can rise more easily to the surface. Areas where extension has occurred show many manifestations of thermal activity, such as volcanic areas and regions of geothermal activity. Faults can be important pipelines for rising heat. The heat is transported by hot fluids, which produce hot springs and hot underground water, and by liquid rock, or magma, which rises to the surface to form volcanoes and lava flows. In New Mexico, there is a direct correlation between crustal extension and young faulting, volcanism and geothermal activity. Most of the geothermal areas in the state are low grade; they contain subsurface water below 275°F. These hot-water reservoirs are formed by rising internal heat, which raises the temperature of the underground water. Sometimes a magma body high in the crust will also add heat to the reservoir. If it can be pinpointed, this type of geothermal reservoir is ideal for space heating, since water of this temperature is more than adequate for heating homes and greenhouses.

The large volcanic fields which extend from the eastern border of central Arizona to the northeastern corner of New Mexico are not so obviously related to the Rio Grande rift. This zone of young volcanic activity, mostly less than six million years old, follows another, much deeper, northeasterly trending fracture in the crust. This fracture has not caused surficial movement, although it is also undergoing extension. Where this fracture zone intersects the Rio Grande rift north of Albuquerque, a very large volcanic complex, the Jemez Mountains, has formed. Large volumes of magma, which have moved upward along faults from deep in the earth, created this volcanic edifice.

The Jemez Mountains are the site of the only known high-grade geothermal reservoir in New Mexico. Here a cooling magma body about one million years old provides a local "hot spot," and subsurface water reaches more than 500°F in local reservoirs. Water and steam of this temperature can be used to generate electricity, and an electric power station is planned for the Jemez Mountains geothermal area.

The major areas with potential geothermal resources in New Mexico are, from north to south: Ojo Caliente, Jemez Mountains, Socorro, Truth or Consequences, the Mesilla Valley–Las Cruces region, and the Animas Valley. Other areas with possible geothermal reservoirs are: the Taos area, Las Vegas area, San Ysidro–Rio Puerco Valley region, Albuquerque basin, and southern Tularosa Valley.

J. F. Callender

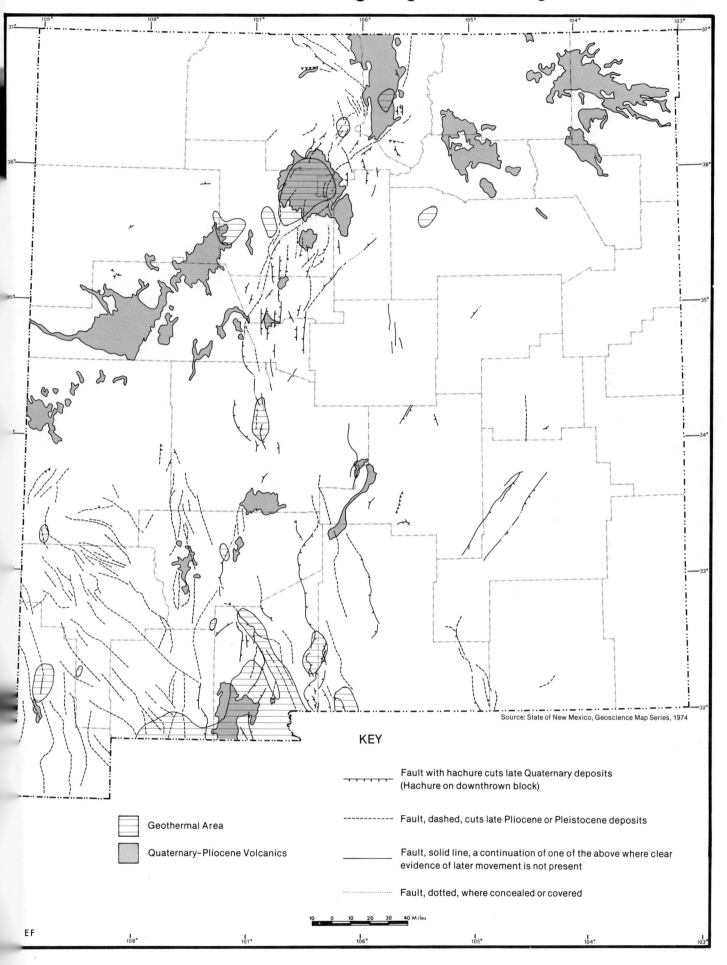

Source: State of New Mexico, Geoscience Map Series, 1974

KEY

⊥⊥⊥⊥⊥⊥   Fault with hachure cuts late Quaternary deposits
(Hachure on downthrown block)

----------   Fault, dashed, cuts late Pliocene or Pleistocene deposits

▭ Geothermal Area

———————   Fault, solid line, a continuation of one of the above where clear
evidence of later movement is not present

▨ Quaternary-Pliocene Volcanics

················   Fault, dotted, where concealed or covered

10   0   10   20   30   40 Miles

E F

landforms

New Mexico, the fifth largest state in the Union, has 121,666 square miles of extremely diverse topographic and geologic terrain. The total topographic relief is greater than 10,000 feet. The highest mountain, Wheeler Peak, located 30 miles south of the Colorado border in the Sangre de Cristo Mountains, reaches an elevation of 13,160 feet above sea level, while the lowest point, Red Bluff Reservoir on the Pecos River near the southern boundary of the state, lies a little less than 3,000 feet above sea level. The elevation of most of New Mexico, however, is between 5,000 and 10,000 feet above sea level. Less than one-third of the state lies below 5,000 feet, principally along the eastern border with Texas. Other areas below 5,000 feet include the Rio Grande Valley from the state's southern boundary to a short distance north of Albuquerque, the Jornada del Muerto and Tularosa Valley, and thousands of square miles of aggraded plains in the southwestern part of the state.

Approximately 1,000 square miles of New Mexico rise above an altitude of 10,000 feet. This includes peaks of the southern Rocky Mountains in the north-central part of the state, particularly in the Sangre de Cristo and Jemez Mountains. Smaller areas with elevations above 10,000 feet occur on Mount Taylor and in the Sandia and Manzano Mountains in the central part of the state, and on the Magdalena, San Mateo, Capitan and Mogollon Mountains and Sierra Blanca in the southern part. Map 1 illustrates the distribution of these major landforms and many other landform features.

Topographically, New Mexico can be divided into four principal divisions: the southern Rocky Mountain Province, the Intermontane Plateaus, the Basin and Range Province, and the Great Plains Province.

The southern Rocky Mountains Province includes only a small part of the state along its northern border and is generally thought to terminate at the southern end of the Nacimiento Mountains and the Sangre de Cristo Range (north of Glorieta Mesa).

The Intermontane Plateaus include two large sections of the Colorado Plateau Province: the Navajo section in northwestern New Mexico consisting of young but canyoned plateaus of moderate relief; and the Datil section to the south including complete lava flows or extensive remnants, numerous volcanic necks, and other extrusive and intrusive igneous rock masses.

The Basin and Range Province also has two sections in New Mexico: the Mexican Highland section, consisting mainly of isolated ranges, which are largely fault-block mountains, separated by aggraded desert plains; and the Sacramento section comprised of mature block mountains with gently tilted strata, block plateaus and extensive bolsons.

The Great Plains Province has three divisions. The Raton section is the most varied of the three consisting of a trenched or deeply eroded peneplain surmounted by dissected lava-capped plateaus and buttes. The High Plains section (with three unconnected parts) consists of extensive, high level, fluvial plains and is the least dissected part of the state. The Pecos Valley is composed of late mature to old, nearly level plains, somewhat younger and at lower levels than the High Plains section.

The Southern Rocky Mountains and the ranges in the Basin and Range Province, separated by wide, deeply alluviated valleys, form a belt 50 to 100 miles wide from east to west and extend from the northern to the southern boundary of the state. These ranges, in a broad way, divide the plateau, lava, and canyon lands of western New Mexico from the plains and generally lower topographic relief of the eastern part.

Rodman E. Snead

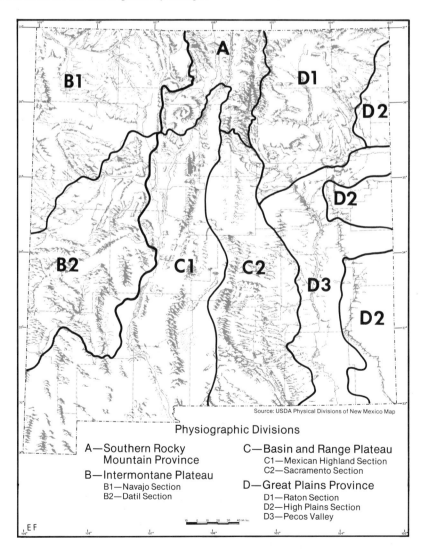

Source: USDA Physical Divisions of New Mexico Map

Physiographic Divisions

A—Southern Rocky
  Mountain Province

B—Intermontane Plateau
  B1—Navajo Section
  B2—Datil Section

C—Basin and Range Plateau
  C1—Mexican Highland Section
  C2—Sacramento Section

D—Great Plains Province
  D1—Raton Section
  D2—High Plains Section
  D3—Pecos Valley

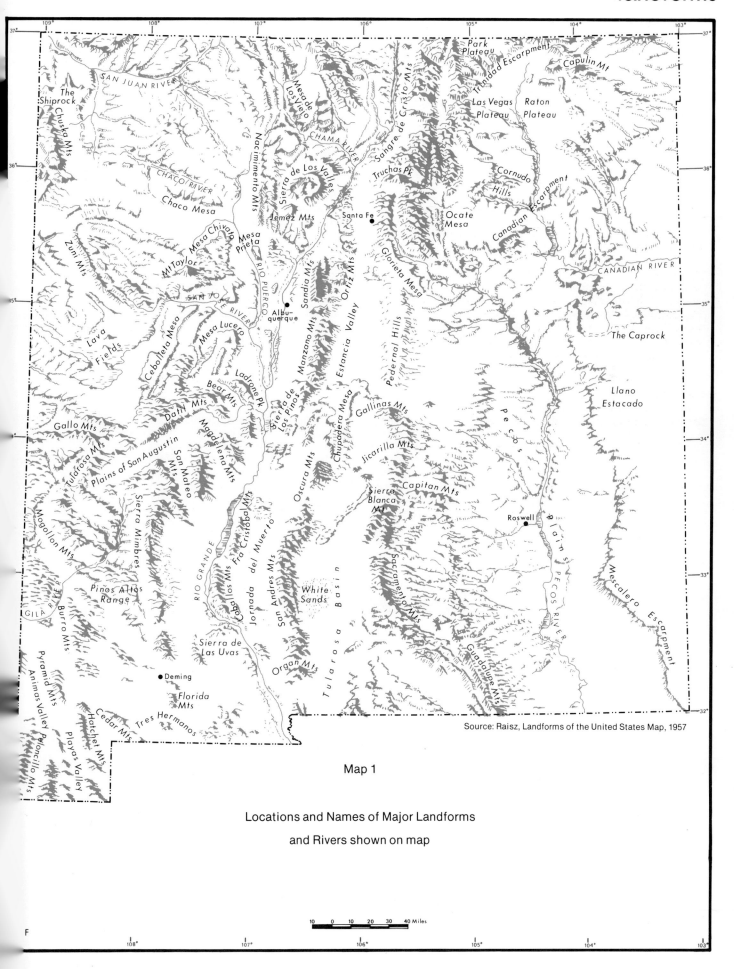

Source: Raisz, Landforms of the United States Map, 1957

Map 1

Locations and Names of Major Landforms

and Rivers shown on map

10 0 10 20 30 40 Miles

temperature

Temperatures in New Mexico are quite variable, both seasonally and topographically. A maximum of 116°F has been recorded at both Artesia (July 14, 1934) and Orogrande (June 29, 1918), while a minimum of −50° was recorded at Gavilan in Rio Arriba County, on February 1, 1951. An unofficial report of −57° was received from Ciniza, in the western mountains, on January 13, 1963. The state has also seen temperatures as low as −36° in April, and 5° in May. Carlsbad recorded 100° on February 24, 1904.

Those extremes aside, the temperatures around the state can be looked at in terms of altitude, latitude, exposure, and season.

Altitude and latitude—While both altitude and latitude influence temperature, the altitude of a station is considerably more important than the latitude. There may be only a 3° difference in mean annual temperature between two stations at similar elevations at opposite ends of the state (northeast and southwest). However, two stations only 15 miles apart, but differing in altitude by 5,000 feet differ in mean annual temperature by 16° or about 3° for every 1,000 feet difference in elevation. If one compares the topographical map with the mean annual temperature map of New Mexico, the relationship between altitude and temperature is striking. Yet other factors must also be considered.

Exposure—The exposure and lay of the land also have an effect on temperature. Solar insolation obviously is greater on a south-facing slope than on a north-facing slope. The contrast is more marked in deep, narrow valleys with an east-west orientation. North-south mountain ranges also have interesting temperature variances due to exposure. The maximum temperature is higher on the west flank than on the east, even though the solar insolation on each flank may be equal. This is because the east flank receives sunlight in the early morning, when temperatures are low to begin with. By the time the sun passes over to the west flank, casting the east face in shadow, the air on the west flank has already warmed considerably. The sun now warms air that has been warming since sunrise. Most mountain ranges in New Mexico are oriented north-south, and the west side nearly always has higher maximum temperatures than the east. Examples are the Sandias, Manzanos, Sacramentos, Sangre de Cristos and Guadalupe Mountains.

Indirectly related to exposure and topography are drainage winds and the pooling of cold air in basins. Air drainage occurs most markedly on clear, still nights. An excellent example of this is in the Rio Grande Valley. At night, air from the high mountains and mesas flanking the valley is cooled by contact with the colder ground. This air, being heavy and close to the ground, cascades down the slopes and builds up in the valley. It then moves down the valley, much like water flowing down the river. This mechanism brings cold air from the mountains and the north to the southern areas of the state.

In basins, like the San Juan Valley and the Estancia Valley east of Albuquerque, cold air also runs downhill but is trapped in the basin. At times, especially in winter, this air remains in the basin throughout the warmest part of the day. This explains why the temperature at Farmington may be lower than that at Chama in the nearby mountains.

Season—July is normally the warmest month in New Mexico and January the coldest. The second half of the year is warmer than the first half: August is warmer than June, September warmer than May, and October warmer than April. Temperatures in the summer months show relatively little variation, while there is a fairly large variation during the winter. This is because of the frequent storms and invasions of cold air into the state during the winter months. In summer, the mechanism for these invasions, the mid-latitude westerlies, is almost non-existent.

June and July are the warmest months mostly due to clear skies and light winds. Moist, shower-producing air from the Gulf of Mexico covers only the eastern plains during this period, and is effectively blocked from entering the western two-thirds of the state by a wall of mountains. In mid to late July, moist, unstable air is moved into the western sections by consistent southerly winds. During the rest of the summer, daily insolation is greatly reduced in the mid-afternoon hours by convective clouds and showers. Mountain areas are dramatically cooler because of frequent cloud cover and higher altitudes.

Bill Eisenhood

TABLE: AVERAGE DAILY TEMPERATURE, 1931-1960

Weather Station Divisions	Average Temperature (°F)*												
	Jan	Feb	Mar	Apr	May	Jun	Jul	Aug	Sep	Oct	Nov	Dec	A
Northwestern Plateau	28	33	39	48	57	66	72	70	63	52	38	30	
Northern Mountains	27	30	36	45	53	62	66	65	59	49	36	29	
Northeastern Plains	35	39	45	54	63	73	76	75	68	57	44	37	
Central Valley	36	41	47	56	65	74	77	76	69	58	44	37	
Central Highlands	32	35	40	49	57	66	68	67	62	52	40	34	
Southeastern Plains	40	44	50	59	67	76	78	77	71	61	48	42	
Southern Desert	41	45	51	59	67	77	80	78	72	62	49	42	
Southwestern Mountain	32	35	41	48	56	66	70	68	62	52	40	34	

*Average temperature = high + low / 2 (rounded to nearest degree).

Source: Climate of New Mexico pp. 13, 14 and 17.

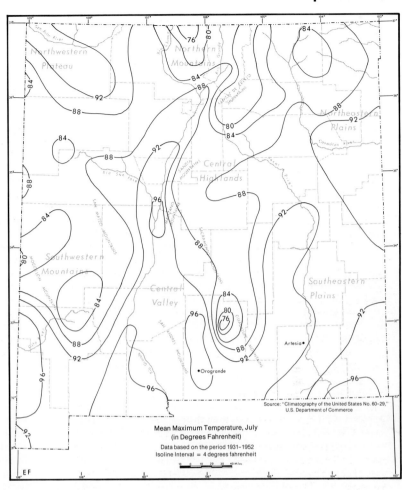

Mean Maximum Temperature, July
(in Degrees Fahrenheit)

Data based on the period 1931–1952
Isoline Interval = 4 degrees fahrenheit

Source: "Climatography of the United States No. 60–29,"
U.S. Department of Commerce

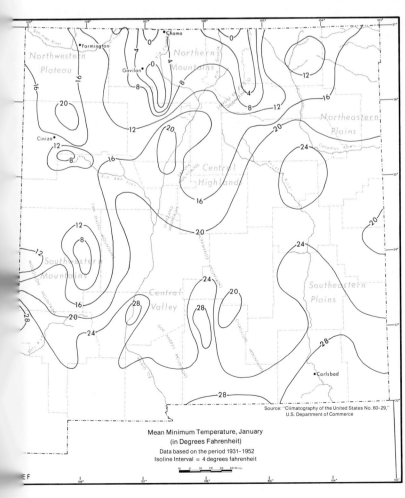

Mean Minimum Temperature, January
(in Degrees Fahrenheit)

Data based on the period 1931–1952
Isoline Interval = 4 degrees fahrenheit

Source: "Climatography of the United States No. 60–29,"
U.S. Department of Commerce

9

precipitation

Although New Mexico is a relatively dry state, there are numerous exceptions to the idea of a barren, dry, lifeless landscape. Several areas of the state, in fact, receive from 30–45 inches of rainfall per year (the terms rainfall and precipitation refer to all forms of precipitation).

The heaviest rains occur in the mountains. The Sangre de Cristo Mountains of northern New Mexico represent the wettest area of the state, with some stations on the eastern faces receiving well over 40 inches annually. The Jemez Mountains to the west across the Rio Grande Valley also receive relatively large amounts of precipitation. The southern mountains receive less precipitation than do the northern ranges.

Areas of moderate rainfall (12–17 inches) are the relatively flat, high plateaus and mesas, including the Plains of San Augustin in western New Mexico and much of the eastern one-third of the state.

Areas of slight precipitation are commonly the flatter, lower elevation regions, such as the northwest plateau, the Rio Grande Valley and most of the southern valleys excluding the southeastern plains. Some of these areas come close to being true desert.

Topography plays a major role in the distribution of precipitation. When rain is created with the aid of the terrain, the rainfall is usually termed orographic precipitation. Sometimes, as in the winter, the moist air is literally forced up a slope and precipitation is enhanced. At other times, such as in the summer, higher terrain heated by the sun in turn heats nearby air. The result is that air over a mountain is warmer than air at the same elevation over a valley. The warmer air then rises, creating the typical summertime showers that for periods may form over the mountains every day.

It is generally true that higher terrain receives higher amounts of precipitation, however, there are exceptions. For example, the southwestern plains, though they are as much as 2000 feet lower in elevation, receive considerably more rainfall than the northwestern plains. To understand this seeming contradiction, it is necessary to look at where the moisture in New Mexico comes from.

There are three major sources of moisture in New Mexico: the northwest winds which bring moisture from the cool Pacific Ocean across California, Oregon, and Washington, chiefly in winter; the southwest winds that at times bring showers to southern Arizona and southwest New Mexico (the source is the warm Pacific along Baja California); and the Gulf of Mexico which is by far the major moisture source for the state. In spring and summer, the rainiest months, the state receives the bulk of its moisture from southeasterly and southerly winds from the Gulf.

Springtime and especially early June, is a fairly dry time for most of the state, except for the eastern plains. During the spring most Pacific storms sweep well to the north through the northern and central Rockies, while the Bermuda High circulates moist, unstable air northwestwardly across Texas and into New Mexico's southeast and eastern plains. Thunderstorms are very common, including sporadic outbreaks of severe weather. The north-south oriented mountains separating the eastern plains from the rest of the state effectively block the moist air, and the western two-thirds of the state remain dry. But by early July, the circulation changes. Gulf air moves from the south into all of New Mexico, signalling the onset of the thunderstorm season (which lasts until mid-September) for the western section of the state.

Autumn is another dry period with a slowdown in rainfall through November. By late November and early December, the cyclonic storms with their Pacific moisture sweep south and result in snow in the western and northern mountains and also in the higher mountains of the south. At times, very large amounts of snow fall in the desert areas, but these storms are infrequent.

Occasionally, a winter storm moving toward New Mexico from the northwest will be slowed by the Rocky Mountains. As the eastern portion of the storm emerges out over the Colorado plains, it rushes southward unimpeded. The cold air rapidly fills the eastern plains, winds blow from the northeast, and pressures rise rapidly in the east while holding steady in the west. Fog and low clouds with drizzle, and at times freezing rain, are the result of the air being lifted by the sloping terrain as it moves from east to west across the plains. Eventually, if the cold air is deep enough, it will move through the canyons and sometimes over the mountains, finally covering the whole state and bringing snows with it. In cases like the above, the storm moving in from the northwest appears to be moving in from the east, like water flowing around a rock.

Bill Eisenhood

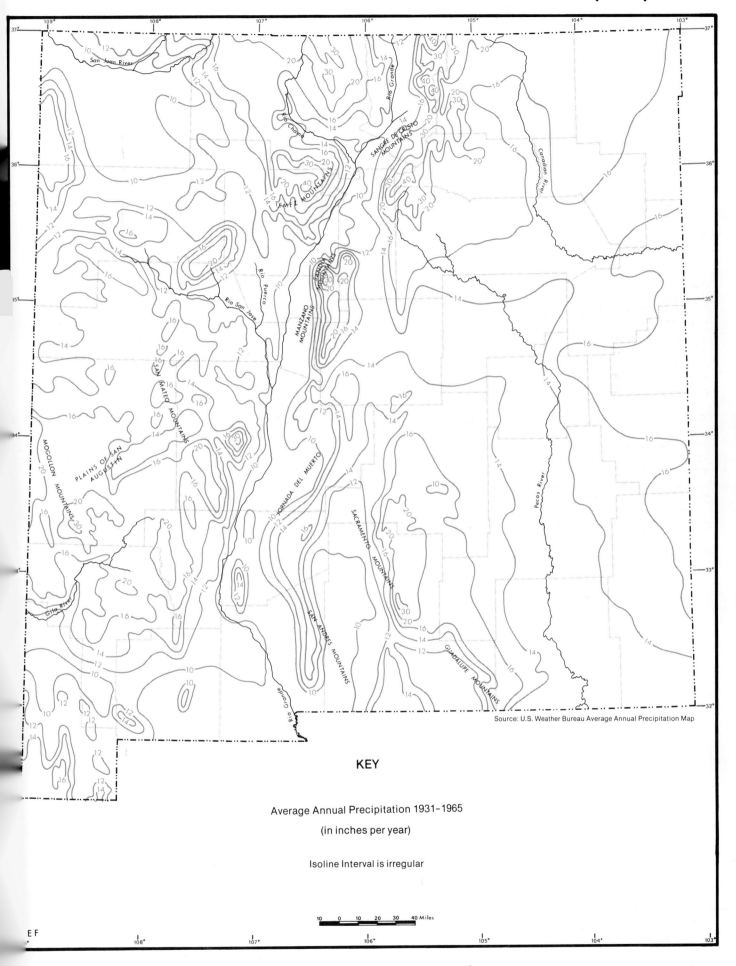

Source: U.S. Weather Bureau Average Annual Precipitation Map

KEY

Average Annual Precipitation 1931–1965

(in inches per year)

Isoline Interval is irregular

10 0   10   20   30   40 Miles

E F

frost conditions

Frost may occur whenever the temperature drops below 32°F (0°C). If the temperature is low enough to severely damage the staple vegetative products of a local area, the frost is referred to as a "killing frost." The plant-surviving period, referred to as a frost-free season, is the interval reported by the National Weather Service between the last killing frost in spring and the first killing frost in the fall.

A frost-free season has local variations of up to 100 days from an expected average, and is a climatic interval difficult to predict. Santa Fe, for example, had an average 164-day frost-free season over a thiry-year period (1931-1961) that reached extremes of up to 209 days (+45 days from expected) in 1934 and down to 113 days (−51 days from average) in 1961. These local variations can be attributed to wind, topography, latitude and altitude.

The most influential factor in the length of the frost-free season is the local wind condition and terrain or topography. A sheltered valley which prohibits or impedes wind flow will allow the more dense cold air to settle in lower areas, increasing the severity of frost. This physical property of weather activity is frequently the cause of frost damage to plants in low lying areas while the vegetation of nearby higher elevations escapes danger. If warm wind mixes with descending cool air on the downslope of a hill, frost in the lower elevations may be delayed.

The variability in the length of the frost-free season has been found to increase with higher latitude and increasing elevation. Since New Mexico covers only six degrees of latitude (31°N to 37°N), the latitudinal factor would not be expected to be as significant on frost activity as is the elevation. Areas of the same general elevation, located in the southern and northern extremities of the state, have approximately the same average number of days between frosts. Deming (32° 20′N latitude) and Clovis (34° 30′N latitude), both at approximately 4300 foot elevation, have 200-day and 198- day average frost-free seasons respectively. Much of the difference that occurs between these two stations can be attributed to the orientation of local mountain ranges and prevailing wind conditions. This would also explain the difference in the average length of frost-free seasons between Deming and Alamogordo (17-days), both of similar latitude and altitude.

The effect of elevation on frost activity can be very dramatic in New Mexico (Table I). The average period free of frost in Red River (8676 ft) is less than half as long as that of Bloomfield (5794 ft). Local topography may contribute to this large variation of 82 days: Red River is confined to a narrow valley surrounded by alpine peaks, whereas Bloomfield is in a wide valley characterized by much less of a change in relief. The altitudinal effect on frost occurrence can be demonstrated by Red River and nearby Eagle Nest (8200 ft), the only two stations in the state to report no days without frost in the years of 1931 and 1938.

It should be noted that a frost-free season is slightly longer than the growing season. Plant growth does not normally occur below temperatures in the low 40's. Also, freezing temperature does not necessarily mean sudden death to all crops. Many types of vegetation, including fruits, can tolerate light frosts and even temperatures as low as the mid-20's. The most dangerous frosts occur after a period of unusually warm spring weather which promotes the growth of fruit blossoms and tender shoots of certain crops. Defense measures such as smudge pots, misting with water sprays, and other cover devices are usually relied on to decrease damage.

Jerry L. Williams and Howard Morgan

TABLE I: EXTREME DURATIONS—FROST FREE SEASONS 1931-1961

Map Letter		Year Longest	(Days)	Year Shortest	(Days)	Average	Latest Spring	Range (Days)	Earliest Fall	Range (Days)
A	Bloomfield	1950	203	1936	151	165	5-20-60	37	9-26-34	39
B	Chaco Canyon	1957	179	1961	105	141	6-18-37	69	9-4-61	57
C	Silver City	1952	229	1960	120	181	5-20-60	55	9-30-45	41
D	Hachita	1934	248	1959	153	215	5-10-53	59	10-5-59	56
E	Red River	1936	113	1931	0	83	Frost all year — 1931 and 1938			
F	Truchas	1956	169	1961	81	129	— — —	—	— — —	—
G	Santa Fe	1934	209	1961	113	164	5-25-60	48	9-3-61	66
H	Albuquerque	1931	232	1952	173	203	5-4-44	42	10-11-46	35
I	Socorro	1943	226	1938	170	197	5-11-53	51	10-12-46	31
J	Elephant Butte	1954	255	1951	205	228	4-13-33	41	10-31-58	56
K	Las Cruces	1934	254	1937	217	221	4-6-33	84	9-30-45	36
L	Ruidoso	1943	140	1950	71	102	6-23-47	33	8-18-50	63
M	Estancia	1934	176	1944	95	138	6-9-51	42	9-8-44	43
N	Carlsbad	1938	241	1957	217	218	4-18-40	36	10-26-56	42
O	Clovis	1934	245	1954	163	199	5-14-53	30	10-3-43	49
P	Clayton	1934	229	1945	147	166*	5-29-47	55	9-28-45	54

*1921-1950

Source: Climate of New Mexico, State Planning Office, 1973

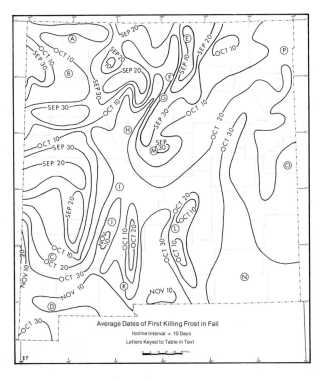

Average Dates of First Killing Frost in Fall

Isoline Interval = 10 Days

Letters Keyed to Table in Text

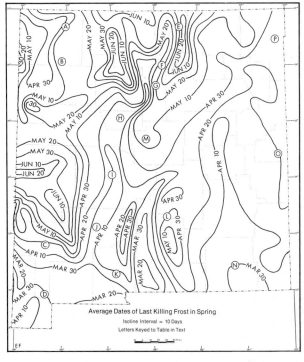

Average Dates of Last Killing Frost in Spring

Isoline Interval = 10 Days

Letters Keyed to Table in Text

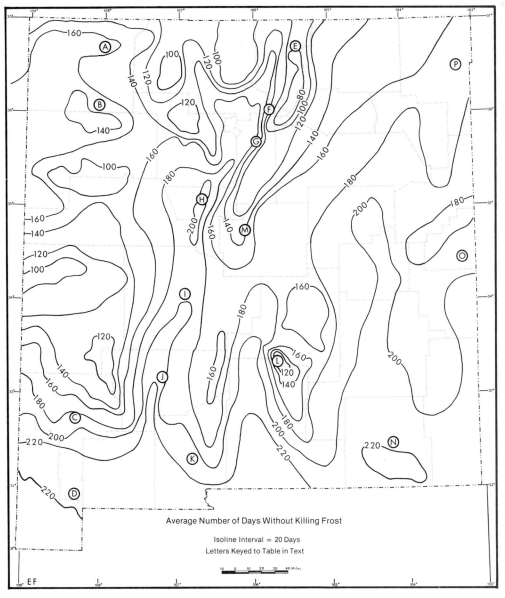

Average Number of Days Without Killing Frost

Isoline Interval = 20 Days

Letters Keyed to Table in Text

evaporation

Evaporation from the earth's surface supplies moisture to the atmosphere and is the source of rainfall and other forms of precipitation. Worldwide, most of this evaporation comes from oceans, seas, lakes, and rivers. However, over land surfaces, soils and vegetation contribute moisture to the atmosphere in much greater total amounts than do local bodies of water. Evaporation from a forested area averages about 50 percent more than from a body of water equal in area.

Within the continental United States the amount of precipitation exceeds the amount of evaporation only in a very few areas. These include parts of the Atlantic Coast area, the eastern Gulf Coast, western Washington, and the northern part of the Great Lakes region. Elsewhere, evaporation is much greater than precipitation, and in most western and southwestern areas (including New Mexico), evaporation is two to five times greater than precipitation.

The evaporation of water from the tissues of living plants is called transpiration. The amount of water needed by a plant to increase the dry matter within the plant by one pound is called its water requirement. Stated in pounds, this figure may range from 350 pounds for corn to 500 for wheat to 640 for potatoes, to 1,000 pounds for alfalfa. In utilizing this great amount of water, plants tend to emit a great deal of moisture through transpiration. A single corn plant may lose almost a gallon of water per day during its period of rapid growth. A mature, large tree may lose up to 10 gallons or more water per day. Fortunately, the deep root systems of such plants enable them to tap supplies of water deep in the subsoil.

The combined loss of water through evaporation from soils and transpiration of plants is called evapotranspiration. Actual evaporation is usually less than the maximum possible because insufficient water is available to satisfy the evaporating power of the atmosphere. The term potential evapotranspiration is used to indicate the total evaporating capacity of the atmosphere when the water supply in the ground is unlimited.

Evaporation is influenced by many factors. On an open water surface solar radiation, air temperature, relative humidity, wind, water turbidity, and water temperature greatly affect evaporation. From bare soil, evaporation is also affected by soil texture and depth of water table. Transpiration is affected by root systems, stage of growth, and the complexity of the plant structure above the ground. In light of this, few instruments are available to totally measure potential evapotranspiration. This stimulated the development of a formula to compensate for unobtainable data. The most widely accepted formula developed by Thornthwaite, calculates potential evapotranspiration (PE) by eliminating all factors except mean temperature and length of day, assuming all other factors such as wind, humidity, and solar radiation vary together.

From the agricultural point of view, potential evapotranspiration and its derivative, moisture deficit, are of the highest significance since they indicate the water needs of crops. A knowledge of the seasonal and geographical changes in the potential evapotranspiration of different areas would indicate the water requirements for storage or irrigation. Evaporation loss must be cal-

culated when storing water in dams and ponds. It has been estimated that the evaporational loss from Elephant Butte Reservoir is enough to irrigate over 50,000 areas of cropland.

Map 3 illustrates formulated potential evapotranspiration amounts in inches per year. The PE attains a maximum of 35.3 inches at Carlsbad in the southeast and falls to 17.4 on Sandia Crest. Lower values seem to be consistent with most mountain areas. In the eastern plains, the PE decreases from 34 inches in the south to 22 in the north. The largest PE values are found in areas of high summer temperatures and strong winds.

Potential evapotranspiration in the southern Rio Grande Valley is almost as high as in the Carlsbad area. Elephant Butte Dam is in a high PE area (34.6 inches) which continues northward through the valley to Albuquerque, where the annual PE is 30.9 inches.

The Average Annual Moisture Deficit map indicates the potential evapotranspiration less the rainfall and the stored soil water. The comparison of this map with the Annual Potential Evapotranspiration map shows significant changes in the location of maximum and minimum values. The greatest annual moisture deficit is the middle and southern Rio Grande Valley with a deficit of over 26 inches at Elephant Butte Dam and 22.2 inches at Albuquerque. These two areas are characterized by a combination of high summer temperatures and low annual rainfall averages as well as intense solar radiation. Carlsbad, with 21 inches annual moisture deficit has the advantage of a greater annual rainfall. In general, higher annual rainfall in the eastern plains of New Mexico results in lower moisture deficits.

The southwestern desert areas show a greater soil moisture deficit than does the southeast. Northward in the mountain area of greater rainfall, the annual moisture deficit becomes less. If the northwestern portion of New Mexico is compared with the northeast, the maps indicate a similar potential evapotranspiration annual rate, but a larger moisture deficit exists in the northwest. This is attributed to the annual rainfall in the northeast being twice that of the northwest.

For the more practical purpose of calculating water needs during the growing season of crops, the values indicated on the map for the annual frost-free season moisture deficit can be used. The frost-free season is that time elapsing between the average dates of the last killing frost in spring and the first killing frost in fall. The actual growing season is slightly less due to the inability of some vegetable crops to survive or produce at all variations of frost-free temperature ranges.

Potential evapotranspiration rates vary by the month and are highest in summer and lowest in winter. There is now increasing evidence that solar radiation largely controls evaporation rates. In New Mexico, the combination of higher altitudes and greater percentage of sunshine certainly contributes to a higher evaporation rate. Thus the widespread use of agricultural irrigation techniques in the state are perhaps more necessary than they would be in other regions with similar precipitation averages.

Howard Morgan

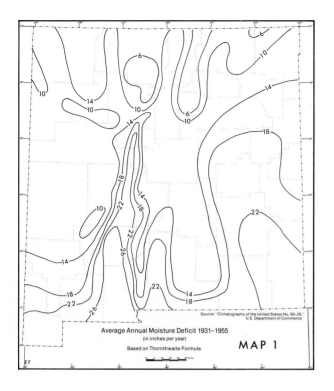

Source: "Climatography of the United States No. 60–29,"
U.S. Department of Commerce

Average Annual Moisture Deficit 1931–1955
(in inches per year)

Based on Thornthwaite Formula

MAP 1

E F

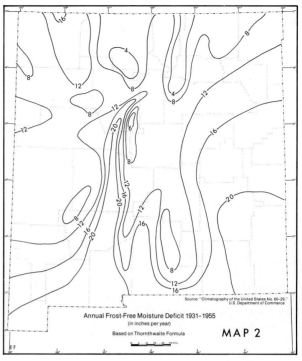

Source: "Climatography of the United States No. 60–29,"
U.S. Department of Commerce

Annual Frost-Free Moisture Deficit 1931–1955
(in inches per year)

Based on Thornthwaite Formula

MAP 2

E F

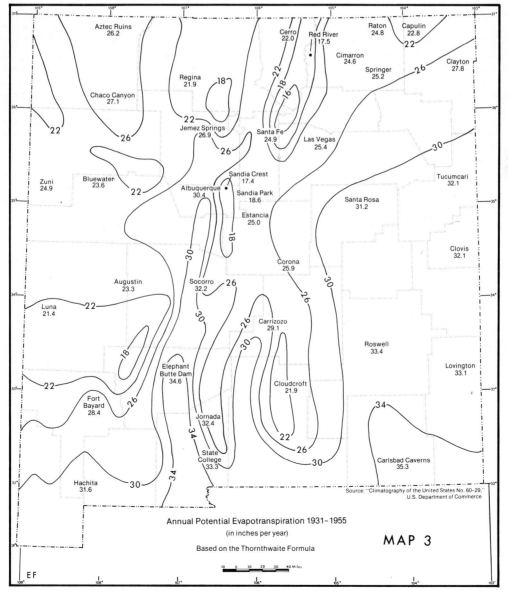

Aztec Ruins
26.2

Cerro
22.0

Red River
17.5

Raton
24.8

Capulin
22.8

Cimarron
24.6

Springer
25.2

Clayton
27.8

Regina
21.9

Chaco Canyon
27.1

Jemez Springs
26.9

Santa Fe
24.9

Las Vegas
25.4

Tucumcari
32.1

Zuni
24.9

Bluewater
23.6

Albuquerque
30.4

Sandia Crest
17.4

Sandia Park
18.6

Santa Rosa
31.2

Clovis
32.1

Estancia
25.0

Augustin
23.3

Socorro
32.2

Corona
25.9

Luna
21.4

Carrizozo
29.1

Roswell
33.4

Lovington
33.1

Elephant
Butte Dam
34.6

Cloudcroft
21.9

Fort
Bayard
28.4

Jornada
32.4

Carlsbad Caverns
35.3

State
College
33.3

Hachita
31.6

Source: "Climatography of the United States No. 60–29,"
U.S. Department of Commerce

Annual Potential Evapotranspiration 1931–1955

(in inches per year)

Based on the Thornthwaite Formula

MAP 3

E F

hydrology

In New Mexico hydrologic systems generally coincide with topographic or surface drainage basins, though in some areas water movement is underground from one basin to another. Most of the hydrologic systems in New Mexico extend across the state boundaries. The hydrologic units (subdivisions of the large systems) can be defined arbitrarily as small topographic basins tributary to the large basins.

New Mexico lacks large perennial streams, and the few that are considered to be perennial are at times nearly dry. Much more common are sandy washes that infrequently are filled for a short time by storm runoff. The principle streams that drain the broad plains of eastern New Mexico are the Cimarron, Canadian, and Pecos Rivers. The Rio Grande, San Juan, and Gila Rivers drain most of the mountains and high plateaus of the central and western parts of the state. There are several large basins in the central and southwestern areas that have interior drainage.

Rivers are the major source of water in the state, and dams on several of these rivers provide important reservoirs for irrigation, fishing, and recreation. The major reservoirs are Elephant Butte and Caballo on the Rio Grande; Conchas on the Canadian; and Navajo on the San Juan.

The predominance of the Rio Grande is striking. This river is the fifth longest in North America, totaling 1885 miles of which about 470 miles cross the state of New Mexico. The Rio Grande and the San Juan are the only important rivers in New Mexico with sources outside the state. The Rio Grande begins as a clear Rocky Mountain stream fed by springs at an elevation of more than 12,000 feet in the San Juan Mountains of Colorado. The river enters New Mexico through the Rio Grande gorge and flows south through the center of the state following the Rio Grande trough. When the Rio Grande leaves New Mexico just north of El Paso, the river and its tributaries have drained an area of over 32,207 square miles in New Mexico and Colorado.

The San Juan River is approximately 400 miles long, with 115 miles in northwestern New Mexico. It enters the state at Navajo Reservoir, and after passing through the Navajo Dam flows through the Farmington area supplying water to the irrigated farmland along the wide river valley. Near the Utah border, in the four-corner region, the San Juan enters the Colorado Plateau where it has carved an S-shaped canyon, "The Goose Necks," over 1,000 feet deep.

The Cimarron, a tributary to the Arkansas, and the North Canadian rivers begin in northeastern Union County, and flow east into Oklahoma. The Canadian River, originating in Colfax County and also a tributary to the Arkansas, drains the eastern slopes of the Sangre de Cristo Range, the southern flank of which drains into the Pecos River. The Pecos starts in Mora County, northcentral New Mexico, in the high peaks of the Southern Rockies. After leaving the mountains it flows through the eroded plains of the Pecos Valley. The Pecos has carved a valley 1,000 feet deep and 30 to 50 miles wide extending almost to Roswell. From Roswell the river widens into a basin which closes somewhat to a broad shallow valley at the Texas–New Mexico border. On the western side of the Continental Divide the principal rivers are the San Juan, Little Colorado, and Gila, all tributaries of the Colorado, which flows into the Gulf of California.

The Gila River, beginning in the mountains of southwestern New Mexico, drains much of the water from the Mogollon, Burro and Pinos Altos Mountains as well as the Black Range. Although the Gila is 110 miles long in New Mexico, it travels 540 miles through the arid southwest to its mouth in the Gulf of California.

Rodman E. Snead

TABLE SUMMARY OF LENGTH, DISCHARGE AREA, AND DISCHARGE FIGURES FOR TEN RIVERS IN NEW MEXICO

Rivers	Total Length	Approx. Length in N.M.	Discharge area (sq. mi.)	Aver. Runoff acre-feet per year thru 1963	Date	Peak Discharge Cubic ft. per Sec. (cfs)	Cfs per sq. mi.
Rio Grande at El Paso	1885	470	32,207	636,400	6-12-05	24,000	.75
Canadian at Logan	906	250	11,141	178,000	9-30-04	278,000	25.0
Pecos near Red Bluff	926	367	19,540	185,800	5-24-41	52,600	2.69
Cimarron near Folsom	692	75	895	7,460	5-17-28	4,500	4.80
Gila at N.M. Ariz. border	650	110	3,360	110,000	9-29-41	39,500	11.8
San Juan at Shiprock	400	115	12,900	1,683,000	8-11-29	v80,000	6.20
Rio Puerco near Bernado	170	125	6,220	37,790	10-11-04	50,000	1.82
Rio Chama near Chamita	140	120	3,144	404,000	5-22-20	k15,000	4.78
Jemez below Jemez Canyon Dam	60	70	1,040	37,280	8-29-43	16,300	15.7
Mimbres near Faywood	80	80	460	9,480	8-04-39	20,000	45.5

v = Maximum recorded; the flood of Oct. 6, 1911, may have exceeded 130,000 ft.
k = August 1893, Oct. 2, 1904, July 25, 1905, Aug. 17, 1915, and May 30, 1957.

The table provides average daily runoff over several years, but actual flows fluctuate greatly with long-term, seasonal, short-term and even diurnal variations. Also, river basin conditions have not remained static over the period recorded; the effects of artificial regulation and water withdrawn must be added to natural variations in precipitation, melt rate, groundwater flow, and evapotranspiration losses.

LIST OF MAJOR DRAINAGE BASINS

Arkansas River Basin
1-1 Canadian River basin above mouth of Cimarron Creek
1-2 Cimarron River basin
1-3 North Canadian River basin
1-4 Mora River basin
1-5 Canadian River basin, Cimarron Creek-Mora River
1-6 Ute Creek basin
1-7 Canadian River basin, below Ute Dam
1-8 Canadian River basin, Mora River-Conchas Dam
1-9 Canadian River basin, Conchas Dam-Ute Dam

Southern High Plains
2-1 Frio Draw Basin
2-2 Running Water Draw basin
2-3 Northern Lea basin
2-4 Southern Lea basin

Pecos River Basin
3-1 Pecos River basin above Gallinas River
3-2 Pecos River basin, Gallinas River-Alamogordo Reservoir
3-3 Vaughn Plains
3-4 Pecos River basin, Alamogordo Reservoir-Arroyo de la Mora
3-5 Pecos River basin, Arroyo de la Mora-Rio Hondo
3-6 Mescalero Pediment
3-7 Rio Hondo basin
3-8 Pecos River basin, Rio Hondo-Lake McMillan
3-9 Pecos River basin, Lake McMillan-State Line
3-10 Querecho Plains—San Simon Swale

Central Closed Basins
4-1 Estancia basin
4-2 Northern Jornado del Muerto
4-3 Northern Tularosa basin
4-4 Southern Jornado del Muerto
4-5 Southern Tularosa basin
4-6 Salt basin

Rio Grande Basin
5-1 Rio Chama basin
5-2 Rio Grande basin, Colorado line-Espanola
5-3 Rio Puerco basin above Rio San Jose
5-4 Jemez River basin
5-5 Rio Grande basin, Espanola-Bernalillo
5-6 Rio San Jose basin
5-7 Albuquerque area
5-8 Rio Salado basin
5-9 Rio Puerco basin below Rio San Jose
5-10 Rio Grande basin, Isleta-San Acacia
5-11 Rio Grande basin, San Acadia-San Marcial
5-12 Rio Grande basin, San Marcial-Elephant Butte dam
5-13 Rio Grande basin, Elephant Butte Dam-Radius Spri
5-14 Rio Grande basin, Radium Springs-El Paso

Western Closed Basins
6-1 North Plains
6-2 San Augustin Plains

San Juan River Basin
7-1 San Juan River basin
7-2 Chaco River basin

Lower Colorado River Basin
8-1 Puerco River basin
8-2 Zuni River basin
8-3 Carrizo Wash basin
8-4 San Francisco River basin
8-5 Gila River basin
8-6 San Simon Creek basin

Southwestern Closed Basins
9-1 Animas basin
9-2 Mimbres River basin
9-3 Playas basin
9-4 San Louis basin
9-5 Hachita basin
9-6 Wamel basin

Source: *Mineral and Water Resources of New Mexico;* New Mexico Bureau of Mines and Mineral Resources, 1977.

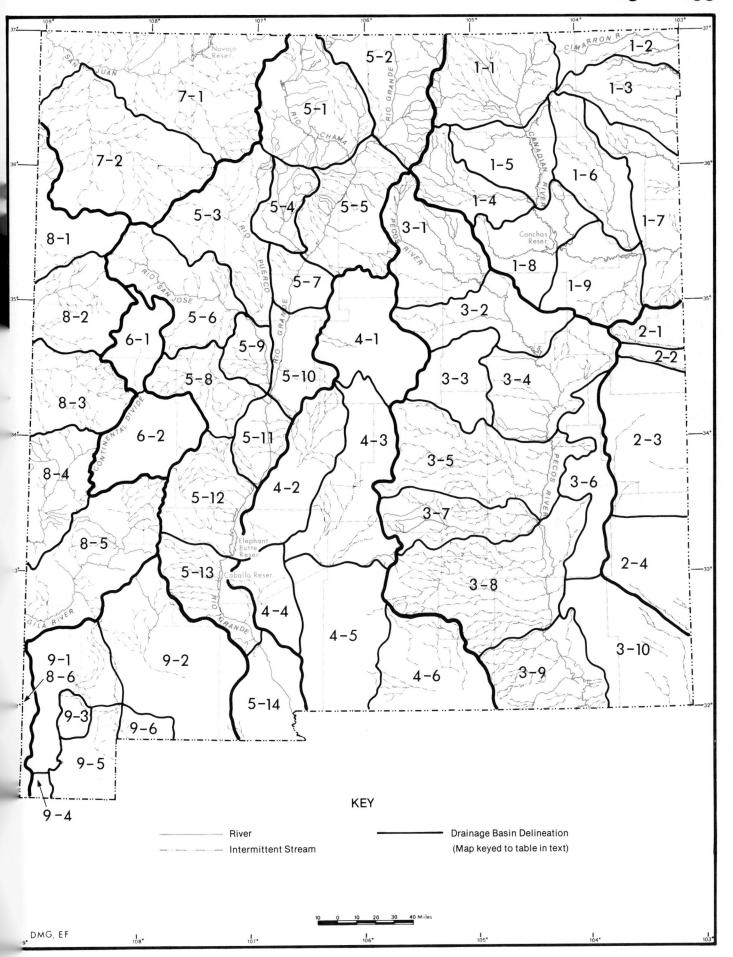

KEY

——————— River   ——————— Drainage Basin Delineation

—·—·—·— Intermittent Stream   (Map keyed to table in text)

10 0 10 20 30 40 Miles

DMG, EF

aquifers

Fresh ground water in New Mexico varies both in depth and availability and relies on spring runoff and intermittent rainfall to recharge the aquifers. All ground water is found in aquifers, which are rocks or sediments containing water and which are able to conduct that water to wells or springs. Some areas of the state have exposures of igneous or metamorphic rocks formed by volcanic and heat compression which are relatively dry. Limited quantities of water from these igneous or metamorphic rocks are available where they are fractured or weathered but these areas are likely to be discontinuous. Perched water zones are not shown on the associated maps. Perched ground water is unconfined ground water separated from a main ground water body by an unsaturated zone. Perched ground water, although common in New Mexico, is of little importance and rarely developed.

In general, ground water conditions are presented as being more or less static; however, this usually is not the actual situation. Aquifers continually receive water by seepage from streams and to a lesser extent by direct precipitation, and in some areas by seepage from irrigation. Water is also discharged naturally from aquifers into streams, through evaporation from the soil and by evapotranspiration of plants. The primary artificial discharge is by wells in intensively irrigated areas. Water levels within aquifers may fluctuate greatly, mostly in areas where water has been developed for irrigation. Increased discharge can cause general depletion of the ground water, subsidence of the materials locally above the sites of heavy pumping, and higher pumping costs due to energy requirements in bringing the water to the surface.

Not all areas within New Mexico have an adequate supply of water. Geologic conditions result in varying depths to the ground water supply. In several areas of the state the water table is more than 500 feet below ground. In southwestern Eddy County and the high country of northern Grant County and southern Catron County, the water table is at least 1000 feet below the surface. In one small area along the southern flank of the Jemez Mountains the depth to water is probably more than 1500 feet. In most of the valleys and plains areas the depth to water is less than 200 feet, and it is in this depth range that water for irrigation use has been most intensively developed. In some areas of the state, it is difficult to develop suitable supplies of fresh ground water as the aquifers are relatively impermeable and yield little water to wells, or contain soluble materials which cause the water to be saline. Eddy, Chaves and Otero counties have areas of highly saline water and approximately 75% of all New Mexico counties have some saline ground water.

In many areas of the state, ground water data is too sparse to delineate the aquifer thickness with confidence. Aquifer thickness ranges are illustrated on the map and it is assumed that areal anomalies of thickness may exist.

The thickest known aquifer in New Mexico containing fresh water is in the unconsolidated sand and gravel within the Rio Grande Valley. Near Albuquerque more than 3000 feet of aquifer is thought to be present. From Socorro northward to southern Rio Arriba County the thickness of the aquifer ranges from less than 1000 feet to more than 3000 feet. Within the valley in the vicinity of Las Cruces, as much as 2000 feet of aquifer may be present. Most of the fresh water in the Rio Grande Valley is received from the highland areas of Colorado and New Mexico. The water moves to nearby stream channels and then to the Rio Grande drainage system, downward to the water table. It has been estimated that 55,000 acre-feet of fresh ground water flows annually southward out of highlands and into the Rio Grande Valley.

Michael Inglis

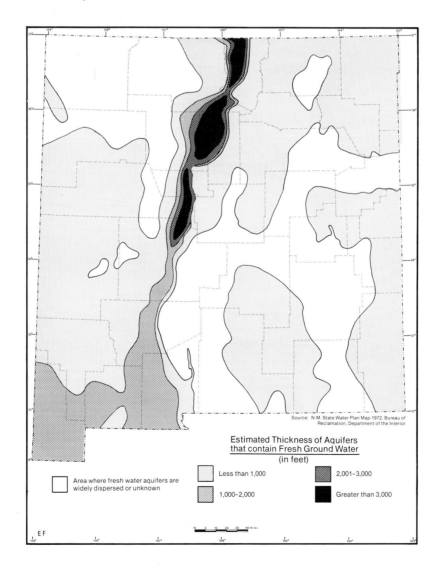

Source: N.M. State Water Plan Map-1972, Bureau of Reclamation, Department of the Interior

Estimated Thickness of Aquifers that contain Fresh Ground Water
(in feet)

Area where fresh water aquifers are widely dispersed or unknown

Less than 1,000

1,000-2,000

2,001-3,000

Greater than 3,000

aquifers

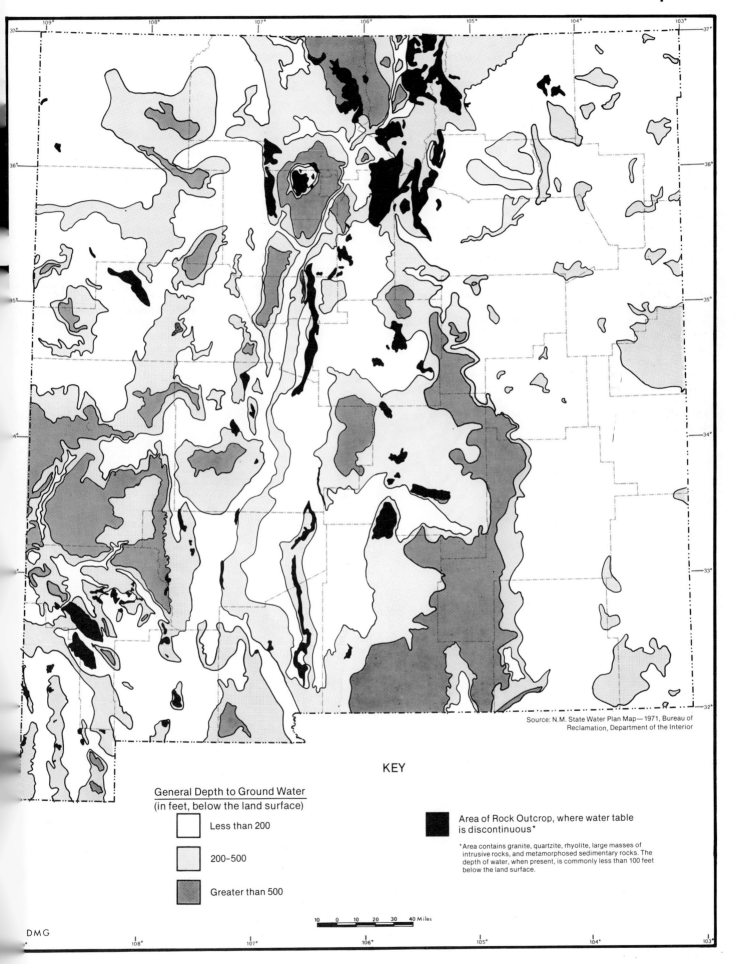

KEY

General Depth to Ground Water
(in feet, below the land surface)

☐ Less than 200

▨ 200–500

▨ Greater than 500

■ Area of Rock Outcrop, where water table
is discontinuous*

*Area contains granite, quartzite, rhyolite, large masses of
intrusive rocks, and metamorphosed sedimentary rocks. The
depth of water, when present, is commonly less than 100 feet
below the land surface.

Source: N.M. State Water Plan Map—1971, Bureau of
Reclamation, Department of the Interior

10 0 10 20 30 40 Miles

DMG

soils

The five soil Orders in New Mexico are Aridisols, Mollisols, Entisols, Inceptisols and Alfisols. Aridisols are extensive in lower elevations over the southern two-thirds of the state but are replaced in the cooler and moister higher elevations by Mollisols. Entisols occupy the Rio Grande Valley from Santa Fe southward to the Texas-Mexico border.

The northern one-third of the state and far eastern counties are dominated by Mollisols, Entisols and Alfisols. Inceptisols are found in the highest elevations of the San Juan and Sangre de Cristo Mountains.

The northern one-third of the state and far eastern counties are dominated by Mollisols, Entisols and Alfisols. Inceptisols are found in the highest elevations of the San Juan and Sangre de Cristo Mountains.

Other materials of note include the gypsum sands of White Sands National Monument and lavas of the Carrizozo, Grants, and other malpais (lava rockland).

Alfisols are soils having a yellowish or ochre-colored surface underlain by a moderately clay rich (argillic) subsoil. They tend to have relatively high base saturation and high water holding capacity during the growing season. Because of these properties they are, as a whole, intensively used, but problems of compaction and cultivation are very common.

Aridisol soils lack available moisture for mesophytic plant growth for long periods. During most of the year the soil is too salty, or water is held in the soil at tensions above the wilting point of most plants, or both. Frequently they have soil layers inherited from former pluvial periods. Surface horizons are normally light in color, low in organic matter, and have a soft consistency when dry. Vegetation, if it exists without irrigation, consists mostly of ephemeral grasses and scattered xerophytic plants. Most of the surface is bare much of the time and in many instances a surface gravel pavement has formed by deflation of the finer wind blown particles.

Entisols display little evidence of soil horizon development because they are either too young, as in the Rio Grande Valley; or, they are in a state of active erosion, as in the San Juan Basin of New Mexico. Entisols are soils in the sense that they support plant growth but not in the sense that they display the same degree of biological weathering as other soil Orders. They are not restricted to any climatic or vegetational zone.

The definition of **Inceptisols** is unavoidably complicated since they are soils not specifically included in the other nine Orders. They tend to be soils of humid regions that have lost bases and/or iron and aluminum, but which do not display subsoil horizons of accumulation. They may have any kinds of horizons common to other Orders but among the more common ones are brittle layers and cement-like layers below a yellowish surface. Their unique properties include a combination of water available for plant growth for more than three consecutive months, together with one or more horizons of alteration or concentration. They cannot form in arid environments, but otherwise are common from tropical to polar latitudes.

Mollisols are soils that generally have a very dark colored or black surface and a high base saturation. They also contain clay rich, sodium rich, or calcium rich subsoils. Most of the Mollisols have formed under grass vegetation, although in New Mexico they also coincide with mountainous, forested areas. They tend to have high native fertility and moderately high water holding capacities such that both dry land and irrigated agriculture can be practiced.

Stan Morain

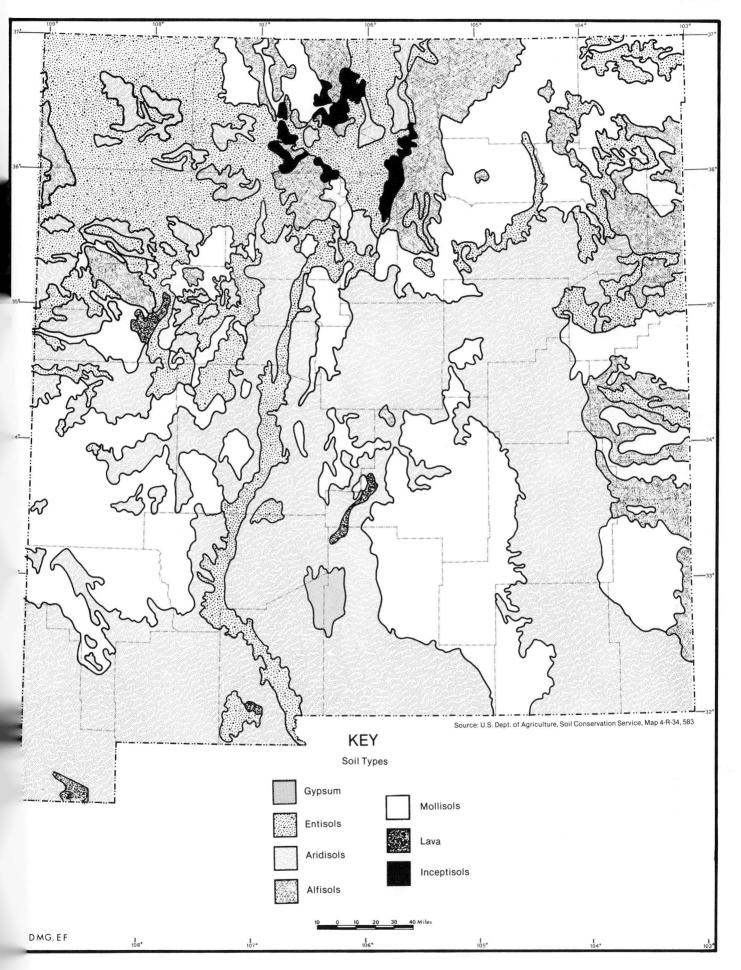

Source: U.S. Dept. of Agriculture, Soil Conservation Service, Map 4-R-34, 583

KEY

Soil Types

Gypsum

Entisols

Aridisols

Alfisols

Mollisols

Lava

Inceptisols

10 0 10 20 30 40 Miles

DMG, EF

vegetation cover types

Within the borders of New Mexico all of the major biomes of the world can be found except tundra and tropical rainforest. From the alpine barrens of Wheeler Peak to the sparse *yucca* of White Sands, environments are favorable to a variety of forest, woodland, grassland and desert plant communities. Elevation, topography and slope orientation, among other factors, all combine to provide local habitats which give New Mexico unmatched scenic beauty.

Ten major types of natural vegetation are mapped together with one category each of cultural (cultivated), barren land, and vegetational complexes. The last category contains numbers to indicate which types comprise the complex. It should be emphasized that the distributions shown here were all interpreted from 1973 satellite photographs and that, as such, represent more of a true picture than would be the case if they were derived by applying principles of ecology alone.

Progressing from higher to lower elevations in the state and from north to south the following types are encountered.

The Sangre de Cristo, San Juan, Jemez, Sandia, Manzano, Sacramento, Chuskas and Black range are all forested with mixtures of spruce (*Picea*), fir (*Abies*), pine (*Pinus*), and aspen (*Populus*) in varying proportions. Toward their lower and drier margins there are increasing admixtures of piñon (*Pinus*) and juniper (*Juniperus*) and in their higher, colder ranges they succumb to alpine barrens (not shown). Many of the intermontane valleys support alpine meadows, while burned and disturbed areas support scrub oak (*Quercus*). The most extensive areas of scrub oak occur in the San Juan, Sandia and Sacramento mountains.

Extensive areas of the state are occupied by juniper woodlands with differential mixtures of piñon or oak. They normally occur on surfaces of alluvial fans or dissected, hilly areas below pine forests and are usually characterized by wide variability in density. Some are nearly continuous while others are essentially grasslands with only occasional stunted specimens. They occur primarily in the central mountains corridor and west central areas of the state.

The distribution of cottonwood (*Populus*) with willow (*Salix*) or salt cedar (*Tamarix*) is limited to a few major river and stream courses throughout the state. Only the most extensive localities can be shown at this map scale. Many of the species, including salt cedar and willows, are deeply rooted to tap ground water. These are referred to as phreatophytes because they are able to absorb free water from the water table. These trees are considered by many to be highly beneficial as a wildlife habitat; by others they are considered to be detrimental consumers of water. The salt cedar is imported and is spreading rapidly throughout the southern half of the state.

Great basin sagebrush (*Artemisia*) is confined largely to the north central section. It is a native type in New Mexico but has been spreading due to heavy grazing. Large stands in the Questa and Chama areas have been drag-chained to clear them of shrubs, then seeded to native, and in some cases, imported grasses.

Saltbush/greasewood (*Atriplex/Sarcobatus*) is localized mainly in the central and southwestern sections of the state. It occurs in low-lying or rugged areas with very low moisture availability and generally saline or alkaline conditions.

Creosote bush (*Larrea*) is the dominant cover type over the southeastern quarter of the state. It extends up the west side of the Rio Grande to Socorro and westward to Deming. Over much of this range, mesquite (*Prosopis*), yucca and cholla (*Opúntia*) have become invasive subdominants through grazing.

The most extensive vegetation distribution in New Mexico is grama (*Bouteloua*) with galleta (*Hilaria*), mesquite or buffalo grass (*Buchloë*). It ranges throughout the state on intermediate slopes between juniper/piñon and great basin sagebrush in the higher elevations and saltbush/greasewood in the lower reaches. In the southern sections its range is terminated by too little rainfall. This type has been highly degraded and altered by grazing since the middle of the last century.

Yucca and cholla represent a dominantly cactus type that occurs in the higher elevations of small mountain ranges in the extreme southwestern part of the state. Local stands can be found from as far north as Santa Fe, southward.

Cultivated land is mainly land removed from the grama grassland type or the cottonwood/willow type along the major water courses.

Stan Morain

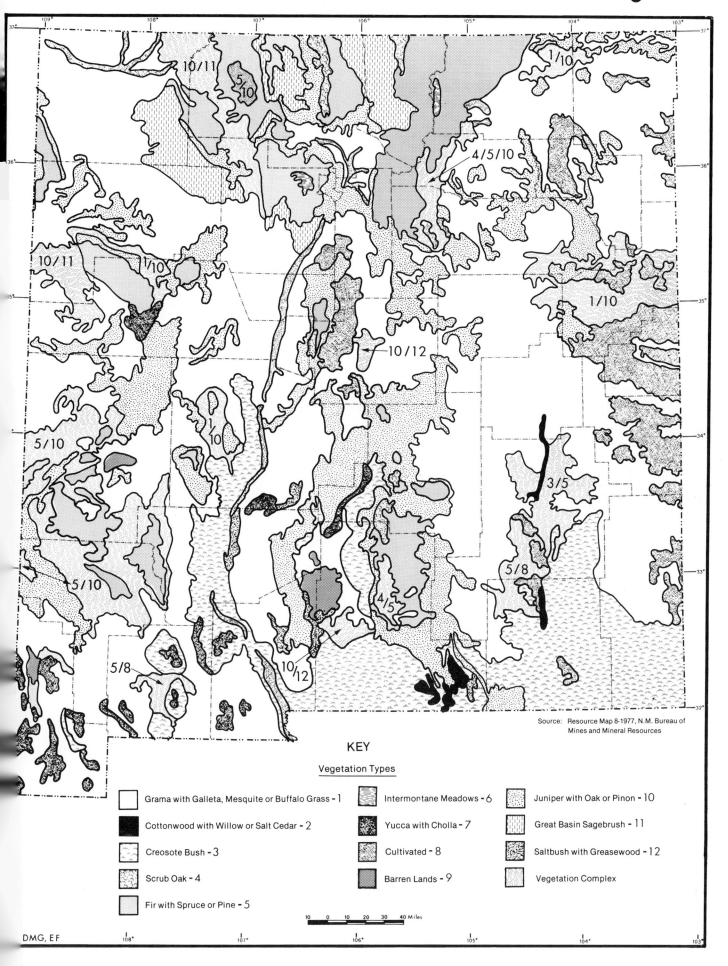

10/11

5/10

1/10

10/11

1/10

4/5/10

1/10

10/12

10/12

1/10

3/5

5/8

5/10

4/5

5/8

5/10

Source: Resource Map 8-1977, N.M. Bureau of
Mines and Mineral Resources

KEY

Vegetation Types

Grama with Galleta, Mesquite or Buffalo Grass - 1

Cottonwood with Willow or Salt Cedar - 2

Creosote Bush - 3

Scrub Oak - 4

Fir with Spruce or Pine - 5

Intermontane Meadows - 6

Yucca with Cholla - 7

Cultivated - 8

Barren Lands - 9

Juniper with Oak or Pinon - 10

Great Basin Sagebrush - 11

Saltbush with Greasewood - 12

Vegetation Complex

10   0   10   20   30   40 Miles

DMG, E F

23

historical landscapes

vertebrate fossil and paleoindian sites

Fossils older than 500 million years to those a few thousand years old are present in sedimentary rocks exposed over most of New Mexico. The map displays the following known vertebrate fossil distributions in New Mexico: Paleozoic sites (600 to 230 million years old), mainly fish, amphibians and early reptiles; Mesozoic sites (230 to 65 million years old), mainly amphibians, reptiles, and dinosaurs; and Cenozoic sites (65 to 1 million years old), mainly primitive to nearly modern mammals. Areas with good deposits of invertebrate fossils are more extensive in New Mexico, but are not shown here because their distribution essentially coincides with the exposures of marine sedimentary rocks indicated on the geologic map. Also not shown are scattered Pleistocene (about 1 million to 10,000 years old) vertebrate fossil sites, some of which also include the implements of PaleoIndian.

PaleoIndian refers to archeological remains dating to the Late Pleistocene Era, when the ancestors of modern American Indians crossed the Bering Land Bridge into North America. Artifacts recovered consist of stone and bone tools, frequently in association with Pleistocene fauna. New Mexico contains the primary type sites of three PaleoIndian assemblages: Sandia, Clovis, and Folsom. There are also type sites such as Firstview Complex and Cody Complex, which are representative of primary site finds outside of the state.

The Sandia assemblage site is Sandia Cave, above Las Huertas Canyon, Bernalillo County. Remains include the diagnostic Sandia points and other stone tools. The only other excavated Sandia site in New Mexico is the Lucy Site, near Lucy, New Mexico.

The Clovis type site is Blackwater Draw Locality 1, seven miles north of Portales. Blackwater Draw El Llano, near Locality 1, has also produced Clovis material. Artifacts consist of diagnostic fluted projectile points, stone scrapers and a variety of bone tools. Faunal remains are diverse; the mammoth is typical of those represented.

The Folsom type site is near Folsom, New Mexico. Elida, about 25 miles southwest of Portales, is also an excavated Folsom site, as is the Rio Rancho site, 15 miles west of Albuquerque. Folsom assemblages contain the finely flaked diagnostic fluted Folsom points, scrapers, knives and borers of stone, and some bone artifacts. At the Folsom type site and elsewhere, Folsom artifacts are associated with *Bison antiquus,* the older and larger ancestor of the modern bison (*Bison bison*). The *Bison antiquus* became extinct around 8000 years ago.

In addition to the type sites, Blackwater Draw and the San Jon site have yielded remains of the Firstview Complex. Complex refers to associated tool and projectile point types and does not necessarily define distinct cultural types. Firstview Complex points are not fluted but are thinned by lateral flaking. The bases of the points are slightly indented. Firstview artifacts have been found in association with *Bison occidentalis,* the smaller successor of *Bison antiquus.*

The final PaleoIndian manifestation over much of New Mexico is the Cody Complex. Near Sapello in San Miguel County is a Cody Complex quarry. Cody Complex artifacts include Eden and Scottsbluff finely transversed flaked points with indented bases, and the Cody knife, a distinctive implement with a transverse cutting edge. Bison are represented at Cody Complex kill sites. Other fauna associated with Cody include cervids, antelope and other large and small mammals.

Three sites in the Guadalupe Mountains have yielded Paleo-Indian remains but are difficult to interpret. Burnet Cave contained a Clovis point and Pleistocene fauna, but the deposit showed some evidence of disturbance. Hermit's Cave contained Pleistocene fauna and a hearth but no diagnostic artifacts. Burro Cienega No. 9 has been interpreted as either Midland Complex or Plainview Complex. The Midland Complex was contemporaneous to the Folsom excavation horizon (9,000 to 8,000 years ago) however, the point types differed in style. The Plainview Complex was similar to and later than the Midland Complex, but with non fluted points.

In addition to these excavated sites, PaleoIndian sites and isolated points are found in many areas of New Mexico. Generally they occur on eroded land surfaces. Areas that have yielded quantities of PaleoIndian remains, as both surface and subsurface finds, are shaded on the map.

PaleoIndian sites are not as well-dated as could be hoped. The Sandia remains may be as old as 25,000 years, but this has been disputed. Clovis artifacts rather consistently date to about 11,500 years ago. The other PaleoIndian complexes date between 10,000 and 7,500 years ago with considerable overlap in available radiocarbon dates.

Barry Kues
Linda Corde

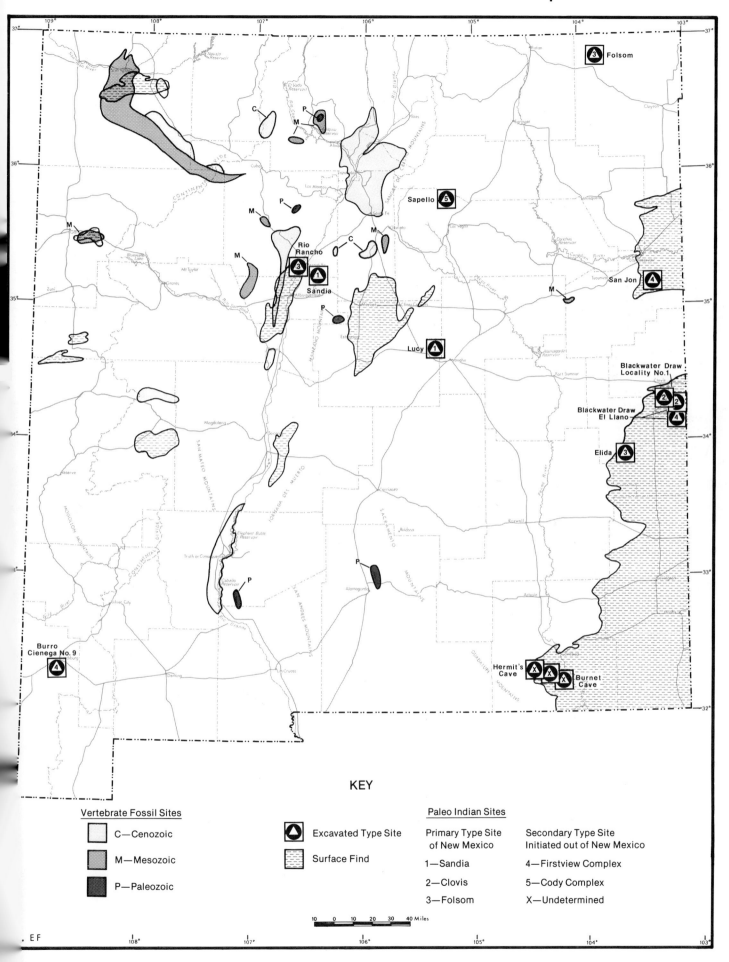

vertebrate fossil and paleoindian sites

Folsom

Sapello

San Jon

Rio Rancho

Sandia

Lucy

Blackwater Draw
Locality No.1

Blackwater Draw
El Llano

Elida

Burro
Cienega No. 9

Hermit's
Cave

Burnet
Cave

KEY

Vertebrate Fossil Sites

C—Cenozoic

M—Mesozoic

P—Paleozoic

Excavated Type Site

Surface Find

Paleo Indian Sites

Primary Type Site of New Mexico	Secondary Type Site Initiated out of New Mexico
1—Sandia	4—Firstview Complex
2—Clovis	5—Cody Complex
3—Folsom	X—Undetermined

10 0 10 20 30 40 Miles

E F

native american settlements

At the end of the Pleistocene, coincident with climatic change and the reduction of grasslands in New Mexico, the PaleoIndian adaptation gave way to a hunting and gathering way of life. Referred to as the Archaic, it focused on plant foods and small game animals (deer, rabbits, antelope, and mountain sheep). Within this context, corn which had been domesticated in Mesoamerica was adopted. Evidence of early corn comes from well-preserved cave deposits such as Tularosa Cave and Bat Cave, dated at 2000 B.C. Not until A.D. 400 or 500 did sedentary village communities appear.

Archeologists recognize two major cultural traditions of village agriculturalists in New Mexico: the Mogollon, named for the Mogollon Mountains, and the Anasazi, a Navajo term for "the ancient ones." The Mogollon centered in southwestern and south-central New Mexico, extending into adjacent portions of Arizona and far south into Chihuahua, Mexico. The Mogollon villages are predominantly composed of semi-subterranean pit houses with interior and exterior storage pits. Ceramics are largely brownwares. Late in Mogollon prehistory, above ground rectangular pueblos were built and black-on-white ceramics made. The ceramics of the Mimbres branch of the Mogollon, along the Mimbres River, are well known. The descendants of the Mogollon may have moved into the Zuni area and along the Rio Grande.

The Anasazi centered on the four-corners area of New Mexico, Arizona, Utah and Colorado, but extended considerably eastward into the Rio Grande area and the eastern periphery along the Cimarron and Pecos Rivers. Originally the Anasazi lived in pit house villages and made gray or black-on-white ceramics. About A.D. 700, most Anasazi were living in rectangular-roomed, above ground villages, retaining the pit houses as ceremonial rooms (or kivas). In some cases, such as in the Taos area and in the Gallina area, pit houses continued to be used as dwellings until A.D. 1250. Some of the most spectacular Anasazi sites are in the San Juan and Chaco Canyon area. These include the ruins of Chaco Canyon National Monument (Pueblo Bonito, Kin Kletso, Una Vida, and Chetro Ketl), the ruin at Aztec National Monument and Salmon Ruin (near Bloomfield), the ruins of villages on the Pajarito Plateau including those in Bandelier National Monument, and Pecos Pueblo.

The San Juan area was abandoned by A.D. 1300. The larger ruins of the Pajarito Plateau and the Rio Grande Valley were founded after this date, although smaller villages in the area are contemporary with those of the four-corners area. It is generally agreed that the modern Pueblo Indians are descendants of the Anasazi, although there is considerable controversy in determining the precise location of the ancestral villages of each pueblo. Shortly before the arrival of the Spaniards in the 16th century, Athapaskan-speaking Indians (Navajos and Apaches) entered New Mexico and lived among the Pueblos. Comanches and Utes also extended their range into New Mexico prior to 1750.

Linda Cordell

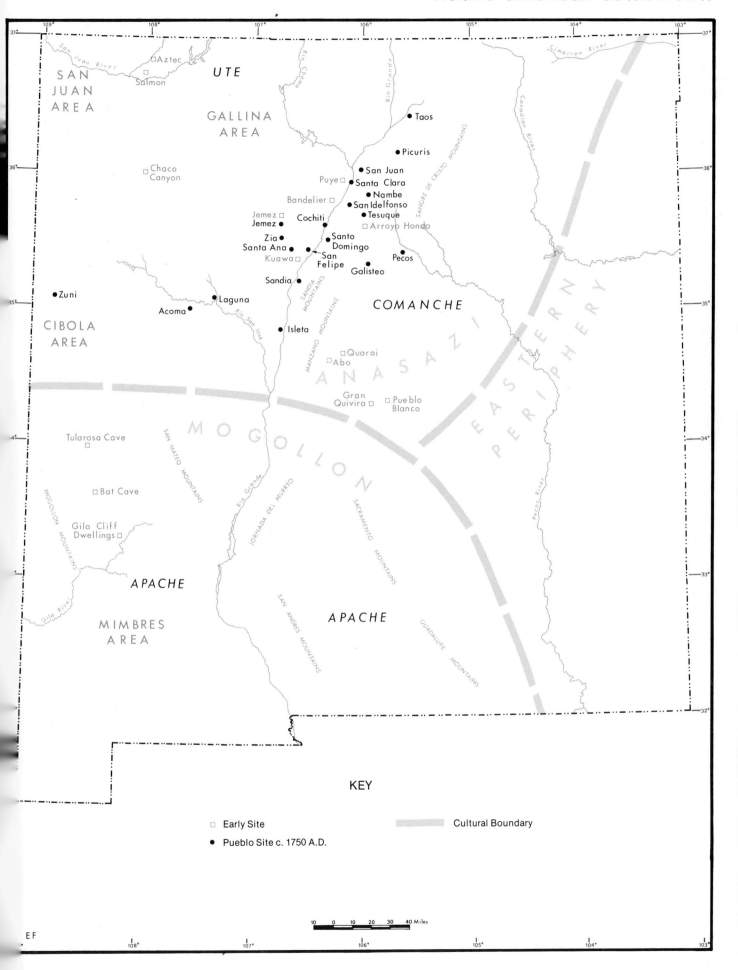

KEY

□ Early Site   ▬▬▬ Cultural Boundary

● Pueblo Site c. 1750 A.D.

E F

spanish exploration

New Mexico quickly became known to the early Spanish explorers and colonists. Two natural highways allowed easy entry for northward moving Spaniards expanding the frontiers of the Viceroyalty of New Spain. These access routes were the Rio Pecos and the Rio Grande del Norte. Native Indian populations were largely distributed along the Rio Grande and its intermittent tributaries. Therefore, it is hardly surprising that early European exploration would focus on such Indian villages as potential sources of supply and geographical intelligence.

Spanish expectations of rich cities, possible duplicates of the Aztec capital of Tenochtitlán (Mexico City), led to rapid scouring of the land in anticipation of material wealth. The first explorers to penetrate the general area were led by Alvar Núñez Cabeza de Vaca of the ill-fated Pánfilo de Narváez colony in Florida. Plagued by misfortune, the expedition attempted to return to civilization via the Gulf of Mexico in hand-crafted, makeshift vessels. A few survivors finally washed ashore on the Texas coast, most of whom were unable to survive the rigors of the first winter. Only four lived to recount their experiences. Alvar Núñez Cabeza de Vaca, Alonso de Castillo Maldonado, Andrés Dorantes, and the latter's Moorish slave, Estevan or Estevanico, became successively slaves, traders, and medicine men. In the latter capacity they gained fame and prestige as they moved from tribe to tribe practicing their newly-found skills. They proceeded slowly westward across Texas and near El Paso the wanderers crossed the Rio Grande. Scholars have discussed and hypothesized at length over possible routes traversed by the party, but because the primary account was written several years ex post facto, the safest statement is that the four travellers and their Indian entourage crossed what was once New Mexico en route to civilization, which they encountered on the Sinaloa, Mexico coast in 1536.

Though Alvar Núñez Cabeza de Vaca did not find any of the legendary fabulous cities in the interior, Indian informants gave rise to increased expectations. Cabeza de Vaca, after prolonged wandering, declined a viceregal offer to head a follow-up reconnaissance and continued his service elsewhere.

Dorantes and Castillo Maldonado also declined a similar viceregal offer but the Viceroy purchased the slave, Estevanico, and assigned him to a new northern exploratory sortie. Named as leader was a much-travelled Franciscan priest, Fray Marcos de Niza, who had recently returned from exploration in Peru and Central America. Roughly reversing Cabeza de Vaca's route, the priest and Estevanico, acting as the guide, set out. They subsequently separated, with the slave serving as advance agent. New power caused Estevancio to make excessive demands on Indians encountered along his itinerary. He frequently sent messages back to Fray Marcos. The last report Marcos received was of rich cities and of Estevanico's death at the hands of the Hawikuh Pueblo natives. Marcos later told a story of continuing onward and claimed he could see a rich city in the distance. There is a question of the veracity of Marcos and of whether he or his Moorish companion ever set foot in today's New Mexico. In any case, they were almost astride its modern boundary.

In New Mexico, Marcos' tale of wealth found eager audience with Viceroy Mendoza, who organized a large scale exploratory expedition. The party, under the leadership of Francisco Vasquez de Coronado, entered New Mexico near the site of Estevanico's death. The Spaniards, attracted to the Rio Grande and its associated Pueblo Indian villages, spent the winter at a native village, located near what is now the town of Bernalillo, but not where the Coronado State Historical Monument today stands.

Exploratory parties visited the northern and eastern areas. They crossed the Pecos River, and visited the Buffalo Plains where the party almost became lost and traversed the Llano Estacado. When no great civilizations nor rich cities materialized, they headed homeward. Interest in New Mexico waned for decades.

As the mining frontier of Central Mexico expanded northward, Spanish interest in the Pueblo Indians was rekindled, with the Franciscans at the forefront. Brother Augustín Rodríguez and ageing frontier Captain Francisco Sánchez Chamuscado joined religious and military forces in 1581 and entered New Mexico from the south along the river highway of the Conchos and Rio Grande. Rodríguez died a martyr, and Chamuscado died en route home. Stories of rich silver mines in the Magdalenas continued to circulate.

Believing that his Franciscan colleagues were still alive, or on that pretext, Father Bernardino Beltrán received permission for a "rescue expedition" which in 1582-83 replicated and added to the achievements of the previous expedition. This sortie left a story of a purported lake of gold to stimulate renewed action and many were eager to go. Some made formal petitions and awaited regal permission while others took unauthorized action. Gaspar Castaño de Sosa, Lieutenant Governor of Nuevo León, in 1589 led a group of colonists up the Pecos River to Pecos Pueblo. They later moved to Santo Domingo Pueblo, where the leader was apprehended by royal authority. It was not until 1598 that an authorized entry occurred under the leadership of Juan de Oñate.

Oñate's expedition carried out the settlement of New Mexico with initial headquarters near modern Española. The leader's lieutenants, among them his nephews Juan and Vicente Zaldivar, explored in various directions. Oñate made a long trip to the "South Sea" of the Pacific, duplicating earlier reconnaissance, and en route left his historic inscription on El Morro.

In future decades Spanish explorers, with various motives, reexplored areas to the northeast, east, and southeast, while missionary activity preserved a knowledge of the west. Only the Ute Indian barrier to the north and northwest defied occasional exploratory penetration. By 1765 even that area was explored during two expeditions by Juan María Antonio Rivera. Subsequent explorations toward the little known north in the 1770's by Fathers Domínguez and Escalante and by Governor Juan Bautista de Anza rounded out initial reconnaissance.

Donald Cutte

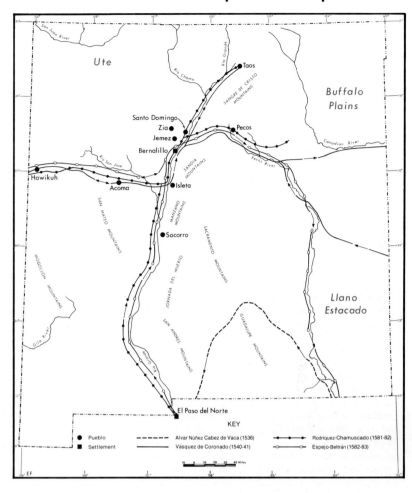

KEY

- ● Pueblo
- ■ Settlement

- – – – Alvar Núñez Cabez de Vaca (1536)
- ——— Vásquez de Coronado (1540-41)

- ●–●–● Rodríquez-Chamuscado (1581-82)
- ○—○—○ Espejo-Beltrán (1582-83)

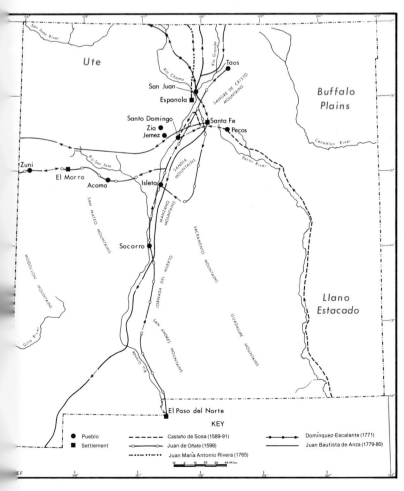

KEY

- ● Pueblo
- ■ Settlement

- – – – Castaño de Sosa (1589-91)
- ○—○—○ Juan de Oñate (1598)
- –·–·– Juan María Antonio Rivera (1765)

- ●–●–● Domínquez-Escalante (1771)
- ——— Juan Bautista de Anza (1779-80)

spanish colonization 1598-1821

Treasure, religious idealism, and strategic factors motivated Spain's movement into New Mexico. Spanish *conquistadores* sought another Tenochtitlán, new gold and silver mines, and labor for their mining operations in Zacatecas and Durango, Mexico. Spain's religious mission as defender of the Roman Catholic faith found potential converts among the sedentary inhabitants of the Rio Grande Pueblos. In addition, the search for the legendary Strait of Anián, a water passage through the North American continent to the China trade, remained a vital force in the push into the northern frontier. Interest in New Mexico heightened after 1579 when the English privateer, Francis Drake, circumnavigated the globe so quickly that Spanish leaders feared the Strait had been located by their greatest enemy.

Permanent occupation of New Mexico began in 1598 when Don Juan de Oñate led 400 men with 130 families, eight Franciscan priests, Indian and black slaves, and thousands of head of cattle into the Rio Grande Valley via El Paso del Norte. As governor of the province he established his capitol (San Juan) at the confluence of the Rio Chama and the Rio Grande north of Española. Oñate consolidated his authority over the pueblos, and the sacking of Ácoma in 1599 decisively aided this process. Franciscans were distributed among the pueblos to Christianize the natives, and the *encomienda* (a labor and tribute system) was also established. Oñate directed expeditions east of the Pecos River to the "buffalo plains" and west to the Colorado River and the Gulf of California to locate fabulous treasures. Growing discontent with Oñate's leadership caused him to resign his governorship. In approximately 1610 the capitol was moved to Santa Fe.

Conflict between church and state characterized seventeenth century New Mexico. Governors and settlers sought material wealth through exploitation of Indian labor while Franciscans attempted to save the natives from abuse and their souls for eternal glory. The inquisition and threat of excommunication kept secular authorities in line. This rivalry, however, did much to undermine Spanish prestige in the Rio Grande Valley. Combined with drought, famine, and devastating Apache and Navajo raids in the 1660's and 1670's, pueblo discontent simmered until Popé, the charismatic leader of San Juan Pueblo, launched the Pueblo Revolt of 1680. This successful rebellion resulted in the founding of El Paso del Norte and the termination of the *encomienda* system. In 1692 Governor Don Diego de Vargas reestablished Spanish authority in the province.

During the eighteenth century, Spain became firmly entrenched in the Rio Grande Valley. Laguna Pueblo had been founded earlier as a western defensive post; Albuquerque was established in 1706 by settlers from Bernalillo; and by the middle of the century posts were established to the north at Abiquiu and Ojo Caliente. By the 1770's settlers had penetrated eastward to the Pecos and Canadian Rivers and westward along the Rio Puerco and into the Mt. Taylor region. In spite of such activity, Spain's posture in New Mexico remained defensive, contending with pressure from Apaches, Navajos, Utes, and Comanches. This pressure compelled some retrenchment late in the century, and caused Spain to rely heavily upon pueblo auxiliary forces to punish these raiders.

New Mexico never attained the economic success its founders had envisioned. Some copper mining activity occurred in the Silver City area while turquoise, silver, and lead deposits were developed near Los Cerrillos. Agricultural endeavors included tobacco, grapes, corn, wheat, chile, and cotton. The most important industry was sheep and cattle grazing. New Mexico relied upon the Chihuahua Trail as part of a world trading network, linking Santa Fe to Spain and the Philippines, for its economic and military sustenance. It usually took three to five years for goods to reach Santa Fe. New Mexican imports included hardware items, church ornaments, and small high-value articles. Exports consisted of hides, cloth, salt, and an illegal slave traffic for silver mines to the south. Trade with Apaches, Utes, Comanches, and Navajos was carried on at the picturesque Taos fair. These Indians attempted to acquire weapons and ammunition in return for hides, tallow, jerky, animals, and slaves.

New Mexico also developed a stratified social structure. At the top were the *ricos* (or dons), wealthy landowners and merchants. They not only possessed economic power but political dominance as well. Associated with them were Franciscan clergy, usually the most educated group in the province. At the bottom of the social scale rested the *pobres* held in debt peonage. The don-peon system was to dominate New Mexico politics and economy until the twentieth century. A significant group were the *genízaros,* composed of non-pueblo detribalized Indians who became Spanish in culture and language. *Genízaros* ultimately acquired political rights and performed a valuable role as a bulwark against external Indian aggression. They settled in Belen, San Miguel, and Abiquiu as advance guards of Spanish civilizations, and their trading contacts with non-pueblo Indians allowed Spanish goods to reach Canada.

Throughout the colonial period New Mexico remained important as a missionary field and as a buffer against foreign encroachment into the silver district of north-central New Spain. Following France's expulsion from North America in 1763, Spain girded itself to administer French Louisiana and to prepare for war against Great Britain. Consequently, Charles III instituted a series of reforms to consolidate Spain's hold on the borderlands. Central to Spanish policy was retrenchment of its military defense line, settlement of Alta California, and reduction of hostile Apache, Navajo, and Comanche forces. New Mexico Governor Don Juan Bautista de Anza skillfully employed might and diplomacy to make peace with the Navajos and Comanches and to urge them to turn on the Apaches. His defeat of Cuerno Verde near Pueblo, Colorado in 1779 and his subsequent negotiation of uneasy Indian alliances proved decisive in easing Comanche pressure from the eastern plains.

By the early 1800's, however, New Mexico became the focus of a new threat from the east: the vanguard of American expansion across the Mississippi River in the form of fur traders and precursors of the Santa Fe trade. Trade with *yanqui* entrepreneurs was discouraged by confiscating goods and incarcerating traders in Santa Fe and Chihuahua City jails. Even so, New Mexican isolation was breached periodically until Spain was expelled from the area in 1821. In 1806-1807 the controversial Pike expedition did much to spark American interest in trade with New Mexico and adjacent areas. All that was necessary to open a new era in New Mexican history was the elimination of Spanish authority in September of 1821.

Stephen Sayles

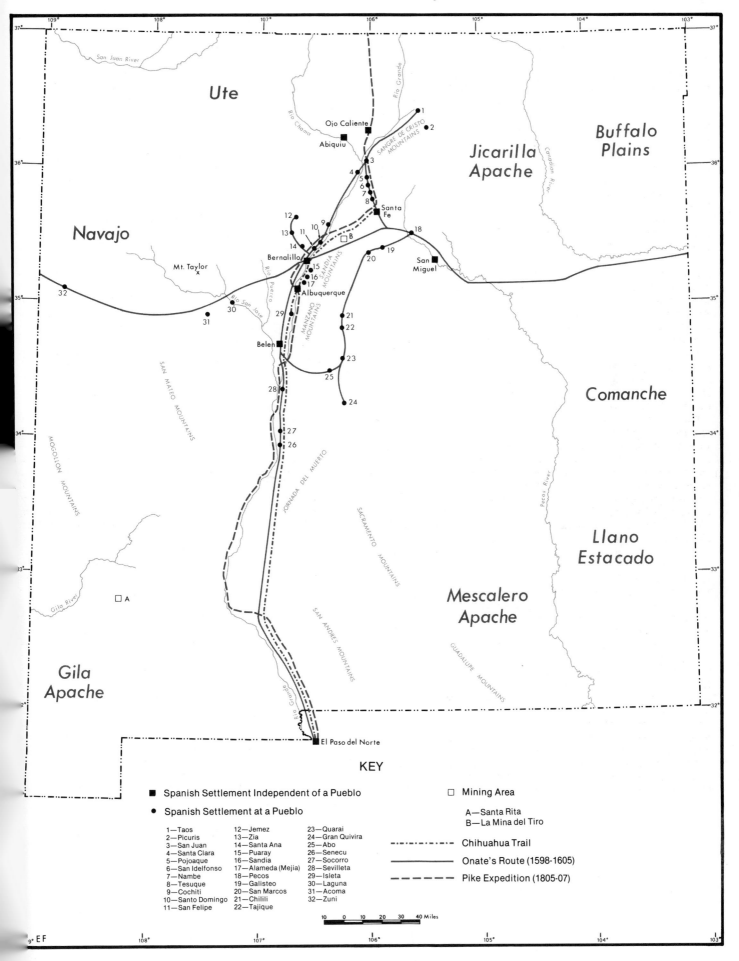

Ute

Navajo

Jicarilla
Apache

Buffalo
Plains

San Juan River

Rio Chama

Ojo Caliente
Abiquiu

1
2

Rio Grande

SANGRE DE CRISTO MOUNTAINS

3
4
5
6
7
8

Santa
Fe

12
13
14

11
10
9

18

B

Bernalillo

Mt. Taylor
x

Rio Puerco

Rio San Jose

15
16
17

Albuquerque

19

20

San
Miguel

Canadian River

32

30
31

29

SANDIA MOUNTAINS

21
22

MANZANO MOUNTAINS

Belen

23

25

28

24

Comanche

27
26

JORNADA DEL MUERTO

SAN MATEO MOUNTAINS

SACRAMENTO MOUNTAINS

Pecos River

Llano
Estacado

MOGOLLON MOUNTAINS

Gila River

□ A

SAN ANDRES MOUNTAINS

Mescalero
Apache

GUADALUPE MOUNTAINS

Gila
Apache

Rio Grande

El Paso del Norte

KEY

■ Spanish Settlement Independent of a Pueblo

● Spanish Settlement at a Pueblo

□ Mining Area

A—Santa Rita
B—La Mina del Tiro

1—Taos
2—Picuris
3—San Juan
4—Santa Clara
5—Pojoaque
6—San Idelfonso
7—Nambe
8—Tesuque
9—Cochiti
10—Santo Domingo
11—San Felipe

12—Jemez
13—Zia
14—Santa Ana
15—Puaray
16—Sandia
17—Alameda (Mejia)
18—Pecos
19—Galisteo
20—San Marcos
21—Chilili
22—Tajique

23—Quarai
24—Gran Quivira
25—Abo
26—Senecu
27—Socorro
28—Sevilleta
29—Isleta
30—Laguna
31—Acoma
32—Zuni

—··—··—··— Chihuahua Trail

—————— Onate's Route (1598-1605)

— — — — Pike Expedition (1805-07)

10 0 10 20 30 40 Miles

E F

mexican control 1821-1846

In September 1821 Mexico became independent from Spain. New Mexico declared its allegiance to the new Republic of Mexico and following elections in January 1822 sent a delegation to the Mexican Congress. Its government was dominated until 1837 by the *jefe político* (political chief) and thereafter by the governor. Beneath the executive was a weak assembly. *Ayuntamientos* (city councils) governed such larger towns as Santa Cruz de La Cañada, Santa Fe, and Taos, while smaller communities retained their *alcaldes* (magistrates) who dispensed justice subject to review from the supreme court in Chihuahua. In January 1824 New Mexico joined the Mexican provinces of Chihuahua and Durango as a single state. Durango resisted this union, however, and New Mexico's status as a territory continued until 1837 when it became a department under the centralist Constitution of 1836. It remained a department until August 1846 when the area fell to the United States Army of the West.

Internal political chaos in Mexico City, dominated by General Antonio López de Santa Ana, diverted Mexican attention from its northern frontier. Consequently, New Mexico developed a sense of regionalism and autonomy from Mexican rule as it struggled against strong pressure from hostile tribes along its perimeter.

Contemporary observers described New Mexicans as a generous, and gracious people who possessed strong patriarchal family ties. New Mexico's pastoral economy continued to be dominated by sheep with some copper mining at Santa Rita del Cobre. Bands of *ciboleros* hunted buffalo on the Llano Estacado while *comancheros* (Indian traders) brought trade goods to the eastern plains in return for Comanche plunder and captives.

Local and regional dons dominated New Mexican politics and economy through debt peonage. Local dons provided jobs, health care, and loans to their *peones* in exchange for their personal and political loyalty. Education in New Mexico was virtually nonexistent. Dons had their sons educated in Durango or St. Louis and resisted efforts to establish primary schools in such communities as Albuquerque, Belen, Taos, San Miguel, and Santa Fe. There were few, if any, qualified teachers available, and funding through city councils was difficult to obtain. A printing press arrived in Santa Fe in 1834, however, and a weekly newspaper was published for a short period.

Mexico City did exert significant influence upon New Mexican lives. Liberal land legislation of the 1820's opened the area up to huge land grants to foster settlement. These massive grants, often in hundreds of thousands of acres, were made primarily in north-central New Mexico where the grantees had access to good land and water. Important grants included the Beaubien and Miranda grants (later the Maxwell grant), the Mora grant, the Las Vegas grant, the Montoya grant along the Canadian River, and the Ortiz land grant, site of the 1820's gold rush settlements of Dolores and Tuerto. These and similar grants would dominate New Mexican politics until the 1900's.

Anti-clerical liberals in the Mexican Congress also enacted mission secularization legislation. In 1828 they pushed through the Expulsion Act to expel Spanish-born *gachupines* (literally, "wearer of spurs," referring to pure blood Spaniards born in Spain as opposed to *criollos* who were pure blood Spaniards born in the Americas) from Mexico. In reality, this meant removal of the Franciscan priests from the New Mexican field, leaving the territory desperate for religious instruction. Mexican-born secular priests replaced the Franciscans in Taos, Belen, Albuquerque, San Miguel and elsewhere. Without the rigid discipline of the Francis-

can order, the quality of religious instruction and activity declined in spite of occasional visits from the Bishop of Durango. This decline gave fresh impetus to the *penitente* movement in northern New Mexico. Only the arrival of Bishop Jean Baptiste Lamy in 1851 brought discipline to New Mexico Catholicism.

The dominating motif of this era was the coming of the American fur traders and the Santa Fe trade. Taos was the base for mountain men and fur traders exploiting beaver areas in the southern Rockies, Pecos River, and rich Gila River Valley of southwestern New Mexico and Arizona. Such mountain men as Ewing Young and William Wolfskill, along with New Mexican merchants like Antonio Armijo, opened the Old Spanish Trail into southern California in 1829-1830. New Mexican sheep were moved west, and California mules were moved east to Santa Fe and eventually to Missouri.

The Santa Fe trade dominated New Mexican economic life for decades. Simultaneous with Mexican independence, *yanqui* trader William Becknell opened up Santa Fe to American trade goods. New Mexican and Chihuahua gold and silver were exchanged for high value goods and manufactured products. The trade pioneered the use of wagon caravans across the plains over the Santa Fe Trail which opened in the 1820's. The stranglehold of Chihuahua City merchants on Santa Fe commerce was ultimately broken by better quality and less expensive American goods. Anglo-Hispanic relations were exacerbated by arbitrary Mexican regulations and custom duties. Moreover, Texan independence under the Treaty of Velasco in 1836 included land claims into New Mexico. Texan leaders were anxious to divert the Santa Fe trade and invaded New Mexico periodically between 1841 and 1843 to fulfill their expansionist designs. The Texas-Santa Fe expedition of 1841, however, terminated disastrously near Anton Chico, and the subsequent brutal march of Texan prisoners down the Rio Grande to El Paso inflamed ethnic tensions throughout the Rio Grande Valley.

New Mexico notions of autonomy were dashed in 1835 with the appointment of Albino Pérez as governor of the territory. Pérez was an outsider and attempted to ingratiate himself with New Mexicans by marrying a local woman. As an official of the central government, however, he was also compelled to enforce the Constitution of 1836 by restricting village authority through direct taxation. Efforts to curb local authority sparked a revolution in Santa Cruz de La Cañada and other northern pueblos in 1837. Rebel forces defeated Pérez' army and beheaded the governor. José González of Taos was elected governor, but his accession disappointed Manuel Armijo of Albuquerque who had participated in the revolt. Appointed governor by Mexico City, Armijo defeated and executed González in January 1838 at Santa Cruz de La Cañada.

As a native New Mexican, Armijo enjoyed public support, but his character and patriotism have been ravaged by prejudicial accounts of *yanqui* observers. He remained governor of the department until 1846 when he fled before the American Army of the West in the early stages of the Mexican War. Suspicion remains that he may have been bribed by trader James Magoffin not to make a stand against the invaders. It is doubtful that Armijo could have made little more than a token defense. When the invaders entered Santa Fe without resistance on August 18, 1846, New Mexico began a new period of political and economic development.

Stephen Sayles

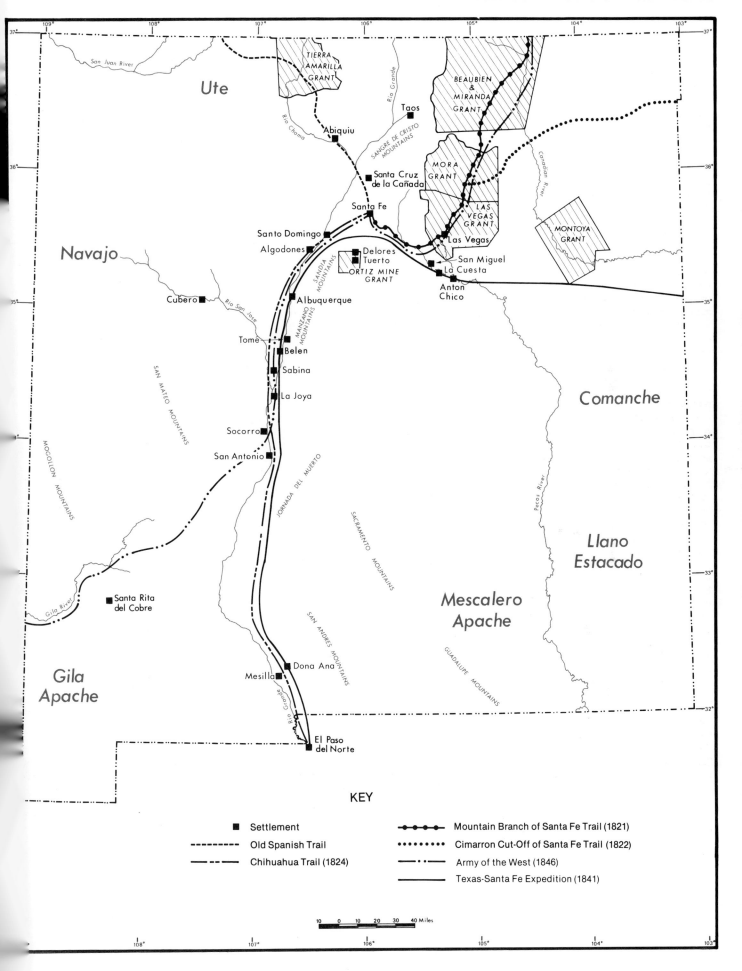

Ute

TIERRA AMARILLA GRANT

San Juan River

Rio Grande

Taos

Rio Chama

Abiquiu

BEAUBIEN & MIRANDA GRANT

SANGRE DE CRISTO MOUNTAINS

Santa Cruz de la Cañada

MORA GRANT

Navajo

Santa Fe

Canadian River

LAS VEGAS GRANT

Santo Domingo

Las Vegas

Algodones

MONTOYA GRANT

Delores
Tuerto

San Miguel

SANDIA MOUNTAINS

La Cuesta

ORTIZ MINE GRANT

Anton Chico

Cubero

Rio San Jose

Albuquerque

MANZANO MOUNTAINS

Tome

Comanche

SAN MATEO MOUNTAINS

Belen

Sabina

La Joya

Socorro

San Antonio

MOGOLLON MOUNTAINS

JORNADA DEL MUERTO

SACRAMENTO MOUNTAINS

Pecos River

Llano
Estacado

Gila River

Santa Rita del Cobre

SAN ANDRES MOUNTAINS

Mescalero
Apache

SAN AGUSTIN

Gila
Apache

Mesilla

Dona Ana

Rio Grande

GUADALUPE MOUNTAINS

El Paso
del Norte

KEY

■ Settlement

● ● ● Mountain Branch of Santa Fe Trail (1821)

- - - - Old Spanish Trail

• • • • Cimarron Cut-Off of Santa Fe Trail (1822)

– · – · Chihuahua Trail (1824)

– · · – Army of the West (1846)

——— Texas-Santa Fe Expedition (1841)

10 0 10 20 30 40 Miles

land grants

New Mexico land theoretically belonged to the Spanish Crown and, after the Plan of Iguala, 1821, it became the domain of the Mexican government. Spanish and Mexican land grants were designed to colonize and develop unoccupied lands and to defend against foreign encroachment and hostile nomadic tribes. Land grants in New Mexico were of three types: proprietary grants given to individuals; community grants given to ten or more families or to pueblo communities; and the *sitio*, or ranch, grants which varied in size from one square league during the colonial period to hundreds of thousands of acres during the Mexican period.

Spanish land grants concentrated along the Rio Grande and its tributaries between Taos and Belen. Mexican grants tended to be larger and were located on the periphery of existing grants. Texan independence in 1836 compelled such New Mexican leaders as Governor Manuel Armijo to issue massive grants to New Mexican citizens. Should the American occupation of Santa Fe occur, it was intended to keep as much New Mexican land in Mexican hands as possible. Accordingly, large grants such as Sangre de Cristo, Beaubien-Miranda, Nolan, Vigil and St. Vrain, and Conejos were issued in northern New Mexico and southern Colorado during the 1840's in the wake of renewed Texan-Mexican conflict along the Rio Grande.

Spanish and Mexican land grants were protected under the Treaty of Guadalupe-Hidalgo, 1848, which terminated the Mexican War. Hispanic residents were guaranteed the rights of American citizenship, but strict enforcement of treaty provisions was not maintained in the following years. Consequently, land grant controversies have been a major theme of New Mexican history since the 1840's. At issue was the conflict between Anglo and Hispanic land laws and customs, indefinite land grant boundaries, inability of many claimants to prove legitimacy of titles, development of the Santa Fe Ring and its satellites to obscure and manipulate title ownership, and political and legal entanglements leading to major political violence in territorial New Mexico. In 1891, following unsuccessful efforts, Congress established machinery to quiet title to these grants with the Court of Private Land Claims. By 1904 the work of this body was ostensibly completed. Even so, land grant issues remain a vexing New Mexican issue due to the unfulfilled promise of the Treaty of Guadalupe-Hidalgo. This attitude was manifestly displayed by Reies Lopez Tijerina's raid on Tierra Amarilla courthouse in June 1967.

Stephen Sayles
Jerry L. Williams

TABLE: LAND GRANTS

Map No.	Grant	Date	Acreage
SPANISH INDIAN GRANTS			
1	Picuris	1689	14,959
2	San Juan	1689	12,213
3	Santa Clara	1689	12,224
4	San Ildefonso	1689	15,413
5	Pojoaque		11,593
6	Nambe		12,560
7	Tesuque	1689	16,706
8	Cochiti	1689	22,763
9	Santo Domingo	1689	65,571
10	San Felipe	1689	30,285
11	Pecos	1689	16,000
12	Santa Ana	1689	15,406
13	Zia	1689	16,282
14	Jemez	1689	17,314
15	Sandia	1689	22,883
16	Isleta	1689	109,362
17	Laguna	1689	17,403
18	Acoma	1689	94,159
19	Zuni	1689	17,636
20	Taos	1793	15,400
SPANISH GRANTS (1650-1799)			
21	Piedre Lumbre	1766	49,749
22	J. J. Lobato		205,616
23	Plaza Colorado	1739	7,577
24	Plaza Blanca	1739	8,955
25	Abiquiu	1754	13,000
26	Polvadera	1766	35,761
27	Antonio de Abeyta	1736	721
28	Ojo Caliente	1793	2,244
29	Martinez or Godoi	1716	61,605
30	Antoine Leroux (Vigil)	1742	
31	Gijosa	1715	16,240
32	Cristoval de la Serna	1710	22,232
33	San Fernando de Taos	1799	1,817
34	Rancho del Rio Grande	1795	91,813
35	Santa Barbara	1796	30,638
36	Las Trampas	1751	19,030
37	Sebastian Martin	1751	51,387
38	Black Mesa	1743	19,171
39	Bartolome Sanchez		
40	Santa Cruz	1767	4,567
41	Santo Domingo de Cundiyo	1743	2,137
42	Nuestra Senora del Rosario San Fernando Y Santiago	1754	14,768
43	F. M. Vigil		8,254
44	Juan de Gabaldon	1752	10,690
45	Santiago Ramirez	1744	272
46	Santa Fe	@1660	@16,000
47	Jacona	1702	6,952
48	Caja del Rio	1742	66,848
49	Ramon Vigil	1746	31,209
50	Canada de Cochiti	@1740	19,112
51	Ojo de San Jose	1768	
52	Cañon de San Diego	1798	116,286
53	M&S Montoya	1767	
54	Ignacio Chavez	1768	47,258
55	Felipe Tafoya	1767	4,340
56	Bartolome Fernandez	1767	25,424
57	San Mateo Spring	1754	4,350
58	San Ysidro	1786	11,476
59	Ojo del Borrego	1768	16,079
60	La Majada	1716	54,404
61	Mesita de Juana Lopez	1782	
62	Cieneguilla	1693	3,202
63	Pacheco	1769	581
64	Sitio de Juana Lopez	@1750	1,086
65	Sitio de Los Cerrillos	1788	572
66	San Marcos Pueblo	1754	1,895
67	Los Cerrillos	1788	1,479
68	Sebastian de Vargas	1728	13,434
69	Cañada de Los Alamos	1785	12,068
70	Atalaya Hill	1735	319
71	Lamy		16,547
72	San Miguel del Bado	1794	5,024
73	Bernalillo	1701	3,404
74	San Antonio de las Huertas	1767	4,763
75	Alameda	1710	79,346
76	Bernabe Montano	1753	44,070
77	Cañada de Los Alamos	1768	4,096
78	Agua Salada	1769	
79	Paguate	1796	
80	Elena Gallegos	1716	35,084
81	Atrisco	1768	67,491
82	Antonio Sedillo	1769	86,249
83	Pajarito	1746	28,724
84	Gutierres & Sedillo		21,676
85	San Clemente	1716	37,099
86	Nicolas Duran de Chavez	1768	46,655
87	Lo de Padilla	1716	51,940
88	Tome	1739	121,594
SPANISH GRANTS (1800-1820)			
89	Antonio Ortiz	1819	163,291
90	Los Trnigos	1815	7,342
91	Alexander Valle	1808	@300
92	Arroyo Hondo	1815	
93	Galisteo	1814	
94	Cañon de Carnae	1819	
95	San Cristoval	1815	81,031
96	Santa Rosa de Cubero	1815	
97	Ojo del Espirita Santo	1815	113,141
98	Nuestra Senora de la Luz de las Lagunitas	1820	39,184
99	Cebolleta	1807	199,567
100	Gigante		
101	San Juan		
102	El Rito		
103	Sevilleta	1819	272,193
104	Socorro	1815	17,371
105	Pedro Armendaris #34	1820	447,534
106	Pedro Armendaris #33	1820	
SPANISH GRANTS (1821-1829)			
107	Tecolote	1824	41,123
108	Anton Chico	1822	378,537
109	Preston Beck	1823	318,690
110	Jose Perea	1825	17,712
111	Agua Negra	1824	17,361
112	Pablo Montoya	1824	655,468
113	Casa Colorado	1823	131,779
114	Manzano	1829	17,360
115	Bracito	1823	14,808
116	J.M.S. Baca		3,531
MEXICAN GRANTS (1830-1853)			
117	Tierra Amarilla	1832	525,515
118	Sangre de Cristo	1843	1,038,195
119	Beaubien & Miranda (Maxwell)	1841	1,714,764
120	Petaca	1836	@350
121	Mora	1835	827,889
122	John Scolly	1846	21,701
123	Las Vegas	1835	431,653
124	Baca Location #2	1835	99,298
125	Baca Location #1	1835	90,424
126	Ortiz Mine	1833	69,458
127	Tejon	1840	12,801
128	San Pedro	1839	20,094
129	Chilili	1841	41,481
130	Tajique	1834	7,185
131	Torreon	1841	14,146
132	La Salina	1846	@600
133	Cubero	1834	16,490
134	Bosque de Apache	1845	
135	B. F. Edwards		640
136	Dona Ana Bend Colony	1839	35,399
137	Mesilla Civil Colony #1	1853	21,628
138	Santo T. de Yturbide	1853	9,622
139	Refugio Colony #1	1852	15,000
140	Refugio Colony #2	1852	
141	Santa Teresa		8,479

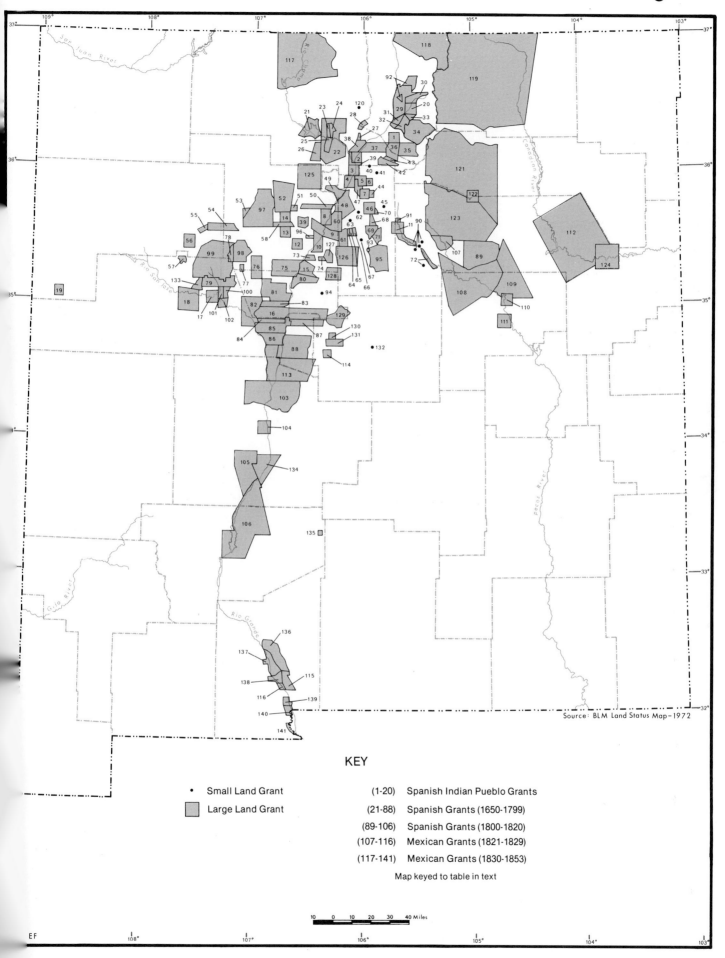

Source: BLM Land Status Map–1972

KEY

• Small Land Grant	(1-20)	Spanish Indian Pueblo Grants
Large Land Grant	(21-88)	Spanish Grants (1650-1799)
	(89-106)	Spanish Grants (1800-1820)
	(107-116)	Mexican Grants (1821-1829)
	(117-141)	Mexican Grants (1830-1853)

Map keyed to table in text

10 0 10 20 30 40 Miles

territorial period conflicts

Territorial New Mexico was a violent place. The initial conquest by American troops in 1846 was virtually bloodless, although Doniphan's Missouri Volunteers encountered sharp resistance at Brazito during their march into Mexico. In 1847 a revolt flared in northern New Mexico with uprisings at Taos and Mora. American forces decisively defeated the rebels at La Cañada, El Embudo, and Taos. Minor skirmishes at La Cuesta, Las Vegas, and La Cienega ended the rebellion.

Beginning in 1846, the United States established military posts throughout the territory to protect the inhabitants. The most important site was Fort Union, which became the army's main supply base in the region. Other forts guarded against depredations by particular Indian tribes: Cantonment Burgwyn and Fort Lowell against the Jicarilla Apaches; Fort Wingate against the Navajos; Forts McLane, Cummings, and Bayard against the Chiricahua and Gila Apaches; Fort Stanton against the Mescalero Apaches; and Fort Bascom against the Comanches. To supervise the Navajos who were resettled at Bosque Redondo Reservation, Fort Sumner was established. Guarding the Rio Grande valley were Forts Craig, Selden, and Fillmore, among others.

Several posts were significant in the defense of New Mexico against a Confederate invasion during the Civil War. In 1861 Confederate units forced the surrender of Fort Fillmore's garrison, which had retreated to San Augustin Springs. During 1862 a larger Confederate force invaded the territory and won a major battle at Valverde, but was unable to capture Fort Craig. Proceeding northward to Santa Fe, the Confederates clashed again with Federal troops at Apache Cañon and Pigeon's Ranch in Glorieta Pass. Lacking supplies, the invaders then withdrew southward into Texas. Federal forces followed, with a brief skirmish at Peralta.

After the Civil War, New Mexico's military posts resumed supervision of the Indians. Before 1861, major campaigns had been waged against the Navajos, Jicarilla Apaches, and Mescalero Apaches. In the post-war period, columns from northeastern New Mexico broke the power of the Comanches, while troops in the southwest battled the Chiricahua Apaches until 1886.

Even after the decline of military operations, New Mexico Territory remained the scene of conflict. In addition, vigilante activities occurred in Albuquerque, Las Vegas, and Socorro during the early 1880's. Instances of political assassination were noted as late as the 1890's.

Glen Robertson

TABLE: WAR AND CONFLICT SITES

⊗ Mexican War Sites	⊙ Civil War Sites
1. Brazito	1. San Agustin Springs
2. Taos	2. Valverde
3. Mora	3. Apache Cañon
4. La Cañada	4. Pigeon's Ranch
5. El Embudo	5. Peralta
6. La Cuesta	
7. Las Vegas	
8. La Cienega	

● Indian War Sites	▲ Civilian Conflict Sites
	1. Albuquerque
	2. Colfax County
1. Agua Caliente	3. Lincoln County
2. Cieneguilla	4. San Juan County
3. Chuska Valley	5. Las Vegas
4. Bear Springs	6. Socorro
5. Manzano	
6. West of Sabinal	
7. San Mateo Mountains	■ Forts and Camps
8. Cuchillo Negro	
9. Black Range	(named on map)
10. Gavilan Cañon	
11. Guadalupe Cañon	
12. Hatchet Mountains	
13. Doña Ana	
14. Mesilla	
15. Hembrillo Cañon	
16. Snakehand Springs	
17. Peñasco Cañon	
18. Dog Cañon	
19. Round Mountain	
20. Blazers Mill	
21. Fort Stanton	
22. Placitas	

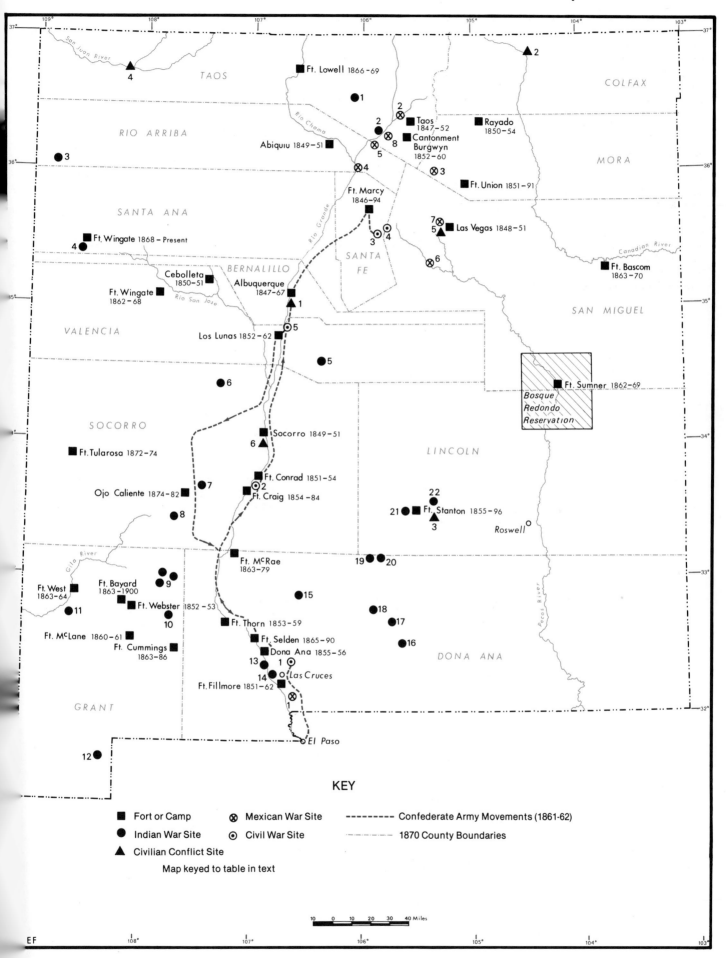

Ft. Lowell 1866-69

● 1

2 ⊗ 2

⊗ Taos
1847-52

■ Rayado
1850-54

Abiquiu 1849-51 ■

⊗ 8
⊗ 5

Cantonment
Burgwyn
1852-60

⊗ 4

⊗ 3

Ft. Union 1851-91

Ft. Marcy
1846-94

7 ⊗
5 ▲ Las Vegas 1848-51

● 3

⊙ 4
3 ⊙

▲ 4 ■ Ft. Wingate 1868-Present

⊗ 6

● 4

Ft. Bascom
1863-70

Cebolleta
1850-51 ■

Albuquerque
1847-67 ■

Ft. Wingate
1862-68 ■

Rio San Jose

▲ 1

SAN MIGUEL

⊙ 5

Los Lunas 1852-62

● 5

Bosque
Redondo
Reservation

■ Ft. Sumner 1862-69

● 6

■ Socorro 1849-51
▲ 6

LINCOLN

Ft. Tularosa 1872-74 ■

■ Ft. Conrad 1851-54
⊙ 2

Ojo Caliente 1874-82 ■

● 7

■ Ft. Craig 1854-84

● 8

22 ●

21 ● ■ Ft. Stanton 1855-96
▲ 3

Roswell ○

Ft. McRae
1863-79

19 ● ● 20

Ft. West
1863-64 ■

Ft. Bayard
1863-1900 ■

● ●
● 9

● 15

● 18

Ft. Webster 1852-53 ■

10

■ Ft. Thorn 1853-59

● 17

Ft. McLane 1860-61 ■

■ Ft. Selden 1865-90
Dona Ana 1855-56

● 16

● 11

DONA ANA

Ft. Cummings
1863-86 ■

13 ● ● 1 ⊙

● 12

14 ● ○ Las Cruces

Ft. Fillmore 1851-62 ⊙
1 ⊗

GRANT

○ El Paso

KEY

■ Fort or Camp   ⊗ Mexican War Site   - - - - - Confederate Army Movements (1861-62)

● Indian War Site   ⊙ Civil War Site   — · — · — 1870 County Boundaries

▲ Civilian Conflict Site

Map keyed to table in text

10 0 10 20 30 40 Miles

E F

the frontier period 1846-1912

The frontier era in the West has been vividly portrayed on the movie screen and in novels as a period of lawlessness and of armed conflict. Although romanticized names such as Billy the Kid and Black Jack Ketchum have received much publicity, the events they participated in were not as significant as the settlement story of the Anglo Americans. During the second half of the 19th century, rapid growth occurred outside the Spanish and Mexican land grant areas. Boom towns resulted from the discovery of gold, silver, and other rare minerals in the hills and remote mountain areas, and settlements grew to serve the cattlemen and the homesteaders who began to file into the vast grassland areas. Because much of this settled area was outside of the former Spanish and Mexican sphere of influence, transportation links between the new settlements had to be developed for passengers, freight, and mail. These routes were frequently carved out and maintained by hand labor from the various towns competing with each other to become part of mail route and stagecoach lines. With the introduction of the railroad to the territory in the 1880's a new set of towns and populated strips evolved. The competition between places to attract a railway company was intense as the future of many towns relied upon access to the railroad.

The territory was officially proclaimed part of the United States by the Treaty of Guadalupe Hidalgo in 1848, a full two years after General Kearney had entered Santa Fe and placed the Mexican territory under American military control. The treaty retained the land grant property rights that were legally held under Mexican law, which in effect closed out a large area of the state to Anglo settlement. From 1820 to 1850, merchants, mountainmen, and prospectors entered the territory with visions of economic opportunity; many others who came with the wagon trains were invalids seeking a dry-climate cure for the fevers and epidemics that ravaged the early settlers of the Mississippi Basin.

So many health-seekers came to the territory during the period of Mexican rule (1821-1846) that the U.S. Congress designated specific depots for collecting invalids along the Santa Fe Trail, and after 1825 the U.S. Army provided a military escort to the limits of the territory. Later (1860-1890) the territory was recognized as a sanitorium for tubercular patients, and health migrants from the industrial east were added to the increasing flow of invalids to New Mexico. It has been estimated that health-seekers constituted 20% to 25% of the total immigration into the southwest during the 19th century. Thermal springs, abundant in New Mexico, were perceived as healing waters, and practically every hot spring in the territory became a resort before 1912. Sanitoriums and health facilities were available at practically every major town in New Mexico at the turn of the century, and two military stations (Fort Bayard and Fort Stanton) became sanitoriums for military patients.

Many of the remaining American immigrants who were not seeking a health cure arrived in search of mineral wealth. Prospectors' holes peppered the mountains of New Mexico during the entire 19th century, but the pace of prospecting accelerated after the first 'gold rush' of the West which occurred at Old Placers (later Delores) near Cerrillos in the late 1820's. By 1850 there were mining camps in the Organ Mountains near Las Cruces and in the Jicarilla Mountains in northern Lincoln County. Prospectors were beginning to uncover rich lodes which attracted a flow of miners from the gold fields of California. Gold was found in the Moreno Valley of western Mora County, and the mining boomtown of Elizabethtown grew so rapidly in population (2200 by 1870) and fame that the mountain settlement was selected as the first county seat of Colfax County in 1869. Pinos Altos and Steeple Rock mining districts were rapidly developing in the southwest and gold lodes were discovered in the Sacramento Mountains of Lincoln County. Significant deposits of silver were uncovered near Magdalena in 1863 and many new mining districts opened in the 1870's.

American ranchers and farmers began to arrive after the Civil War seeking the abundant grasslands in the eastern half of the territory and along the high plateau near the western border. Many of the early cattlemen came from Texas, attracted by the abundant grama grasses of the eastern plains, where the headquarters of the Chisum and Slaughter ranches were established along the lower Pecos River. It is estimated the cattle stock of New Mexico in-

creased from 57,000 head in 1870 to around 350,000 head in 1880. U.S. military posts in Arizona, Colorado, and Wyoming made demands for meat on Texas and New Mexican ranchers, initiating a network of long distance cattle trails (Goodnight, Chisum, Slaughter) that crisscrossed the territory. Livestock ranching and the control of land and water rights were the bases of large empires that formed in the late 19th century. The eastern half of San Miguel County was owned in 1872 by the Consolidated Land, Cattle Raising, and Wool Growing Company and in 1883 most of the land presently occupied by Union County was controlled by the Prairie Cattle Company. The southern half of Santa Fe County was divided in the 1880's between the Boston and New Mexico Cattle Company and the Kentucky Land and Stock Company. Thomas Catron, a financial wheeler-dealer of this period, and a partner in many of the above named companies, formed an empire called the American Valley Company in the northern half of what is presently Catron County.

The large stock herds and ranching emphasis in the territory presented another economic opportunity in the form of cattle rustling. Bands of rustlers established well known operation centers in isolated sections of New Mexico and every county was affected to some degree by their activities. At first cattle rustled in Mexico were driven into the territory and sold to American ranchers and cattle companies at rendezvous places near the San Agustin Plain. As the herds increased in New Mexico the rustler's attention turned to them. The most serious incident occurred in the 1880's when a rustler's war developed in Doña Ana County. The territorial militia had to be ordered by the governor to subdue the thirty-to-forty member rustlers' army that terrorized ranchers near Las Cruces.

The territories of the West hoped to stimulate population growth by encouraging farmers to settle on land opened for donation land claims in the 1850's. The first claim for a 160-acre section of New Mexico was in Doña Ana County in 1858. To receive land, the claimant had to occupy and cultivate it, a stipulation that was frequently open to fraud or overlooked. Many of the donation claims were also unrecognized or disputed as surveys were inaccurate or not properly recorded. By 1884, the final year of entry, almost 52,000 acres had been awarded under the donation land claim system with an additional 73,000 acres claimed by claimants who did not meet the full requirements. The national program called the Homestead Act followed the territorial donation claim system and also based the grant size on the 160-acre parcel thought necessary to support a family in a fertile farming community. The weakness of the Homestead Act for New Mexico was that a plot as small as 160 acres of semi-arid countryside was unlikely to support a family. Only 50% of the original homestead entries by 1892 were in areas climatically capable of supporting crops. Practically all homesteading occurred in the high plains and river valleys east of the mountains and in scattered grassland areas near the Arizona border. Wherever there was a concentration of homesteaders, commercial townsite arose to serve the scattered community. Most of these small towns had short lives and disappeared with the farmers after several seasons of insufficient crop production.

To connect the old Hispanic plazas, mining camps, cowtowns, homestead villages, and later railroad towns, an elaborate system of overland and buckboard stage companies evolved. Most of the companies were short-line feeder routes connecting isolated places to regional and national overland stage routes. The first era of stagecoaching in New Mexico opened in 1849 with a thirteen-day passenger trip between Kansas City and Santa Fe. By the beginning of the railroad period in 1880 there were over thirty-five private stage companies on record that covered a total distance in excess of 800 miles within the territory. To make a stage route profitable, a line would apply for mail contracts or an express parcel freight contract.

By the twentieth century, the main purpose of the stage was to connect communities not located on a railroad line. The railroad mileage increased so rapidly during the American Territorial period that the peak coverage within New Mexico was reached at the time of statehood in 1912.

Jerry L. Williams

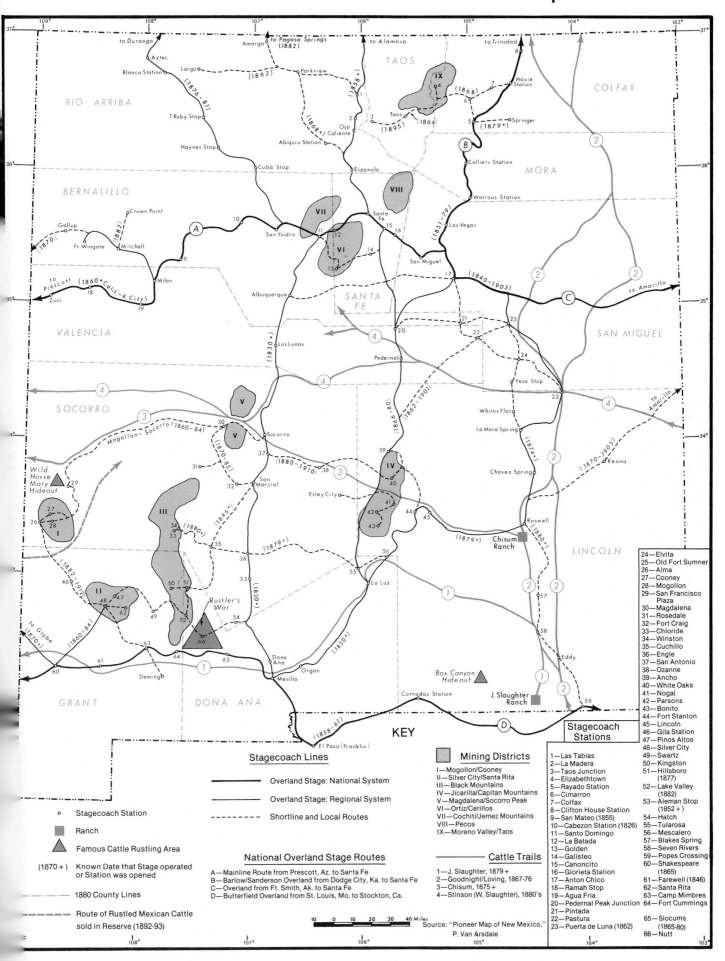

the frontier period 1846-1912

to Durango
Aztec
Amargo   to Pagosa Springs (1882)   to Alamosa   to Trinidad
8
TAOS   IX   COLFAX
Blanco Station   Largo   (1862)   Parkview   4   (1868)   7   Hoxie Station
RIO ARRIBA   (1876-81)   1   6
T Ruby Stop   (1858+)   (1895)   Taos   (1864)   5   Springer
Haynes Stop   (1868+)   Ojo Caliente   (1879+)
Abiquiu Station   B
Cuba Stop   Espanola   Colliers Station   MORA
BERNALILLO   VIII   Watrous Station
Crown Point   Santa Fe   15   Las Vegas   (1851-79)
Gallup   (1882)   VII   11   16
(1870)   Mitchell   San Ysidro   12   San Miguel
Ft. Wingate   10   VI   14   17   (1840-1903)   C   to Amarillo
9   13   SAN MIGUEL
to Prescott   (1860+Calif-K.City)   Milan   Albuquerque   SANTA FE   (1830+)   20   4   2
18   19   Zuni   Los Lunas   4   21   22   (1870-1905)   to Amarillo
VALENCIA   Pedernal   Yeso Stop   24   4
4   4   Whites Flat   25
SOCORRO   3   V   La Mora Spring   (1874+)   Kenna
30   V   Socorro   (1870-85)   37   39   Chavez Springs   (1862-1901)
Wild Horse Mary Hideout   129   31   (1880-1970)   38   IV   40   Roswell   (1880+)
27   32   San Marcial   3   41   44   45   Chisum Ranch
26   28   I   34   (1880+)   35   42   43   LINCOLN
II   33   36   55   (1879+)
46   48   47   (1879+)   53   La Luz   1   2   2
62   50   51   Rustler's   54   56   57
49   52   War   Tularosa   58   Eddy
to Globe   (1870+)   63   66   Dona Ana   Box Canyon Hideout   J. Slaughter Ranch   59
61   60   64   65   Organ   Cornudas Station   D
Deming   Mesilla   KEY   103°
GRANT   DONA ANA   (1858-61)   Source: "Pioneer Map of New Mexico,"
El Paso (Franklin)   P. Van Arsdale

KEY

Stagecoach Lines

——— Overland Stage: National System
——— Overland Stage: Regional System
- - - - Shortline and Local Routes

○ Stagecoach Station

▦ Ranch

▲ Famous Cattle Rustling Area

(1870+) Known Date that Stage operated or Station was opened

———— 1880 County Lines

———— Route of Rustled Mexican Cattle sold in Reserve (1892-93)

Mining Districts
I—Mogollon/Cooney
II—Silver City/Santa Rita
III—Black Mountains
IV—Jicarilla/Capitan Mountains
V—Magdalena/Socorro Peak
VI—Ortiz/Cerillos
VII—Cochiti/Jemez Mountains
VIII—Pecos
IX—Moreno Valley/Taos

National Overland Stage Routes
A—Mainline Route from Prescott, Az. to Santa Fe
B—Barlow/Sanderson Overland from Dodge City, Ka. to Santa Fe
C—Overland from Ft. Smith, Ak. to Santa Fe
D—Butterfield Overland from St. Louis, Mo. to Stockton, Ca.

Cattle Trails
1—J. Slaughter, 1879 +
2—Goodnight/Loving, 1867-76
3—Chisum, 1875 +
4—Stinson (W. Slaughter), 1880's

10 0 10 20 30 40 Miles

Stagecoach Stations
1—Las Tablas
2—La Madera
3—Taos Junction
4—Elizabethtown
5—Rayado Station
6—Cimarron
7—Colfax
8—Clifton House Station
9—San Mateo (1855)
10—Cabezon Station (1826)
11—Santo Domingo
12—La Batada
13—Golden
14—Galisteo
15—Canoncito
16—Glorieta Station
17—Anton Chico
18—Ramah Stop
19—Agua Fria
20—Pedernal Peak Junction
21—Pintada
22—Pastura
23—Puerta de Luna (1862)
24—Elvita
25—Old Fort Sumner
26—Alma
27—Cooney
28—Mogollon
29—San Francisco Plaza
30—Magdalena
31—Rosedale
32—Fort Craig
33—Chloride
34—Winston
35—Cuchillo
36—Engle
37—San Antonio
38—Ozanne
39—Ancho
40—White Oaks
41—Nogal
42—Parsons
43—Bonito
44—Fort Stanton
45—Lincoln
46—Gila Station
47—Pinos Altos
48—Silver City
49—Swartz
50—Kingston
51—Hillsboro (1877)
52—Lake Valley (1882)
53—Aleman Stop (1852+)
54—Hatch
55—Tularosa
56—Mescalero
57—Blakes Spring
58—Seven Rivers
59—Popes Crossing
60—Shakespeare (1865)
61—Farewell (1846)
62—Santa Rita
63—Camp Mimbres
64—Fort Cummings
65—Slocums (1865-80)
66—Nutt

41

railroad development

The history of railroading in New Mexico can be viewed as the story of the growth of the Atchison, Topeka, and Santa Fe Railroad (henceforth called the Santa Fe) and the reaction of its competitors to this expansion. The Santa Fe linked New Mexico to the Pacific and the Midwest and was the only rail system to completely traverse the state in both north-south and east-west directions. Its routing also determined the eventual routes of the Southern Pacific and the Denver and Rio Grande, its two major competitors within the state. Acquisitions of small lines by companies seeking to gain new rights-of-way and alliances formed between competing companies were often attempts to develop a system within New Mexico capable of competing with the Santa Fe.

The original intent was to construct the Santa Fe rail line along the main route of the famous Santa Fe Trail, from Kansas to Santa Fe via Trinidad, Colorado, and then southward to Mexico City. As construction of the railroad proceeded in segments from the western terminus of the Kansas Pacific, the Santa Fe Trail shrank in length and in economic importance to New Mexico. The final eastern terminus of the stage and freight service on the Trail was Las Vegas until 1880 when the railroad was extended to Lamy.

The entry of the Santa Fe Railroad into the New Mexico territory was not easy. The physical barrier of the Raton Pass imposed severe construction difficulties on the financially strained company. At the same time the Santa Fe had to wage a small railroad war with the Denver and Rio Grande (D&RG) for right-of-way through the pass. The D&RG withdrew from the conflict and shifted its narrow gauge track further west, entering New Mexico along the headwaters of the Rio Grande. The Santa Fe also ran into an unreceptive territorial legislature that attempted to block the entry of the line until a financial construction guarantee was made that was beyond the capability of the company. This political barrier was circumvented only by locating a previous railroad bill that enabled the railroad to enter the territory under the name of a New Mexico corporation.

In 1878 the first Santa Fe locomotive entered New Mexico under the charter of the "New Mexico and Southern Pacific Company." By September 1879 the Raton tunnel was completed and the rail line advanced rapidly southward, reaching Lamy by February 1880. The first workshops and switching yards of the railroad in New Mexico were located in Las Vegas. The city of Santa Fe, which gave its name to the railroad company, is located in a basin that is undesirable terrain for through-line railroad construction. So the territorial capitol, and largest city in the southwest in 1880, was an eighteen-mile branch line away from the main route of the Santa Fe at Lamy. In 1880 the railroad reached Albuquerque (April) and San Marcial (October), where additional workshops and switching yards were constructed. San Marcial was completely destroyed by floods in 1929 and little evidence remains of the former railroad center. By 1881 the Santa Fe junctioned at Rincon and extended to Deming (March) and El Paso (June).

Major railroad construction occurred in 1880 in New Mexico as the Southern Pacific, the second railroad to enter the territory, proceeded southeastward from San Francisco through southern Arizona to El Paso, where connection was made with the Texas and Pacific Railroad. In 1880 the Southern Pacific reached Lordsburg (October) and Deming (December), and entered El Paso a month before the Santa Fe did (May, 1881). The Denver and Rio Grande entered New Mexico in 1880 by two routes: one from Alamosa, Colorado to Espanola (The "Chile Line"); and the other from Antonito, Colorado to Chama across the Cumbres Pass. The route that reached Espanola in 1880 was extended only to Buckman, on the western bank of the Rio Grande River, and did not cover the fifteen mile difference to Santa Fe until 1886, the year the capitol became a main-line terminal. Also in 1880, the St. Louis and San Francisco Railroad Company began construction from Isleta to Arizona after acquiring the massive land rights granted by the U.S. Congress to the bankrupt Atlantic and Pacific Railroad. The St. Louis and San Francisco was completed from the Rio Grande to Gallup and reached the Colorado River before the company went bankrupt. The line was acquired by the Santa Fe Railroad in 1897.

In 1890 the Pecos Valley Railroad completed a route along the Pecos River from a junction with the Texas and Pacific at Pecos, Texas to the town of Eddy (Carlsbad). This service was extended to Roswell in 1894. The Pecos Valley Company was reorganized as the Pecos Valley and Northeastern and, combined with the Panhandle and Santa Fe Company, opened service through Clovis to Amarillo, Texas in 1899. The Pecos River railroad system was acquired by the Santa Fe Railroad in 1901. Shortly after this acquisition the Santa Fe then constructed the Belen Cutoff, connecting Clovis to Belen, a more direct route to Kansas than the mountainous northern route. The connection provided the Santa Fe with a complete east-west axis across the state, which is the most travelled line in New Mexico today, and made Belen the logical site for the Santa Fe railway center of New Mexico. The importance of Clovis as a gateway to the east (as is Gallup on the west) made this small plains town a railway center and the location of the now abandoned Santa Fe technical training school.

Around 1900 the El Paso and Southwestern Railroad was constructed by the Phelps-Dodge Mining Corporation from its smelters in Arizona to the main line at El Paso. This company later connected to (and acquired) the El Paso and Rock Island that joined with the Chicago, Rock Island and Pacific (henceforth called the Rock Island) at Santa Rosa in 1902. When good coking coal was discovered in 1901 at Dawson, near Cimarron, the Phelps-Dodge Company constructed a railroad from Tucumcari to the coal fields, connecting with the Santa Fe at the main junction town of French. By 1908, all Phelps-Dodge railway holdings were incorporated under the name of El Paso and Southwestern. In 1924, the Southern Pacific acquired the El Paso and Southwestern and the Arizona and New Mexico railroads. The last main line to be constructed in New Mexico was the Texas and Northwestern built to the oil field centers of Lea County in 1928.

Numerous short feeder lines were built from the two major systems to places of varying economic importance. The Carthage branch (1906), La Ventana route (1933), Capitan route (1899), Russia and Cloudcroft Railway (1898), and several spurs around Raton and Gallup, were built for coal and timber used for fuel and construction by the railroads and in the mining industries. Agricultural railroads, like the New Mexico Central (The "Pinto Line") and the Elkhart and Santa Fe, were main line feeder routes that opened the Estancia Valley and northeastern plains, respectively, to large scale bean production.

Total main line rail mileage in New Mexico appears to have peaked around 1914 (see table). Since 1925, the abandonment and dismantling of unprofitable routes continued at a fairly steady rate (25 miles per year) until 1970. Extensive line abandonment occurred during the depression years of the 1930's when the Southern Pacific discontinued service on all connections between the former El Paso and Southwestern route, and its existing main line through Deming. The Santa Fe abandoned Service to Cimarron and Des Moines, and the aforementioned "beanfield" railroads went out of business. When oil replaced coal as engine fuel after World War II, most of the rail lines to coal fields were abandoned, including the extension from Tucumcari to Dawson. The Denver and Rio Grande discontinued service from Alamosa to Santa Fe in the 1940's and completely closed its operations throughout northern New Mexico during the 1950's and 1960's.

Although railroads continue to close uneconomical branch services in the state, construction of new routes continues. At present the Santa Fe has petitioned to construct the longest rail spur ever built in the state: from Prewitt (near Grants) to the strippable coal deposits near Bisti in the Chaco Basin. As coal attains new importance as an energy fuel following the 1970's oil shortage, there may be more railroad interest in the coal rich area of northwestern New Mexico.

Jerry L. Williams

MAIN LINE RAIL MILEAGE* IN NEW MEXICO

Year	Mileage	Year	Mileage
1880	643	1945	2583
1890	1284	1950	2464
1912	3002	1963	2164
1914	3124	1970	2046
1926	3096	1975	1984
1930	2981		

*excludes sidings and switching yards

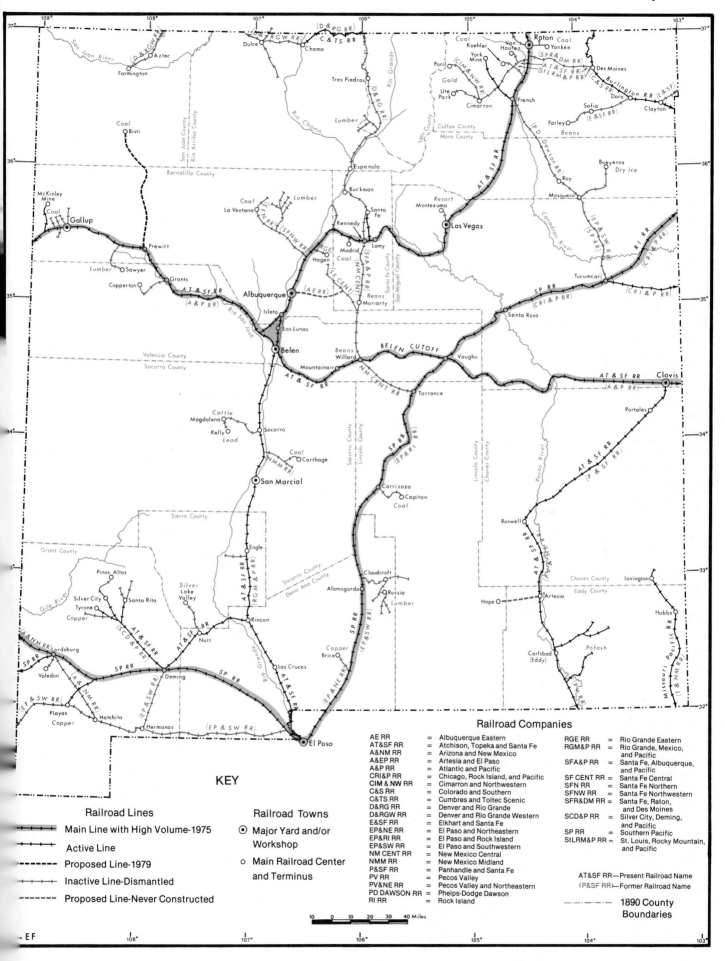

KEY

Railroad Lines

- ┼┼┼┼┼ Main Line with High Volume-1975
- ┼┼┼┼ Active Line
- ─ ─ ─ Proposed Line-1979
- ┼┼┼┼ Inactive Line-Dismantled
- ─ ─ ─ Proposed Line-Never Constructed

Railroad Towns

- ◉ Major Yard and/or Workshop
- ○ Main Railroad Center and Terminus

Railroad Companies

AE RR	=	Albuquerque Eastern	RGE RR	= Rio Grande Eastern
AT&SF RR	=	Atchison, Topeka and Santa Fe	RGM&P RR	= Rio Grande, Mexico, and Pacific
A&NM RR	=	Arizona and New Mexico		
A&EP RR	=	Artesia and El Paso	SFA&P RR	= Santa Fe, Albuquerque, and Pacific
A&P RR	=	Atlantic and Pacific		
CRI&P RR	=	Chicago, Rock Island, and Pacific	SF CENT RR	= Santa Fe Central
CIM & NW RR	=	Cimarron and Northwestern	SFN RR	= Santa Fe Northern
C&S RR	=	Colorado and Southern	SFNW RR	= Santa Fe Northwestern
C&TS RR	=	Cumbres and Toltec Scenic	SFR&DM RR	= Santa Fe, Raton, and Des Moines
D&RG RR	=	Denver and Rio Grande		
D&RGW RR	=	Denver and Rio Grande Western	SCD&P RR	= Silver City, Deming, and Pacific
E&SF RR	=	Elkhart and Santa Fe		
EP&NE RR	=	El Paso and Northeastern	SP RR	= Southern Pacific
EP&RI RR	=	El Paso and Rock Island	StLRM&P RR	= St. Louis, Rocky Mountain, and Pacific
EP&SW RR	=	El Paso and Southwestern		
NM CENT RR	=	New Mexico Central		
NMM RR	=	New Mexico Midland		
P&SF RR	=	Panhandle and Santa Fe	AT&SF RR—Present Railroad Name	
PV RR	=	Pecos Valley	(P&SF RR)—Former Railroad Name	
PV&NE RR	=	Pecos Valley and Northeastern		
PD DAWSON RR	=	Phelps-Dodge Dawson	─ ─ ─ 1890 County Boundaries	
RI RR	=	Rock Island		

10 0 10 20 30 40 Miles

43

new mexico 1912

According to the 1910 census 327,301 people lived in New Mexico Territory, an increase of 67.6% since 1900. Most of this population increase was in rural settlements in the eastern counties. Ten towns had over 2,500 residents including Albuquerque with 11,020, Roswell with 6,172, Santa Fe with 5,072, and Raton with 4,539. New Mexico had 26 counties, eight of which were organized after 1900. By 1910 the eastern plains were dominated by transplanted Texans, Oklahomans, Arkansans, and Missourians with their racial and ethnic biases and Democratic politics. Traditional Republican strength remained in the less populated northern counties dominated by Hispanic dons.

Throughout the territorial period (1850-1911) Anglo politicians had adapted themselves to the don system that had dominated the area for centuries. Statehood politics became inextricably intertwined with land grant, mining, lumber, livestock, and railroad issues. The Santa Fe Ring, a nebulous collection of Anglo and Hispano politicos, attorneys, territorial officials, and judges, exploited these issues for its own pecuniary and political gain. Ring partisans generally supported statehood under the leadership of Elkins and Catron, a Santa Fe based law firm, but such obstacles as sectionalism, nativism, and religious bigotry doomed the movement to failure.

Meanwhile, territorial economy boomed with the coming of the Atchison, Topeka, and Santa Fe Railroad in 1879. By 1881 construction had moved southward past Rincon and at Deming connected with the Southern Pacific heading east to El Paso. The Deming connection gave New Mexico a transcontinental railroad link. A branch line hooked Santa Fe to the railroad at Lamy. Other railroad lines later connected the Rio Grande Valley to Arizona via Grants and Gallup. Railroad construction opened the territory to national markets for agricultural and livestock products. Small branch lines to mining districts like Kelly, Madrid, and Silver City materially benefitted gold, silver, lead, and coal operations. Tourist and health industries became important as immigration to New Mexico increased substantially, a trend abetted by creation of the Bureau of Immigration.

The Pecos Valley development during the 1880's and 1890's dramatically affected territorial politics. Railroads linked the valley to Pecos City, Texas in the south, and to Amarillo, Texas in the northeast, inducing significant immigration from Texas and adjacent states. By 1910 Roswell had become the major political and economic center of southeastern New Mexico, now popularly called "Little Texas." Visionary irrigation schemes promoted by Charles Eddy, Pat Garret, and James J. Hagerman and exploitation of vast artesian water supplies greatly benefitted local agricultural industries. Livestock producers thrived as external markets became more accessible. Construction of the Belen cut-off line at the turn of the century made Clovis an important gateway community on the eastern plains.

Along with economic development and population increase came continued pressure for statehood after 1900. Large landholders, railroaders, lumbermen, and miners who exploited the public domain with little or no restraint tended to oppose the movement. Statehood meant higher taxation to support local governmental operations which until that time had been financed by the federal government. Some landholders like Thomas Benton Catron of Santa Fe supported statehood because of expected increases in land values. Statehood was nearly achieved in 1905 when a "jointure" bill linked New Mexico and Arizona as a single state.

Although it received congressional and presidential support Arizona rejected "jointure" fearing New Mexican political and economic dominance. In October 1909 at the Alvarado Hotel in Albuquerque, southern New Mexico politician Albert B. Fall persuaded President William H. Taft to support the lobby for New Mexico statehood. On June 20, 1910, Taft signed the enabling bill, and New Mexico subsequently held elections for a state constitutional convention.

One hundred delegates met in Santa Fe in September 1910 to draft the state constitution. Seventy-one of the delegates were Republican, including all 33 Hispanic delegates led by Solomon Luna, don of Valencia County and the largest sheep rancher in the territory. Harvey B. Fergusson of Albuquerque headed the 29-member Democratic delegation which actively sought progressive political reforms. Under the leadership of Luna, Fall, Catron, and the Republican Old Guard, however, the delegates prepared a conservative document designed to protect railroad, mining, and livestock interests. In this period of national progressive politics the constitution contained no provisions for direct election of senators, recall, initiative, referendum, or women's suffrage. Consequently, most of the Democratic delegation refused to accept the final document.

Luna, however, obtained specific voting and education guarantees for Hispanic residents; namely, that the state legislature was to use both the English and Spanish languages, that voting rights could not be abridged on basis of race, color, religion or literacy in English or Spanish, and that no child could be deprived of an equal education on the same grounds. Moreover, amendment procedures were made so stringent that Hispanic guarantees and vested interests were protected from popular action. Luna's efforts were aided by Octaviano A. Larrazolo, a Democratic non-delegate. Disappointed over previous electoral defeats in Little Texas, Larrazolo left the Democratic Party when its delegates opposed the state constitution. This created a power struggle within the Republican Party between Luna and Larrazolo for control of the Hispanic vote, a struggle that concluded in 1912 when Luna drowned in a vat of sheep dipping fluid.

On January 6, 1912, New Mexico formally entered the union as the forty-seventh state. Statehood engineered a revolution in New Mexico politics matched only by the impact of the New Deal during the thirties. In the 1911 elections Democrats scored impressive upsets against the entrenched Old Guard. Larrazolo's promotion of Hispanic pride badly split the Republican organization and enabled a Little Texan, William C. McDonald, to become governor. Democrats shrewdly selected Ezequiel Cabeza de Baca, a Las Vegas publisher, for lieutenant governor and diverted Hispanic votes to their slate. Old Guard partisans, however, dominated the legislature and elected Fall and Catron to the United States Senate.

The first two decades of statehood witnessed a Democratic-Republican balance of power. Personalities dominated state politics as they had for centuries. Larrazolo's dream of becoming don of all Hispanic voters never materialized. Ironically, it was Bronson M. Cutting, a wealthy New York Protestant, who became the don of New Mexico politics until his death in 1935. Muted and overt ethnic tensions between Little Texas and the northern Hispanic counties characterized state politics until the New Deal fatally undermined the don system in the 1930's.

Stephen Sayles

1910—POPULATION OF TOWNS AND SETTLEMENTS

= (500-1000)		= (500-1000)		= (500-100)		= (500-100)		= (1000-2500)	
Anthony	@520	Fierro	@500	Roy	@820	Portales	1292		
Anton Chico	@500	Galisteo	@500	San Marchal	@800	Santa Rita	@1950		
Aztec	~509	Gibson	@900	San Rafael	@530	Socorro	1580		
Bernalillo	@900	Hachita	@500	Santa Rosa	@750	Vaughn	@1050		
Capitan	@500	Kenna	@530	Sunnyside	@550	Wagon Mound	@1300		
Carrizozo	@850	Knowles	@500	Sunnyside	@500	Willard	@1050		
Central	@900	Lincoln	@800	Tierra Amarilla	@780				
Chama	@500	Llano	@880	Van Houten	@790		= (2500-5000)	
Cimarron	791	Los Lunas	@500			Clovis	3255		
Clapham	@610	Melrose	@950		= (1000-2500)	Dawson	3050		
Clayton	970	Mogollon	@770	Alamogordo	1948	Las Cruces	3856		
Corona	@500	Monument	@820	Artesia	1885	Las Vegas City	3755		
Dona Ana	@500	Mora	@500	Belen	@1150	Las Vegas Town	3179		
El Rito	@550	Mountainair	@720	Carlsbad	1736	Raton	4539		
Endee	@540	Nara Vesa	@500	Deming	1864	Silver City	3217		
Engle	@500	Ocate	@550	Gallup	2204	Tucumcari	2526		
Estancia	517	Orogrande	@750	Kelly	1015				
Farmington	785	Park View	@700	Koehler	@1070		= (5000)	
		Rincon	@500	Lordsburg	@1100	Albuquerque	11020		
				Magdalena	@1150	Roswell	6172		
Source: U.S. Census of Population: 1910				Mesilla	1271	Santa Fe	5072		
"Population of Minor Civil Divisions"				Old Albuquerque	2143				

POPULATION AND COUNTY CHANGE 1900-1910

County	1900	1910	Population Change	%
Bernalillo	28,630	23,605	Area reduced by boundary change	
Chaves	4,773	16,850	+12,077	253
Colfax	10,150	18,460	+8,310	82
Curry	----	11,443	New county	
*Doña Ana	10,137	12,893	Area reduced by boundary change	
Eddy	3,229	12,400	+9,171	284
Grant	12,883	14,813	Area reduced by boundary change	
Guadalupe	5,429	10,927	Area reduced by boundary change	
*Lincoln	4,953	7,822	+2,868	58
Luna	----	3,913	New county	
McKinley	----	12,900	Area increased by boundary change	
Mora	10,304	12,611	+2,307	22
Otero	4,791	7,069	+2,278	48
Quay	----	14,912	New county	
*Rio Arriba	13,777	16,624	+2,847	21
Roosevelt	----	12,064	New county	
San Juan	4,829	8,504	+3,675	76
San Miguel	22,053	22,930	+877	04
Sandoval	----	8,579	New county	
*Santa Fe	14,658	14,770	$112	01
Sierra	3,153	3,538	+385	12
Socorro	12,195	14,761	+2,566	21
Taos	10,889	12,008	+1,119	10
Torrance	----	10,119	New county	
Union	4,528	11,404	+6,876	152
Valencia	13,895	13,820	Area reduced by boundary change	

*Minor boundary alterations—distorts calculation of % for comparison

44

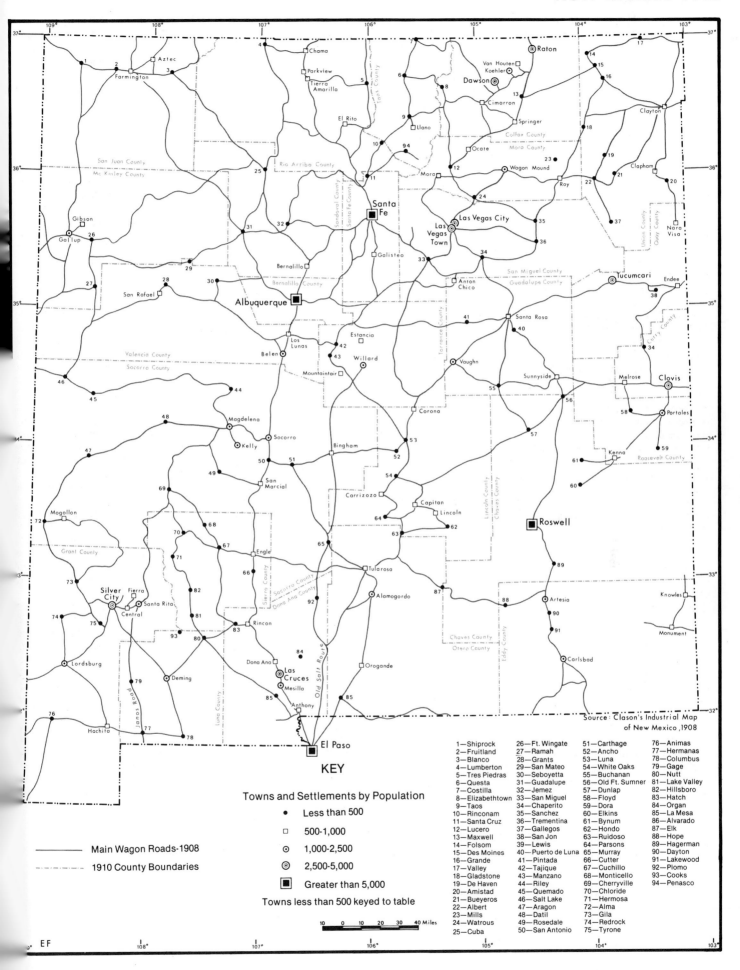

new mexico 1912

KEY

Towns and Settlements by Population

- • Less than 500
- ▫ 500-1,000
- ⊙ 1,000-2,500
- ◉ 2,500-5,000
- ■ Greater than 5,000

Towns less than 500 keyed to table

—— Main Wagon Roads-1908

–·– 1910 County Boundaries

10 0 10 20 30 40 Miles

Source: Clason's Industrial Map of New Mexico, 1908

1—Shiprock	26—Ft. Wingate	51—Carthage
2—Fruitland	27—Ramah	52—Ancho
3—Blanco	28—Grants	53—Luna
4—Lumberton	29—San Mateo	54—White Oaks
5—Tres Piedras	30—Seboyetta	55—Buchanan
6—Questa	31—Guadalupe	56—Old Ft. Sumner
7—Costilla	32—Jemez	57—Dunlap
8—Elizabethtown	33—San Miguel	58—Floyd
9—Taos	34—Chaperito	59—Dora
10—Rinconam	35—Sanchez	60—Elkins
11—Santa Cruz	36—Trementina	61—Bynum
12—Lucero	37—Gallegos	62—Hondo
13—Maxwell	38—San Jon	63—Ruidoso
14—Folsom	39—Lewis	64—Parsons
15—Des Moines	40—Puerto de Luna	65—Murray
16—Grande	41—Pintada	66—Cutter
17—Valley	42—Tajique	67—Cuchillo
18—Gladstone	43—Manzano	68—Monticello
19—De Haven	44—Riley	69—Cherryville
20—Amistad	45—Quemado	70—Chloride
21—Bueyeros	46—Salt Lake	71—Hermosa
22—Albert	47—Aragon	72—Alma
23—Mills	48—Datil	73—Gila
24—Watrous	49—Rosedale	74—Redrock
25—Cuba	50—San Antonio	75—Tyrone
		76—Animas
		77—Hermanas
		78—Columbus
		79—Gage
		80—Nutt
		81—Lake Valley
		82—Hillsboro
		83—Hatch
		84—Organ
		85—La Mesa
		86—Alvarado
		87—Elk
		88—Hope
		89—Hagerman
		90—Dayton
		91—Lakewood
		92—Plomo
		93—Cooks
		94—Penasco

45

new mexico 1940

In 1940 many Americans were only vaguely aware of New Mexico's location, and few knew what part it played in the nation's economic and social development. Indeed, it often seemed that large numbers of Americans were unaware that New Mexico was part of the Union. This can be understood somewhat when one considers the status of New Mexico at that time. The state ranked 41st in total population and was one of the most sparsely settled states. The shaded areas on the map indicate where population density exceeded four persons (approximately one family) per square mile. In the remainder of the state the *average* population density was such that any family could be separated from its nearest neighbor by at least one mile. Large parts of the state were, for all purposes, uninhabited.

The largest city, Albuquerque, had only 35,449 people, and only six cities exceeded a population of 10,000. Table 1 lists all incorporated places with at least 1,000 inhabitants. The largest settlements were located in the north-central and southeast areas of the state. West of the Rio Grande only Gallup, a rail and mining center, and Silver City, also a mining town, had populations exceeding 5,000 and only four other towns had over 1,000 citizens. Overall, urban areas of 2,500 people or more contained 33 percent of the state's population. An additional 7 percent lived in non-urban incorporated places.

Over half the population lived on farms and produced about $48,000,000 worth of products (Table 2). Livestock, primarily cattle and to a much lesser extent, sheep, were the most valuable farm commodity. Major herd concentrations were in Grant County in the southwest; Chaves, Lea, and Lincoln counties in the southeast; Union County in the northeast; and San Juan County in the northwest. Forage crops were important in Chaves and Doña Ana counties, but the most valuable single crop was cotton. Production was valued at almost $3,000,000 in Doña Ana County and exceeded $1,250,000 in both Chaves and Eddy counties.

Another major segment of the economy was retail trade. Sales exceeded $125,000,000 and were dispersed throughout the state, roughly in proportion to population. Mineral industries were second only to retail trade in value of products. Petroleum associated products were the most valuable mineral resource. County statistics are unavailable but production centered on the extreme southeast and northwest regions of the state. Other mineral products listed in order of importance included copper, gold, silver, and zinc in Grant County; potash in Eddy and Lea counties; and coal in Colfax and McKinley counties.

The least important segment of the economy was manufacturing. It employed fewer than 4,000 workers and produced only $25,000,000 worth of products. The most important manufactured goods were associated with mineral industries and agriculture, petroleum refining, sawmills, bakeries, and food processing. Population centers in Bernalillo, Chaves, Eddy, and Otero counties accounted for most of the production although some manufacturing was found in every county except Harding.

On the eve of American entry into World War II, New Mexico was a little-known, sparsely settled state whose economy had not yet recovered fully from the depression. However, the state played a surprisingly important role in the war effort. As part of the early effort to halt the Japanese conquest of the Pacific, New Mexicans suffered heavy losses in the Bataan Death March. At home, because of its small population and open spaces, New Mexico was chosen as the location for secret development of the atomic bomb (first exploded at the Trinity Site in Socorro County) and as an area for the internment of POW's. At various times camps at Roswell and Lordsburg held over 10,000 German and Italian prisoners. Partly as a result of the war, the federal government has since become a major employer in New Mexico and can be considered an important contributor to the state's economy.

Paul McAllister

TABLE 1—INCORPORATED PLACES OF 1,000 OR MORE

Map Key	Place	Population	Map Key	Place	Population
1	Albuquerque	35,449	18	Clayton	3,188
2	Santa Fe	20,325	19	Lordsburg	3,101
3	Roswell	13,482	20	Belen	3,038
4	Las Vegas*	12,362	21	Hot Springs (Truth or Consequences)	2,940
5	Hobbs	10,619			
6	Clovis	10,065	22	Santa Rosa	2,310
			23	Farmington	2,161
7	Las Cruces	8,385	24	Lovington	1,916
8	Raton	7,607	25	Fort Sumner	1,669
9	Carlsbad	7,116	26	Mountainair	1,477
10	Gallup	7,041	27	Carrizozo	1,457
11	Tucumcari	6,194	28	Tularosa	1,446
12	Portales	5,104	29	Vaughn	1,331
13	Silver City	5,044	30	Magdalena	1,323
			31	Springer	1,314
14	Artesia	4,071	32	Eunice	1,227
15	Alamogordo	3,950	33	Jal	1,157
16	Socorro	3,712	34	Roy	1,138
17	Deming	3,608			

*Las Vegas City and Las Vegas Town combined.

TABLE 2—THE ECONOMY IN 1940

Activity	Number Units	Employees	Wages & Salaries (millions)	Value Products (millions)
Agriculture	32,830 Farms	178,349*	NA	47.8
Retail Trade	6,617 Stores	12,846	11.6	125.8
Mineral Industries	273 Companies	9,271	7.0	59.4
Manufacturing	272 Companies	3,772	3.8	25.1

*Total farm population.   NA not available.

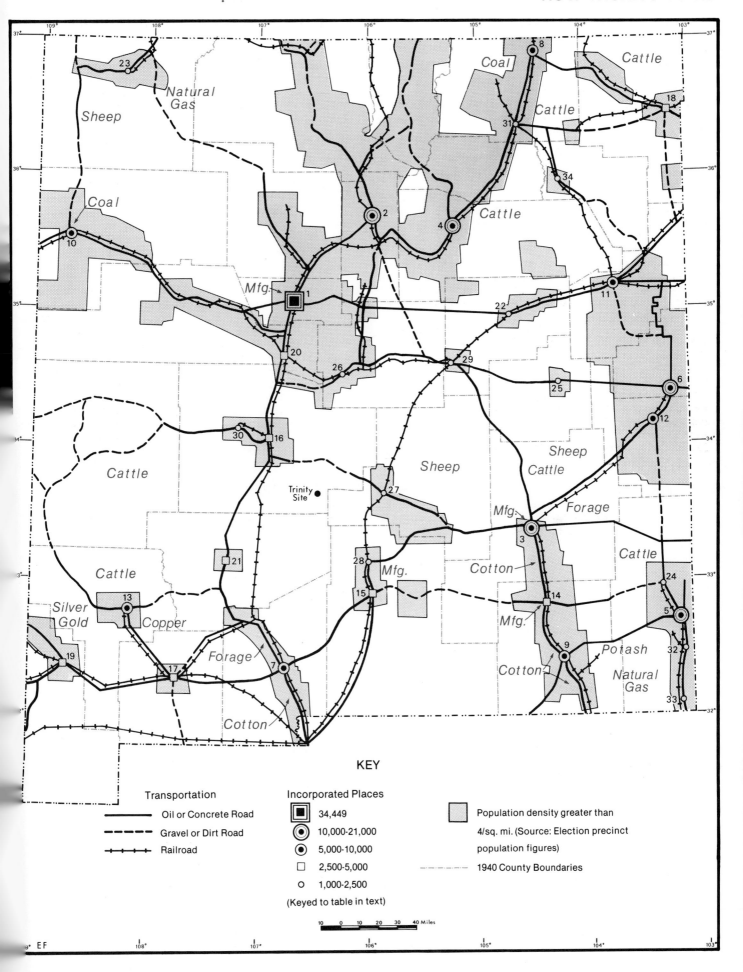

KEY

Transportation

——— Oil or Concrete Road

– – – Gravel or Dirt Road

+–+–+ Railroad

Incorporated Places

■ 34,449

◉ 10,000-21,000

● 5,000-10,000

□ 2,500-5,000

○ 1,000-2,500

(Keyed to table in text)

Population density greater than
4/sq. mi. (Source: Election precinct
population figures)

– · – · 1940 County Boundaries

10 0 10 20 30 40 Miles

county boundaries

New Mexico's counties vary greatly in area and population. Los Alamos is the smallest county with only 69,120 acres; Catron is the largest county with 4,414,720 acres. In terms of population, Harding County with a 1975 estimate of 1,200 inhabitants, is the smallest, while Bernalillo (county seat, Albuquerque) is the largest with an estimated 365,200 people. The counties also have an interesting variety of names. Five presidents, all Republicans, have been honored as have one vice president and two United States senators. Eleven other counties are named for governors or locally prominent individuals. Thirteen of the thirty-two county names are Anglo in origin. Nineteen county names are Spanish, even though it wasn't until the area became part of the United States that counties were formed.

New Mexico, under Spanish and Mexican control, was separated into three major districts reflecting the Spanish-Mexican concept of centralized government. American political tradition emphasized the importance of local governments, and when New Mexico became a territory of the United States, counties were created.

The territory's small population, concentrated along the Rio Grande Valley, required few counties to deal with government functions. However, the vastness of the territory (it then included Arizona and part of southern Colorado) called for counties of huge proportions and unusual shapes. The nine counties existing in 1852 were basically horizontal strips stretching from Texas to California. Santa Fe was a small rectangle very similar to its present size and location. Santa Ana and Rio Arriba counties stretched from the Rio Grande westward to Arizona. San Miguel County ran eastward from the Rio Grande to the Texas border.

New Mexico changed radically during the 1860's. Colorado Territory annexed a portion of the extreme north, and Arizona became a separate territory in 1863. Mora County had been created in the northeast corner, and as the population increased due to mining and ranching, three new counties were formed in 1869. During the 1870's there were numerous redefinitions of county boundaries but no new county creations. In fact, Santa Ana County was abolished, the only instance in New Mexico history in which a county with an organized government was disbanded. The coming of the railroads and increased population growth, due to further mining and ranching efforts, led to the creation of eight more counties during the 1880's and 1890's.

These new counties were organized mainly in the south and northwest portions of the state and brought the total number to twenty by the turn of the century.

Soon after 1900 new counties were added on the eastern plains and in the central part of the territory. With a total of twenty-six counties New Mexico became the forty-seventh state on January 6, 1912. During the first decade after statehood, five additional counties were created along the eastern and southwestern borders. Little need was felt for any additional counties, and except for relatively minor boundary adjustments and the inclusion of Los Alamos, the counties of 1921 are the same as those of today.

Los Alamos became the thirty-second county in the state as a result of the federal government's activities during World War II. It was in this area of New Mexico that the government's atomic energy research was conducted. The work required extreme secrecy, and early in the war isolated and mountainous portions of Santa Fe and Sandoval counties were placed under the exclusive jurisdiction of federal authorities. In 1949 Congress returned the area to state jurisdiction and within two weeks Los Alamos became the state's newest county.

Counties throughout the United States have usually been formed in response to the need of citizens to be closer to their government. County creations, of course, have occurred for other reasons as well: a sense of local pride; supposed economic benefits; desire to acquire or dominate local political offices; and efforts to increase or decrease party strength in state legislatures. But perhaps one of the more unusual reasons for creating a new county occurred in New Mexico in 1899 when Otero County (named for the incumbent governor) was formed to prevent a locally prominent rancher from facing a murder trial in an unfriendly county seat. Plans for a railroad and increased population were the justifications presented to the legislature in defense of the county creation.

While sentiments in the twentieth century seem to dictate that there will be no new counties in New Mexico, efforts to reduce the number of counties have aroused strong feelings and have failed. Unless the political climate changes or unusually heavy population growth occurs in the less densely settled areas, New Mexico will probably retain its present thirty-two counties.

Paul McAllister

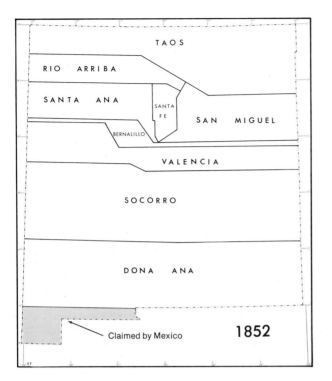

Claimed by Mexico

1852

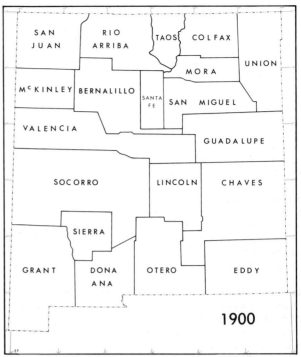

1900

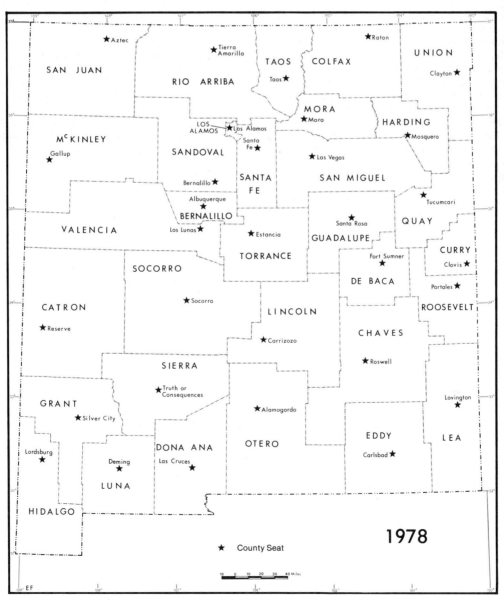

★ County Seat

1978

distribution of place names

The names people choose to designate and describe their environment say a great deal about the history and cultural heritage of an area. Names such as Arroyo Hondo (deep wash), Black Lake, Cloudcroft, and Tierra Amarilla (yellow earth) originate from man's perceptions of the physical environment. They reflect the history of different cultural groups, just as do those places named for important individuals: Carson, Lincoln, Montezuma, and San Juan. The place names of New Mexico reflect rather accurately the multi-cultural character of the state.

The cultural heritage of New Mexico is based upon two major ethnic divisions: Native American and European. But more realistically, it is the product of at least three very prominent cultural groupings: Indian, Spanish, and Anglo. While all three of the major cultural groups have made contributions to the place names of the state, they have not done so in equal proportions.

New Mexico has perhaps the most apparent manifestation of pre-European history and culture found in the contiguous United States, but that influence is not reflected in the number of Indian place names. Of the 453 names shown on the maps, only 17 or 3.8 percent can be considered of Indian origin. These places are found, with only two exceptions, in the northern half of the state. The greatest concentration is on or near the northwestern Indian reservations. The small number of locations with Indian names may be attributed in part to the methodology employed in this study. The places represented on the maps are either post offices in existence during 1977 or settlements shown on a standard road map of the state. Indian place names are primarily descriptive of the physical environment, for example, Toadlena (water bubbling up). Physical features such as canyons, creeks, and mountains as well as national and state monuments, parks, forests, and other recreation areas are not included.

Language differences also contribute to the small number of Indian place names. The several unwritten Indian dialects produced communication problems not only among Indian, Spanish, and Anglos but also among the various Indian pueblos and tribes. As a result, the numerically dominant population groups (at first Spanish and now Anglo) often corrupted Indian names or replaced them entirely.

The second group to affect the cultural landscape of New Mexico was the Spanish. Entering the southwest in the sixteenth century, they had great difficulty in establishing any effective control, but during the seventeenth century they finally became the dominant element in north-central New Mexico and along portions of the Rio Grande Valley. The Spanish brought with them a spiritual homogeneity in the form of Roman Catholicism which they tried to impose upon the Indians. Missions and mission settlements extended the Spanish influence farther and faster than it would have spread under secular settlement alone. The combination of Spanish governmental, religious, and individual initiatives imposed upon the various Indian groups resulted in New Mexico having the strongest Spanish heritage of any state.

Spanish place names are not only more common than Indian names, they also encompass a wider variety of usages. In addition to the physical environment, Spanish place names often represent individuals and places important in history: saints of the Catholic Church, government and royal officials, early explorers and set-tlers. Today Spanish place names constitute 46 percent of the state total and are found unevenly dispersed throughout New Mexico.

The greatest concentration of Spanish names is found, quite naturally, in the areas of early Spanish dominance: the northcentral part of the state (Mora, Rio Arriba, San Miguel, Santa Fe, and Taos counties) and the Rio Grande Valley. Other significant concentrations are found along the Rio Hondo in Lincoln County and the Rio San Jose in Valencia County. What is as interesting and significant as the river valley concentrations is the lack of Spanish place name concentrations along the periphery of the state. This can be attributed to the chronology of governmental changes in the territory.

Mexico secured its independence from the Spanish Empire in 1821, and almost simultaneously Americans began to intrude upon the New Mexico province. The Santa Fe Trail introduced Anglo-Americans and their ways into the very heart of Spanish culture. Within three decades New Mexico became a territory of the United States, and the Anglo influence has been increasing ever since.

Anglo place names duplicate the usage patterns of the Indians and Spanish and go a step further. In addition to the physically descriptive, the individual and the historically significant, they include acronyms (words formed by combining initial letters or parts of words) and names of other places in the United States. Examples of acronyms are Jal (cattle brand of John A. Lynch of east Texas), Maljamar (named for children of William Mitchell, president of a local oil company), and Gamerco (from Gallup American Coal Company). Miami and Des Moines are examples of names transferred from other areas of the country. Just as Anglos now comprise the largest population group in New Mexico, so do Anglo place names form the largest category (49.7 percent). Anglo names do not greatly outnumber Spanish nor have they made significant inroads into the predominantly Spanish regions. The area of greatest Anglo concentration is the eastern plains where homesteaders and cattlemen, mainly from Texas and Oklahoma, settled in the late nineteenth and early twentieth centuries. Other concentrations include the farming and ranching areas in the southern third of the state; mining areas in the southwest; and mining, railroad, and Mormon settlements in the northwest.

While Anglo and Spanish place names tend to form fairly distinct clusters, there is considerable intermingling as Anglo names appear in every county and Spanish ones in all but two. It is also important to keep in mind that place names do not always reflect the ethnic or cultural stock which founded a particular settlement. There are Anglo settlements with Spanish names and Spanish settlements that have taken Anglo names. Surprisingly there are only rare examples of Spanish and Anglo names being combined to form place names. Glenrio is one example: Anglo "Glen" combined with Spanish "rio."

New Mexico can expect continued population growth as Americans migrate to this "Sun Belt" state. Wherever these migrants choose to live, in already established settlements or new communities, it appears very likely that the derivation of place names will tell us less and less about the culture of the specific areas.

Paul McAllister

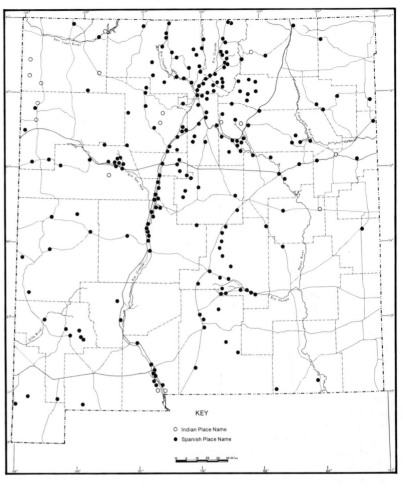

KEY

O Indian Place Name

● Spanish Place Name

10 0 10 20 30 40 Miles

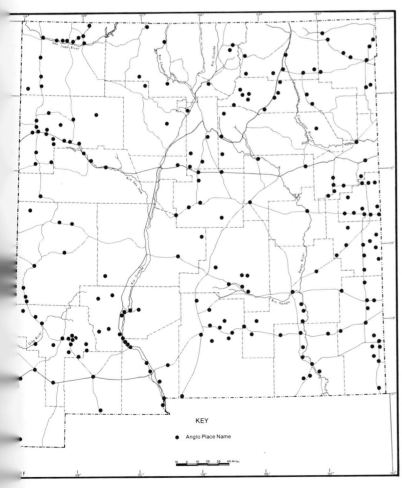

KEY

● Anglo Place Name

10 0 10 20 30 40 Miles

abandoned places

The cultural landscape of New Mexico is a surface complicated by relics of former residents. Many abandoned artifacts of the Indian and Spanish periods have disintegrated and are difficult to locate. This section describes the more visible abandoned sites of the Spanish and Anglos, who occupied New Mexico in the 19th and 20th centuries. The towns they constructed were either central to their farming areas, dispersed in linear patterns along rail lines and highways, or clustered in inhospitable mountainous environments where the earth was yielding a precious mineral.

An abandoned place is a settlement that no longer has the economic attraction that was instrumental in its creation, and presently exists as a shadow of its former self. The list that follows is not inclusive of all vacated towns and villages constructed during this period. To assure a degree of permanence to the site, only those that were allocated post office functions were admitted to the map. The presence of a post office indicated that the settlement was a central point for an area larger than the town. The dispersed population may have been larger than the approximated resident population.

Jerry L. Williams

ABANDONED PLACES — 1978

County/ Map # Town Name	Post Office	Location	Economics	Population Estimates	Present Status
CATRON COUNTY					
A1 Alma	(1882-1931)	7 mi. N of Glenwood	Ranching/Trade	1890-@220	10 residents
A2 Pleasanton	(1882-1886)	4 mi. S of Glenwood	Farming	@250	25 residents
A3 Collins Park	(1908-1955)	45 mi. NE of Reserve	Ranching	@50	abandoned
A4 Prineville/Mangus	(1905-1943)	16 mi. S of Quemado	Ranching	1940-@70	4 residents
A5 Hickman	(1937-1955)	25 mi. ENE of Quemado	Ranching	1910-@75	abandoned
M1 Clairmont	(1881-1883)	19 mi. NNE of Glenwood	Gold	@200	2 residents
M2 Cooney	(1884-1915)	15 mi. NE of Glenwood	Gold/Silver	1889-@600	abandoned
M3 Mogollon	(1890-1973)	13 mi. NE of Glenwood	Gold/Silver	1910-@950	35 residents
M4 Graham	(1895-1904)	7 mi. ENE of Glenwood	Gold/Smelter	@200	Catwalk St. Park
M5 Fluorine	(1910-1918)	57 mi. SSE of Reserve	Gold	@300	abandoned
CHAVES COUNTY					
A6 Olive	(1909-1938)	63 mi. NE of Roswell	Ranching	@50	abandoned
A7 Elk	(1894-1954)	52 mi. ENE of Alamogordo	Ranching/Sawmill	@75	3 residents
T1 Elkins	(1907-1970)	37 mi. NE of Roswell	RR/Homestead	1940-@120	2 residents
T2 Boaz	(1907-1955)	40 mi. NE of Roswell	RR/Trade	@50	abandoned
O1 Acme	(1906-1946)	25 mi. NE of Roswell	Gypsum/Cement	1935-@200	abandoned
COLFAX COUNTY					
A8 Farley	(1929-1932)	33 mi. E of Springer	Farm/RR Terminus	1940-@520	20 residents
A9 Bell	(1891-1933)	16 mi. E of Raton	Farm/Homestead	1940-@120	abandoned
M6 Sugarite	(1912-1944)	9 mi. NNE of Raton	Coal	1930-@500	2 residents
M7 Yankee	(1906-1922)	8 mi. NE of Raton	Coal	1915-@300	3 residents
M8 Gardiner	(1897-1940)	3 mi. W of Raton	Coal	1900-@900	abandoned
M9 Blossburg	(1881-1905)	5 mi. W of Raton	Coal	1893-@1000	abandoned
M10 Swastika/Brilliant	(1919-1954)	6 mi. NW of Raton	Coal	1929-@500	abandoned
M11 Brilliant	(1906-1935)	7 mi. NW of Raton	Coal	1907-@350	abandoned
M12 Van Houton	(1902-1952)	14 mi. SW of Raton	Coal	1930-@720	abandoned
M13 Koehler	(1907-1957)	16 mi. SW of Raton	Coal	1920-@2000	NRA gun club
M14 Dawson	(1900-1954)	14 mi. NE of Cimarron	Coal	1935-@9000	1 resident
M15 Baldy	(1888-1926)	16 mi. WNW of Cimarron	Gold/Copper	1897-@200	Philmt. Scout Ranch
M16 Elizabethtown	(1868-1931)	31 mi. NW of Cimarron	Gold	1870-@2000	4 residents
M17 Midnight	(1895-1898)	35 mi. NW of Cimarron	Gold	@200	abandoned
T3 Lynn	(1891-1910)	6 mi. N of Raton	RR Section	@100	abandoned
T4 Old Abbott	(1881-1936)	19 mi. SE of Springer	RR/Ranching	@120	2 residents
T5 Colmor	(1887-1965)	11 mi. S of Springer	RR/Trade	1930-@250	4 residents
T40 French	(1908-1945)	9 mi. N of Springer	Farm/RR Junction	1930-@360	abandoned
O2 Colfax	(1908-1921)	28 mi. SW of Raton	Trade/RR	1910-@300	abandoned
O3 Catskill	(1890-1905)	20 mi. W of Raton	Charcoal/Lumber	1900-@600	abandoned
CURRY COUNTY					
A10 Hollene	(1907-1953)	27 mi. N of Clovis	Dry Farm	1940-@150	3 residents
A11 Preston/Bellview	(1907-1914)	30 mi. NNE of Clovis	Ranching	1930-@200	abandoned
A12 Field	(1907-1924)	25 mi. NW of Clovis	Ranching	1940-@170	8 residents
DE BACA COUNTY					
A13 Ricardo	(1908-1954)	10 mi. SW of Ft. Sumner	Homestead/Ranching	1920-@290	abandoned
A14 Elvira	(1908-1924)	20 mi. WNW of Ft. Sumner	Ranching	@20	abandoned
A15 Dunlap	(1907-1961)	34 mi. SW of Ft. Sumner	Homestead	1930-@70	2 residents
T6 Agudo	(1909-1914)	6 mi. SSW of Ft. Sumner	RR/Trade	1906-@30	abandoned
T7 Buchanan	(1907-1940)	30 mi. W of Ft. Sumner	RR Section	1915-@90	abandoned
O4 LaLande	(1906-1955)	7 mi. E of Ft. Sumner	College/RR	1920-@100	4 residents
O5 Guadalupe	(1905-1908)	12 mi. NW of Ft. Sumner	Shrine/Ranching	1920-@110	abandoned
DONA ANA COUNTY					
M18 Plomo	(1902-1903)	46 mi. NE of Las Cruces	Lead	@100	U.S. Missile Range
M19 San Augustin	(1876-1888)	18 mi. ENE of Las Cruces	Silver/Lead	1884-@100	U.S. Missile Range
T8 Afton	(1924-1941)	20 mi. W of El Paso	RR Section	1950-@140	6 residents
O6 Crater	(1933-1935)	26 mi. W of Las Cruces	Trade	1930-@50	abandoned
EDDY COUNTY					
A16 Queen	(1905-1920)	40 mi. SW of Carlsbad	Ranching	1920-@90	abandoned
A17 Lakewood	(1904-)	20 mi. NNW of Carlsbad	Tomato Factory	1915-@270	15 residents
A18 Dayton	(1903-1944)	26 mi. NNW of Carlsbad	Ranch/RR	1950-@500	abandoned
A19 Hope	(1890-)	40 mi. NW of Carlsbad	Orchards/Ranching	1920-@700	50 residents
M20 Globe	(1915-1923)	12 mi. NW of Carlsbad	Gypsum	1915-@400	abandoned
GRANT COUNTY					
M21 Carlisle	(1884-1896)	42 mi. W of Silver City	Gold/Silver/Copper	1890-@150	abandoned
M22 Gold Hill	(1886-1906)	15 mi. ENE of Lordsburg	Gold	1897-@125	abandoned
M23 Malone	(1884-1888)	15 mi. NE of Lordsburg	Gold	1904-@75	abandoned
M24 Paschal	(1882-1883)	15 mi. SW of Silver City	Copper	1882-@400	under mine dumps
M25 Leopold	(1904-1914)	11 mi. SW of Silver City	Copper	1907-@600	open pit mine
M26 Old Tyrone	(1906-1921)	13 mi. SW of Silver City	Copper	1920-@4060	open pit mine
M27 Black Hawk	(1884-1887)	16 mi. W of Silver City	Silver	1885-@700	abandoned
M28 Fleming	(1883-1887)	11 mi. W of Silver City	Silver	1885-@150	abandoned
M29 Pinos Altos	(1867-1964)	7 mi. N of Silver City	Gold/Silver	1870-@2000	300 residents
M30 Georgetown	(1875-1903)	18 mi. NE of Silver City	Silver	1880-@540	abandoned
M31 Old Santa Rita	(1881-1954)	15 mi. E of Silver City	Copper	1915-@2500	open pit mine
M32 Vanadium	(1912-)	10 mi. E of Silver City	Vanadium	1900-@400	60 residents
M33 Old Hachita	(1882-1898)	45 mi. SW of Deming	Silver/Lead/Copper	1884-@300	7 residents
T9 New Hachita	(1902-)	39 mi. SW of Deming	RR depot/Ranching	1925-@400	50 residents
O7 Faywood Springs	(1879-1881)	21 mi. NW of Deming	Hot Spring Resort	@75	abandoned
GUADALUPE COUNTY					
A20 Sombrio	(1906-1936)	28 mi. W of Santa Rosa	Ranching	1930-@100	abandoned
A21 Pintada	(1909-1947)	24 mi. W of Santa Rosa	Ranching	1920-@310	15 residents
A22 San Ignacio	(1908-1946)	18 mi. W of Santa Rosa	Ranching	1920-@130	abandoned
A23 Riddle/Borcia	(1909-1920)	17 mi. S of Santa Rosa	Ranching	1917-@50	abandoned
A24 Los Tanos	(1907-1925)	11 mi. NE of Santa Rosa	Ranching	1915-@50	abandoned
M34 Guadalupe	(1900-1941)	15 mi. WSW of Santa Rosa	Copper/RR Section	@80	abandoned
O8 Cuervo	(1902-)	18 mi. NE of Santa Rosa	Trade/RR depot	1920-@200	10 residents

ABANDONED PLACES — 1978

County/ Map #	Town Name	Post Office	Location	Economics	Population Estimates	Present Status
HARDING COUNTY						
A25	Cone	(1908-1935)	43 mi. SSW of Clayton	Homestead/Ranch	1920-@30	abandoned
A26	Yates	(1922-1931)	22 mi. NE of Roy	Homestead/Trade	1925-@50	2 residents
A27	Solano	(1907-)	10 mi. SE of Roy	Ranching/RR	1920-@260	16 residents
T10	Mills	(1898-)	11 mi. NNW of Roy	RR/Milling	1920-@670	3 residents
HIDALGO COUNTY						
A28	Cloverdale	(1913-1943)	32 mi. S of Animas	Ranching	1925-@80	abandoned
M35	Valedon	(1917-1932)	3 mi. SW of Lordsburg	Gold/Silver	1920-@1250	abandoned
M36	Pyramid	(1882-1897)	9 mi. S of Lordsburg	Silver	1895-@100	abandoned
M37	Sylvanite	(1908-1913)	20 mi. ESE of Animas	Gold/Copper	1908-@100	abandoned
T11	Steins	(1888-1944)	19 mi. W of Lordsburg	Stage depot/RR	1919-@200	abandoned
T12	Shakespeare/Ralston	(1870-1885)	2 mi. S of Lordsburg	Stage depot/Silver	1884-@200	2 residents
LEA COUNTY						
A29	Knowles	(1902-1944)	9 mi. N of Hobbs	Ranching	1910-@500	dismantled
A30	Plainview	(1907-1930)	15 mi. NNE of Lovington	Homestead Town	1930-@130	abandoned
A31	King	(1908-1918)	13 mi. NE of Lovington	Homestead Village	1920-@25	abandoned
A32	Scott	(1909-1921)	32 mi. NNW of Hobbs	Homestead Town	1915-@40	dismantled
M38	Ochoa	(1917-1940)	14 mi. W of Jal	Oil Town	1920-@90	dismantled
M39	Lea	(1929-1931)	21 mi. SW of Hobbs	Oil Town	1930-@50	abandoned
LINCOLN COUNTY						
A33	Rebenton	(1896-1928)	19 mi. NE of Carrizozo	Bean Farming	1910-@130	2 residents
A34	Spindle	(1917-1920)	25 mi. NE of Carrizozo	Ranching	1915-@80	abandoned
A35	Richardson	(1895-1928)	25 mi. ENE of Carrizozo	Ranching/Trade	@50	5 residents
A36	Encinosa	(1915-1920)	22 mi. E of Carrizozo	Ranching/Trade	1920-@170	3 residents
A37	Lincoln	(1873-)	32 mi. SE of Carrizozo	Farm/County Seat	1890-@800	55 residents
A38	Arabela	(1901-1929)	40 mi. E of Carrizozo	Ranching	1925-@100	15 residents
A39	Lon	(1934-1942)	30 mi. ESE of Corona	Homestead/Ranch	1930-@70	abandoned
M40	Jicarilla	(1892-1942)	27 mi. NNE of Carrizozo	Gold	1935-@250	5 residents
M41	White Oaks	(1880-1954)	11 mi. NE of Carrizozo	Gold	1890-@830	25 residents
M42	Parsons	(1888-1926)	12 mi. NNW of Ruidoso	Gold	1890-@200	abandoned
M43	Bonito City	(1882-1911)	10 mi. NNW of Ruidoso	Silver	1910-@190	under Bonito Lake
M44	Estey City	(1901-1910)	37 mi. WSW of Carrizozo	Copper	1920-@120	U.S. Missile Range
T13	Coalara	(1903-1905)	1 mi. NW of Capitan	Railroad Coal	1905-@150	abandoned
T14	Oscuro	(1901-1951)	17 mi. SW of Carrizozo	RR Section/Gold	1890-@300	10 residents
O9	Ancho	(1902-1969)	26 mi. NE of Carrizozo	Bricks/Gypsum	1910-@440	6 residents
LUNA COUNTY						
A40	Waterloo	(1911-1922)	10 mi. N of Columbus	Farming	1910-@40	abandoned
M45	Cookes/Cookes Peak	(1889-1914)	29 mi. NNE of Deming	Silver/Lead	1900-@100	abandoned
M46	Chance City/Fullerton	(1885-1922)	23 mi. WSW of Deming	Lead	@50	abandoned
T15	Hermanas	(1903-1925)	32 mi. SSW of Deming	RR Section	1930-@75	abandoned
T16	Hondale	(1908-1934)	15 mi. SSW of Deming	RR Depot/Farming	1920-@50	3 residents
T17	Myndus/Akela	(1913-1941)	20 mi. E of Deming	RR Section	1930-@340	2 residents
T18	Florida	(1928-1940)	14 mi. NE of Deming	RR Section	1940-@100	4 residents
T19	Nutt	(1881-1939)	27 mi. NE of Deming	RR Junction	1930-@80	2 residents
McKINLEY COUNTY						
A41	Page	(1913-1916)	25 mi. SE of Gallup	Farming/Lumber	1930-@480	abandoned
M47	Defiance	(1881-1887)	12 mi. SW of Gallup	Coal/Trade Post	@70	abandoned
M48	Mentmore	(1917-)	8 mi. W of Gallup	Coal/Mission	1950-@1300	10 residents
M49	Allison	(1913-1937)	3 mi. NW of Gallup	Coal	1910-@550	30 residents
M50	Clarkville	(1898-1908)	6 mi. NW of Gallup	Coal	1920-@780	abandoned
M51	Gamerco	(1923-)	3 mi. N of Gallup	Coal	1925-@1800	250 residents
M52	Heaton	(1909-1922)	2 mi. N of Gallup	Coal	1920-@350	abandoned
M53	Gibson	(1890-1947)	5 mi. ENE of Gallup	Coal	1910-@850	abandoned
T20	Perea	(1915-1920)	15 mi. ESE of Gallup	RR Junction	@50	abandoned
O10	Savoia	(1882-1887)	30 mi. SSE of Gallup	Trading Post/Lumber	@30	abandoned
MORA COUNTY						
A42	Shoemaker	(1882-1957)	10 mi. ENE of Watrous	Ranching/RR	1930-@120	10 residents
A43	Tiptonville	(1876-1898)	23 mi. SW of Wagon Mound	Ranching/Farming	1890-@230	abandoned
A44	La Cueva	(1868-1969)	5 mi. SE of Mora	Milling/Ranching	1860-@570	8 residents
A45	Ocate	(1866-)	24 mi. NW of Wagon Mound	Ranching/Lumber	1900-@830	35 residents
A46	Naranjos	(1886-1917)	20 mi. NW of Wagon Mound	Ranching/Farming	1920-@175	2 residents
A47	Aurora	(1902-1921)	20 mi. SSW of Cimarron	Ranching	@50	abandoned
O11	Lucero	(1885-1936)	7 mi. NE of Mora	Lumber/Ranch	1900-@300	20 residents
O12	Loma Parda	(1872-1900)	6 mi. NW of Watrous	Trade/Military	1870-@420	abandoned
O13	Valmora	(1916-)	5 mi. NE of Watrous	Sanitorium/RR	@200	15 residents
OTERO COUNTY						
A48	Avis	(1903-1930)	37 mi. SE of Alamogordo	Ranching	1910-@75	5 residents
A49	Three Rivers	(1883-1973)	17 mi. N of Tularosa	Ranching/RR	1930-@320	5 residents
M54	Brice/Jarilla	(1899-1920)	30 mi. SSW of Alamogordo	Gold/Turquoise	1919-@330	abandoned
M55	Orogrande	(1905-)	32 mi. SSW of Alamogordo	Gold/Smelting	1920-@550	40 residents
T21	Valmont	(1917-1922)	10 mi. S of Alamogordo	Railroad/Trade	1930-@75	abandoned
O14	Orange	(1904-1925)	78 mi. SE of Alamogordo	Trading Post	1910-@60	abandoned
O15	Russia	(1904-1906)	25 mi. ESE of Alamogordo	Lumber	@50	abandoned
O16	Marcia	(1923-1942)	12 mi. ESE of Alamogordo	Lumber	1930-@270	abandoned
QUAY COUNTY						
A50	Hassell	(1907-1948)	20 mi. NE of Ft. Sumner	Ranching	@70	5 residents
T22	Hudson	(1908-1926)	12 mi. NNE of Tucumcari	RR Section	1950-@85	abandoned
T23	Obar	(1908-1953)	38 mi. NE of Tucumcari	RR Section/Trade	1920-@150	abandoned
T24	Endee	(1886-1955)	12 mi. ENE of San Jon	RR Section/Highway	1930-@275	abandoned
RIO ARRIBA COUNTY						
A51	Gavilan	(1929-1946)	25 mi. N of Cuba	Ranching	@50	3 residents
M56	Hopewell	(1894-1906)	23 mi. SE of Chama	Gold/Lumber	@300	abandoned
M57	Monero	(1884-1963)	15 mi. W of Chama	Coal/RR	1930-@360	6 residents
M58	Gobernador	(1916-1942)	25 mi. SW of Dulce	Gold/Lumber	1930-@210	abandoned
T25	Amargo	(1881-1923)	25 mi. W of Chama	RR/Stage Junction	@70	burned down
O17	Azotea	(1887-1893)	13 mi. W of Chama	Lumber	1895-@500	abandoned
ROOSEVELT COUNTY						
A52	Judson	(1907-1918)	25 mi. SE of Elida	Homestead Village	@25	abandoned
A53	Inez	(1908-1930)	20 mi. SSE of Portales	Homestead Town	1920-@130	3 residents
T26	Delphos	(1905-1940)	12 mi. SW of Portales	RR Section/Trade	1930-@40	abandoned
T27	Kenna	(1902-)	35 mi. SW of Portales	RR/Stage Depot	1930-@110	5 residents
O18	Bethel	(1902-1907)	10 mi. W of Portales	Church School	1905-@70	abandoned
SANDOVAL COUNTY						
A54	Miller/Guadalupe	(1898-1905)	38 mi. SSW of Cuba	Farm/Ranching	1890-@160	2 residents
A55	Cabezon/La Posta	(1891-1949)	34 mi. SSW of Cuba	Farm/Stage Depot	1940-@320	abandoned
M59	Copper City	(1883-1890)	3 mi. E of Cuba	Copper	1880-@240	abandoned
M60	Senorito	(1901-1924)	4 mi. SSE of Cuba	Copper	1910-@50	abandoned
M61	La Ventana	(1925-1932)	14 mi. S of Cuba	Coal/Coke	1900-@450	5 residents
M62	Albermarle	(1901-1903)	42 mi. NNW of Albuquerque	Gold	@70	abandoned
M63	Bland	(1894-1935)	39 mi. N of Albuquerque	Gold/Silver	1900-@610	1 resident
M64	Woodbury/Allerton	(1894-1903)	33 mi. NW of Albuquerque	Gold/Lumber	1897-@50	abandoned
M65	Hagen (& Coyote)	(1902-1931)	30 mi. NE of Albuquerque	Coal	1926-@500	abandoned
T28	La Bajada	(1870-1872)	26 mi. SW of Santa Fe	Freight Depot/Trade	1890-@150	10 residents

ABANDONED PLACES — 1978

County/ Map # Town Name	Post Office	Location	Economics	Population Estimates	Present Status
SAN JUAN COUNTY					
A56 Largo	(1885-1927)	25 mi. E of Farmington	Farm/Ranch/Trade	1890-@220	abandoned
A57 Jewett/Liberty	(1884-1920)	17 mi. W of Farmington	Farming	@300	15 residents
SAN MIGUEL COUNTY					
A58 La Linedre	(1878-1942)	21 mi. SE of Las Vegas	Farming	1910-@200	2 residents
A59 Mishawaka	(1910-1911)	18 mi. ESE of Las Vegas	Farming	1910-@50	abandoned
A60 Cherryvale	(1910-1926)	28 mi. E of Las Vegas	Homestead Farm	1920-@100	15 residents
A61 Old Garita	(1918-1927)	48 mi. SE of Las Vegas	Ranching	1930-@75	abandoned
A63 Sanchez	(1898-1927)	45 mi. E of Las Vegas	Ranching/Trade	1910-@165	4 residents
M66 San Geronimo	(1922-1944)	19 mi. W of Las Vegas	Gold/Ranching	1900-@450	20 residents
M67 Mineral City	(1881-1883)	25 mi. WNW of Las Vegas	Gold	@500	10 residents
M68 Tererro	(1927-)	16 mi. N of Pecos	Gold/Silver/Lead	1920-@600	3 residents
O19 Old Trementina	(1901-1950)	45 mi. ESE of Las Vegas	Mission/Ranching	1930-@530	abandoned
O20 Mesa Rica	(1938-1941)	51 mi. WNW of Tucumcari	Trade/Construction	1935-@500	abandoned
O21 Los Alamos	(1878-1919)	13 mi. NNE of Las Vegas	Trade/Ranching	1900-@170	10 residents
O22 San Miguel	(1851-1910)	22 mi. SW of Las Vegas	Territorial Prison	1860-@550	20 residents
SANTA FE COUNTY					
A64 Juana Lopez	(1866-1870)	12 mi. SW of Santa Fe	Ranching	1890-@75	abandoned
A65 Stanley	(1907-)	42 mi. S of Santa Fe	Farming/RR	1910-@200	25 residents
M69 Bonanza City	(1880-1883)	13 mi. SW of Santa Fe	Silver/Lead	1882-@220	abandoned
M70 Carbonateville	(1879-1899)	15 mi. SW of Santa Fe	Turquoise/Silver	1884-@150	abandoned
M71 Los Cerrillos	(1880-)	20 mi. S of Santa Fe	Gold/Silver/Copper	1990-@1150	100 residents
M72 Madrid	(1896-1966)	24 mi. SSW of Santa Fe	Coal	1930-@1500	45 residents
M73 Delores	(1887-1901)	32 mi. S of Santa Fe	Gold	1840-@1500	abandoned
M74 Golden	(1880-1928)	33 mi. NE of Albuquerque	Gold	1884-@400	15 residents
M75 San Pedro	(1881-1918)	30 mi. NE of Albuquerque	Gold/Copper	1890-@510	8 residents,
T29 Waldo	(1920-1926)	22 mi. SSW of Santa Fe	RR Junction/Coke	1925-@100	abandoned
O24 Buckman	(1899-1903)	15 mi. NW of Santa Fe	Lumber/Railhead	@75	abandoned
SIERRA COUNTY					
A67 Monticello	(1881-)	21 mi. NNW of T. or C.	Farm/Ranching	1910-@650	35 residents
M76 Grafton	(1881-1904)	37 mi. NW of T. or C.	Gold/Silver	1886-@350	abandoned
M77 Winston/Fairview	(1881-)	28 mi. NW of T. or C.	Silver/Ranching	1885-@1000	30 residents
M78 Chloride	(1881-1956)	30 mi. NW of T. or C.	Silver	1895-@250	10 residents
M79 Hermosa	(1884-1929)	28 mi. W of T. or C.	Gold/Silver	1890-@210	abandoned
M80 Andrews/Gold Hill	(1898-1907)	7 mi. NE of Hillsboro	Gold	1905-@100	abandoned
M81 Hillsboro	(1897-)	30 mi. SW of T. or C.	Gold/County Seat	1920-@820	200 residents
M82 Kingston	(1882-1957)	9 mi. W of Hillsboro	Silver	1890-@860	50 residents
M83 Tierra Blanca	(1892-1903)	7 mi. SW of Hillsboro	Silver	1900-@100	2 residents
M84 Lake Valley	(1882-1955)	13 mi. S of Hillsboro	Silver	1884-@1000	3 residents
M85 Shandon/Pittsburg	(1904-1906)	14 mi. S of T. or C.	Gold	1905-@50	abandoned
T30 Robinson	(1882-1883)	35 mi. NW of T. or C.	RR Speculation	1880-@60	abandoned
T31 Engle	(1881-1955)	17 mi. E of T. or C.	RR/Cattle Railhead	1910-@480	6 residents
SOCORRO COUNTY					
A68 Riley	(1890-1931)	42 mi. NW of Socorro	Ranching/Gold	@150	3 residents
A69 Contreras	(1919-1935)	25 mi. N of Socorro	Farm/Ranch	1865-@350	25 residents
A70 Claunch	(1930-)	53 mi. ENE of Socorro	Bean Farming	1940-@280	5 residents
M86 Tokey	(1919-1932)	19 mi. SE of Socorro	Coal	1930-@150	abandoned
M87 Carthage	(1883-1951)	20 mi. SE of Socorro	Coal	1920-@450	abandoned
M88 Rosedale	(1899-1928)	24 mi. SW of Magdalena	Gold	1900-@140	abandoned
M89 Kelly	(1883-1945)	4 mi. S of Magdalena	Lead/Zinc	1910-@1015	abandoned
T32 San Marcial	(1869-1944)	30 mi. S of Socorro	Railroad/Farm	1920-@600	4 residents
T33 Scholle	(1908-1970)	32 mi. SE of Belen	RR Section/Trade	1940-@120	abandoned
O25 Park City/La Smelta	(1892-1894)	1 mi. SW of Socorro	Smelter	1892-@300	abandoned
TAOS COUNTY					
M90 Amizette/Twining	(1893-1910)	14 mi. NE of Taos	Gold/Copper	1897-@250	mountain resort
M92 LaBelle	(1895-1901)	8 mi. NE of Red River	Gold	1900-@100	private resort
T34 Barranca Station	(1881-1890)	21 mi. SW of Taos	RR Depot/Stage	@50	abandoned
TORRANCE COUNTY					
A71 Eastview	(1890-1919)	10 mi. NE of Mountainair	Ranching	@50	abandoned
A72 Pinos Wells	(1884-1919)	29 mi. SW of Vaughn	Ranching	1920-@160	4 residents
A73 Gran Quivira	(1904-1968)	19 mi. SE of Mountainair	Ranching	1940-@40	abandoned
T35 Progresso	(1894-1930)	14 mi. SE of Willard	RR/Ranching	1930-@30	5 residents
T36 Negra	(1902-1972)	27 mi. ENE of Willard	RR Section/Trade	@35	abandoned
T37 Pedernal	(1917-1955)	21 mi. ENE of Willard	RR Section/Ranch	1930-@125	abandoned
T38 Lucy	(1915-1942)	12 mi. ENE of Willard	RR/Homestead/Trade	1925-@50	abandoned
UNION COUNTY					
A74 Centerville	(1907-1944)	42 mi. S of Clayton	Homestead/Ranch	1915-@50	abandoned
A75 Hayden	(1908-1970)	30 mi. SSW of Clayton	Ranch/Trade	1930-@220	5 residents
A76 Clapham	(1888-1954)	22 mi. SW of Clayton	Homestead/Ranch	1925-@50	abandoned
A77 Sofia	(1914-1926)	36 mi. W of Clayton	Bean Farming	1930-@80	3 residents
A78 Grenville	(1888-)	27 mi. NW of Clayton	Ranch/Dairy/RR	1920-@500	20 residents
A79 Seneca	(1908-)	14 mi. NNE of Clayton	Farming	1925-@100	5 residents
T39 Mt. Dora	(1908-)	18 mi. WNW of Clayton	RR Junction/Ranch	1920-@200	10 residents
O26 Amistad	(1907-)	33 mi. S of Clayton	Seminary/Ranch	1930-@110	20 residents
A80 Gladstone	(1880-)	36 mi. E of Springer	Ranching	1930-@65	4 residents
VALENCIA COUNTY					
M93 Copperton	(1901-1911)	23 mi. W of Grants	Copper		abandoned
T40 Correo	(1914-1959)	30 mi. W of Albuquerque	RR Section/Trade	@75	6 residents
O27 Sawyer	(1909-1916)	19 mi. W of Grants	Lumber	@100	abandoned
O28 Paxton Springs	(1929-1930)	15 mi. SW of Grants	Lumber	@50	2 residents

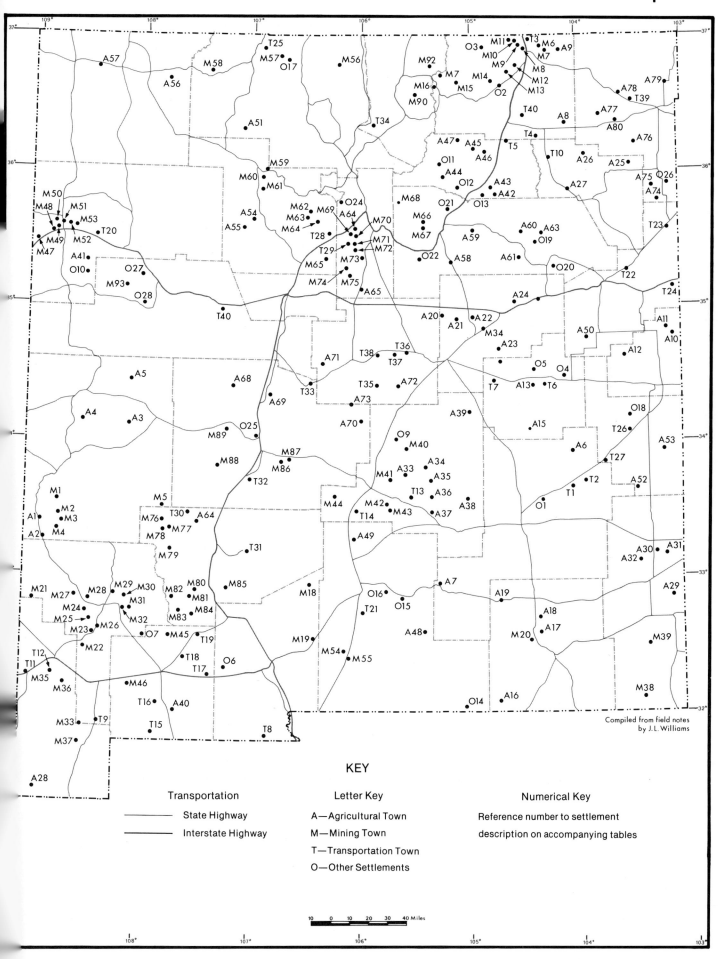

KEY

Transportation

— State Highway

— Interstate Highway

Letter Key

A—Agricultural Town

M—Mining Town

T—Transportation Town

O—Other Settlements

Numerical Key

Reference number to settlement
description on accompanying tables

Compiled from field notes
by J. L. Williams

10 0   10   20   30   40 Miles

population characteristics

population change 1930-1970

The population of New Mexico increased from 423,317 in 1930 to 1,017,055 in 1970, a gain of over 140%. While steady growth characterized general population change throughout the state, the county population trends varied widely. The decade from 1930 to 1940 marked an increase of 25.6% in the state's population. However, nine counties experienced higher rates of growth, ranging from 244.3% in Lea County to 28.7% in Taos County, while four counties (Colfax, Harding, Hidalgo, and Union) lost population.

During the next decade, 1940 to 1950, population growth in New Mexico accelerated slightly with an increase of 28.1%. Once again, the percentage of population growth in eight counties exceeded the percentage increase of population in the state. The largest increase, 109.9%, was recorded in Bernalillo County. Contrasting this growth, the number of counties which lost population increased to fourteen, with losses ranging from −31.1% in Harding County to −1.4% in Rio Arriba County.

The most discrepant population trends occurred from 1950 through 1960. This decade marked the largest increase in the state's population, 39.6%, and significant increases in many of the counties. Bernalillo County's population continued to grow with a gain of 80% while the population in San Juan and Otero Counties more than doubled with increases of 191.4% and 148%, respectively. At the same time, half of the counties experienced a loss in population. The average decrease among these counties was −14.8%.

From 1960 to 1970, population growth decelerated significantly throughout New Mexico. The increase in the state's population dropped to 6.9%, less than 1.0% annually. Over half of the counties experienced a population decrease, including counties such as San Juan and Lea which had been experiencing significant growth.

The shift in population trends can be attributed to emigration from New Mexico. Only three counties, Bernalillo, Grant, and Sierra, experienced net immigration between 1960 and 1970.

Lynn Wombold

POPULATION CHANGE BY COUNTY: NEW MEXICO

County	Population 1930	Population 1940	% Change 1930-1940	Population 1950	% Change 1940-1950	Population 1960	% Change 1950-1960	Population 1970	% Change 1960-1970
Bernalillo	45,430	69,391	52.7	145,673	109.9	262,199	80.0	315,774	20.4
Catron	3,282	4,881	48.7	3,533	−27.6	2,773	−21.5	2,198	−20.7
Chaves	19,549	23,980	22.7	40,605	69.3	57,649	42.0	43,335	−24.8
Colfax	19,157	18,718	−2.3	16,761	−10.5	13,806	−17.6	12,170	−11.8
Curry	15,809	18,159	14.9	23,351	28.6	32,691	40.0	39,517	20.9
De Baca	2,893	3,725	28.8	3,464	−7.0	2,991	−13.7	2,547	−14.8
Dona Ana	27,455	30,411	10.8	39,557	30.1	59,948	51.5	69,773	16.4
Eddy	15,842	24,311	53.5	40,640	67.2	50,783	25.0	41,119	−19.0
Grant	19,050	20,050	5.2	21,649	8.0	18,700	−13.6	22,030	17.8
Guadalupe	7,027	8,646	23.0	6,772	−21.7	5,610	−17.2	4,969	−11.4
Harding	4,421	4,374	−1.1	3,013	−31.1	1,874	−37.8	1,348	−28.1
Hidalgo	5,023	4,821	−4.0	5,095	5.7	4,961	−2.6	4,734	−4.6
Lea	6,144	21,154	244.3	30,717	45.2	53,429	73.9	49,554	−7.3
Lincoln	7,198	8,557	18.9	7,409	−13.3	7,744	4.5	7,560	−2.4
Los Alamos	------	------	---	10,476	---	13,037	24.4	15,198	16.6
Luna	6,247	6,457	3.4	8,753	35.6	9,839	12.4	11,706	19.0
McKinley	20,643	23,641	14.5	27,451	16.1	37,209	35.5	43,208	16.1
Mora	10,322	10,981	6.4	8,720	−20.6	6,028	−30.9	4,673	−22.5
Otero	9,779	10,522	7.6	14,909	41.7	36,976	148.0	41,097	11.1
Quay	10,828	12,111	11.8	13,971	15.4	12,279	−12.1	10,903	−11.2
Rio Arriba	21,381	25,352	18.6	24,997	−1.4	24,193	−3.2	25,170	4.0
Roosevelt	11,109	14,549	31.0	16,409	12.8	16,198	−1.3	16,479	1.7
Sandoval	11,144	13,898	24.7	12,438	−10.5	14,201	14.2	17,492	23.2
San Juan	14,701	17,115	16.4	18,292	6.9	53,306	191.4	52,517	−1.5
San Miguel	23,636	27,910	18.1	26,512	−5.0	23,468	−11.5	21,951	−6.5
Santa Fe	19,567	30,826	57.5	38,153	23.8	44,970	17.9	54,774	21.8
Sierra	5,184	6,962	34.3	7,186	3.2	6,409	−10.8	7,189	12.2
Socorro	9,611	11,422	18.8	9,670	−15.3	10,168	5.1	9,763	−4.0
Taos	14,394	18,528	28.7	17,146	−7.5	15,934	−7.1	17,516	9.9
Torrance	9,269	11,026	19.0	8,012	−27.3	6,497	−18.8	5,290	−18.6
Union	11,036	9,095	−17.6	7,372	−18.9	6,068	−17.7	4,925	−18.9
Valencia	16,186	20,245	25.1	22,481	11.0	39,085	73.8	40,576	3.7
State	423,317	531,818	25.6	681,187	28.1	951,023	39.6	1,017,055	6.9

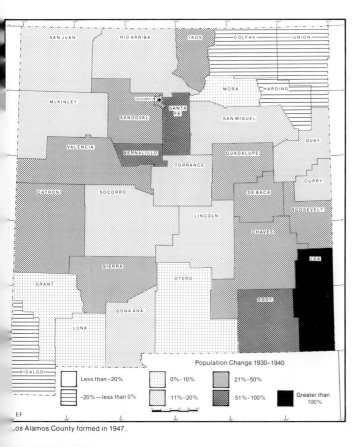

Population Change 1930-1940

Less than -20%	0%-10%	21%-50%
-20%—less than 0%	11%-20%	51%-100%
		Greater than 100%

* Los Alamos County formed in 1947.

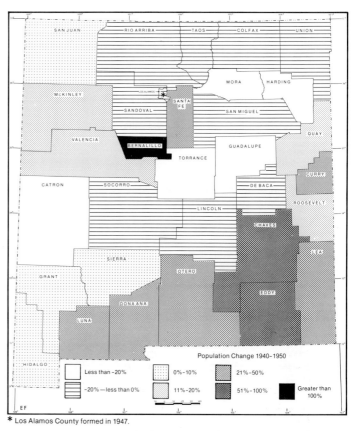

Population Change 1940-1950

Less than -20%	0%-10%	21%-50%
-20%—less than 0%	11%-20%	51%-100%
		Greater than 100%

* Los Alamos County formed in 1947.

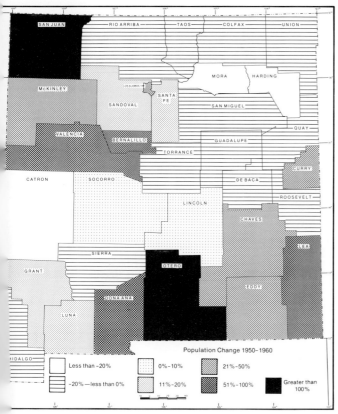

Population Change 1950-1960

Less than -20%	0%-10%	21%-50%
-20%—less than 0%	11%-20%	51%-100%
		Greater than 100%

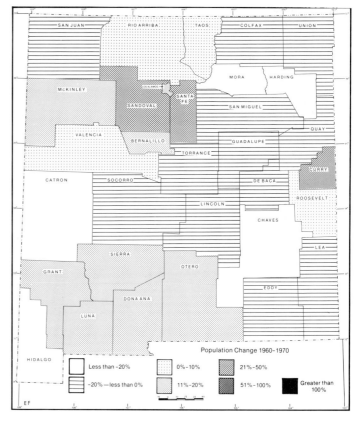

Population Change 1960-1970

Less than -20%	0%-10%	21%-50%
-20%—less than 0%	11%-20%	51%-100%
		Greater than 100%

59

population growth 1970-1977

During the 1970's, the annual rate of population growth in New Mexico more than doubled. Between 1970 and 1977, the population grew at an average annual rate of 2.3% (17% for the seven-year period). Natural increase (births minus deaths) accounted for most of this growth.

Natural increase dominated the population growth in the non-metropolitan counties while net migration accounted for most of the growth in the metropolitan counties of Bernalillo and Sandoval. Contrary to the national trend from 1970 to 1977, the population in metropolitan counties increased more rapidly than population in nonmetropolitan counties (20.6% for metropolitan counties compared to 15.3% for nonmetropolitan counties). However, there were some exceptions to this general trend.

The population increase in the Albuquerque (Bernalillo County) area was exceeded in eight nonmetropolitan counties: Hidalgo, Lincoln, Luna, McKinley, San Juan, Sierra, Torrance and Valencia. Growth may be attributed to recent metal mining activities in Hidalgo County; a retirement subdivision in Luna County; resort development and tourism in Lincoln and Sierra counties; and the proximity of Albuquerque in Torrance County. In Valencia County, population growth was stimulated by its eastern proximity to Albuquerque and the developing energy resources in its western portion.

The 1970-1977 population growth rates shadow a more recent slow-growth period in New Mexico. Between 1970 and 1975, the average annual percent increase in New Mexico's population was 2.4%, but this rate dropped to 2.0% between 1975 and 1977. Similarly, growth in the metropolitan counties dropped from an average of 3.0% annually to 2.1%. Eight nonmetropolitan counties experienced a slower rate of growth between 1975 and 1977.

These shifts in population change are due primarily to changing migration rates. While a decline in natural increase might be expected from the general decrease in fertility rates, the average decline among the counties was only 0.1%. However, the decrease in migration rates among counties with a decreasing rate of population change averaged 1.4%. Similarly, the average increase in migration rates among counties with an increasing rate of change was 1.5%.

While natural increase still comprises most of the population growth in the state, migration effected the changes in population trends from the 1970-1975 period to the 1975-1977 period. With declining birth rates, natural increase will ultimately be supplanted by net migration as the dominant factor of population change in New Mexico.

Lynn Wombold

TABLE: ESTIMATES OF THE POPULATION, 1977: NEW MEXICO COUNTIES[1]

	July 1, 1977 (Provisional)	July 1, 1976 (Revised)	July 1, 1975 (Revised)	April 1, 1970[2] (Census)	Change 1970-1977 Number	Percent	Components of Change 1970-1977[3] Births	Deaths	Net Migration Number	Percent
New Mexico[2]	1,190,000	1,172,000	1,144,000	1,017,055	173,000	17.0	156,000	58,000	75,000	7.3
Bernalillo	377,900	369,400	362,600	315,774	62,100	19.7	43,700	16,000	34,400	10.9
Catron	2,500	2,500	2,400	2,198	300	15.6	300	100	200	10.1
Chaves	49,300	48,500	47,600	43,335	5,900	13.7	5,500	3,200	3,700	8.5
Colfax	12,800	13,300	13,000	12,170	600	5.2	1,600	900	(Z)	(Z)
Curry	41,100	40,900	43,300	39,517	1,600	4.0	7,100	2,000	−3,500	−9.0
De Baca	2,500	2,600	2,600	2,547	(Z)	−.5	200	200	(Z)	.5
Dona Ana	83,900	82,300	79,600	69,773	14,100	20.3	11,400	3,000	5,700	8.2
Eddy	45,500	45,300	42,900	41,119	4,300	10.5	5,300	2,700	1,700	4.1
Grant	24,500	24,300	24,600	22,030	2,500	11.4	3,500	1,300	300	1.5
Guadalupe	4,900	4,900	4,900	4,969	−100	−2.2	600	300	−400	−8.1
Harding	1,200	1,300	1,200	1,348	−100	−11.1	100	100	−200	−12.0
Hidalgo	6,200	6,200	5,800	4,734	1,500	31.6	900	400	1,000	20.2
Lea	52,900	53,100	51,600	49,554	3,400	6.8	7,500	2,500	−1,600	−3.2
Lincoln	10,300	10,000	9,700	7,560	2,700	35.8	1,000	500	2,200	29.1
Los Alamos	17,100	16,500	16,100	15,198	1,900	12.7	1,300	300	1,000	6.4
Luna	14,400	14,700	14,400	11,706	2,700	23.2	2,000	1,000	1,700	14.7
McKinley	56,100	54,800	51,100	43,208	12,900	29.8	10,400	2,700	5,200	11.9
Mora	4,800	4,900	4,800	4,673	200	3.5	500	300	−100	−1.3
Otero	42,300	42,400	42,500	41,097	1,200	3.0	7,100	1,700	−4,200	−10.3
Quay	11,200	11,300	11,300	10,903	300	2.8	1,300	1,000	(Z)	−.4
Rio Arriba	27,600	28,000	27,800	25,170	2,500	9.8	4,700	1,700	−600	−2.3
Roosevelt	16,500	16,500	16,600	16,479	100	.4	2,100	1,000	−1,000	−6.0
Sandoval	24,000	23,600	22,800	17,492	6,600	37.5	3,600	1,400	4,300	24.4
San Juan	70,800	68,000	64,500	52,517	18,300	34.9	10,400	2,700	10,700	20.3
San Miguel	22,700	23,200	23,300	21,951	800	3.4	3,300	1,400	−1,100	−4.9
Santa Fe	65,200	64,300	62,000	54,774	10,400	19.0	7,800	3,100	5,700	10.4
Sierra	8,800	8,800	8,300	7,189	1,600	22.5	600	1,100	2,000	28.5
Socorro	9,900	10,200	9,900	9,763	200	1.9	1,600	700	−700	−7.4
Taos	19,800	19,800	19,300	17,516	2,300	13.1	2,700	1,100	700	4.1
Torrance	6,800	6,700	6,400	5,290	1,500	28.6	700	400	1,200	22.8
Union	4,900	4,900	4,900	4,925	(Z)	.2	500	400	−100	−2.5
Valencia	51,400	48,900	46,100	40,576	10,800	26.6	6,600	2,200	6,400	15.8

Z Less than 50 persons or less than .05 percent.

[1] State estimates are rounded to the nearest thousand, county estimates to the nearest hundred.

[2] The State total includes all corrections to the 1970 census made subsequent to the release of the official counts. The official 1970 count for New Mexico was 1,016,000.

[3] Births and deaths are based on reported vital statistics from April 1, 1970 to December 31, 1976 with extrapolations to June 30, 1977. Net migration is the difference between net change and natural increase.

population growth 1970-1977

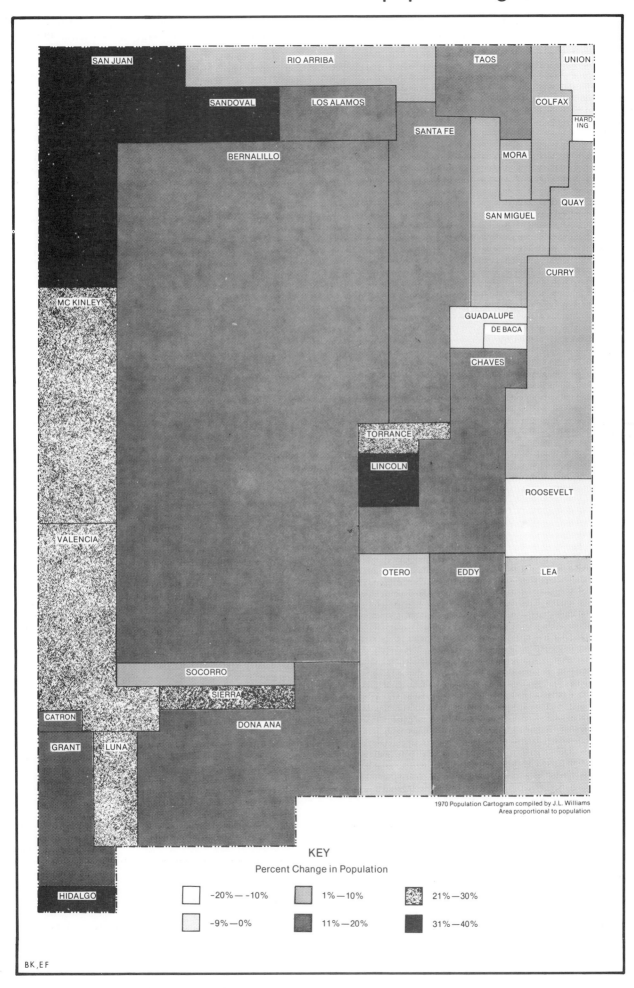

1970 Population Cartogram compiled by J.L. Williams
Area proportional to population

KEY
Percent Change in Population

-20% — -10%   1% — 10%   21% — 30%
-9% — 0%   11% — 20%   31% — 40%

BK,EF

61

population origins 1970

As a result of the decline in immigration to New Mexico during the 1960's the majority of the state's population was native. In only seven counties in 1970 were most of the residents born outside New Mexico. Five of these counties, Chaves, Curry, Lea, Eddy and Otero, are located in the southeast section of the state. Since many of the migrants to New Mexico came from Texas, the proximity to Texas undoubtedly influenced the distribution of out-of-state residents in this area.

Residents born outside the United States comprised less than 2.0% of the population in over half of New Mexico counties. Those counties with the highest proportions of foreign-born residents included Doña Ana and Hidalgo, 8.3% each; Luna, 6.6% and Grant and Sierra, 4.0% each. Each of these counties is located in the southwest sector of the state near the border with Mexico.

Lynn Wombold

POPULATION ORIGINS: 1970

County	Total Replies	Born in State	Born out of State	Foreign Born
Bernalillo	302,179	151,784	144,259	6,136
Catron	2,002	1,250	719	27
Chaves	40,677	19,551	19,825	1,301
Colfax	11,755	8,195	3,304	256
Curry	37,502	14,041	22,604	497
De Baca	2,464	1,595	812	57
Dona Ana	66,018	31,905	28,662	5,451
Eddy	39,162	18,345	19,934	888
Grant	20,989	13,514	6,629	846
Guadalupe	4,867	4,268	552	47
Harding	1,264	947	299	18
Hidalgo	4,567	2,574	1,614	378
Lea	47,234	14,241	32,271	722
Lincoln	6,855	4,179	2,613	63
Los Alamos	14,494	5,058	9,285	151
Luna	10,893	5,766	4,404	723
McKinley	41,058	30,624	10,016	418
Mora	4,488	4,171	291	26
Otero	38,726	14,534	23,073	1,119
Quay	10,687	6,096	4,529	62
Rio Arriba	23,418	20,472	2,740	206
Roosevelt	16,007	8,102	7,759	146
Sandoval	16,802	13,497	3,112	193
San Juan	49,728	27,729	21,648	351
San Miguel	20,380	16,386	3,391	603
Santa Fe	50,322	35,682	13,958	682
Sierra	6,875	3,064	3,537	274
Socorro	9,163	6,697	2,265	201
Taos	16,617	13,593	2,928	96
Torrance	4,981	3,586	1,361	34
Union	4,655	2,655	1,983	17
Valencia	39,142	27,876	10,746	520

Source: U.S. Bureau of the Census, "Census of Population"—1970.

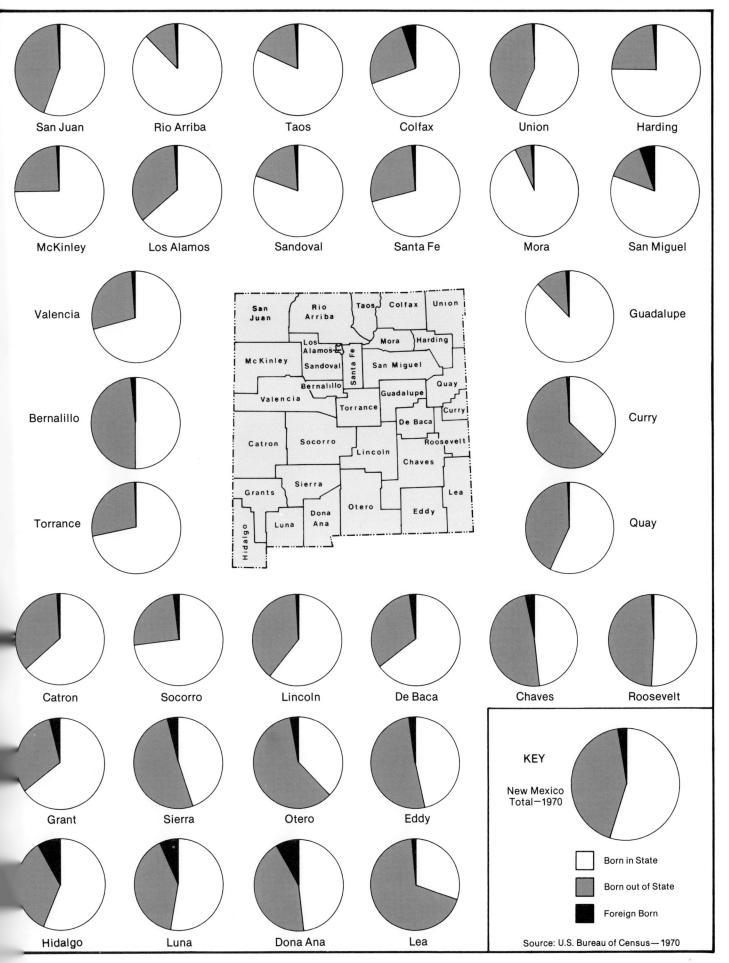

San Juan

Rio Arriba

Taos

Colfax

Union

Harding

McKinley

Los Alamos

Sandoval

Santa Fe

Mora

San Miguel

Valencia

Guadalupe

Bernalillo

Curry

Torrance

Quay

Catron

Socorro

Lincoln

De Baca

Chaves

Roosevelt

Grant

Sierra

Otero

Eddy

Hidalgo

Luna

Dona Ana

Lea

KEY

New Mexico
Total—1970

☐ Born in State

▨ Born out of State

■ Foreign Born

Source: U.S. Bureau of Census—1970

population density 1975

With a statewide population density fewer than ten persons per square mile, New Mexico may be regarded as a lightly populated state. This by no means implies that the area is underpopulated even though vast land tracts are nearly uninhabited.

Several factors contribute to the peculiar distribution of population in New Mexico. Natural elements such as soils, water, and climate are important in determining where people can survive and were strong influences on the early settlement patterns in the state. The land grants relocated Indian settlers into reservations and established vast land tracts for the Spanish and Mexican residents who concentrated in the northern mountains and along the major river valleys. Economics, such as commercial agriculture, rail and road transport, and mining, were major factors for explaining more recent concentrations of people.

Water is the most important factor in describing where people are in New Mexico. Alluvial flood plains along the main surface channels of the San Juan, Rio Grande, and Pecos rivers are clearly visible on the map as ribbons of high population density. The flow of the Rio Grande and San Juan during the growing season was a major attraction for historic (and prehistoric) settlement of Indian and Hispanic peoples. The use of a reliable water resource for surface irrigation continued until recently to be the primary motivation for population concentration and growth along these rivers. Although surface flow is vital to agricultural irrigation, the accumulation of population along the lower Pecos River (Chaves and Eddy counties) is related to the abundance of artesian water that percolates to the surface when the pressure of overlaying material is penetrated. There are other water-associated concentrations in Torrance, Luna, Otero, and Roosevelt counties where settlements are found over large underground aquifers. Recent technology has provided economical ways to pump water from the underground reservoirs to the surface.

Sections along the San Juan, Rio Grande, and Pecos rivers that appear to be lightly populated are areas of either deep canyons with little agricultural potential or are large tracts of land reserved by the state and federal governments as nesting regions for migratory waterfowl. The Canadian and Gila rivers are major drainage systems that are lightly populated as they are either flanked by steep-rising canyon walls, or the surface flow in the summer is unpredictable. Large sections of the map that presently show very light densities were at one time heavily settled by farmers who were attracted to the fertile soil and the opportunity to acquire 160-acre homesteads. Following a long drought cycle when much of the area was reduced to dust storms and diminished subsurface water supplies, the farmer was replaced by the rancher and one household would occupy space previously held by as many as one hundred households.

Many of the dispersed pockets of moderate population densities are not related to reliable locations of water. Settlements attracted by railroad and highway development concentrated near junctions and railroad maintenance sidings. Mining communities account for other pocket concentrations. Employment opportunities available in these numerous small towns once offered important supplementary support for residents of nearby subeconomic homesteads. Although many of the economic reasons for the founding of these small centers have been abandoned, some of the services have remained and support a moderately-populated local hinterland.

The land grant history is not clearly reflected in the chaotic pattern of population density in northcentral New Mexico. The Spanish and Mexican land grants were surveyed as geometric patterns, but the settlement patterns within the granted tracts were linear stretches confined to the narrow tributary valleys that carried spring snow melt out of the high mountains. The Indian land grants show up very clearly on the map if the reservation is very small or if the population is concentrated in pueblos. The Navajo reservation of McKinley and San Juan counties is extensive and people live in very small villages or scattered homesteads. Navajo concentrations that appear on the map are water-related such as areas supplied by perennial springs. But even here the density varies greatly by season or year and there is no accurate way to account for population densities on the Navajo reservation.

Twentieth century concentrations have focused on energy resource locations in New Mexico. Gas and oil have greatly expanded the population along the San Juan River and attracted immigrants to Lea County. Coal has been responsible for pockets of high densities at various times in Colfax, McKinley, San Juan, and Santa Fe counties. The former areas of shaftmining (Raton, Madrid) that dominated local production for half a century have declined concurrently with the rise of surface mining that has brought new employment and population density increase to other centers (Farmington, Gallup). The mining of uranium fuel spawned a population boom in western Valencia and eastern McKinley counties. Grants, a small village in the 1950's, expanded rapidly as the uranium center, and today is the largest town in Valencia County, attracting mineworkers from as far away as Albuquerque.

The urban population densities appear on the table to be exceptionally high compared with densities of non-urban areas of the state. However, compared with urban densities of the midwestern and northeastern United States where densities generally exceed 10,000 and 20,000 persons per square mile, the New Mexico cities appear to have low concentrations of people. Most urban areas are horizontal stretches of single-family subdivision housing with very little application of vertical construction of residential units. Albuquerque, which spreads over ninety square miles and is the major area of population concentration in New Mexico, has approximately 40 percent of its area in low density housing. The commuting hinterland of this metropolitan area affects the overall population densities of neighboring Valencia and Sandoval counties by attracting people to the area of the Rio Grande Valley accessible to Albuquerque.

The urban concentrations have added to the demand for water. Cities, which are heavy users of water, compete with farming areas for available supplies, and the former usually emerge victorious. Supply and demand of water resources is normally the modern criterion for measuring the carrying capacity of the land in the arid southwest. Many scientists have speculated that population demand for water in New Mexico has already exceeded the replenishment rate of this necessary resource. If this is true, the low density appearance of the state may already represent an overpopulated area.

Jerry L. Williams

TABLE POPULATION DENSITIES—1975

COUNTY County Subarea	1975 Land Area in sq. mi.	1975 Population	Population Density Per sq. mi.	COUNTY County Subarea	1975 Land Area in sq. mi.	1975 Population	Population Density Per sq. mi.	COUNTY County Subarea	1975 Land Area in sq. mi.	1975 Population	Population Density Per sq. mi.
BERNALILLO	1169.0	362,600	310.2	LEA	4393.0	51,600	11.7	SANDOVAL	3714.0	22,800	6.1
Albuquerque	88.7	279,401	3150.0	Hobbs	16.6	27,660	1666.3	SAN JUAN	5500.0	64,500	11.7
Rest of County	1080.3	83,199	77.0	Lovington	4.5	9,270	2060.0	Farmington	17.5	27,802	1588.7
CATRON	6897.0	2,400	0.3	Jal	5.1	2,637	517.1	Aztec	3.6	4,157	1154.7
				Eunice	1.3	2,508	1929.2	Rest of County	5478.9	32,541	5.9
CHAVES	6084.0	47,600	7.8	Rest of County	4365.5	9,525	2.2				
Roswell	25.2	37,980	1507.1	LINCOLN	4858.0	9,700	2.0	SAN MIGUEL	4741.0	23,300	4.9
Rest of County	6058.8	9,620	1.6	Ruidoso	2.3	3,442	1496.5	Las Vegas	3.2	15,101	4719.1
COLFAX	3764.0	13,000	3.5	Rest of County	4855.7	6,258	1.3	Rest of County	4737.8	8,199	1.7
Raton	5.6	7,757	1385.2	LOS ALAMOS	108.0	16,100	149.1	SANTA FE	1902.0	62,000	32.6
Rest of County	3758.4	5,243	1.4	LUNA	2957.0	14,400	4.9	Santa Fe	29.9	44,937	1502.9
CURRY	1403.0	43,300	30.9	Deming	3.9	10,511	2695.1	Rest of County	1872.1	17,063	9.1
Clovis	13.5	31,734	2350.7	Rest of County	2953.1	3,889	1.3	SIERRA	4156.0	8,300	2.0
Rest of County	1389.5	11,566	8.3	McKINLEY	5454.0	51,100	9.4	T or C	9.6	5,207	542.4
DE BACA	2356.0	2,600	1.1	Gallup	8.1	16,948	2092.3	Rest of County	4156.4	3,093	0.7
DONA ANA	3804.0	79,600	20.9	Rest of County	5445.9	34,152	6.3	SOCORRO	6603.0	9,900	1.5
Las Cruces	18.9	40,336	2134.2	MORA	1940.0	4,800	2.5	Socorro	12.5	6,014	481.1
Rest of County	3785.1	39,264	10.4	OTERO	6638.0	42,500	6.4	Rest of County	6590.5	3,886	0.6
EDDY	4167.0	42,900	10.3	Alamogordo	2.3	23,535	10232.6	TAOS	2256.0	19,300	8.6
Carlsbad	12.6	22,955	1821.8	Tularosa	2.1	3,045	1450.0	Taos	5.6	2,700	494.6
Artesia	3.5	10,199	2914.0	Rest of County	6633.6	15,920	2.4	Rest of County	2250.4	16,530	7.3
Rest of County	4150.9	9,746	2.3	QUAY	2875.0	11,300	3.9	TORRANCE	3346.0	6,400	1.9
GRANT	3970.0	24,600	6.2	Tucumcari	5.4	7,349	1360.9	UNION	3816.0	4,900	1.3
Silver City	6.5	9,464	1456.0	Rest of County	2869.6	3,951	1.4	Clayton	3.1	2,943	949.4
Bayard	0.7	2,918	4168.6	RIO ARRIBA	5840.0	27,800	4.8	Rest of County	3812.9	1,957	0.5
Rest of County	3962.8	12,218	3.1	Espanola	4.6	7,380	1604.3	VALENCIA	5656.0	46,100	8.2
GUADALUPE	2998.0	4,900	1.6	Rest of County	5838.4	20,420	3.5	Grants	6.4	8,583	1341.1
HARDING	2134.0	1,200	0.6	ROOSEVELT	2454.0	16,600	6.8	Belen	5.2	5,825	1120.2
HIDALGO	3447.0	5,800	1.7	Portales	4.5	10,339	2297.6	Rest of County	5644.4	31,692	5.6
Lordsburg	8.3	4,120	496.4	Rest of County	2449.5	6,261	2.6	NEW MEXICO	121412.0	1,144,000	9.4
Rest of County	3438.7	1,680	0.5					Urban Areas > 2500[a]	444.3	710,927	1600.1
								Non-Urban Areas[b]	120967.7	433,073	3.6

Source: U.S. Census Bureau, 1975.
a—including Los Alamos County
b—excluding Los Alamos County

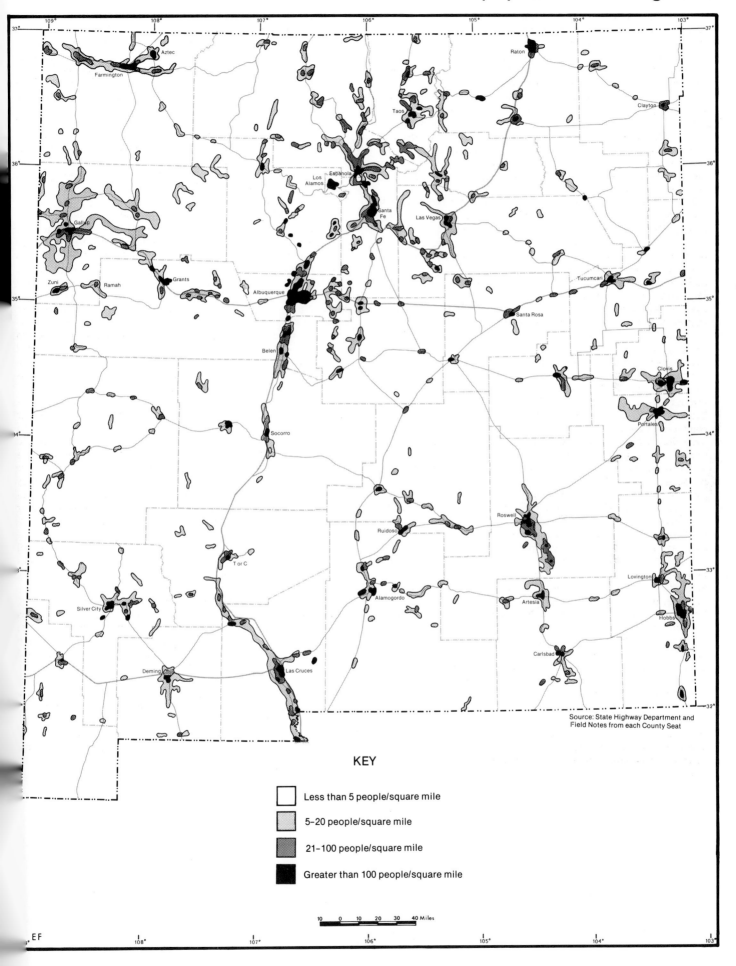

KEY

☐ Less than 5 people/square mile

▨ 5–20 people/square mile

▦ 21–100 people/square mile

■ Greater than 100 people/square mile

Source: State Highway Department and
Field Notes from each County Seat

10 0 10 20 30 40 Miles

ethnic distribution 1970

New Mexico is essentially tricultural as Indian, then Hispanic, and finally Anglo peoples found the area attractive for settlement. Although interbreeding has occurred between Indian, Hispanic, and Anglo, the distribution of the three ethnic populations clearly illustrates enclaves of single group dominance. The separation of cultures results from the sequence of occupation, the economic demands of the different settler groups, and the solutions to conflicts in search for security between the ethnic groups.

Indians, who were the first of the three cultures to settle in New Mexico, occupy vast land tracts in the western half of the state. This land was established for them by Hispanic and Anglo administrators to confine and control the Indian population. Most of the designated Indian areas were occupied by the tribes when the other cultures arrived, but the surveyed boundaries completely ignored many ancient Indian settlement sites and ancestral burial grounds.

The Pueblo Indians occupy arable lands along the Rio Grande and San Jose river valleys. This was the area of pueblo settlement when the Spanish and Mexican explorers arrived in the 17th century, and became the location of early land protection grants to the Indians. The high incidence of Indian population in Rio Arriba, Santa Fe, Sandoval, and Valencia counties results directly from these Spanish land grants. A large land area in northwestern New Mexico was granted to the Navajo Indians during the Territorial Period of the late 19th century as a resolution of conflict between the U.S. government and the Navajo nation. Administered from the tribal center at Window Rock, Arizona, the Navajo land covers much of McKinley and San Juan counties, accounting for the high proportion of Indian population in those areas. The U.S. government provided land for some of the other local tribes which resisted Anglo settlement during the late Territorial Period. The Ute and Jicarilla Apache tribes were allocated land in the northern counties of San Juan and Rio Arriba, and the Mescalero Apaches were placed on a reservation in northern Otero County. Land was not provided in New Mexico for the Comanche Indians, who controlled much of the eastern half of the state during the periods of Hispanic and Anglo settlement. As no Indian group was designated land east of the mountains, the eastern counties became populated entirely by the Hispanic and Anglo cultures.

Hispanics of Mexican, Spanish, and Christianized Indian origins settled along the Rio Grande and its tributaries on arable lands not granted to the Indians. They also occupied the upper Pecos Valley, the grazing lands along the foothills of the high mountains between the Rio Grande and Pecos rivers, and the high country of the north-central portion of the state. Most of the His-

panic centers of settlement were also grants of land from Spanish and Mexican administrators as ex post facto rights to territories claimed by families established in those areas. These grants became protected areas for Hispanic descendants of early settlers, and when recognized by the American government, they became areas of refuge from the Anglo pioneers. This partly explains the high concentrations of Hispanics in Rio Arriba, Taos, Mora, San Miguel, Guadalupe, Santa Fe, Torrance, and Socorro counties. The high proportion of Hispanic population in Colfax, Grant, Hidalgo, and Luna counties results from the later import of labor from Mexico to operate the Anglo industries in agriculture and mining.

The term "Anglo" depicts the English-speaking American immigrant who began arriving in large numbers by the mid-19th century. Anglos predominate on the eastern plains and the western border counties, and have an agricultural economy based on cattle, sheep, and wheat farming. The counties of Curry, Roosevelt, Lea, Chaves, and Eddy had the soil and climate to support limited dryland and irrigation farming. These counties, and to a lesser degree the western counties of Catron and Hidalgo, became populated by Anglo "nesters" during the American land settlement program of the Homestead Acts around the turn of the century. The Anglo population expanded into the southeastern plains counties when Texas cattlemen and oilmen moved into most of the areas unoccupied by the homesteaders. Many Anglos were also drawn to the mineral wealth of Lincoln, Sierra, Grant, and Colfax counties, and to the scientific anomaly called Los Alamos that was born of the nuclear age. Migrations of Anglos from the midwestern and northeastern areas of the United States to the sunbelt of New Mexico can be expected to alter the future ethnic proportions of resort and retirement counties such as Doña Ana, Luna, Lincoln, Bernalillo, Santa Fe, and Taos.

The Black population of New Mexico is very small. About one-third of the Blacks live in Albuquerque, and significant proportions are found in the Texas border counties of Curry, Lea, Otero, and Doña Ana. The immigration of Blacks to New Mexico is related to agricultural and oil field employment in the east and to railroad opportunities along the Rio Grande. The small group listed as "other" on the table consists of minority populations of Orientals and mixed groups who are generally listed by the census as "Unclassified."

Jerry L. Williams

TABLE 1: NEW MEXICO'S ETHNIC/RACIAL POPULATION BY COUNTY IN 1970

	Anglo	Hispanic	Indian	Black	Other	Total		Anglo	Hispanic	Indian	Black	Other	Total
New Mexico	527,539* (51.9)**	388,364 (38.2)	72,757 (7.2)	19,535 (1.9)	7,812 (0.8)	1,016,007	Mora	433 (9.3)	4,226 (90.5)	–	–	8 (0.2)	4,667
Bernalillo	180,022 (57.0)	120,760 (38.2)	5,840 (1.8)	6,691 (2.1)	2,465 (0.8)	315,778	Otero	27,970 (68.1)	9,305 (22.6)	1,622 (3.9)	1,850 (4.5)	351 (0.9)	41,098
Catron	1,234 (56.2)	926 (42.2)	8 (0.4)	5 (0.2)	19 (0.9)	2,192	Quay	6,779 (62.2)	3,895 (35.7)	16 (0.1)	120 (1.1)	90 (0.8)	10,900
Chaves	28,951 (66.8)	11,986 (27.6)	605 (1.3)	1,420 (3.3)	372 (0.9)	43,334	Rio Arriba	2,779 (11.0)	19,390 (77.0)	2,754 (10.9)	47 (0.2)	201 (0.8)	25,171
Colfax	5,563 (45.7)	6,450 (53.0)	44 (0.4)	60 (0.5)	51 (0.4)	12,168	Roosevelt	13,616 (82.7)	2,488 (15.1)	93 (0.6)	113 (0.7)	163 (1.0)	16,473
Curry	29,665 (75.0)	6,668 (16.9)	123 (0.3)	2,525 (6.4)	534 (1.4)	39,515	Sandoval	4,130 (23.6)	6,443 (36.8)	6,797 (38.9)	18 (0.1)	106 (0.6)	17,494
De Baca	1,494 (59.0)	1,038 (41.0)	–	–	–	2,532	San Juan	27,562 (52.4)	6,094 (11.6)	18,440 (35.0)	299 (0.6)	224 (0.4)	52,619
Dona Ana	32,349 (46.4)	35,093 (50.3)	209 (0.3)	1,339 (1.9)	781 (1.1)	69,771	San Miguel	3,719 (16.9)	17,861 (81.4)	91 (0.4)	93 (0.4)	190 (0.9)	21,954
Eddy	27,533 (67.0)	12,395 (30.1)	81 (0.2)	901 (2.2)	210 (0.5)	41,120	Santa Fe	18,126 (33.7)	34,037 (63.3)	1,097 (2.0)	267 (0.5)	231 (0.4)	53,758
Grant	9,315 (42.3)	12,330 (56.0)	82 (0.4)	118 (0.5)	185 (0.8)	22,030	Sierra	4,575 (63.7)	2,554 (35.6)	11 (0.2)	4 (0.0)	35 (0.5)	7,179
Guadalupe	827 (16.7)	4,120 (83.0)	–	–	19 (0.4)	4,966	Socorro	3,160 (32.4)	5,726 (58.7)	706 (7.2)	67 (0.7)	100 (1.0)	9,759
Harding	676 (50.3)	665 (49.4)	4 (0.3)	–	–	1,345	Taos	1,850 (10.5)	14,167 (80.9)	1,193 (6.8)	29 (0.2)	280 (1.6)	17,519
Hidalgo	1,881 (39.8)	2,786 (59.0)	17 (0.4)	18 (0.4)	23 (0.5)	4,725	Torrance	2,474 (46.8)	2,781 (52.7)	4 (0.1)	–	23 (0.4)	5,282
Lea	40,267 (81.3)	6,138 (12.4)	174 (0.4)	2,612 (5.3)	364 (0.7)	49,555	Union	3,471 (70.7)	1,394 (28.4)	5 (0.1)	–	39 (0.8)	4,909
Lincoln	4,806 (63.6)	2,560 (33.9)	83 (1.1)	41 (0.5)	68 (0.9)	7,558	Valencia	13,839 (34.1)	20,158 (49.7)	6,080 (15.0)	195 (0.5)	262 (0.6)	40,534
Los Alamos	12,395 (81.6)	2,607 (17.2)	70 (0.5)	60 (0.4)	63 (0.4)	15,195							
Luna	6,019 (51.4)	5,383 (46.0)	4 (0.0)	233 (2.0)	59 (0.5)	11,698							
McKinley	10,059 (23.3)	5,940 (13.7)	26,504 (61.3)	410 (0.9)	296 (0.7)	43,209							

*Total number of ethnic/racial population by county.
**Percent of ethnic/racial population by county.

Source: U.S. Bureau of the Census, 1970, General Population Characteristics.

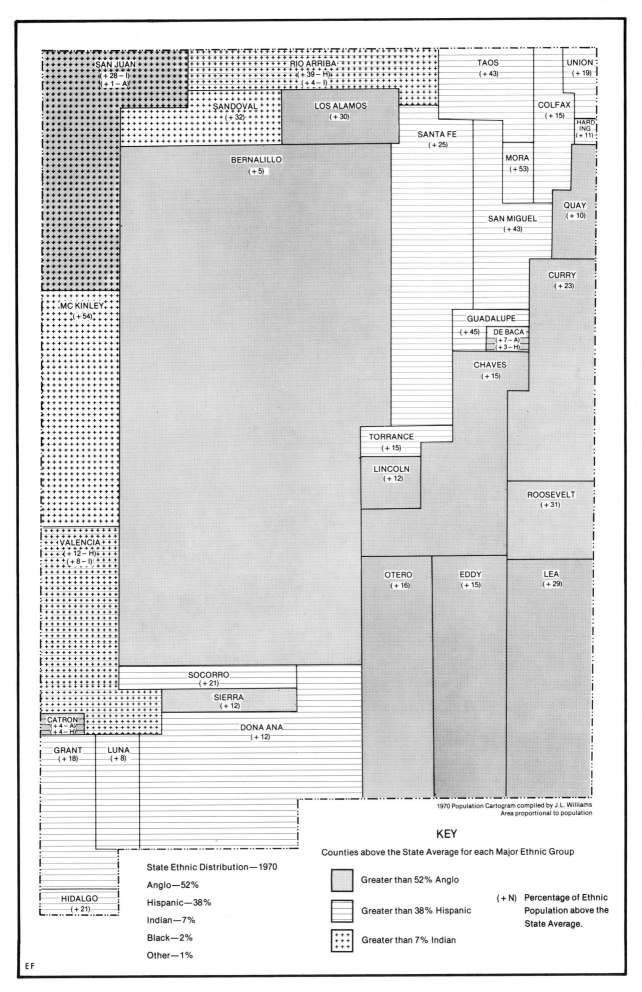

SAN JUAN
(+ 28 – I)
(+ 1 – A)

RIO ARRIBA
(+ 39 – H)
(+ 4 – I)

TAOS
(+ 43)

UNION
(+ 19)

SANDOVAL
(+ 32)

LOS ALAMOS
(+ 30)

COLFAX
(+ 15)

HARD
ING
(+ 11)

SANTA FE
(+ 25)

BERNALILLO
(+ 5)

MORA
(+ 53)

QUAY
(+ 10)

SAN MIGUEL
(+ 43)

CURRY
(+ 23)

MC KINLEY
(+ 54)

GUADALUPE
(+ 45)

DE BACA
(+ 7 – A)
(+ 3 – H)

CHAVES
(+ 15)

TORRANCE
(+ 15)

LINCOLN
(+ 12)

ROOSEVELT
(+ 31)

VALENCIA
(+ 12 – H)
(+ 8 – I)

OTERO
(+ 16)

EDDY
(+ 15)

LEA
(+ 29)

SOCORRO
(+ 21)

SIERRA
(+ 12)

CATRON
(+ 4 – A)
(+ 4 – H)

DONA ANA
(+ 12)

GRANT
(+ 18)

LUNA
(+ 8)

HIDALGO
(+ 21)

1970 Population Cartogram compiled by J.L. Williams
Area proportional to population

KEY

Counties above the State Average for each Major Ethnic Group

State Ethnic Distribution—1970

Anglo—52%

Hispanic—38%

Indian—7%

Black—2%

Other—1%

Greater than 52% Anglo

Greater than 38% Hispanic

Greater than 7% Indian

(+ N)   Percentage of Ethnic
Population above the
State Average.

EF

sex-age characteristics 1970

Sex-age characteristics, presented in the standard pyramidal form on a county basis, reveal interesting variations within the state of New Mexico. The rural counties lacking in job opportunities (Catron, Eddy, De Baca, Harding, Mora, Quay, Roosevelt, Sierra, Torrance, and Union) have significant inversions in the young employment-age midsection of the pyramids. The absence of this 20-to-45-year age group indicates that a major export of the county is labor. These counties also are noted as areas of the state where more than ten percent of the population is over 65 years of age. This implies that either the previous generation did not migrate for employment, or that the rural area is still attractive to the elderly and those on fixed retirement incomes. Conversely, the areas that are urban or near major employment centers (Bernalillo, Curry, Doña Ana, McKinley, Otero, Santa Fe, Taos, and Valencia) maintain a standard pyramidal shape, from the broad base to the age peak at the top.

Distortions are evident in the 20-to-30-year age group categories in which university populations account for over ten percent of the total county population and the bulk of the student population is imported from outside of the county (Doña Ana, 16%; Roosevelt, 23.5%; and San Miguel, 9.4%). Irregular sex imbalances are represented by the large number of males in the 20-to-25-year interval for Curry and Otero counties and in the 15-to-20-year interval for Colfax County. The Curry County imbalance may be the consequence of the Santa Fe Railroad training school and Canon Air Force Base located in the Clovis area. The Otero situation may be explained by the location of Holloman Air Force Base south of Alamogordo. Since there is no major male-oriented institution in Colfax County, the youthful imbalance may be the result of the inclusion of Boy Scouts at the Philmont Scout Ranch near Cimarron during the census enumeration.

A unique age distribution occurs in Sierra County where nearly one-fourth of the population is over the age of 65. The high median age of 43.7 years (which does not vary significantly from a 42.4-year median in 1960) is the result of large annual pilgrimages of fixed income retirees to the Truth or Consequences area to benefit from the dry climate and agglomeration of mineral baths. There have been significant increases in the median age between 1960 and 1970 in De Baca (9.1 years), Harding (6.0 years), Torrance (6.0 years), and Union (4.1 years) counties which may indicate either an increase in the emigration of school graduates or an increased immigration of elderly during the intercensal years. A few counties (Grant, Hidalgo, and Roosevelt) have increased their youthfulness with the decline in median age since 1960. Few counties will likely reach the low median age of McKinley County (19.2 years) in which nearly 50% of the population is under 18 years of age. McKinley also has one of the lowest proportions of population over 65 years in the state. The figures for Los Alamos indicate that few of the scientists employed there decide to remain in retirement. The pyramid for this county also reflects the opportunities for middle-aged professionals at the scientific laboratories and the lack of employment opportunities for the high school graduate and 20-to-30-year age group.

New Mexico, with a median age in 1970 of 23.9 years, is a youthful state. Since 1970 the cost of energy and successive severe winters in the north have initiated a movement referred to as the "sunbelt migration." A major element of this migration is the relocation of retired persons from the northern states to the low energy cost areas of the south. If New Mexico becomes a destination state, the immigrant population shall significantly alter the median ages and social characteristics of the counties in which they settle.

Jerry L. Williams

TABLE: SEX-AGE CHARACTERISTICS: 1970

County	Over 65 yrs.	% of Total	Under 18 yrs.	% of Total	Median Age			1960 Median
					Total	Male	Female	
Bernalillo	19,348	6.1	121,197	38.4	24.4	23.8	25.1	23.8
Catron	271	12.3	775	35.3	31.3	31.4	31.3	27.5
Chaves	3,909	9.0	6,922	16.0	25.9	23.8	27.8	22.9
Colfax	1,497	12.3	4,646	38.2	28.9	26.8	31.1	25.9
Curry	2,919	7.4	14,962	37.9	23.6	23.1	24.4	23.9
DeBaca	461	18.1	824	32.4	38.0	37.0	38.6	28.9
Dona Ana	3,715	5.3	28,190	40.4	22.0	21.8	22.2	21.8
Eddy	3,642	8.9	15,546	37.8	27.2	25.3	28.8	23.7
Grant	1,733	8.0	8,470	38.4	24.6	24.2	25.0	25.3
Guadalupe	466	9.4	2,201	44.3	22.4	21.4	23.3	20.5
Harding	197	14.6	490	36.4	34.2	35.3	32.9	28.2
Hidalgo	415	8.8	1,993	42.1	24.5	23.3	25.6	24.7
Lea	2,665	5.4	19,379	39.1	25.9	25.4	26.4	24.0
Lincoln	875	11.6	2,549	33.7	32.0	30.9	32.9	29.7
Los Alamos	314	2.1	6,449	42.4	26.7	26.5	26.9	25.1
Luna	1,197	10.2	4,706	40.2	27.0·	25.3	28.3	24.1
McKinley	1,885	4.4	20,899	48.4	19.2	18.7	19.6	18.0
Mora	556	11.9	2,021	43.2	22.6	22.8	22.4	19.0
Otero	1,684	4.1	17,151	41.7	22.4	22.2	22.8	22.3
Quay	1,358	12.5	3,879	35.6	30.2	29.1	31.3·	26.8
Rio Arriba	1,869	7.4	11,370	45.2	21.0	20.2	21.6	19.0
Roosevelt	1,627	9.9	5,091	30.9	23.8	23.5	24.2	25.1
Sandoval	1,259	7.2	7,809	44.6	21.3	21.0	21.5	18.6
San Juan	2,563	4.9	24,182	46 0	20.7	19.9	21.2	20.0
San Miguel	2,181	9.9	8,177	37.3	23.4	22.8	24.1	22.2
Santa Fe	4,211	7.8	21,153	39.4	24.8	24.0	25.7	24.5
Sierra	1,778	24.7	2,046	28.5	43.6	43.7	43.5	42.4
Socorro	749	7.7	3,876	39.7	22.9	22.0	23.9	21.6
Taos	1,624	9.3	7,428	42.4	23.3	22.9	23.7	19.6
Torrance	629	11.9	2,012	38.0	28.4	27.7	29.1	22.4
Union	758	15.4	1,751	35.6	33.2	32.6	33.7	29.1
Valencia	2,266	5.6	18,072	44.6	21.6	21.3	21.8	20.1
State Totals	70,611	6.9	396,196	39.0	23.9			

Source: U.S. Bureau of Census, Census of Population—1970.

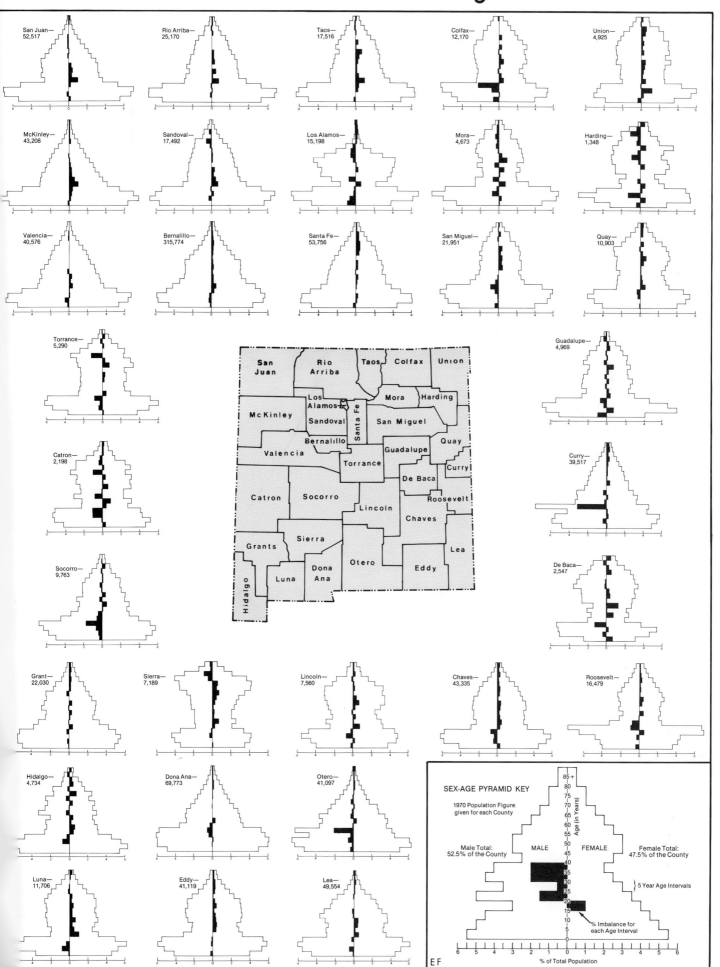

SEX-AGE PYRAMID KEY

1970 Population Figure
given for each County

Male Total:
52.5% of the County

MALE   FEMALE

Female Total:
47.5% of the County

5 Year Age Intervals

% Imbalance for
each Age Interval

% of Total Population

69

family income characteristics 1970

Two discernible distribution patterns of median family income are evident in New Mexico. The northern counties represent a region of sharp contrast: counties with a high median family income (Santa Fe and Bernalillo) are juxtaposed to those counties with a very low median family income (Mora, San Miguel, and Torrance). This contrast in northern New Mexico reflects varying employment opportunities: oil, natural gas and uranium mining in the northwest (San Juan and McKinley); federal and state employment in the north-central area (Los Alamos and Santa Fe); and farming or ranching in the northeast (Union, Harding, and San Miguel). Counties which illustrate a low median family income lack major private employment and depend on state or local government resources (administration, schools and hospitals) for limited employment opportunities.

Unlike northern New Mexico with its sharp contrasts, the southern region has only a gradational change between counties, with the exception of Sierra County, which has no major employer and is characterized by a large inflow of social security retirees attracted to the mineral springs. The U.S. Forest Service, farming or ranching, and large state institutions are major sources of income throughout southern New Mexico. Copper mining in the southwest (Grant and Hidalgo) and potash, oil and natural gas mining in the southeast (Lea and Eddy) are major factors increasing regional income levels. The White Sands Missile Range and Holloman Air Force Base in south-central New Mexico are major income resources for Otero and Doña Ana counties.

There is an indirect relationship between median family income and the percent of families below poverty level in New Mexico. Counties such as Los Alamos, Santa Fe, Bernalillo, Valencia, Lea and Eddy with a high median family income have a small percent of families below poverty level, while counties with a low median family income (Sandoval, Rio Arriba, Taos, Mora, San Miguel, Guadalupe, Torrance and De Baca) have a large percent of families below poverty level. San Juan deviates from this indirect relationship between family income and poverty level in that it is a county with both a high median family income and more than one of every five families below poverty level. This may be attributed to the small portion of the work force engaged in energy industries that receive relatively high incomes.

Although median family income provides a generalized pattern of wealth and poverty in New Mexico by county, the extreme contrasts of high and low income levels which might exist are obscured. Income levels fluctuate sharply, and a median value cannot accurately represent all income levels of a county. Pockets of poverty in counties with a high median family income are not shown with these median values. Instead, the middle value in a range of high to low income characterizes each county.

Karleene Smith

	Family Income Characteristics				Poverty Level Characteristics			
	Median Family Income [1]	Mean Wage/Salary Income	Mean Nonfarm Self-employment Income	Mean Farm Self-employment Income	% of Families below Poverty Level [2]	% of Families Receiving Public Assistance Income	% of Families with Female Head of Household	% of Civilian Male Heads of Household <65 years old in Labor Force
Bernalillo	$ 9,031	$ 9,568	$8,044	$1,164	13.0	23.2	37.9	70.8
Catron	6,630	7,248	4,693	8,442	14.3	19.5	4.9	63.5
Chaves	7,212	7,747	8,620	6,536	20.4	15.5	31.1	74.1
Colfax	6,596	7,193	5,539	4,022	20.1	15.7	24.4	76.3
Curry	$ 7,162	$ 7,617	$8,847	$8,018	15.1	17.7	30.3	79.3
DeBaca	5,663	5,121	4,685	7,526	24.5	16.9	8.7	85.2
Dona Ana	7,395	8,166	7,770	2,924	20.5	15.4	23.2	79.6
Eddy	7,870	7,884	7,832	7,353	17.8	17.1	24.9	80.3
Grant	$ 7,898	$ 8,143	$7,937	$3,532	11.9	16.6	26.5	74.3
Guadalupe	4,885	5,977	5,702	3,717	37.9	32.9	23.0	63.6
Harding	6,500	5,269	6,210	3,886	28.3	8.1	15.1	78.9
Hidalgo	6,568	6,686	5,501	7,167	21.7	14.8	16.0	81.1
Lea	$ 8,703	$ 8,850	$8,522	$3,535	12.5	15.3	29.3	77.7
Lincoln	6,522	6,587	8,443	5,216	20.7	9.4	18.6	83.6
Los Alamos	15,273	14,895	4,650	872	2.1	—	32.5	82.9
Luna	6,472	7,152	5,687	5,641	20.5	29.4	31.1	72.1
McKinley	$ 6,783	$ 7,719	$8,450	$2,004	33.7	22.8	24 9	61.1
Mora	3,100	3,968	4,180	4,322	57.3	27.6	21.0	66.8
Otero	8,117	8,745	5,406	2,888	12.3	13.9	34.1	72.0
Quay	6,794	6,617	6,951	4,749	19.3	25.8	22.4	76.2
Rio Arriba	$ 5,544	$ 6,627	$4,651	$2,241	34.3	25.8	21.0	63.9
Roosevelt	6,273	6,103	5,459	5,475	21.5	14.8	13.9	72.1
Sandoval	5,479	6,331	5,213	1,942	37.5	29.6	16.8	59.2
San Juan	8,150	8,647	7,778	976	21.7	18.9	26.8	52.7
San Miguel	$ 4,595	$ 5,918	$7,734	$2,365	39.2	27.0	27.0	66.6
Santa Fe	8,018	8,690	8,965	3,516	18.2	23.3	31.0	79.4
Sierra	4,833	6,206	3,902	4,650	23.9	12.8	14.8	79.4
Socorro	6,360	6,749	4,489	4,075	29.5	20.0	18.0	50.7
Taos	$ 5,308	$ 6,772	$6,037	$2,904	35.8	33.9	25.7	55.8
Torrance	4,920	5,437	6,063	5,615	32.6	24.3	18.6	74.9
Union	5,295	5,327	8,424	4,302	26.2	7.0	23.7	86.9
Valencia	7,610	7,948	6,754	2,707	18.5	24.7	24.3	68.7
NEW MEXICO	$ 7,849				18.5			

[1] The Bureau of the Census defines a family as "a household head and one or more other persons living in the same household who are related to the head by blood, marriage, or adoption." Appendix B, p. 13.

[2] "The [poverty] index provides a range of poverty income cutoffs adjusted by such factors as family size, sex of the family head, number of children under 18 years old, and farm and nonfarm residence." The weighted average threshold at the poverty level in 1969 for all families was $3,388. Appendix B, pp. 29, 30.

Source: U.S. Bureau of the Census, *Census of Population: 1970, General Social and Economic Characteristics, Final Report PC(1)-33, New Mexico,* Table 124 and Appendix B, pp. 13, 29, and 30.

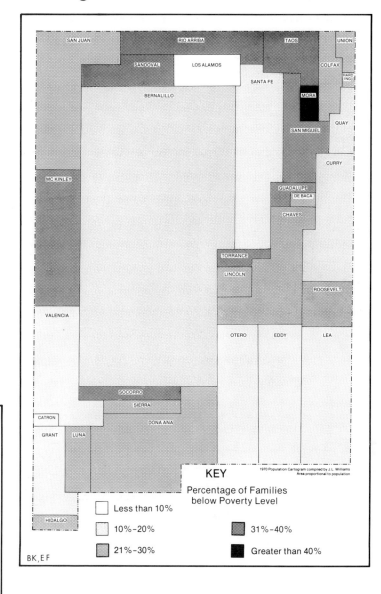

KEY

Percentage of Families
below Poverty Level

☐ Less than 10%

☐ 10%–20%

▨ 21%–30%

▨ 31%–40%

■ Greater than 40%

1970 Population Cartogram compiled by J. L. Williams
Area proportional to population

BK,EF

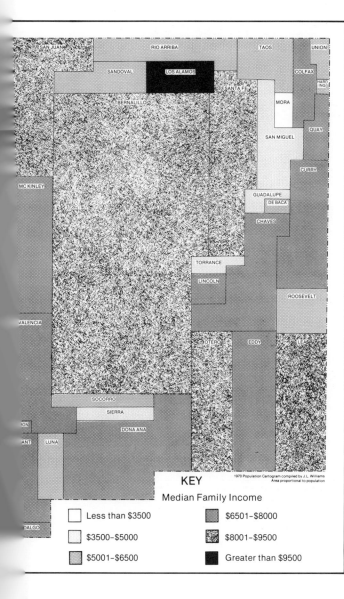

KEY

Median Family Income

☐ Less than $3500

☐ $3500–$5000

▨ $5001–$6500

▨ $6501–$8000

▨ $8001–$9500

■ Greater than $9500

1970 Population Cartogram compiled by J. L. Williams
Area proportional to population

housing characteristics 1950-1970

Housing statistics, frequently referred to as indicators of growth and economic status, present interesting patterns in New Mexico when viewed on a county basis. Housing construction figures mirror the demand for dwelling units reflected by the migration and/or the changing economic climate of each area. This is apparent in the recent housing construction within the expanding oil and gas fields of San Juan, Lea, and McKinley counties. Construction has been boosted in McKinley County by the post-1960 development of the Gallup-Grants-Laguna uranium fields. Recent construction in Sandoval, Bernalillo, and Valencia counties is related to the rapid growth of the Albuquerque metropolitan area. The commercial-industrial economy of this urban center has created bedroom communities along the Rio Grande Valley in Valencia and Sandoval counties. Since 1975 commuters have also spread eastward through Tijeras Canyon into the northwest quarter of Torrance County. The housing growth of Bernalillo County has a greater impact when viewed in raw figures: over one-third (69,000) of the total dwelling units constructed in the state from 1950 to 1970 were built in the Bernalillo-Albuquerque urban area.

Recent construction in Los Alamos, Doña Ana, and Otero counties can be attributed to federal expansion and investment in Los Alamos Scientific Laboratories, White Sands Missile Base, and Holloman Air Force Base, respectively. Many of the southern border counties (Luna, Doña Ana, Otero, and Eddy) experienced a steady increase in housing since 1960 in response to immigrant retirees seeking sunbelt accommodations. This form of demand has intensified dramatically with the mid-1970 energy shortage and harsh winter conditions in the upper midwest and northeast quarter of the United States. A large increase in Hidalgo County housing can be expected from 1970 to 1980. A new ore smelter has been developed in the southeastern portion of the county and an urban service center is being constructed to accommodate nearly 1000 residents.

In contrast to these southern and northwestern sectors of recent construction (or growth) is the obvious lack of recent housing demand in the northeastern quarter of the state. The agricultural counties of Union, Harding, Mora, and San Miguel experienced little economic stimulus during the period 1950 to 1970, resulting in an estimated emigration of nearly one-fourth of the area's population. The majority of settlements in these counties are small rural villages built with local adobe and stone building materials that require recurrent maintenance to avoid deterioration of the units. Much of the construction recorded in these northeastern counties is predominantly replacement of delapidated dwellings. According to the 1970 census, nearly 90% of the housing units in Harding County predated 1950, as did four out of five units in Union County. Population estimates for 1975 have indicated little migration change for this area. Thus, housing construction will be expected to follow a slow-growth (or no-growth) trend.

The table demonstrates the rural-urban dichotomy apparent in portions of the state. Catron, Mora, Harding, De Baca, Taos, and Rio Arriba counties were classified as 100% rural in the 1970 census of Housing and Population. Statistically these same counties stand out as dispersed rural settlement areas, lacking plumbing and/or full kitchen facilities in the houses, with a corresponding low proportion of units connected to any public water or sewage system. Counties that are more than 80% urbanized (Bernalillo, Chaves, Curry, Lea, Los Alamos, and Otero) show a strong statistical contrast to the first group. Los Alamos stands out as an anomaly within the state as its entire population of housing units is connected to public water and sewage.

The intercensal estimates for 1975 have indicated a significant increase in population since 1970 for many of the New Mexico counties. Some areas (Chaves, Doña Ana, Lincoln, McKinley, Rio Arriba, San Juan, and Valencia) have completely reversed large emigration flows that have existed since 1950. If these estimates hold true, there will be a large increase in housing for these areas during the decade of the 1970's.

Jerry L. Williams

COUNTY	Total Units	% Lack Some Plumbing	% Lack Complete Kitchens	% With More Than One Person/Room	% On Public Water	% On Individual Well Water	% On Public Sewer	% On Septic Tank or Cesspool	COUNTY	Total Units	% Lack Some Plumbing	% Lack Complete Kitchens	% With More Than One Person/Room	% On Public Water	% On Individual Well Water	% On Public Sewer	% On Septic Tank or Cesspool
Bernalillo	98,634	3.0	2.0	9.7	84.1	15.3	82.5	16.0	McKinley	10,586	36.8	33.0	38.0	66.2	13.3	61.5	5.9
Catron	957	26.3	14.3	12.2	29.4	58.3	11.4	54.2	Mora	1,750	58.4	47.9	19.7	33.1	46.5	12.5	27.9
Chaves	17,786	3.5	8.7	8.5	88.0	10.0	86.0	12.0	Otero	12,098	2.9	2.6	10.9	91.8	4.6	81.1	16.3
Colfax	4,804	13.5	9.7	12.3	80.7	11.9	70.8	19.0	Quay	4,256	6.0	8.0	9.8	76.1	23.4	66.3	30.9
Curry	12,401	1.3	2.1	9.7	91.1	8.7	87.3	12.0	Rio Arriba	7,503	38.1	28.6	25.0	40.3	42.9	26.9	31.9
De Baca	1,247	11.3	11.1	7.1	64.5	32.4	46.3	47.8	Roosevelt	5,759	3.5	5.1	7.7	66.5	32.6	62.0	35.1
Dona Ana	19,815	7.2	4.3	15.2	78.0	20.5	70.6	25.0	Sandoval	4,785	33.9	26.9	30.7	52.1	29.4	25.3	39.8
Eddy	15,070	5.0	7.5	9.7	90.8	7.4	77.2	19.3	San Juan	14,960	19.0	17.6	23.9	74.9	11.9	63.2	17.8
Grant	6,946	9.0	4.9	13.7	82.3	15.4	70.1	22.9	San Miguel	7,214	35.2	20.4	16.2	71.5	14.8	52.1	15.4
Guadalupe	1,649	31.9	19.6	20.1	80.1	10.5	54.0	16.0	Santa Fe	16,135	5.7	3.9	15.5	82.7	16.3	74.2	21.
Harding	621	34.9	25.4	9.5	51.2	41.4	26.1	48.8	Sierra	3,743	11.9	6.7	8.4	80.1	17.4	64.9	28.
Hidalgo	1,548	5.2	3.4	18.3	72.8	25.6	70.0	27.4	Socorro	3,029	19.9	13.7	16.9	66.4	28.2	54.8	29.
Lea	17,158	2.4	3.5	10.1	83.8	15.6	81.2	17.7	Taos	6,216	40.2	36.0	17.3	40.1	39.7	18.0	35.
Lincoln	4,950	9.7	7.0	6.2	52.5	16.9	31.3	32.6	Torrance	1,919	21.4	10.2	13.8	60.4	37.2	37.5	46
Los Alamos	4,706	0.2	0.2	5.4	100.	0.0	100.	0.0	Union	1,993	10.4	10.7	7.8	66.4	30.9	54.8	34
Luna	3,927	7.3	3.3	15.0	76.1	23.2	67.7	28.2	Valencia	11,554	18.5	12.6	22.6	60.1	35.6	45.8	38
									NEW MEXICO	325,715	9.9	8.2	13.6	78.3	17.2	70.8	20

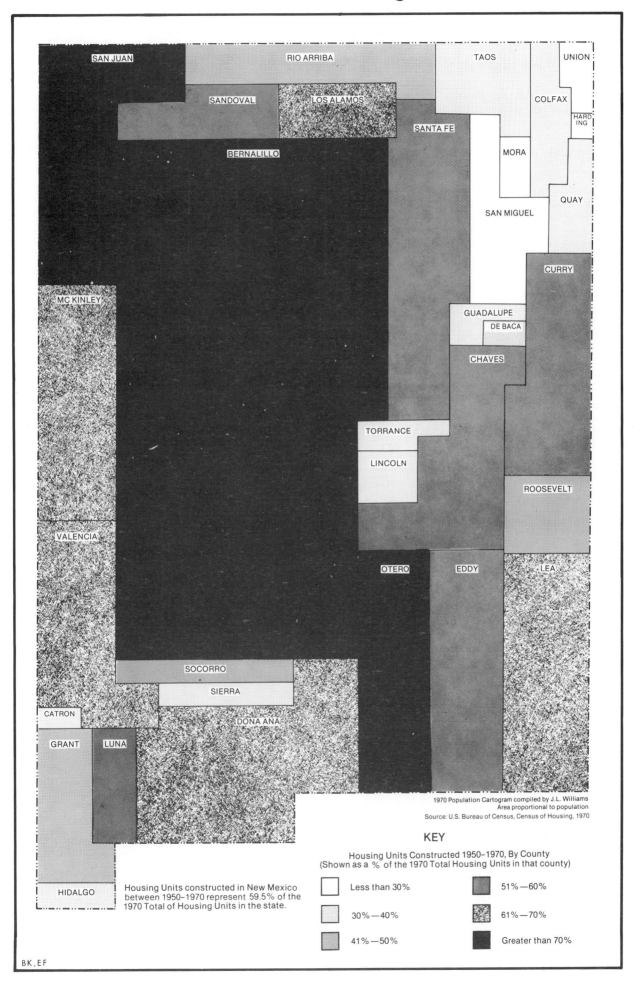

SAN JUAN

RIO ARRIBA

TAOS

UNION

SANDOVAL

LOS ALAMOS

COLFAX

HARD ING

SANTA FE

BERNALILLO

MORA

MC KINLEY

SAN MIGUEL

QUAY

CURRY

GUADALUPE

DE BACA

CHAVES

TORRANCE

LINCOLN

ROOSEVELT

VALENCIA

OTERO

EDDY

LEA

SOCORRO

SIERRA

CATRON

DONA ANA

GRANT

LUNA

HIDALGO

1970 Population Cartogram compiled by J.L. Williams
Area proportional to population
Source: U.S. Bureau of Census, Census of Housing, 1970

KEY

Housing Units Constructed 1950–1970, By County
(Shown as a % of the 1970 Total Housing Units in that county)

Housing Units constructed in New Mexico
between 1950–1970 represent 59.5% of the
1970 Total of Housing Units in the state.

Less than 30%

51%—60%

30%—40%

61%—70%

41%—50%

Greater than 70%

BK,EF

medical facilities

The location of medical facilities in New Mexico in 1978 demonstrates a high correlation to population distribution. Albuquerque, with an estimated 30.3% of the state's population in July, 1977 (360,000 of 1,190,000), also had 36.4% of the short-term and long-term medical beds (2790 of 7667). In 1978 the Albuquerque metropolitan area had 55.7% of the medical doctors in the state, 41.6% of the licensed pharmacists, 45.3% of the practicing dentists, and 52% of the employed registered nurses. Special facilities and trained medical specialists, such as those of the burn treatment center at the publicly-funded Bernalillo County Medical Center (BCMC), are also located in Albuquerque. BCMC is operated in conjunction with the well-staffed University of New Mexico Medical School. Through the services of the Kirtland Air Force Base emergency helicopter rescue facilities, Albuquerque has an outreach capability that covers the entire state.

While hospital distribution is largely determined by local public policy and economic resources, doctors and dentists locate according to job opportunities and individual tastes. Most concentrate in areas such as Albuquerque, Santa Fe, and Taos. This has a detrimental effect on the rural counties that have difficulty attracting and retaining medical personnel. A number of counties (De Baca, Hidalgo, Catron, Guadalupe, Torrance, Mora, and Harding) have fewer than three doctors and/or dentists to serve an extensive land area of dispersed population. Harding County has neither a practicing doctor nor a dentist, while Hidalgo County has the highest population per doctor ratio in the state.

Many rural residents are not only isolated from medical personnel, but must also be transported great distances to reach an emergency facility. Five counties in 1978 (Catron, Torrance, Guadalupe, Harding, and Mora) did not have a hospital or immediate care facility. The figure of 2400 people per hospital bed in Sandoval County is misleading as most of the population is located along the northern urban fringe of Albuquerque and is dependent on facilities outside of the county. Most of the Catron County patients must be transported to hospitals in Socorro, Silver City, or Springerville, Arizona. Emergency cases from Torrance, Sandoval, and Guadalupe counties are transported to Albuquerque while patients in Mora and Harding counties rely on treatment at the facilities in Tucumcari and Las Vegas. Relief to the medical shortage in Guadalupe County is expected in 1979 with the reopening of a small hospital in Santa Rosa. Rural counties with higher than expected numbers of doctors (Sierra, McKinley, and Los Alamos) usually are the location of special state or federally funded hospitals.

Over one hundred-fifty emergency vehicles serve most of the inhabited areas of the state. Many medical vehicles are operated by rural fire departments and serve only the tax district of the fire station. First aid training for drivers and ambulance personnel is the responsibility of the Emergency Medical Services Academy located at BCMC in Albuquerque. The emergency vehicles and medical facilities throughout the state are linked together through an Emergency Health Communications network, which enables isolated portions of the state to be within minutes of an airborne team of specialists from Albuquerque.

Jerry L. Williams

MEDICAL CHARACTERISTICS

County	Provisional Population (a) 1975	1977	Total Physicians (MD's) 1978 (b)	1977 Population/1978 MD	Total Physicians (MD's) 1976 (b)	1975 Population/1976 MD	Primary MD's 1976 Family and General Practice	Internal Medicine	Obstetrics/Gynecology	Pediatrics	Licensed RN's–1978	Employed RN's–1978	1977 Population/RN Employed–1978	Nurse Midwives–1978	Dentists (DDS)–1978	1977 Population/Dentist–1978	Pharmacies–1978	Primary Care Clinics–1978	Short Term Hospital Beds–1978	1977 Population/Hospital Bed–1978	1977 Population Over Age 65 (c)	Nursing Home (NH) Beds–1978 (d)	1977 Population Over Age 65/NH Bed–1978	Intermediate Care Facility (ICF) Beds 1978 (d)	1977 Population Over Age 65/
Bernalillo	365,200	377,900	1,065	355	936	386	153	188	95	89	3,003	2,078	163	8	210	1,800	73	8	2,109	179	23,052	127	182	554	42
Catron	2,300	2,500	1	2,500	1	2,300	1	0	0	0	5	1	2,500	0	4	----	0	4	0	----	308	0	----	0	---
Chaves	48,200	49,300	64	770	45	1,071	15	4	4	3	218	162	304	0	15	3,287	14	0	233	212	4,437	0	---	134	33
Colfax	12,900	12,800	14	914	16	806	6	2	1	0	43	30	427	0	6	2,133	7	0	82	156	1,574	0	---	52	30
Curry	43,200	41,100	36	1,142	30	1,303	7	4	2	3	110	70	587	0	15	2,740	27	1	136	302	3,041	0	---	208	15
De Baca	2,600	2,500	1	2,500	2	1,300	2	0	0	0	7	5	500	0	0	----	2	1	25	100	453	0	---	44	10
Dona Ana	80,000	83,900	88	953	68	1,154	20	13	8	8	281	200	419	0	23	3,648	15	4	160	524	4,447	0	---	119	37
Eddy	42,400	45,500	36	1,264	33	1,285	13	3	4	2	170	115	396	0	17	2,676	17	1	168	271	4,050	24	169	232	17
Grant	24,600	24,500	20	1,225	19	1,295	8	4	3	1	98	61	402	0	7	3,500	4	0	65	377	1,936	58	33	29	67
Guadalupe	4,900	4,900	2	2,450	2	2,450	2	1	0	0	6	3	1,633	0	1	4,900	1	3	0	----	461	0	---	0	---
Harding	1,200	1,200	0	----	0	----	0	0	0	0	2	1	1,200	0	0	----	0	1	0	----	176	0	---	0	---
Hidalgo	5,700	6,200	2	3,100	1	5,700	1	0	0	0	13	8	775	0	1	6,200	2	0	25	248	539	0	---	82	7
Lea	51,200	52,900	39	1,356	34	1,506	21	2	1	3	168	106	499	0	12	4,408	18	0	180	294	2,857	0	---	207	14
Lincoln	9,500	10,300	7	1,471	6	1,583	9	0	0	1	35	20	515	0	4	2,575	4	1	38	271	1,195	0	---	0	---
Los Alamos	15,900	17,100	32	534	23	691	2	7	2	5	181	126	136	0	9	1,900	6	0	84	204	359	0	---	0	---
Luna	14,500	14,400	7	2,057	4	3,625	4	0	0	0	38	29	497	0	4	3,600	3	0	52	277	1,469	0	---	34	43
McKinley	51,200	56,100	87	645	82	624	26	9	7	11	165	107	524	4	5	11,200	5	1	353	159	2,468	0	---	64	39
Mora	4,900	4,800	1	4,800	1	4,900	1	0	0	0	7	4	1,200	0	1	4,800	0	2	0	----	571	0	---	0	---
Otero	42,700	42,300	31	1,365	26	1,442	10	4	5	1	183	122	347	0	8	5,287	7	0	119	355	1,734	0	---	70	25
Quay	11,400	11,200	3	3,733	6	1,900	5	0	1	1	28	18	622	0	2	5,600	4	3	58	193	1,389	0	---	54	26
Rio Arriba	28,000	27,600	23	1,200	20	1,400	14	2	1	0	76	54	511	0	9	3,067	7	7	80	345	2,042	0	---	0	---
Roosevelt	16,300	16,500	11	1,500	5	3,260	7	1	2	0	33	20	825	1	4	4,125	6	1	32	516	1,634	0	---	67	24
Sandoval	22,600	24,000	16	1,500	9	2,511	8	1	0	1	83	34	705	0	4	6,000	5	5	10	2,400	1,728	0	---	0	---
San Juan	65,300	70,800	57	1,242	54	1,209	25	3	3	4	197	115	616	9	23	3,078	13	3	204	347	3,611	0	---	62	58
San Miguel	23,500	22,700	27	841	21	1,119	6	4	2	2	82	60	378	2	7	3,243	5	3	51	445	2,247	9	250	344	---
Santa Fe	62,000	65,200	138	472	120	517	24	20	5	13	399	259	252	2	48	1,358	18	2	271	241	5,086	0	---	159	32
Sierra	8,500	8,800	17	518	14	607	6	0	0	1	39	26	338	0	1	8,800	3	0	100	88	2,147	0	---	25	87
Socorro	9,800	9,900	5	1,980	5	1,960	5	0	1	0	33	23	430	1	3	3,300	2	0	42	236	762	0	---	0	---
Taos	19,300	19,800	27	733	23	839	14	3	2	1	69	39	508	1	9	2,200	3	4	33	600	1,841	0	---	0	---
Torrance	6,400	6,800	2	3,400	4	1,600	4	0	1	0	12	5	1,360	0	0	----	3	1	0	----	809	0	---	0	---
Union	4,900	4,900	5	980	2	2,450	2	0	0	0	23	15	327	0	2	2,450	2	0	38	129	755	0	---	33	22
Valencia	46,000	51,400	19	2,705	16	2,875	16	4	1	1	123	67	767	0	14	3,671	10	2	68	756	2,878	0	---	60	48
New Mexico			625		696								298			2,565				247			351		2

Source: Health Services Registry, 1978 New Mexico Statistical Summary.

(a) Estimates from Bureau of Business and Economic Research—UNM
(b) Civilian, excluding osteopathic doctors
(c) Population over age 65 approximated by multiplying the 1977 population estimate by the percent over 65 in 1970
(d) Do not include mental retardation facilities nor homes not available to the general public

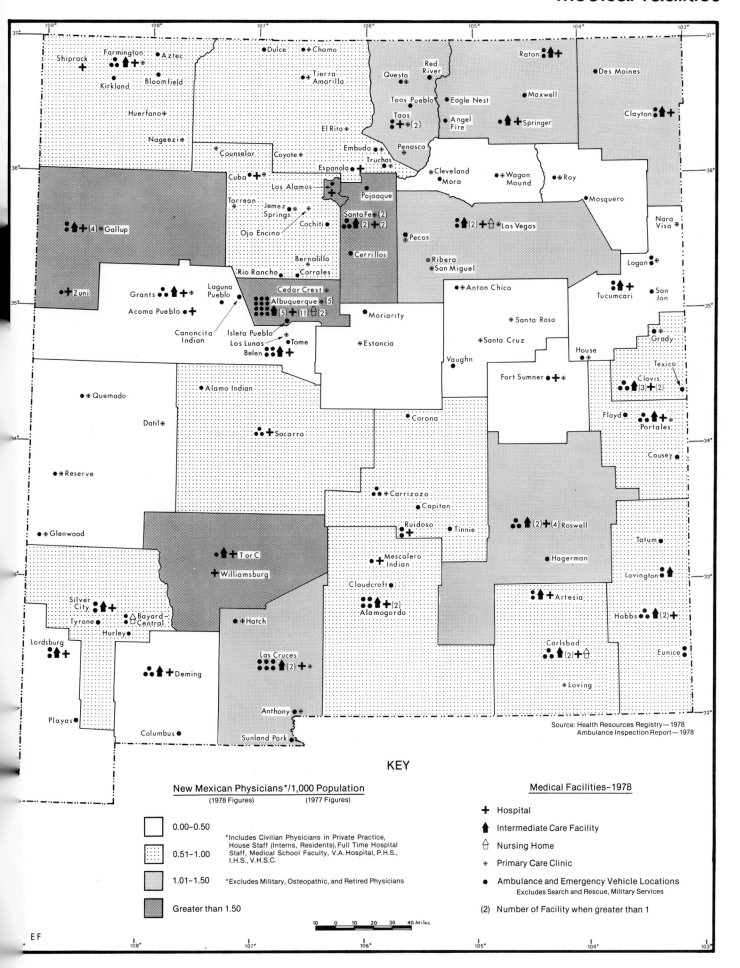

Source: Health Resources Registry—1978
Ambulance Inspection Report—1978

KEY

New Mexican Physicians*/1,000 Population

(1978 Figures) (1977 Figures)

☐ 0.00-0.50

*Includes Civilian Physicians in Private Practice, House Staff (Interns, Residents), Full Time Hospital Staff, Medical School Faculty, V.A. Hospital, P.H.S., I.H.S., V.H.S.C.

⠿ 0.51-1.00

▦ 1.01-1.50

*Excludes Military, Osteopathic, and Retired Physicians

■ Greater than 1.50

10 0 10 20 30 40 Miles

Medical Facilities-1978

✚ Hospital

▲ Intermediate Care Facility

⌂ Nursing Home

⊕ Primary Care Clinic

● Ambulance and Emergency Vehicle Locations
Excludes Search and Rescue, Military Services

(2) Number of Facility when greater than 1

E F

natality and mortality

The **natality rate**, sometimes called the Crude Birth Rate, is the number of births per 1,000 population; the **mortality rate**, referred to as the Crude Death Rate, is the number of deaths per 1,000 population. The difference between these two rates is known as the rate of natural increase or decrease. Combined with the net migration rate for an area, the natural increase or decrease rate is useful in providing an estimate of population change. *Vital Statistics of the United States* provides the figures used in the calculation of birth and death rates. The Bureau of the Census provides the figures used in the calculation of the population. Since, in the past, the Bureau of the Census conducted cennial counts, one must estimate other years. The more years from cennial count, the less accurate the estimate, as the state and county totals become skewed without an updated count. The problem of estimation is coupled with the census problem of inconsistency. In 1970 the New Mexico population estimate for the state was 1,016,000, whereas the summation of the county estimates totaled 1,017,055. The correction of this error was not released until 1974, and all mortality-natality rates had to be adjusted accordingly. The New Mexico Health and Social Services Department also provides annual birth and death statistics which differ from those released by the Census Bureau.

Natality and Mortality rates can be closely related to the age, sex, economic, health, educational, and religious structures of a population. Birth rates may reflect the number of females of child-bearing age and is closely associated with the fertility rate of a population. Fertility rate, or the number of births per 1,000 women aged 15-44, is low for women aged 15-19 and peaks in the 20-24 age group. Thereafter it slowly declines with increasing age. The death rate is high for infants, relatively low for ages 1-39, and continues to increase with advancing age from about age 40. Alterations to the natality-mortality rates by county may be explained by the access of the population to health services and the education and acceptance of birth control methods and proper health maintenance.

Counties within New Mexico that have high birth rates, (McKinley, Rio Arriba, Hidalgo) are generally in the less urbanized areas where a majority of the population is involved in agriculture. The more urbanized the area (Santa Fe, Bernalillo) the lower the birth rate as children do not have the same economic value as those in a more isolated area. The low birth rates in non-urban places such as Harding and Sierra counties, are a result of the out migration of population in the main child-bearing age group. High death rates in New Mexico are normally associated with counties that have a large number of elderly residents. Sierra County and the famous Hot Springs at Truth or Consequences have attracted old people from the midwest with arthritic problems for many years. Most of them live out their years in the hotels and bath houses of T or C. Extremely low death rates may be attributed to either a small percentage of elderly population in the area or to the presence of excellent health facilities. The elderly will often vacate an area that does not provide suitable health facilities

and resettle in an area that has abundant health care places. The anomaly to this is that often a place with good facilities may have an exceptionally high death rate simply due to the large proportion of elderly who reside there.

The infant mortality rate (IMR) is defined as the number of infant deaths under one year divided by the live births in that year and multiplied by 1,000. This measurement reflects not only quality of health care and of transportation and communication systems, but also reflects on population characteristics such as education and income levels. It may also indirectly describe infant health status (weight and congenital conditions).

New Mexico has several unique features that make interstate comparisons difficult. Its population is essentially tricultural: 52% Anglo, 38% Hispanic, 7% Indian, 2% Black, and 1% classified as other. The impact of each major cultural group should be considered. But *Vital Statistics of the U.S.* lists only Whites (Anglos and Hispanics), Blacks, and others (Indians, Japanese, Chinese, etc.). The Black population, relatively small, contributes little statistically to the overall picture of infant mortality. The Indian population, although only 7% of the state total, is larger in several counties (McKinley, 61%; Sandoval, 39%; and San Juan, 35%), and may have a high correlation with the IMR in those areas.

One-third of the state's population resides in the Albuquerque urban area which provided the main urban IMR characteristic of New Mexico. There are only 11 other cities with a population greater than 10,000. As a result, direct in-state comparisons of IMR's are difficult, if not inaccurate. Intrastate comparisons are needed as they reflect the general conditions within New Mexico.

New Mexico's state IMR, in absolute terms, has decreased with time. As late as 1940, it was 100. This means that one infant in ten died before his first birthday. In 1975, it was 18.25 or one infant in 55 died before his first birthday. This reduction implies an increase in the quality of infant care in New Mexico.

When analyzing the IMRs, the size of New Mexico's population must be considered. Seven counties had fewer than 5,000 people in the 1970 U.S. Census: Catron (2,198), De Baca (2,547), Guadalupe (4,969), Harding (1,348), Hidalgo (4,734), Mora (4,673), and Union (4,925). Small populations can skew IMR's. The smallest populated counties, Catron, De Baca, and Harding, have erratic rates. Although Harding has a very high IMR, only three infants died in five years, all in 1970.

The last five years of available data for New Mexico counties, 1970-1974, show definite pockets of low IMR's. Bernalillo, Catron, De Baca, Santa Fe, and Torrance counties have the lowest rates. Other counties with low rates are Chaves, Colfax, Curry, Doña Ana, Grant, Los Alamos, and Roosevelt. IMR's have declined in the past and as health and education conditions improve, should continue to decline in the future.

Richard G. Rogers

TABLE 1

AREA	1970-1974 BIRTH RATE/1000	1970-1974 DEATH RATE/1000	INFANT MORTALITY RATES/1000 BIRTHS	AREA	1970-1974 BIRTH RATE/1000	1970-1974 DEATH RATE/1000	INFANT MORTALITY RATES/1000 BIRTHS
NEW MEXICO	20.06	7.32	19.67	McKinley	30.87	8.08	23.96
Bernalillo	18.01	6.42	14.98	Gallup			12.08
Albuquerque			14.98	Mora	17.03	9.74	25.19
Catron	14.32[c]	8.75[c]	6.17[a]	Otero	23.71	5.63	21.26
Chaves	17.14	9.33	19.26	Alamogordo			19.55
Roswell			17.22	Quay	17.14	12.15	20.96
Colfax	18.48	10.44	18.53	Rio Arriba	25.07	8.24	20.07
Curry	24.06	6.65	19.92	Roosevelt	17.83	8.44	17.43
Clovis			19.32	Portales			14.54
De Baca	12.84[c]	13.46[c]	12.05[a]	Sandoval	23.52	8.65	22.50
Dona Ana	21.29	5.65	15.88	San Juan	23.63	6.63	28.27
Las Cruces			18.09	Farmington			31.85
Eddy	17.01	8.91	25.23	San Miguel	20.08	8.45	22.12
Carlsbad			25.78	Santa Fe	18.94	7.36	14.12
Artesia			30.34	Santa Fe			13.92
Grant	21.14	8.02	19.83	Sierra	10.61	19.26	39.60
Guadalupe	17.96	8.82	13.57	Socorro	22.37	9.17	22.06
Harding	8.90[c]	9.82[c]	51.72[b]	Taos	21.10	8.61	21.22
Hidalgo	24.28	10.23	29.11	Torrance	16.58	9.90	14.05
Lea	20.12	6.74	27.19	Union	15.88	11.25	32.42
Hobbs			30.15	Valencia	20.60	7.04	24.01
Lincoln	17.02	8.34	24.22				
Los Alamos	12.07	3.16	17.22				
Luna	21.14	10.97	20.13				

[a] less than 100 births 1970-1974
[b] less than 200 births 1970-1974
[c] distortion possible due to low population base

Source: U.S. Department of Health, Education and Welfare. *Vital Statistics of the United States, 1970-1974.*

TABLE 2. INFANT DEATH RATES—ROCKY MOUNTAIN STATES AND U.S.

	1960		1970		1973	
	White	Nonwhite	White	Nonwhite	White	Nonwhite
United States	22.9	43.2	17.8	30.9	15.8	26.2
Arizona	26.6	60.8	16.0	28.0	14.2	21.6
Colorado	26.9	44.0	19.7	23.5	16.2	23.2
Idaho	22.7	33.3	17.3	11.6	16.9	21.6
Montana	24.2	34.5	21.2	24.7	18.7	26.0
Nevada	29.6	33.9	22.2	37.0	19.6	15.6
NEW MEX.CO	30.9	52.8	19.5	28.9	19.0	25.7
Utah	18.8	54.0	14.9	17.5	12.4	20.5
Wyoming	27.5	48.6	19.6	27.6	18.7	13.0

Sources: U.S. Department of Commerce, *Statistical Abstract of the United States*, selected years and Bureau of Business and Economic Research, New Mexico Statistical Abstract—1977.

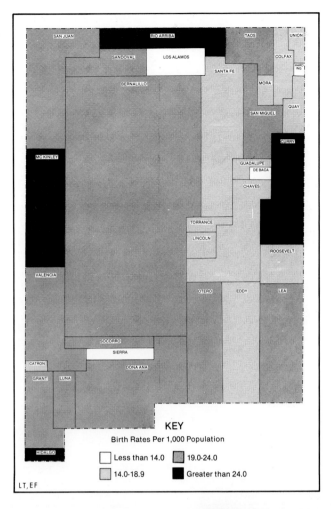

KEY

Birth Rates Per 1,000 Population

Less than 14.0   19.0-24.0

14.0-18.9   Greater than 24.0

LT, EF

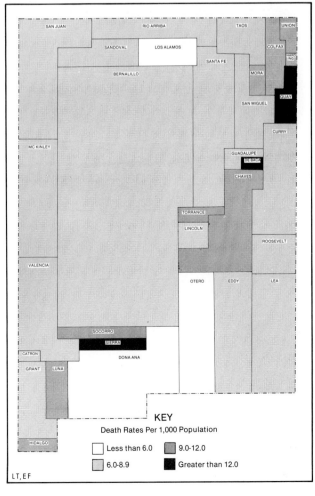

KEY

Death Rates Per 1,000 Population

Less than 6.0   9.0-12.0

6.0-8.9   Greater than 12.0

LT, EF

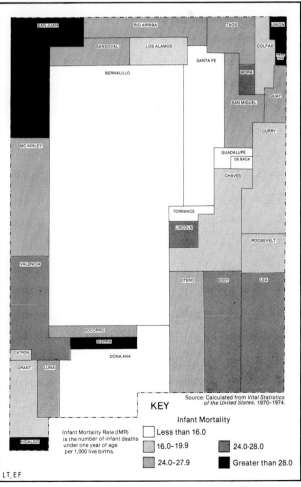

Source: Calculated from *Vital Statistics of the United States*, 1970–1974.

KEY

Infant Mortality

Infant Mortality Rate (IMR) is the number of infant deaths under one year of age per 1,000 live births.

Less than 16.0

16.0–19.9   24.0-28.0

24.0–27.9   Greater than 28.0

LT, EF

77

suicide in new mexico

The suicide rate in New Mexico is significantly (and consistently) higher than the national rate, in spite of the fact that New Mexico has few stress elements generally associated with high suicide rates. New Mexico has a relatively low population, and natural stress elements such as tornadoes, floods, and other weather extremes are rare.

The pattern of suicide rates in the state asks several questions to which there are presently no clear conclusions. Why are the highest rates consistently in large counties of extremely low population densities (Catron, Sierra, Socorro, Guadalupe, Quay)? Some of the most urbanized or rapidly growing areas, normally associated with social stress, have the lowest suicide rates in New Mexico (San Juan, Los Alamos, Doña Ana). It is also curious that two counties

with about the same population have such wide variation in rates on a yearly basis (i.e., Chaves and Curry counties). There have been no research answers to these and other questions about suicide in New Mexico.

Table 1 illustrates several demographic phenomena of social significance in which New Mexico rates exceed national rates. These indicators suggest that New Mexicans experience greater social stresses than do the general United States population. Are the indicators coincidental oddities or are they unexplained correlated phenomena? If there is some unrecognized correlation, these social characteristics are long overdue for some careful and extensive research to unravel the relationships.

Leo Yates and Byron B. King

TABLE 1: SELECTED 1976 DEMOGRAPHIC DATA—NEW MEXICO AND THE UNITED STATES

Phenomena	New Mexico Number	Rate	United States Number	Rate	% N.M. Rate Exceeds U.S. Rate
Marriage[a]	15,616	13.4	2,133,000	9.9	35.5
Divorce[a]	9,128	7.8	1,077,000	5.0	56.0
Suicide[b]	215	18.4	26,832	12.5	47.3
Motor Vehicle Accidents[b]	541	43.7	N/A	21.9	99.5
Homicides[b]	130	12.2	N/A	9.1	34.1

a—rate per 1,000 population
b—rate per 100,000 population
N/A—not available

TABLE 2: SUICIDES IN NEW MEXICO BY COUNTY
(rates per 100,000 estimated population)

County	1971 no.	rate	1972 no.	rate	1973 no.	rate	1974 no.	rate	1975 no.	rate	1976 no.	rate	1977 no.	rate	1971-1977 no.	rate
Bernalillo	51	15.5	53	15.6	68	19.2	79	22.1	66	18.2	64	17.5	91	24.0	67.4	18.9
Catron	2	90.9	1	45.5	1	45.2	1	40.0	0	0.0	0	0.0	0	0.0	0.7	31.7
Chaves	6	13.2	8	17.2	6	12.9	4	8.6	10	21.0	8	16.3	10	20.3	7.4	15.6
Colfax	3	24.8	1	8.3	1	8.1	1	7.8	4	30.8	2	15.0	5	39.1	2.4	19.1
Curry	1	2.4	4	9.8	5	11.7	4	9.3	2	4.6	4	9.4	6	14.6	3.7	8.8
De Baca	0	0.0	1	40.0	0	0.0	0	0.0	1	38.5	0	0.0	1	40.0	0.4	16.9
Dona Ana	5	7.0	6	8.2	11	14.8	1	1.3	10	12.6	7	8.5	6	7.2	6.6	8.5
Eddy	6	14.7	6	14.7	7	17.0	8	19.3	7	16.3	2	4.4	6	13.2	6.0	14.2
Grant	2	8.9	4	17.7	5	21.3	4	16.8	2	8.1	5	20.8	4	16.3	3.7	15.7
Guadalupe	0	0.0	1	20.4	0	0.0	1	20.4	4	81.6	1	20.4	2	40.8	1.3	26.2
Harding	0	0.0	0	0.0	0	0.0	1	83.3	0	0.0	1	76.9	0	0.0	0.3	22.9
Hidalgo	0	0.0	0	0.0	2	42.6	2	37.0	1	17.2	1	16.7	0	0.0	0.9	16.2
Lea	5	10.1	2	4.0	4	8.2	4	8.0	7	13.6	11	20.2	7	13.2	5.7	11.0
Lincoln	1	12.8	4	50.0	0	0.0	1	10.8	2	20.6	2	19.8	3	29.1	1.9	20.4
Los Alamos	1	6.5	0	0.0	1	6.5	3	19.5	2	12.4	1	6.1	4	23.4	1.7	10.6
Luna	2	16.4	3	24.0	3	22.9	2	14.6	1	6.9	2	13.7	3	20.8	2.3	17.0
McKinley	9	20.1	9	19.2	13	26.4	12	24.6	10	19.6	19	33.9	13	23.2	12.1	23.9
Mora	1	21.7	0	0.0	0	0.0	1	20.8	3	62.5	0	0.0	1	20.8	0.9	18.0
Otero	7	16.7	3	7.3	5	12.0	12	28.4	5	11.8	9	21.6	7	16.5	6.9	16.3
Quay	2	17.7	4	36.4	4	36.0	2	17.9	4	35.4	3	26.8	3	26.8	3.1	28.1
Rio Arriba	7	27.1	4	15.4	6	22.6	5	18.2	10	36.0	8	28.9	5	18.1	6.4	23.8
Roosevelt	2	12.0	1	6.0	1	6.0	3	17.5	3	18.1	3	18.2	3	18.2	2.3	13.2
Sandoval	3	16.1	2	10.4	8	38.5	9	40.2	7	30.7	9	38.5	3	12.5	5.6	26.1
San Juan	10	18.7	8	14.4	7	11.9	8	13.0	11	17.1	7	10.3	13	18.4	7.1	14.8
San Miguel	3	13.6	5	21.6	3	12.6	2	8.5	4	17.2	5	21.6	5	22.0	3.9	16.
Santa Fe	8	14.5	7	12.1	10	16.8	18	29.7	16	25.8	14	21.9	14	21.2	12.4	20.
Sierra	3	41.1	3	38.5	3	37.5	4	50.0	1	12.0	1	11.5	1	11.4	2.3	28.
Socorro	0	0.0	2	21.1	3	30.9	4	41.2	2	20.2	5	49.5	2	20.2	2.6	26.
Taos	1	5.6	2	11.1	3	16.2	3	16.0	2	10.4	4	20.3	2	10.1	2.4	12.
Torrance	0	0.0	1	18.9	0	0.0	3	48.4	1	15.6	1	14.5	1	14.7	1.0	16.
Union	0	0.0	1	20.8	3	62.5	0	0.0	2	40.8	1	20.4	1	20.4	1.1	23.
Valencia	1	2.4	4	9.5	6	14.0	6	13.6	8	17.4	15	31.0	8	15.6	6.9	14.
NEW MEXICO	142	13.6	150	14.1	189	17.2	208	18.6	208	18.2	215	18.4	230	19.3	191.7	17.
NATIONAL		11.7		12.0		12.0		12.1		12.7		12.5		N/A		

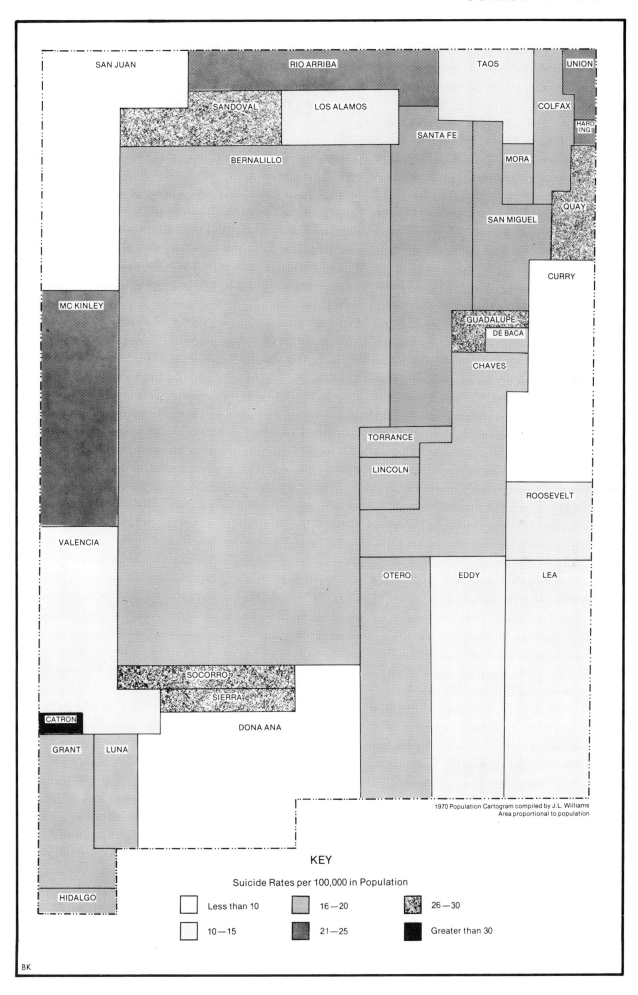

SAN JUAN

RIO ARRIBA

TAOS

UNION

SANDOVAL

LOS ALAMOS

COLFAX

HARD
ING

SANTA FE

BERNALILLO

MORA

QUAY

SAN MIGUEL

MC KINLEY

CURRY

GUADALUPE

DE BACA

CHAVES

VALENCIA

TORRANCE

LINCOLN

ROOSEVELT

OTERO

EDDY

LEA

SOCORRO

SIERRA

CATRON

DONA ANA

GRANT

LUNA

1970 Population Cartogram compiled by J.L. Williams
Area proportional to population

HIDALGO

KEY

Suicide Rates per 100,000 in Population

Less than 10

16—20

26—30

10—15

21—25

Greater than 30

BK

79

cancer in new mexico

The map illustrates average annual cancer mortality rates for New Mexico by county, for the white population, from 1950–1969. The "white" population category includes both Anglo and Spanish–American ethnic groups. Other ethnic groups were not included in the state map because in many counties their relative numbers are very small, and are therefore difficult to show on a statewide basis. However, ethnic distributions are considered in tables 1 and 2. The rates on the map are age-adjusted, to include the number of persons in each given age-group county-by-county, and are statistically corrected, thereby eliminating a bias of higher mortality rates in counties with older populations. Mortality rate per county is derived not from the location of each individual's death, but from the individual's place of residence. This eliminates a bias of higher rates in counties with more hospitals. These "average-annual" rates on the map have varied little since 1974.

The ten types of cancer on the map are those causing the highest mortality in New Mexico. Skin cancer is the most common cancer, however it is not shown in the tables or maps because fatalities from skin cancer are rare. In addition, skin cancer is easily treated by most dermatologists and the incidence is not accurately reported to the New Mexico Tumor Registry.

The geographic distribution of cancer mortality rates in New Mexico shows a rather intriguing pattern. However, the informa-tion should be examined carefully. For instance, mortality rates are higher in counties with a predominantly Anglo population, because the cancer types listed are much more common in Anglos. Many cancers such as breast cancer and leukemia appear to have a greater genetic input than others. When looking at county rates, it is impossible to determine whether a high rate is due to many cases occurring in a few families which could indicate a greater genetic input, or single cases in a lot of families possibly showing a larger environmental input. Hospital facilities should also be considered when examining mortality rates. A cancer may have a higher mortality rate in counties with inadequate treatment facilities, or inefficient screening programs. Also, a county with a very small population will show a much larger increase in mortality rate if one resident dies than a county with a very large population.

The most important conclusions to be drawn from this data are first, that no one environmental factor stands out on the map as a strong correlate with cancer mortality, and second, that a great deal of further research is required before any one environmental source of input can be pinpointed as responsible for enhancing cancer rates.

Denise Glore

TABLE 1: PERCENT OF CANCER INCIDENCE, BY ETHNIC GROUP, IN NEW MEXICO

Cancer Site	Anglo	Spanish-American	American Indian*	Black	Other
Brain	71.1	20.5	6.4	1.3	0.6
Breast	81.6	14.2	2.5	1.3	0.4
Cervix	54.3	29.5	14.4	1.4	0.4
Large Intestine & Rectum	78.4	17.3	2.2	2.0	0.2
Leukemia	70.9	21.1	6.9	1.1	0.0
Lung & Bronchial	81.3	13.3	2.5	2.8	0.0
Pancreas	64.5	30.3	3.5	1.7	0.0
Prostate	67.7	23.7	6.2	2.3	0.1
Stomach	36.9	47.2	12.2	3.2	0.3
% Population of Ethnic Groups in New Mexico	50	36.7	11.2	1.8	0.3

Source: New Mexico Tumor Registry

*The American Indian percentages may be slightly high because residency is difficult to assess on the Navajo Reservation, therefore there is overflow from Arizona.

TABLE 3: COMPARISON OF CANCER MORTALITY RATES BETWEEN NEW MEXICO AVERAGES AND U.S. AVERAGES, FOR WHITE POPULATION, 1950-1969

Cancer Site	Males—NM	Females—NM	Males—U.S.	Females—U.S.
Brain	3.30	2.54	4.42	2.91
Breast	.18	19.01	.28	25.51
Cervix	-----	6.30	-----	8.57
Large Intestine	9.15	10.82	16.54	16.25
Leukemia	7.71	5.23	8.81	5.74
Lung	24.71	6.26	37.98	6.29
Pancreas	8.79	5.92	9.63	5.83
Prostate	15.87	-----	17.84	-----
Rectum	3.39	3.31	7.65	4.82
Stomach	17.96	9.86	15.22	7.70

Source: Mason and McRay, U.S. County Mortality Rates, 1974.

TABLE 2: BY ETHNIC BREAKDOWN, A LIST OF THE MOST COMMON TYPES OF CANCER EXCLUDING SKIN AND CARCINOMA IN-SITU OF THE CERVIX, 1969-1972 IN NEW MEXICO

Ethnic Group and Sex	Site	Percent
Anglo Males	lung and bronchial	21.3
	prostate	18.6
	colon and rectum	12.9
	leukemia and lymphoma	8.6
	urinary bladder	6.1
Anglo Females	breast	30.3
	colon and rectum	14.2
	uterus	7.8
	leukemia and lymphoma	6.8
	lung and bronchial	5.7
Spanish-American Males	prostate	22.2
	stomach	11.5
	lung and bronchial	10.4
	colon and rectum	9.5
	leukemia and lymphoma	9.2
Spanish-American Females	breast	18.0
	cervix	12.1
	colon and rectum	8.7
	stomach	7.2
	leukemia and lymphoma	6.8
American Indian Males	prostate	20.7
	stomach	13.8
	leukemia and lymphoma	12.4
	other and undetermined	8.3
	lung and bronchial	7.6
American Indian Females	cervix	16.3
	breast	15.7
	gall bladder	8.5
	other and undetermined	7.2
	leukemia and lymphoma	6.5
Black Males	prostate	20.6
	lung and bronchial	20.6
	leukemia and lymphoma	9.8
	stomach	7.6
	colon and rectum	6.5
Black Females	breast	19.4
	colon and rectum	19.4
	uterus	6.9
	cervix	5.6
	stomach	5.6

Source: New Mexico Tumor Registry

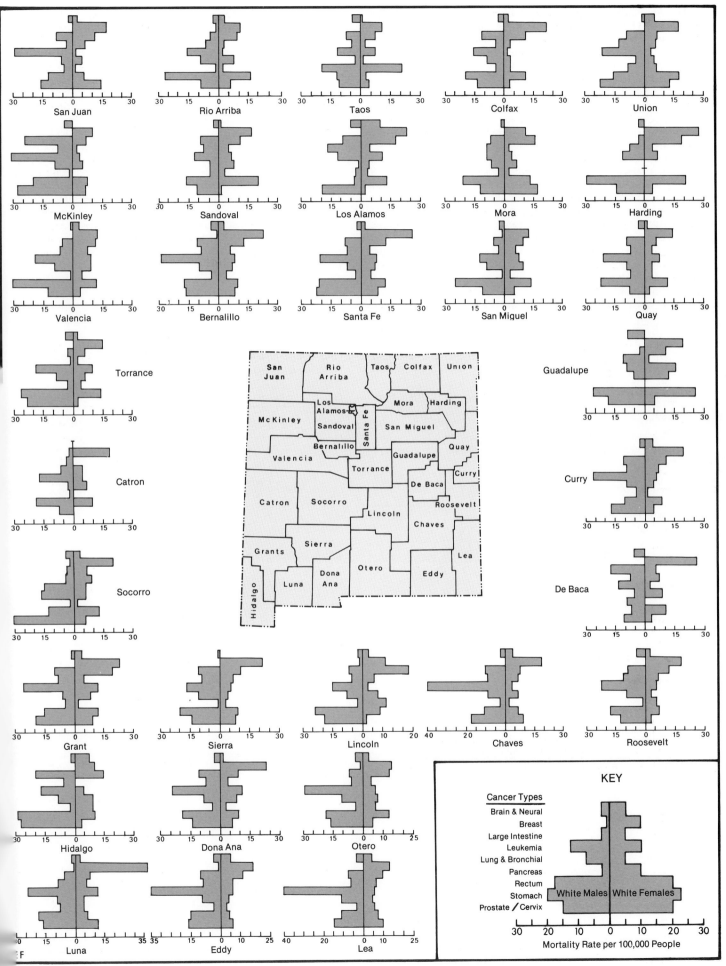

San Juan
Rio Arriba
Taos
Colfax
Union
McKinley
Sandoval
Los Alamos
Mora
Harding
Valencia
Bernalillo
Santa Fe
San Miguel
Quay
Torrance
Guadalupe
Catron
Curry
Socorro
De Baca
Grant
Sierra
Lincoln
Chaves
Roosevelt
Hidalgo
Dona Ana
Otero
Luna
Eddy
Lea

KEY

Cancer Types
Brain & Neural
Breast
Large Intestine
Leukemia
Lung & Bronchial
Pancreas
Rectum
Stomach
Prostate / Cervix

White Males   White Females

30   20   10   0   10   20   30
Mortality Rate per 100,000 People

Data for map and text reviewed by New Mexico Tumor Registry.

81

plague ecology

The Southwestern United States contains one of the world's largest areas inhabited by plague-bearing animals and their plague-transmitting fleas. In temperature regimes found in New Mexico, both hot and cold extremes restrict plague fleas and bacterial activity. Low relative humidity is also an important restricting factor. Plague bacteria typically require 60% relative humidity or higher to be fully active. However, high humidity and moderate temperatures do exist throughout the year in New Mexico in the burrows and on the skin surfaces of rodents, rabbits, and predators. Fleas, while tending to limit the type of mammal they infest to a range of related species or species living in the same environment, are not thought to associate strongly with specific hosts. Thus, of the several species of flea which infest the rock squirrel, at least two have been called aggressive toward humans. The existence of microclimates suitable for fleas and plague bacilli and their continuous presence in the mammalian host populations provide the conditions for occasional human disease in New Mexico. Plague bacilli may for prolonged periods maintain a virtually harmless state of "residency" in some animals until some stress weakens the "host" and the bacilli suddenly reproduce very rapidly. If the stress is associated with a high population density of "hosts" and a high number of fleas on the "hosts," an epidemic in those animals, called an epizootic, is likely to arise.

The flea's role in plague transmission deserves special attention. When the flea encounters an animal sick with plague, having many bacilli in its blood, the bacilli in the blood meal reproduce so fast that they block the flea's digestive system. The flea, unable to digest, gets hungry and again tries to eat but instead pushes the meal plus a few bacilli back into the victim. In humans and many other mammals, one or two bacilli can develop into an infectious population even in healthy individuals. The flea, getting still hungrier, increases the frequency of its attempts to feed, increasing the speed with which the disease spreads. Fleas leave very sick or dying hosts in search of new hosts. Uninfected fleas are especially susceptible to digestive blocking if they have not eaten in a long time when they encounter a sick animal. Thus, during the epizootic, as hosts become harder to find, all flea activity increases and uninfected but hungry fleas more actively seek hosts and more rapidly suffer digestive blockade. Infected fleas, unable to digest, more actively seek meals as they starve.

Recurrence of the disease in the apparent absence of diseased hosts or invasion by sick or infected flea-bearing animals is a subject of some controversy at present. However, under the proper microclimatic conditions, infected fleas may live for over a year without a host. The bacilli may survive prolonged freezing or drying and may endure in burrow soils under good conditions for indefinite periods. The route of reinfection is certainly imaginable along these paths. Also, hibernation, as in marmots and squirrels, may delay the disease effects.

In New Mexico the population of animals constituting one of the world's largest plague "reservoirs" is composed primarily of the squirrel family, including prairie dogs. However, probably all rodents and rabbits may carry plague and plague fleas. Studies in New Mexico have confirmed the presence of the disease in many species. Additionally, predator species, including domestic dogs and cats, may carry plague fleas. While predators are immune to the disease, their habits may provide an avenue of disease transmission to humans and other species.

The plague bacillus, *Yersinia pestis,* causes a very diverse variety of disease states in humans. No clear general characteristic, other than the bacterial agent, groups these diseases or separates them with absolute clarity from other diseases.

Bubonic plague usually appears with an abrupt high fever, high and sometimes pounding heart rate, flushing, aching extremities, and malaise. Occasionally the site of the infecting flea bite develops a blister-like pustule. Seriously swollen lymph nodes called buboes may appear in the neck, throat, armpits, or groin.

Septicemic plague may result from the overwhelming of a lymphatic node defense site (buboe), direct penetration through the lymphatic system to the blood stream, or direct entrance of the bacillus into the blood stream. Buboes may or may not be present, blood is densely populated with bacteria, and most or all the other symptoms of bubonic plague are intensified. Generalized bleeding beneath the skin may appear, giving rise to the historic term, "Black Death."

Pneumonia as a form of plague falls into primary and secondary categories. *Pneumonic plague* arising from bubonic or septicemic plague is secondary. Primary pneumonic plague develops from droplet inhalation or oral contact with contaminated matter. This is the direct human-to-human disease which, appearing in a community, may spread at uncontrollably fast rates. Initial symptoms may be almost absent; a slight mid-chest discomfort may appear early, suddenly followed by abrupt pneumonia, consolidation of parts of the lungs, quantities of lung secretions varying from clear liquid to bloody froth, and extremely dense bacterial populations in the blood. Lymph nodes around the heart and between the lungs may also be drastically enlarged, cutting off breathing. A fever may also develop.

In conclusion, plague in New Mexico is an interesting and potentially very serious problem. Public awareness and scientific study of the disease, and its routes of infection, are and should be increasing. As New Mexico experiences growth in population and broader areas of human activity and development, the control of plague through study and careful outdoor practices becomes increasingly important.

Gordon Venable

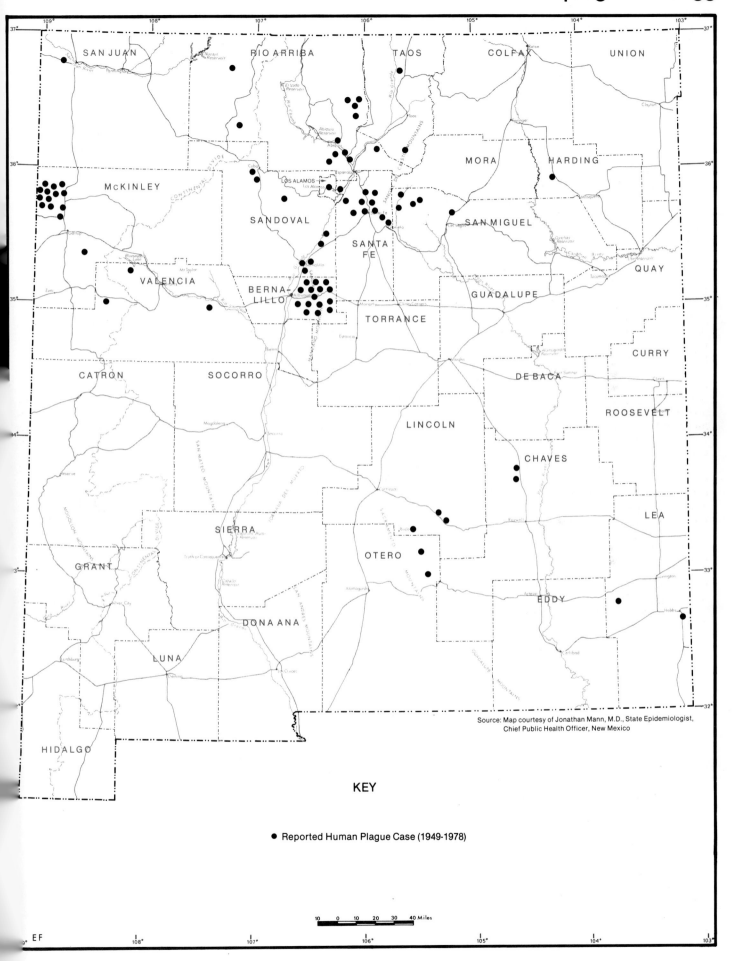

Source: Map courtesy of Jonathan Mann, M.D., State Epidemiologist,
Chief Public Health Officer, New Mexico

KEY

● Reported Human Plague Case (1949-1978)

traffic accidents

The breakdown by county of motor vehicle accident fatality rates in New Mexico shows a preponderance of fatal accidents in the northwest corner of the state, particularly in San Juan and McKinley counties. This skewed distribution reflects the high incidence of highway accidents among the Indian population residing on the reservation in those counties.

Intoxication has been listed as the cause of approximately one third of New Mexico traffic accidents, but these figures may be overly conservative. As of 1979 the state has instituted new criteria and reporting requirements for alcohol-related accidents. The State Police expect these more accurate figures to double the previous figures.

Bernalillo County, which has the highest rate of accidents per vehicle miles, also has, interestingly enough, a relatively low rate of fatalities. This is due to the fact that the county is by far the most urbanized in the state, and accidents there are more likely to occur at slower city speeds.

Overall, there is an increase in fatal traffic accidents statewide, from a low of 540 total deaths in 1974 to 671 in 1977. Two factors may account for this: 1974 was the year speed limits were reduced (these have since increasingly been ignored) and motorcycle helmet laws were repealed in 1977 (the number of motorcycle fatalities almost doubled from 24 in 1976 to 45 in 1978).

Another interesting phenomenon is the statewide rise in fatalities among the age group 25 to 34, from 92 total in 1974, increasing steadily to 158 in 1978. Over half of New Mexico traffic fatalities occur in ages 15 to 34.

Kim Seidler

NEW MEXICO AVERAGE ANNUAL TRAFFIC ACCIDENTS AND FATALITY RATES
(1974 through 1977)

	Total Annual Accidents	Annual Vehicle Miles (millions)	Accidents (per million vehicle miles)	Total Annual Deaths	Annual Deaths (per 100 million vehicle miles)
Bernalillo	16,040.0	2,478.2745	6.465	78.5	3.160
Catron	104.5	50.3085	2.080	5.0	9.970
Chaves	1,981.0	343.2170	5.770	18.0	5.240
Colfax	536.5	159.3140	3.360	5.0	2.955
Curry	1,499.0	242.3200	6.190	10.0	4.125
De Baca	76.5	59.3675	1.290	4.0	6.330
Doña Ana	2,496.0	644.2020	3.865	25.5	3.930
Eddy	1,313.0	308.8785	5.320	12.0	3.900
Grant	735.0	247.8350	2.960	10.0	4.040
Guadalupe	279.0	246.0630	1.130	8.0	3.360
Harding	10.0	15.0655	0.670	0.5	3.210
Hidalgo	167.0	125.7555	1.335	8.5	6.800
Lea	1,674.5	421.4470	3.970	16.0	3.860
Lincoln	584.0	151.5880	3.845	13.0	8.660
Los Alamos	403.0	72.9920	5.520	2.0	3.145
Luna	480.5	234.0580	2.050	10.0	4.110
McKinley	2,464.5	542.1395	4.540	73.0	13.520
Mora	119.0	59.6100	1.990	5.0	7.790
Otero	1,210.0	327.3900	3.700	20.0	6.120
Quay	408.0	252.1540	1.620	12.5	5.010
Rio Arriba	998.0	226.4220	4.400	21.5	9.460
Roosevelt	616.5	151.5130	4.070	6.0	4.125
Sandoval	532.5	300.3170	1.770	28.5	9.590
San Juan	2,719.0	511.8570	5.260	60.0	11.640
San Miguel	968.0	183.2340	5.285	15.0	8.060
Santa Fe	3,348.0	562.4240	5.955	32.5	5.800
Sierra	300.5	95.9030	3.130	4.0	4.400
Socorro	353.0	208.1605	1.700	10.0	4.950
Taos	740.0	152.5970	4.845	17.0	11.100
Torrance	266.0	217.4985	1.220	5.0	2.320
Union	162.0	81.7560	1.980	3.0	3.700
Valencia	1,561.0	567.9230	2.740	34.5	7.460
New Mexico Total	45,483.0	10,241.5830	4.435	582.0	5.680

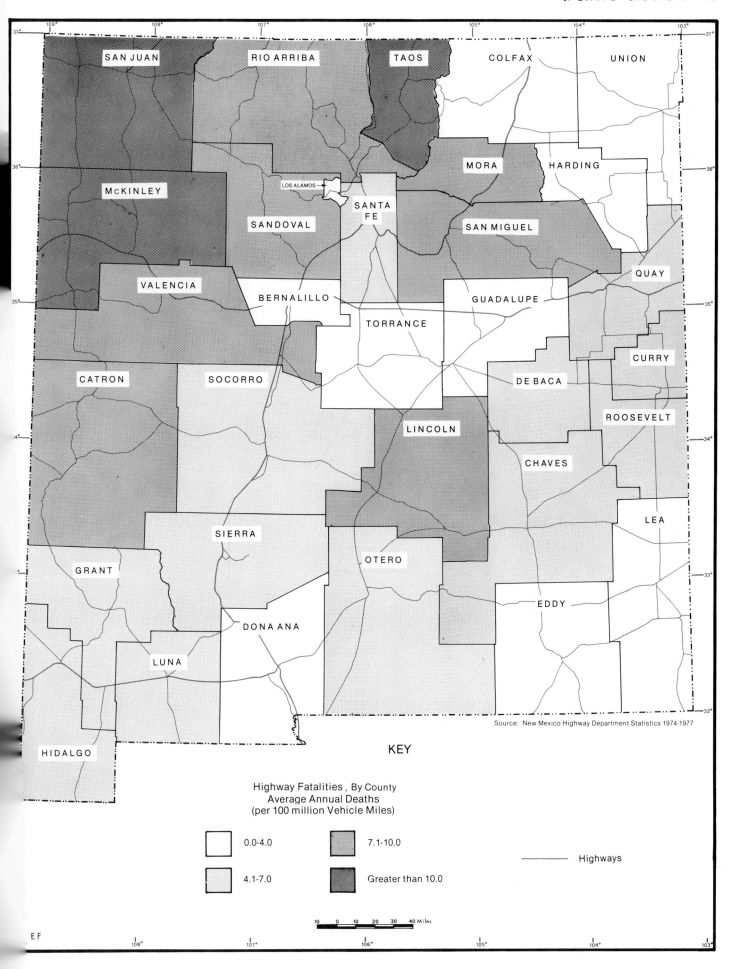

SAN JUAN

RIO ARRIBA

TAOS

COLFAX

UNION

MORA

HARDING

McKINLEY

LOS ALAMOS

SANTA FE

SANDOVAL

SAN MIGUEL

QUAY

VALENCIA

BERNALILLO

GUADALUPE

TORRANCE

CURRY

CATRON

SOCORRO

DE BACA

ROOSEVELT

LINCOLN

CHAVES

LEA

SIERRA

OTERO

GRANT

EDDY

DONA ANA

LUNA

HIDALGO

Source: New Mexico Highway Department Statistics 1974-1977

KEY

Highway Fatalities , By County
Average Annual Deaths
(per 100 million Vehicle Miles)

0.0-4.0		7.1-10.0
4.1-7.0		Greater than 10.0

Highways

10   0   10   20   30   40 Miles

E F

crime rate

New Mexico's crime rate is higher than the national rate, but is less than the rate of two neighboring states. Table 1 compares the crime rate over a five-year period for these areas. The crime rate has increased steadily between 1971 and 1975.

For the five-year period shown in Table 2, 1971-1975, the highest crime rates were found in three counties, Bernalillo, Santa Fe, and San Miguel, and all other counties were below the state average of 50.3 crimes per 1000 population. For 1975 alone, the crime rate has a significantly different statewide pattern with high and moderate crime rates expanding to over one-half the counties. The 1975 rate exceeded the five-year average in all counties but two, Catron and Hidalgo. While crime statistics are not totally reliable, due to reporting procedures, there is no doubt that the crime rate has increased significantly during the past several years.

Paul McAllister

TABLE 1: CRIMES PER 1000 POPULATION, UNITED STATES: 1971-1975

Area	Total Crimes					Violent Crimes[a]					Property Crimes[b]				
	1971	1972	1973[c]	1974	1975	1971	1972	1973	1974	1975	1971	1972	1973[c]	1974	1975
United States	29.1	28.3	41.6	48.5	52.8	4.0	4.0	4.2	4.6	4.8	25.1	24.3	37.4	43.9	48.0
New Mexico	34.7	34.2	49.3	52.1	58.4	3.7	4.2	4.7	4.5	5.4	31.0	30.0	44.6	47.6	53.0
Arizona	35.1	37.5	67.0	82.2	83.4	4.0	4.5	4.8	5.7	5.5	31.1	33.0	62.2	76.5	77.9
Colorado	38.1	40.6	55.0	61.7	66.7	3.7	4.1	4.1	4.3	4.6	34.4	36.5	50.9	57.4	62.1
Texas	27.0	26.5	40.5	47.0	54.1	3.7	3.5	3.8	3.9	3.9	23.3	23.0	36.7	43.1	50.2

[a] Murder, Rape, Robbery, and Assault

[b] Burglary, Larceny, and Motor-Vehicle Theft

[c] Dramatic increase in 1973 due to change in definition of larceny

TABLE 2: CRIMES PER 1000 POPULATION, NEW MEXICO

	5-Year Average 1971-1975			1975				
	Violent Crimes[1]	Property Crimes[2]	Crime Rate	Rank[3] Crime	Rank[3] Population	Violent Crimes[1]	Property Crimes[2]	Crime Rate
Bernalillo	7.0	69.7	76.7	1	1	7.6	74.4	92.0
Catron	1.8	10.2	12.0	32	31	.8	3.8	4.6
Chaves	2.0	37.7	39.7	11	7	2.4	42.8	45.2
Colfax	3.6	16.5	20.1	24	20	4.7	23.1	27.8
Curry	3.0	34.7	37.7	9	9	4.8	42.2	47.0
De Baca	.8	7.5	8.3	30	30	2.3	13.1	15.4
Dona Ana	2.0	41.0	43.0	8	2	2.4	46.4	48.8
Eddy	2.3	37.7	40.0	14	10	2.9	39.3	42.2
Grant	2.7	24.3	27.0	20	13	2.4	30.8	33.2
Guadalupe	4.4	20.4	24.8	18	27	5.9	29.8	35.7
Harding	.8	6.9	7.7	27	32	.0	21.7	21.7
Hidalgo	5.4	35.4	40.8	25	26	5.2	21.0	26.2
Lea	5.5	41.2	46.7	5	5	5.7	56.0	61.7
Lincoln	3.5	28.1	31.6	6	23	6.1	51.3	57.4
Los Alamos	.8	23.2	24.0	23	18	1.4	28.5	29.9
Luna	1.7	34.1	35.8	4	19	2.8	59.1	61.9
McKinley	5.7	28.4	34.1	17	6	7.0	29.8	36.8
Mora	2.7	3.8	6.5	31	29	3.1	7.1	10.2
Otero	1.7	31.3	33.0	15	11	1.3	40.4	41.7
Quay	3.3	43.9	47.2	7	21	6.1	50.4	56.5
Rio Arriba	2.1	16.5	18.6	26	12	4.4	21.3	25.7
Roosevelt	2.0	37.8	39.8	10	17	3.1	42.3	45.4
Sandoval	2.5	11.9	14.4	28	15	2.7	17.6	20.3
San Juan	4.7	29.2	33.9	13	3	6.2	36.8	43.0
San Miguel	5.7	60.8	66.5	3	14	5.5	63.7	69.2
Santa Fe	3.1	56.8	59.9	2	4	4.6	68.0	72.6
Sierra	3.6	32.2	35.8	16	24	2.9	37.6	40.5
Socorro	3.4	23.8	27.2	22	22	2.5	27.9	30.4
Taos	2.3	22.9	25.2	21	16	2.5	30.6	33.1
Torrance	.8	8.2	9.0	29	25	.9	14.7	15.6
Union	2.9	11.3	14.2	18	27	5.3	30.4	35.7
Valencia	2.2	23.7	25.9	12	8	3.4	40.2	43.6
STATE TOTAL	4.4	45.9	50.3	— —	— —	5.1	51.8	56.9

Source: New Mexico 1971-1975, Criminal Offense Statistics.

[1] Murder, Rape, Robbery, Assault

[2] Burglary, Larceny, Motor-Vehicle Theft

[3] Guadalupe and Union tied in crime and population

crime rate

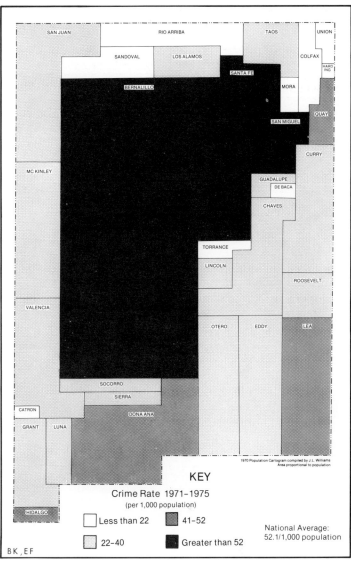

KEY

Crime Rate 1971–1975
(per 1,000 population)

☐ Less than 22   ▨ 41–52

☐ 22–40   ■ Greater than 52

National Average:
52.1/1,000 population

B K , E F

1970 Population Cartogram compiled by J.L. Williams
Area proportional to population

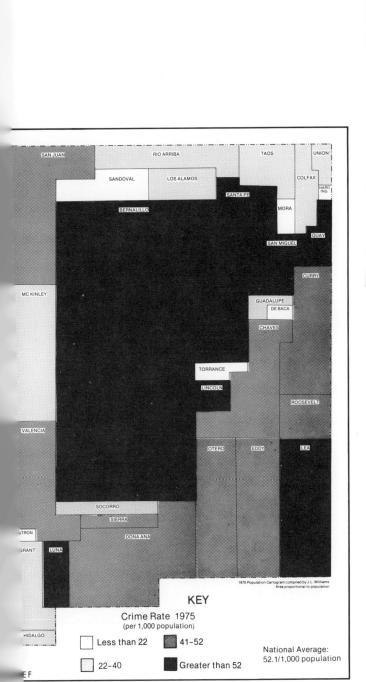

KEY

Crime Rate 1975
(per 1,000 population)

☐ Less than 22   ▨ 41–52

☐ 22–40   ■ Greater than 52

National Average:
52.1/1,000 population

1970 Population Cartogram compiled by J.L. Williams
Area proportional to population

major religious denominations

Religion is an important part of New Mexico's culture. Slightly more than one-half of all Americans (50.4%) do not claim membership in any church, however, almost two of every three New Mexicans (63.3%) adhere to some religious faith. In the Rocky Mountain Region and states adjacent to New Mexico, only Utah with its Latter-Day Saints heritage has a larger percentage of the population claiming church membership.

The Catholic Church, not surprisingly, is the largest denomination in the state as well as in most of the counties. The greatest concentrations of Catholics are found in the areas of early Spanish dominance with over 90 percent of all church members in Mora, Rio Arriba, Sandoval, and Taos counties. The Southern Baptist Convention, with 18.2 percent of all church adherents, is the sec-

ond largest denomination in the state. The greatest Baptist concentration is on the eastern and southern plains, largely a result of the rather heavy immigration from Texas, Oklahoma, and other southern states.

The Baptists and Catholics account for 74.7 percent of all church adherents in New Mexico. The remaining 25.3 percent are divided among 36 denominations. The United Methodist Church ranks third in membership with 9.1 percent and has its greatest concentrations in the easten and southern counties. The Latter-Day Saints (highly concentrated in three western counties) comprise the fourth largest church but have only 3.4 percent of the total church membership.

Paul McAllister

TABLE 1: CHURCH MEMBERSHIP, 1971

Region		% Religious Adherents Claiming Membership in			
	% Total Population Claiming Church Membership	Roman Catholic Church	Southern Baptist Church	United Methodist Church	Latter-Day Saints
United States	49.6	22.1	7.1	5.7	1.0
Total Rocky Mountain States*	52.3	35.3	6.6	6.9	28.8
New Mexico	63.3	56.5	18.2	9.1	3.4
Arizona	47.4	48.7	10.1	6.3	12.7
Colorado	41.5	41.1	5.5	11.3	4.2
Nevada	37.8	49.9	5.0	4.1	25.6
Utah	83.6	5.7	0.8	0.7	89.2
Texas**	56.2	32.0	37.5	13.6	0.7

Data Sources: Douglas W. Johnson, Paul R. Picard, and Bernard Quinn, *Churches and Church Membership in the United States: An Enumeration by Region, State, and County: 1971* (Washington, D.C.: Glenmary Research Center, 1974), and Albuquerque Stake, Latter-Day Saints.

*In addition to listed states includes Idaho, Montana, and Wyoming, but not Texas.
**Texas is not part of Rocky Mountain Region.

TABLE 2: RELIGIOUS PREFERENCE IN NEW MEXICO, 1971

County		% Religious Adherents Claiming Membership in			
	Church Membership as % Total Population	Roman Catholic Church	Southern Baptist Convention	United Methodist Church	Latter-Day Saints*
Bernalillo	60.2	61.9	11.1	9.0	
Catron	52.5	31.8	27.5	1.4	26.0
Chaves	53.0	26.8	37.4	18.4	
Colfax	83.9	73.6	11.4	10.1	
Curry	59.7	25.4	40.9	14.2	
De Baca	68.2	40.3	40.7	14.4	
Dona Ana	60.5	67.2	14.9	7.9	
Eddy	52.5	20.8	42.6	18.3	
Grant	63.0	72.8	12.1	7.5	
Guadalupe	104.2**	86.9	5.3	7.7	
Harding	80.3	64.6	23.9	8.0	
Hidalgo	85.7	73.9	15.7	7.2	
Lea	62.4	14.8	57.7	14.8	
Lincoln	70.0	56.7	21.8	11.5	
Los Alamos	73.7	26.8	12.1	8.5	
Luna	39.7	32.8	28.1	21.9	
McKinley	41.2	51.7	11.0	4.6	21.8
Mora	100.6**	95.7	1.5	----	
Otero	45.5	41.6	29.3	17.8	
Quay	76.3	38.5	43.2	12.5	
Rio Arriba	79.6	92.6	1.6	2.2	
Roosevelt	72.9	31.6	48.9	13.4	
Sandoval	84.5	94.8	1.7	.2	
San Juan	48.6	18.8	31.3	11.1	23.5
San Miguel	63.9	87.0	5.4	3.6	
Santa Fe	72.0	79.4	5.5	6.6	
Sierra	53.3	56.4	23.7	13.1	
Socorro	92.3	79.1	11.1	4.4	
Taos	94.3	93.2	1.8	.8	
Torrance	83.2	66.4	20.8	10.0	
Union	73.8	49.5	26.4	21.3	
Valencia	72.0	81.9	9.9	3.6	
State	63.3	56.5	18.2	9.1	3.4

*Latter-Day Saints data not available by county; these estimates from information provided by Albuquerque Stake, Latter-Day Saints.
**Indicates intercounty movement of church adherents; the church population is greater than total county population.

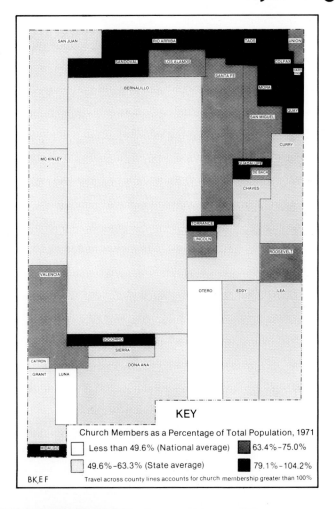

KEY

Church Members as a Percentage of Total Population, 1971

☐ Less than 49.6% (National average) ▨ 63.4%–75.0%

▨ 49.6%–63.3% (State average) ■ 79.1%–104.2%

BK,E F   Travel across county lines accounts for church membership greater than 100%

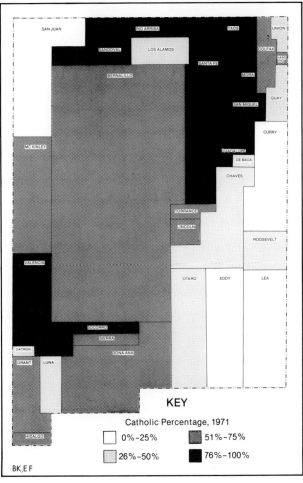

KEY

Catholic Percentage, 1971

☐ 0%–25% ▨ 51%–75%

▨ 26%–50% ■ 76%–100%

BK,E F

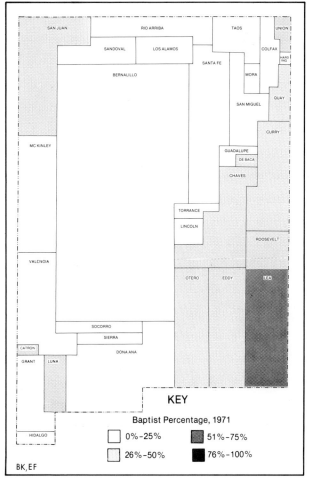

KEY

Baptist Percentage, 1971

☐ 0%–25% ▨ 51%–75%

▨ 26%–50% ■ 76%–100%

BK,E F

marriages and dissolutions

Rates of marriage and dissolutions of marriage per thousand population in New Mexico have consistently remained well above the national levels. These abnormally high rates are in need of explanations that cannot be given with the limited statistical information now available. Such extraordinarily high rates may simply reflect the relative youth of New Mexico's population, the third youngest state in terms of median age.

The number of marriage licenses issued in 1977 increased five percent over the 1976 level after declining for at least two previous years (Table 1). Earlier data are not reliable since accurate records were not kept before 1974. New Mexico, Arizona, and Oklahoma are the only three states in the nation that do not consider marriage a vital record to be centrally recorded.

The marriage rate has been found to vary widely between counties. It is thought that this variance may be due to the high number of out-of-state marriages in county seats of border counties, towns with strong tourist attractions, and towns along the main routes through the state.

"Dissolution of marriage" is the technically correct legal term that includes both divorces and annulments. Since annulments make up less than one percent of legal dissolutions, these are combined with data for divorces. Rates of divorce in New Mexico, based on provisional population estimates, declined in 1977 (Table 2). The decline was very slight, however, and may disappear when population estimates are revised in the 1980 census. What is more notable is that state divorce rates declined or remained stable at a time when national rates continued to increase; however, New Mexico's divorce rate still exceeds the national rate by more than 50 percent.

It is not certain which factors are responsible for the divorce rate variations between counties. As a general rule, in New Mexico lower divorce rates tend to occur in counties with low per capita income, low median educational level, and large unsettled areas remote from population centers. It would be unwarranted to conclude, however, that the poor or those with less education have more stable marriages, for that generalization has been disproved elsewhere. Perhaps geographic mobility helps explain some of the variations in marriage and divorce rates in New Mexico.

Leo Yates

TABLE 1: MARRIAGE RATES PER THOUSAND POPULATION

COUNTY	1977 Number	1977 Rate	1976 Number	1976 Rate	1975 Number	1975 Rate	1974 Number	1974 Rate
Bernalillo	4,756	12.6	4,466	12.1	4,274	11.8	4,434	12.4
Catron	22	8.8	13	5.2	13	5.4	12	4.8
Chaves	678	13.8	650	13.4	685	14.4	695	15.0
Colfax	354	27.7	398	29.9	445	34.2	620	48.4
Curry	905	22.0	960	23.5	984	22.7	948	22.2
De Baca	42	16.8	28	10.8	31	11.9	19	7.0
Dona Ana	1,309	15.6	1,300	15.8	1,364	17.1	1,318	17.0
Eddy	713	15.7	634	14.0	738	17.2	663	16.0
Grant	302	12.3	266	10.9	277	11.3	288	12.1
Guadalupe	44	9.0	61	12.4	59	12.0	62	12.7
Harding	7	5.8	9	6.9	6	5.0	9	7.5
Hidalgo	137	22.1	180	29.0	161	27.8	166	30.7
Lea	970	18.3	924	17.4	976	18.9	932	18.7
Lincoln	155	15.0	118	11.8	161	16.6	125	13.4
Los Alamos	159	9.3	131	7.9	164	10.2	160	10.4
Luna	218	15.1	190	12.9	228	15.8	203	14.8
McKinley	361	6.4	377	6.9	380	7.4	346	7.1
Mora	24	5.0	29	5.9	24	5.0	29	6.0
Otero	702	16.6	632	14.9	640	15.1	669	15.9
Quay	179	16.0	177	15.7	171	15.1	201	17.9
Rio Arriba	83	3.0	77	2.8	56	2.0	91	3.7
Roosevelt	249	15.1	255	15.5	222	13.4	241	14.1
Sandoval	283	11.8	266	11.3	285	12.5	281	12.5
San Juan	827	11.7	790	11.6	772	12.0	683	11.1
San Miguel	182	8.0	237	10.2	208	8.9	251	10.7
Santa Fe	1,146	17.6	1,017	15.8	1,121	18.1	1,087	17.9
Sierra	123	14.0	125	14.2	113	13.6	115	14.4
Socorro	140	14.1	138	13.5	120	12.1	111	11.4
Taos	315	15.9	251	12.7	292	15.1	315	16.8
Torrance	89	13.1	86	12.8	69	10.8	81	13.1
Union	238	48.6	215	43.9	209	42.7	219	42.9
Valencia	673	13.1	616	12.6	542	11.8	512	11.6
State	16,385	13.8	15,616	13.3	15,790	13.8	15,886	14.2
U.S.	2,176,000	10.1	2,154,807	10.0	2,152,662	10.1	2,229,667	10.5
State rate greater by:		36.9%		32.7%		36.6%		35.2%

TABLE 2: DISSOLUTION RATES PER THOUSAND POPULATION

COUNTY	1977 Number	1977 Rate	1976 Number	1976 Rate	1975 Number	1975 Rate	1974 Number	1974 Rate
Bernalillo	3,369	8.9	3,334	9.1	3,016	8.3	2,973	8.3
Catron	19	7.6	9	3.8	10	4.2	3	1.2
Chaves	790	16.0	717	14.6	443	9.3	486	10.5
Colfax	73	5.7	66	5.0	60	4.6	43	3.4
Curry	387	9.4	444	10.4	423	9.8	398	9.3
De Baca	7	2.8	6	2.4	3	1.2	5	1.9
Dona Ana	524	6.2	513	6.3	474	6.0	531	6.9
Eddy	339	7.5	371	8.2	331	7.7	281	6.8
Grant	159	6.5	179	7.5	158	6.4	146	6.1
Guadalupe	12	2.5	14	2.8	11	2.2	8	1.6
Harding	2	1.6	1	0.8	−0−	−0−	2	1.7
Hidalgo	45	7.3	43	7.2	48	8.3	36	6.7
Lea	469	8.9	491	9.0	477	9.2	385	7.7
Lincoln	50	4.9	113	11.2	82	8.5	93	10.0
Los Alamos	99	5.8	90	5.5	83	5.2	69	4.5
Luna	86	6.0	92	6.3	99	6.9	108	7.8
McKinley	156	2.8	154	2.8	166	3.2	190	3.9
Mora	9	1.9	13	2.6	13	2.7	19	4.0
Otero	404	9.6	424	10.2	417	9.8	429	10.2
Quay	73	6.5	84	7.5	73	6.5	81	7.2
Rio Arriba	80	2.9	77	2.8	116	4.2	112	4.1
Roosevelt	104	6.3	115	7.0	89	5.4	93	5.4
Sandoval	154	6.4	118	5.0	102	4.5	110	4.9
San Juan	421	5.9	590	8.7	490	7.6	316	5.1
San Miguel	137	6.0	97	4.2	156	6.7	134	5.7
Santa Fe	345	5.3	341	5.3	373	6.0	359	5.9
Sierra	76	8.6	75	8.5	72	8.7	79	9.9
Socorro	123	12.4	77	7.6	80	8.1	58	6.0
Taos	116	5.9	93	4.7	148	7.7	103	5.5
Torrance	41	6.0	33	4.8	50	7.8	36	5.8
Union	20	4.1	25	5.1	25	5.1	20	3.9
Valencia	454	8.8	319	6.6	325	7.0	186	4.2
State	9,143	7.7	9,128	7.8	8,413	7.4	7,892	7.1
U.S.	1,097,000	5.1	1,083,000	5.0	1,036,000	4.9	977,000	4.6
State rate greater by:		51.0%		54.4%		51.0%		54.3

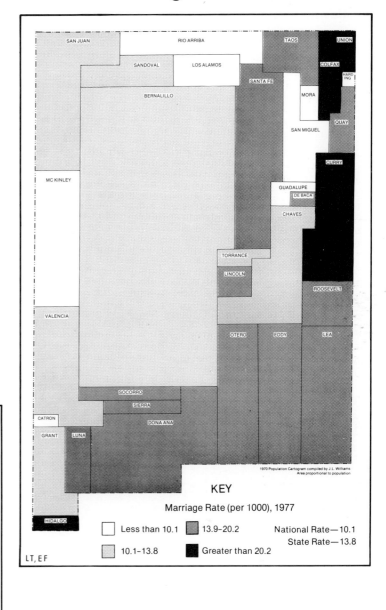

KEY

Marriage Rate (per 1000), 1977

| | Less than 10.1 | | 13.9–20.2 | National Rate—10.1 |
| | 10.1–13.8 | | Greater than 20.2 | State Rate—13.8 |

LT, E F

1970 Population Cartogram compiled by J. L. Williams
Area proportional to population

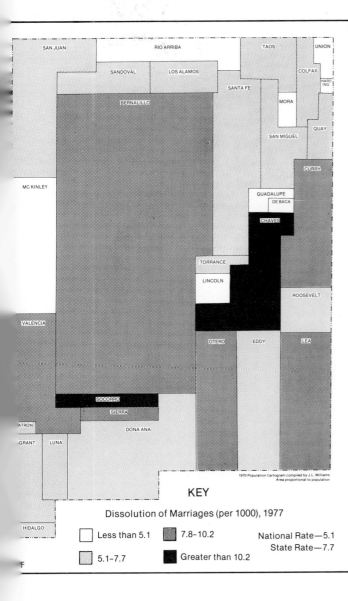

KEY

Dissolution of Marriages (per 1000), 1977

| | Less than 5.1 | | 7.8–10.2 | National Rate—5.1 |
| | 5.1–7.7 | | Greater than 10.2 | State Rate—7.7 |

1970 Population Cartogram compiled by J. L. Williams
Area proportional to population

public school characteristics

The patchwork map of eighty-eight public school districts shows that educational administration is not organized on a county basis. Only in the five counties of De Baca, Los Alamos, Luna, McKinley, and Sierra do the school districts correspond to the county boundaries, with administrative personnel located at the county seats. The delineations of the remaining eighty-three districts are more complex. Large portions of most counties are inaccessible to the populated sectors and many cases are administered by a district headquartered in another county. The present school district boundaries result from consolidations that have occurred over the past twenty-five years. The 374 school districts of New Mexico in 1953-54 (Chaves County with 23 districts; Rio Arriba County with 35; San Miguel County with 35; Sierra County with 22; and Torrance County with 21) had been pared to 265 districts in 1955-56, to 167 districts in 1959-60, and to 91 districts in 1965-66. One of the unfortunate consequences of the consolidation process was the creation of very large districts in areas of sparse population. Twenty-eight school districts had one-way bus routes greater than 50 miles, with four (Animas, Artesia, Fort Sumner, and Gadsden) extending routes more than 70 miles in one direction.

A unique feature of the public school system is the state's method of school finance. As can be observed from the map and table, the districts with lowest pupil-teacher ratios (19, 22, 26, 27, 42, 46, 57, 61, 75) are also those with the lowest indicators of wealth in terms of appraised property. None of these nine districts had more than 200 students enrolled in 1976, which helps to explain the low ratio of students per teacher. Economic survival for many of these dispersed rural school systems with weak local tax bases depends on the state. Over two-thirds of the operating income for seventy-four districts comes directly from the state government, which acts as caretaker for the Trust Lands in New Mexico. The public schools own about eight million acres of Trust Lands which generates over twenty million dollars per year in lease income through the State Land Office.

With the exception of transportation funding, state funds are largely distributed according to a state financial aid formula called the State Equalization Guarantee passed by the 1974 legislature. This formula is calculated according to indicators of a district's need, less some computed measure of a district's wealth. Need reflects costs of early childhood programs (grades 1-3 and grades 7-12), vocational, special, and bilingual education, teacher training and experience, and a sparsity index for low enrollment schools. The wealth of a school district is calculated from the local tax base and local revenue from motor vehicle license fees, the amount of Federal Impact Aid to districts with a large enrollment of dependents of federal government employees, Federal Forest Reserve and Vocational funds, and the Atomic Energy Commission funds (which affect only the Los Alamos district).

The Equalization Guarantee represents forty years (1934-1974) of political compromises. This system of finance, that favors low density rural districts, does not remove all inequities within the school system. This can be seen in the differentials of the assessed value of equipment and property available to students and in the operating budgets per student in each district. The Equalization Formula is still undergoing change, and the right combination of compromises between legislators may alleviate the present imbalances.

Jerry L. Williams

DISTRICT	1975-76 40-Day Average Daily Membership	1972-77 Average Pupil-Teacher Ratio (grades 1-12 per FTE)	1975 Assessed Valuation of Property ($,000's)	1975-76 Operating Funds ($,000's)	1975-76 Local Income (% of Operating Fund)	1975-76 State Income (% of Operating Fund)	1975-76 Federal Income (% of Operating Fund)	1975-76 State Equalization Guarantee Income (%)
1 Alamogordo	8197	21.6	53609	8333	6.2	77.2	16.6	71.3
2 Albuquerque	81651	24.0	911228	83028	11.3	84.8	3.9	79.5
3 Animas	524	18.5	19591	642	27.9	70.8	1.3	53.6
4 Artesia	3269	20.6	188899	3729	49.7	47.5	2.8	39.5
5 Aztec	1896	21.7	34972	2208	17.7	73.9	8.4	66.9
6 Belen	3700	21.6	70251	3653	18.3	79.3	2.4	71.5
7 Bernalillo	2868	19.6	19156	3103	8.9	68.1	23.0	59.1
8 Bloomfield	2288	21.2	71155	2676	27.1	59.1	13.8	43.4
9 Capitan	258	18.9	8956	419	20.8	76.7	2.5	64.7
10 Carlsbad	6385	22.4	150333	7195	20.6	74.1	5.3	68.0
11 Carrizozo	368	16.5	4886	583	10.6	86.4	3.0	79.8
12 Central	5122	22.0	167942	5876	27.1	32.9	40.0	23.4
13 Chama Valley	960	17.7	6278	1152	6.6	89.2	4.2	79.8
14 Cimarron	445	18.0	20158	601	30.0	68.9	1.1	62.1
15 Clayton	993	17.5	14091	1368	11.3	87.4	1.4	66.3
16 Cloudcroft	288	17.6	6304	428	14.3	77.3	8.4	67.8
17 Clovis	8672	21.1	72235	8836	8.8	81.4	9.8	74.4
18 Cobre	2471	21.4	105439	2411	41.9	56.5	1.6	47.9
19 Corona	143	11.5	10093	311	30.7	68.3	1.0	47.3
20 Cuba	1011	18.2	9880	1946	5.5	75.0	16.5	28.9
21 Deming	3719	22.8	52272	3798	12.6	87.1	0.3	78.4
22 Des Moines	174	11.7	3023	358	8.0	91.0	1.0	71.5
23 Dexter	641	17.6	5755	791	8.0	90.4	1.6	83.3
24 Dora	247	15.7	11996	449	26.4	72.8	0.8	53.9
25 Dulce	638	17.8	21269	837	28.6	31.0	40.4	22.9
26 Elida	126	9.7	4415	274	15.8	83.4	0.8	65.3
27 Encino	102	10.7	3781	212	17.5	81.6	0.9	72.2
28 Espanola	5834	21.9	14291	6385	2.7	88.0	9.3	80.4
29 Estancia	620	20.8	7621	738	10.6	87.4	2.0	68.8
30 Eunice	735	20.2	112751	1212	95.1	4.0	0.9	0.0
31 Farmington	6800	22.8	70392	6449	10.9	85.6	3.5	80.3
32 Floyd	180	14.0	2538	330	7.9	91.2	0.9	78.8
33 Ft. Sumner	486	18.0	9191	586	15.0	84.0	1.0	68.9
34 Gadsden	4743	21.9	42813	4465	10.6	87.6	1.8	79.4
35 Gallup	12208	20.5	89010	12208	7.5	58.0	34.5	48.5
36 Grady	137	12.2	3734	293	12.2	84.0	3.8	66.6
37 Grants	5083	21.6	41740	4870	8.1	83.3	8.6	74.0
38 Hagerman	412	15.3	5077	628	8.4	89.3	2.3	80.6
39 Hatch Valley	951	21.0	7022	1010	7.9	89.8	2.3	84.0
40 Hobbs	7283	21.9	139062	7492	19.2	79.6	1.2	74.0
41 Hondo Valley	230	13.5	4336	401	11.0	87.8	1.2	74.1
42 House	90	9.2	2219	197	10.2	87.8	2.0	70.6
43 Jal	755	19.4	73183	1048	76.4	22.4	1.2	17.3
44 Jemez Mtn.	541	14.8	32508	820	43.8	46.6	9.6	27.1

DISTRICT	1975-76 40-Day Average Daily Membership	1972-77 Average Pupil-Teacher Ratio (grades 1-12 per FTE)	1975 Assessed Valuation of Property ($ 000's)	1975-76 Operating Funds ($ 000's)	1975-76 Local Income (% of Operating Fund)	1975-76 State Income (% of Operating Fund)	1975-76 Federal Income (% of Operating Fund)	1975-76 State Equalization Guarantee Income (%)
45 Jemez Springs	561	17.1	22819	631	36.0	37.9	26.1	25.7
46 Lake Arthur	191	11.7	6037	348	19.4	79.0	1.6	70.7
47 Las Cruces	15327	22.4	120088	14990	8.2	86.1	5.7	79.9
48 Las Vegas City	2438	20.4	21269	2683	8.5	89.1	2.4	82.5
49 Las Vegas Town	2867	20.2	16964	3586	4.7	93.8	1.5	74.3
50 Logan	194	13.1	2491	357	6.2	92.7	1.1	79.6
51 Lordsburg	1218	20.2	16068	1326	11.4	87.6	1.0	76.9
52 Los Alamos	4636	19.1	48850	7344	10.3	40.8	48.9	36.9
53 Los Lunas	3563	23.6	26560	3352	8.7	84.9	6.4	76.3
54 Loving	375	18.3	5302	416	15.0	81.2	3.8	75.5
55 Lovington	2869	21.0	140166	3270	42.4	57.0	0.6	50.2
56 Magdalena	628	19.6	4252	646	7.0	63.0	30.0	57.4
57 Maxwell	146	11.8	1588	267	6.0	93.3	0.7	85.8
58 Melrose	291	16.4	6876	457	14.0	83.6	2.4	68.9
59 Mora	971	18.0	3790	1215	4.4	88.0	7.6	76.6
60 Moriarity	924	19.0	9922	1386	7.7	90.3	2.0	56.0
61 Mosquero	107	8.7	2906	236	11.7	86.7	1.6	73.7
62 Mountainair	409	17.2	6686	532	13.8	81.6	4.6	68.8
63 Ojo Caliente	575	19.5	9555	751	14.4	82.0	3.6	66.7
64 Pecos	790	18.8	3465	914	5.8	91.5	2.7	82.2
65 Penasco	822	19.8	1996	935	2.3	93.3	4.4	79.0
66 Pojoaque	1295	22.7	5289	1420	4.8	82.0	13.2	73.1
67 Portales	2567	20.7	19229	2808	6.8	90.9	2.3	82.3
68 Quemado	206	14.2	7351	411	17.0	74.5	8.5	57.7
69 Questa	955	19.5	19291	1062	19.4	79.1	1.5	71.2
70 Raton	1860	19.9	12822	1929	7.3	90.9	1.8	85.7
71 Reserve	365	18.6	7757	488	17.2	67.6	15.2	55.5
72 Roswell	9632	22.8	88071	768	9.9	87.5	2.6	81.9
73 Roy	152	12.4	2082	296	7.5	90.4	2.1	78.0
74 Ruidoso	1200	22.4	26196	1282	18.4	77.2	4.4	69.7
75 San Jon	132	10.8	3514	320	11.3	87.3	1.4	67.2
76 Santa Fe	11672	21.7	155729	11622	11.0	86.5	2.5	80.0
77 Santa Rosa	1020	18.5	10961	1180	8.8	90.4	0.8	78.6
78 Silver City	3359	20.5	98343	3618	23.8	73.6	1.0	65.3
79 Socorro	1949	21.0	14964	2475	6.6	90.0	3.4	68.4
80 Springer	605	19.4	5053	1182	5.0	94.2	0.8	49.9
81 T. or C.	1567	20.7	20899	1715	12.0	86.2	1.8	76.
82 Taos	3326	22.3	18513	3453	6.1	89.0	4.9	82.
83 Tatum	425	16.4	49026	706	69.3	29.6	1.1	17.
84 Texico	432	16.7	7171	604	11.2	87.6	1.2	83.
85 Tucumcari	2069	21.0	18008	2112	8.5	90.4	1.1	83.
86 Tularosa	1484	20.1	5157	1539	4.3	71.6	24.1	65.
87 Vaughn	226	17.2	4161	341	11.7	87.1	1.2	82.
88 Wagon Mound	248	13.4	3027	419	7.7	87.8	4.5	77.
NEW MEXICO	270885	21.8		290540	13.2	78.6	8.1	70.

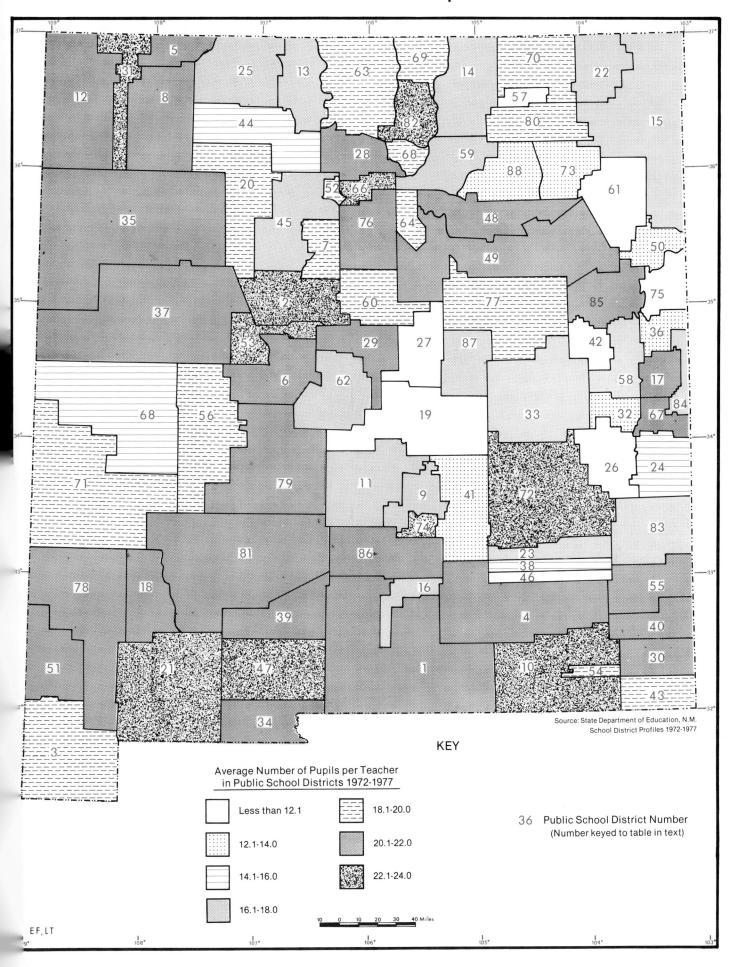

Source: State Department of Education, N.M.
School District Profiles 1972-1977

KEY

Average Number of Pupils per Teacher
in Public School Districts 1972-1977

Less than 12.1

12.1-14.0

14.1-16.0

16.1-18.0

18.1-20.0

20.1-22.0

22.1-24.0

36   Public School District Number
(Number keyed to table in text)

10   0   10   20   30   40 Miles

E F, LT

higher education

Institutes of higher education are those facilities within the state that provide formal post-secondary training with either an academic emphasis or a mix between academic and trade-skill development. Post-secondary school opportunities offered by institutions such as beauty colleges or business schools have not been included in this survey. Although such colleges and schools provide valuable occupational skills, their programs are normally short-term (less than one year), enrollments fluctuate greatly, and statistics are very difficult to obtain. Only those institutes listed by the National Center of Educational Statistics are included in this report.

Approximately 66,000 people attended higher education facilities in New Mexico during the 1977–1978 school year. Over half of these attended the two oldest state-supported institutions: the University of New Mexico (UNM) and New Mexico State University (NMSU). Although many of their functions have converged, NMSU remains a land grant college with emphasis on agriculture, engineering, and applied fields; whereas UNM emphasizes liberal arts, fine arts, graduate study, medicine, and law. The three small state universities offer liberal arts programs and attract students primarily from the region in which they are located. New Mexico Highlands draws heavily from the northeast,

Eastern New Mexico recruits students from the high plains of eastern New Mexico and western Texas, and Western New Mexico has a high enrollment from the southern and southwestern portions of the state.

All of the private institutions, with the exception of the American Indian Arts Institute, are operated by religious organizations. University of Albuquerque and the College of Santa Fe are owned and operated by the Catholic church and are the only private centers of higher education in New Mexico with enrollments greater than 1000 students. Many of the smaller private colleges experience financial difficulties and are forced out of business. A four-year Baptist College at Artesia was a recent economic failure due to declining enrollment.

Although the Albuquerque Technical-Vocational Institute (T-VI) listed 7,500 students enrolled (third highest enrollment in the state), this figure would be reduced one-half or more if only full-time equivalent (FTE) students were considered. This is true for enrollment figures in nearly all two-year and vocational-technical institutions. Most students in these programs are local residents who are enrolled on a part-time basis.

Jerry L. Williams

TABLE: CHARACTERISTICS OF HIGHER EDUCATION INSTITUTIONS IN NEW MEXICO

Type		Name	Location	Established	Funding	1977-78 Enrollment	Degrees Offered
FOUR YEAR AND GRADUATE INSTITUTIONS	1	University of New Mexico	Albuquerque	1889	State	21,912	Associate/Bachelor/ Masters/Ed. Spec./ Doctorate/Medical/Law
	2	New Mexico State University	Las Cruces	1888	State	11,184	Associate/Bachelor/ Masters/Ed. Spec./ Doctorate
	3	Eastern New Mexico Univ.	Portales	1927	State	3,872	Associate/Bachelor/ Masters/Ed. Spec.
	4	New Mexico Highlands U.	Las Vegas	1893	State	2,055	Associate/Bachelor/ Masters
	5	Western New Mexico Univ.	Silver City	1893	State	1,916	Associate/Bachelor/ Masters
	6	New Mexico Institute of Mines and Technology	Socorro	1889	State	1,066	Bachelor/Masters
	7	Albuquerque University	Albuquerque	1920	Private	2,511	Associate/Bachelor
	8	College of Santa Fe	Santa Fe	1947	Private	1,211	Associate/Bachelor
	9	St. John's College	Santa Fe	1964	Private	280	Bachelor/Masters
	10	College of the Southwest	Hobbs	1956	Private	155	Bachelor
BRANCH CAMPUS	1A	University of New Mexico	Gallup	1968	State	815	Associate
	2A	New Mexico State University	Alamogordo	1958	State	1,009	non-degree
	2B	New Mexico State University	Farmington	1956	State	903	non-degree
	2C	New Mexico State University	Carlsbad	1950	State	485	non-degree
	2D	New Mexico State University	Grants	1968	State	378	non-degree
	3A	Eastern New Mexico Univ.	Clovis	1977	State	----	Associate
	3B	Eastern New Mexico Univ.	Roswell	1958	State	897	Associate
SATELLITE CENTER	1B	University of New Mexico	Los Alamos	1970	State	----	non-degree
	1C	University of New Mexico Graduate Center	Santa Fe	1974	State	----	
	1D	University of New Mexico	Belen	1978	State		
	4A	New Mexico Highlands U.	Taos	1977	ENMU	----	non-degree
TWO-YEAR INSTITUTIONS	11	New Mexico Junior College	Hobbs	1965	State	1,054	Associate
	12	New Mexico Military Institute	Roswell	1891	State	898	Associate
	13	Roswell Community College	Roswell		Local		Professional Certificate
	14	Northern New Mexico Community College	El Rito	1969	State	1,800	Associate/Prof. Certificate
	15	Institute of American Indian Arts	Santa Fe	1962	Private	224	Associate
TECHNICAL-VOCATIONAL INSTITUTES	16	San Juan Technical-Vocational	Farmington	--	State	See NMSU #2B	Proficiency Certificate
	17	Luna Vocational-Technical Institute	Las Vegas	1967	State/Local	730	Proficiency Certificate
	18	High Plains Vocational Institute	Clovis	--	State	----	Proficiency Certificate
	19	Southeast Vocational	Hobbs		State	See NMJC #11	Proficiency Certificate
	20	Albuquerque T-VI	Albuquerque	1965	State/Local	7,500	Proficiency Certificate
BRANCH OF VOCATIONAL-TECHNICAL TWO-YEAR INSTITUTES	14A	Northern New Mexico Community College	Espanola	--	NNMCC	included in 14	Certificate
	14B	Northern New Mexico Community College	Santa Cruz	--	NNMCC	included in 14	Certificate
	17A	Luna Vocational-Technical Institute	Springer	1977	LUNA	included in 17	non-degree

Source: *N.C.E.S.* (Natl. Center of Educational Statistics) *Education Directory,* "Colleges and Universities: 1977-1978."

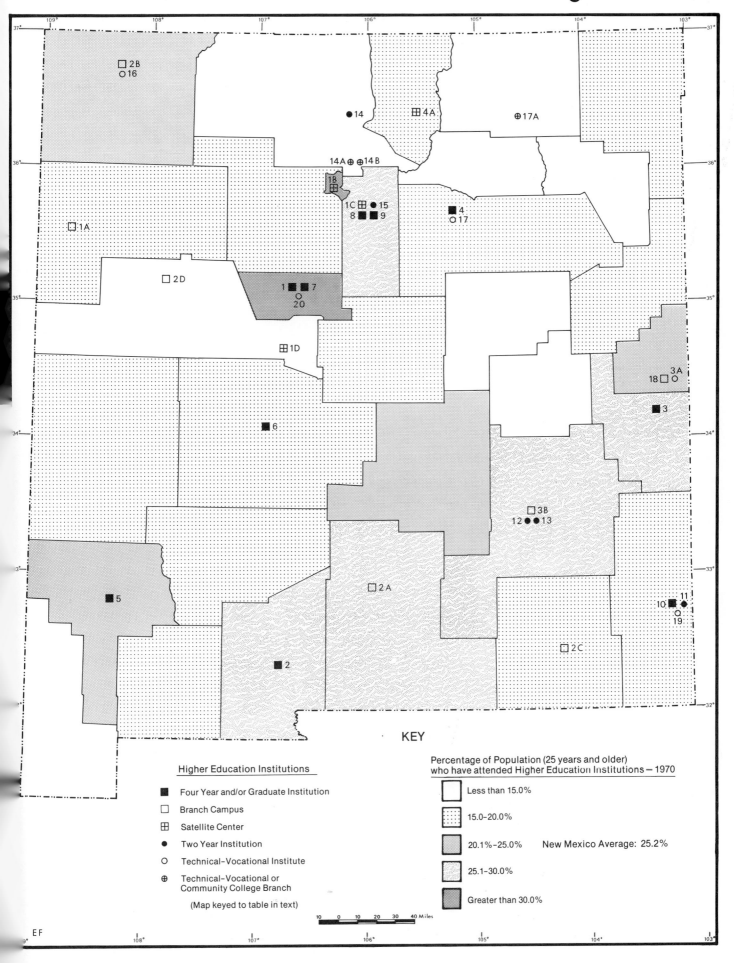

KEY

Higher Education Institutions

■ Four Year and/or Graduate Institution

□ Branch Campus

⊞ Satellite Center

● Two Year Institution

○ Technical-Vocational Institute

⊕ Technical-Vocational or
   Community College Branch

(Map keyed to table in text)

Percentage of Population (25 years and older)
who have attended Higher Education Institutions – 1970

☐ Less than 15.0%

15.0–20.0%

20.1%–25.0%   New Mexico Average: 25.2%

25.1–30.0%

Greater than 30.0%

10   0   10   20   30   40 Miles

E F

urbanization

The 1970 census revealed New Mexico to be a predominantly urbanized state. Nearly 70% of the population lived in an urban place and 26% lived in rural areas but were not classified as farmers. The census defined the urban population as all persons living in places of 2500 inhabitants or more, a broader definition than found in censuses prior to 1950 when only incorporated places greater than 2500 inhabitants were classified as urban. Since 1920 the rural population has been subdivided into farm and non-farm residents. Rural farm residents were classified in 1960 and 1970 as persons living on places of ten acres or more from which sales of farm products were $50 or more during the year preceding the census. A place of less than ten acres outside the urban area could also be classified as rural farm if the sale of farm products exceeded $250 during the year preceding the census. Rural non-farm residents were persons in rural territory who did not live in areas the census defined as farms. Prior to 1960 the census definition of farm and non-farm varied in each report with the probability that the 1920–1950 statistics slightly inflate the size of the farm population.

Less than 40,000 New Mexicans were classified as rural farmers in 1970 with over 30% of these farmers in San Juan (5102), Doña Ana (3817), Roosevelt (3037) and Chaves (2517) counties. The three counties with a high proportion of rural farmers (Catron, Harding, and Union) also had a population density of less than one per square mile with most of the farmers dispersed on large cattle ranches. A much greater number of non-urban counties had a high proportion of rural non-farm population economically dependent on commuting to an urban place for employment. Some non-farm residents were also employed in the local county by federal and state agencies such as the Forest Service and Highway Department or by the utility companies and mining corporations.

Most of the counties have a dominant urban center, with the Albuquerque metropolitan county of Bernalillo influencing the urban and non-farm statistics of neighboring Sandoval, Valencia, and Torrance counties. Other urban places usually dominate only the county in which they are located and most contain over 50% of the county's population. Albuquerque has been the leading urban area of the state since 1900, a result of the railway workshops that located there and the commercial development that followed. Prior to the turn of the century Santa Fe had been the major urban center of the Southwest, but the bypassing of the railroad brought a decline to the economic importance of the former territorial capital. The railroad was also instrumental in the rapid growth of several gateway towns and coal centers during the first quarter of the twentieth century (Gallup, Raton, Clovis, and Las Vegas). In the 1920's mineral resource towns (Santa Rita, Dawson, and Tyrone) blossomed into the ranks of the ten largest cities, but the most rapid climb in the ranks occurred in the 1940's with the entry of the oil boom-town of Hobbs.

Since 1940 little change has happened in the rankings with the exception of Roswell's decline with the closing of the Air Force base in 1967 and the growth of Las Cruces through the economic impact of the nearby White Sands Missile Range in the 1950's. Most significant has been the rapid increase in the size of Albuquerque between 1940 and 1960 when the city far outstripped the growth of any other centers in the state. Since 1960 the rate of increase has lowered somewhat, but with the enormous base of population relative to the rest of the state, a small percentage increase in the growth of Albuquerque has a much greater impact on New Mexico than a larger growth rate anywhere else.

The recent trend of population increase in the state has been called the "sunbelt migration" and consists mainly of people moving into the state from Texas and California or escaping the climate and energy economics of the north. This has brought a rapid 1970–1975 increase in the growth of the southern border towns such as Deming (+26.0%) and Lordsburg (+20.2%), and population booms to resort towns such as Ruidoso (+55.3%). Other cities have increased as commuter satellites of metropolitan areas (Belen, +20.8%) and as new energy resource centers (Farmington, +26.5%). At the same time, cities of a former resource era in the eastern portion of the state continue to decline (Artesia, −1.1%; Eunice, −5.0%; and Portales, −2.0%) as the economic focus is shifted elsewhere.

Jerry L. Williams

Rank Order of Urban Places

1880		1900		1920		1940	
1 Santa Fe	6635	1 Albuquerque	6238	1 Albuquerque	15157	1 Albuquerque	35449
2 Albuquerque	2315	2 Santa Fe	5603	2 Santa Fe	7236	2 Santa Fe	20325
3 Silver City	1800	3 Las Vegas City	3574	3 Roswell	7033	3 Roswell	13482
4 Socorro	1272	4 Raton	3540	4 Raton	5410	4 Hobbs	10619
5 Bernalillo	1223	5 Gallup	2946	5 Clovis	4904	5 Clovis	10065
6 Mora	915	6 Las Cruces	2806	6 Las Vegas City	4318	6 Las Cruces	8385
7 Los Lunas	876	7 Silver City	2735	7 Tyrone (Grant)	4064	7 Raton	7607
8 Ranchos de Atrisco	740	8 Roswell	2049	8 Dawson (Colfax)	4010	8 Carlsbad	7116
9 Corrales	664	9 Santa Rita (Grant)	1874	9 Las Cruces	3969	9 Gallup	7041
10 Lincoln	638	10 Alamogordo	1524	10 Las Vegas Town	3902	10 Las Vegas Town	6421

1950		1960		1970 > 10,000		1975 > 10,000		Area Sq Mi
1 Albuquerque	96815	1 Albuquerque	201189	1 Albuquerque	243751	1 Albuquerque	279401	88.7
2 Santa Fe	27998	2 Roswell	39593	2 Santa Fe	41167	2 Santa Fe	44937	29.9
3 Roswell	25738	3 Santa Fe	33394	3 Las Cruces	37857	3 Las Cruces	40336	18.9
4 Carlsbad	17975	4 Las Cruces	29367	4 Roswell	33908	4 Roswell	37980	25.2
5 Clovis	17318	5 Hobbs	26275	5 Clovis	28495	5 Clovis	31734	13.5
6 Hobbs	13875	6 Carlsbad	25541	6 Hobbs	26025	6 Farmington	27802	8.1
7 Las Cruces	12325	7 Farmington	23786	7 Alamogordo	23035	7 Hobbs	27660	16.6
8 Los Alamos	9934	8 Clovis	23713	8 Farmington	21979	8 Alamogordo	23535	12.3
9 Gallup	9133	9 Alamogordo	21723	9 Carlsbad	21297	9 Carlsbad	22955	12.6
10 Tucumcari	8419	10 Gallup	14089	10 Gallup	14496	10 Gallup	16948	8.1
				11 Las Vegas	13835	11 Las Vegas	15101	3.2
				12 Los Alamos	11310	12 Los Alamos	11340	13.1
				13 Portales	10554	13 Deming	10511	3.9
				14 Artesia	10315	14 Portales	10399	4.5
						15 Artesia	10195	3.5

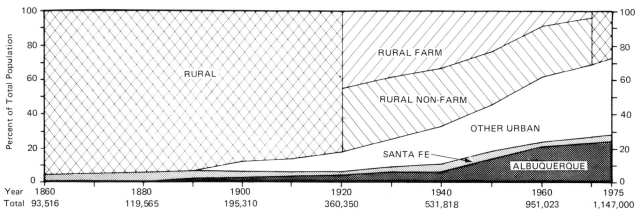

RURAL-URBAN POPULATION DISTRIBUTION: 1860-1975

Year	1860	1880	1900	1920	1940	1960	1975
Total	93,516	119,565	195,310	360,350	531,818	951,023	1,147,000

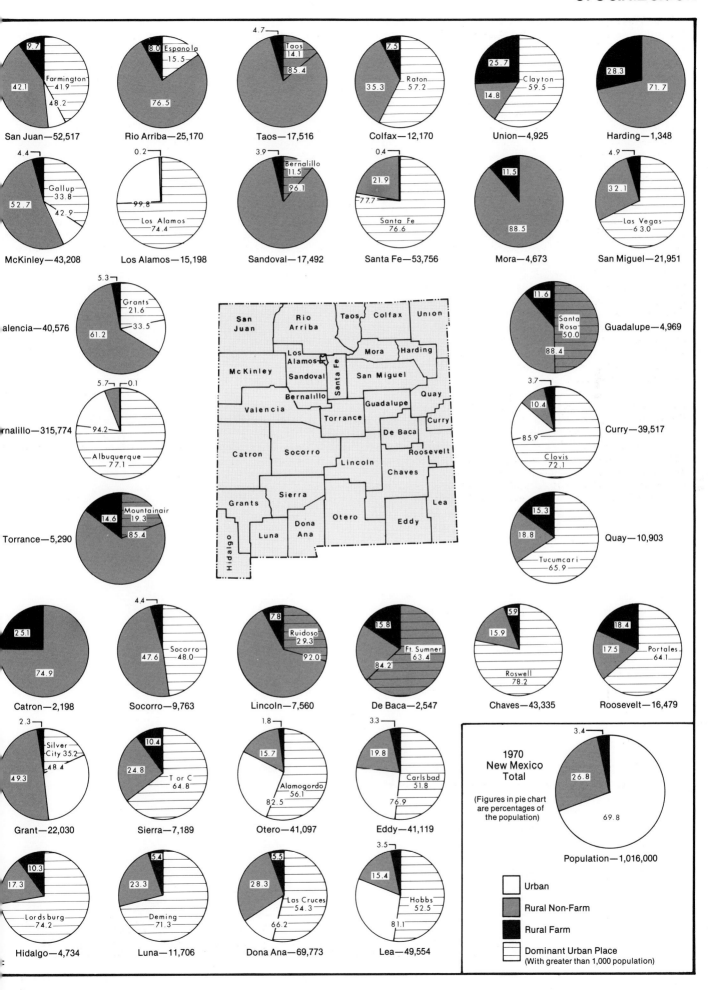

9.7 / 42.1 / 48.2 — Farmington—41.9
San Juan—52,517

8.0 / 76.5 — Espanola—15.5
Rio Arriba—25,170

4.7 / 85.4 — Taos—14.1
Taos—17,516

7.5 / 35.3 — Raton—57.2
Colfax—12,170

25.7 / 14.8 — Clayton—59.5
Union—4,925

28.3 / 71.7
Harding—1,348

4.4 / 52.7 / 42.9 — Gallup—33.8
McKinley—43,208

0.2 / 99.8 — Los Alamos—74.4
Los Alamos—15,198

3.9 / 11.5 / 96.1 — Bernalillo
Sandoval—17,492

0.4 / 21.9 / 77.7 — Santa Fe—76.6
Santa Fe—53,756

11.5 / 88.5
Mora—4,673

4.9 / 32.1 — Las Vegas—63.0
San Miguel—21,951

5.3 / 61.2 / 33.5 — Grants—21.6
Valencia—40,576

5.7 / 0.1 / 94.2 — Albuquerque—77.1
Bernalillo—315,774

14.6 / 85.4 — Mountainair—19.3
Torrance—5,290

11.6 / 88.4 — Santa Rosa—50.0
Guadalupe—4,969

3.7 / 10.4 / 85.9 — Clovis—72.1
Curry—39,517

15.3 / 18.8 — Tucumcari—65.9
Quay—10,903

25.1 / 74.9
Catron—2,198

4.4 / 47.6 — Socorro—48.0
Socorro—9,763

7.8 / 92.0 — Ruidoso—29.3
Lincoln—7,560

15.8 / 84.2 — Ft. Sumner—63.4
De Baca—2,547

5.9 / 15.9 / 78.2 — Roswell
Chaves—43,335

18.4 / 17.5 — Portales—64.1
Roosevelt—16,479

2.3 / 49.3 — Silver City 35.2 / 48.4
Grant—22,030

10.4 / 24.8 — T or C—64.8
Sierra—7,189

1.8 / 15.7 / 82.5 — Alamogordo—56.1
Otero—41,097

3.3 / 19.8 / 76.9 — Carlsbad—51.8
Eddy—41,119

10.3 / 17.3 — Lordsburg—74.2
Hidalgo—4,734

5.4 / 23.3 — Deming—71.3
Luna—11,706

5.5 / 28.3 / 66.2 — Las Cruces—54.3
Dona Ana—69,773

3.5 / 15.4 / 81.1 — Hobbs—52.5
Lea—49,554

1970
New Mexico
Total

(Figures in pie chart
are percentages of
the population)

3.4 / 26.8 / 69.8

Population—1,016,000

☐ Urban
▨ Rural Non-Farm
■ Rural Farm
☐ Dominant Urban Place
(With greater than 1,000 population)

service centers

One way to view the settlement pattern of New Mexico is by a classification system that establishes the relative importance of places within a regional or state-wide network of service centers. A service center is a reflection of population, the local economic base, and site characteristics measured by the degree of accessibility and position relative to competing centers.

Population alone is a misleading indicator of the importance of an area. *Estancia,* a town of approximately 850 people in the rangeland of Torrance County, provides many more services than *Alameda,* a settlement with eight times the population size, located on the northern periphery of Albuquerque. A high-order center may stimulate residential growth in a nearby town without the addition of services, and may be responsible for usurping functions from nearby centers, retarding their population growth.

The adjoining chart identifies a standard method for classifying service centers. The services represent education, health, finance, transportation, communication, and retailing functions. These are not all the services performed in a center, nor necessarily the most common. However they establish relative measures of importance for communities within a regional and state-wide framework.

There are seven types of service centers. The requirements for a *Minimum Service Center* are a post office and a nucleus of 50 people. Also expected are services with a high frequency of demand, including: one or more churches, gas stations, grocery stores, taverns, and perhaps an elementary school. A *Partial Service Center* requires the minimum service criteria, plus two of the following less frequently demanded services: a bank, a high school, and a mortuary. A *Local Service Center* provides the functions of a partial service center with the addition of three of the following: a daily or weekly newspaper, a doctor, a new car dealer, and a public library. A *Community Service Center* requires the functions of a local service center, a level of 12.5 million dollars of annual retail sales, plus two of the following: a hospital, radio station, and airport with hard surface runway. A *Regional Service Center* encompasses the functions of a community service center, has a minimum of 31 million dollars in annual retail trade, and two of the following: a higher education facility, a daily newspaper, and scheduled air service. A *Metropolitan Service Center* differs from a regional service center in that it must have a minimum of 125 million dollars of annual retail sales. A *National Service Center* must have a minimum of one billion dollars of annual retail trade.

Albuquerque, with 1.4 billion dollars of retail sales in 1977, is the only first order (national) center in New Mexico. The six second order (metropolitan) centers are well distributed throughout the state, and, with the exception of Santa Fe, are more than 100 miles from the national center. Farmington, Gallup, and Hobbs have expanded rapidly in size and function over the past decade as resource centers of coal, oil, natural gas, and uranium. Roswell and Las Cruces have evolved as the dominant trade and population centers of the lower Pecos and Rio Grande valleys, respectively. Las Cruces has become a major center in spite of being in the shadow of the national center of El Paso, Texas. Santa Fe owes much of its functional importance as a service center to the income and population associated with state government employment. The combined 1977 retail trade of the six metropolitan centers, which ranged from 224 million dollars at Santa Fe to 141 million dollars at Roswell, was only approximately two-thirds of the retail trade of Albuquerque.

Markets of the six third order (regional) service centers can be found within the intervening spaces between first and second order service centers or in areas isolated by a physical barrier from the higher order centers. Silver City clearly dominates the service functions for a large isolated portion in the southwestern corner of the state, as does Las Vegas for the broad expanse of the northeast. Alamagordo, which nearly meets the retail criteria to be classified metropolitan, is the dominant service center of the Tularosa Valley. The proximity of Clovis ($116 million) to Portales ($33 million) and the retail competition between them has significantly reduced the dominance of either center in the eastern plains region. There are thirteen fourth order (community) service centers that provide for the needs of much smaller market areas (although distances may range far in lightly populated areas such as the northeast and southwest).

Only eight settlements were classified as fifth order (local) service centers. Most of these (Aztec, Clayton, Estancia, Ft. Sumner, Santa Rosa, and Lordsburg) were possibly elevated to this status by their selection as the site of the county seat. Sixth order (partial) service centers usually indicated the presence of a high school and a bank. Mortuaries, which are lesser-demanded services, are rarely found below the fourth order center in New Mexico. Thirty-six sites were classified as partial service centers. The remaining one hundred eighty-three seventh order (minimum) centers are found dispersed along highways and river valleys or concentrated as numerous small villages in the north-central region of the state.

Jerry L. Williams

SERVICE	symbol	Population of at least 50	Post Office	Bank	High School	Mortuary	Newspaper	Medical Doctor	New Car Dealer	Public Library	$12.5 million in retail sales (1977)	Hospital	Radio Station	Airport—Hard Surface	$31 million in retail sales (1977)	Institute of Higher Education	Daily Newspaper	Scheduled Air Service	$125 million in retail sales (1977)	$1 billion in retail sales (1977)
Minimum	●			2 out of 3			3 out of 4													
Partial	⊖											2 out of 3				2 out of 3				
Local	⊕																			
Community	◉																			
Regional	◉																			
Metropolitan	◎																			
National	✪																			

Source: *Trade Centers and Trade Areas of the Upper Midwest,* Borchert and Adams, 1963.

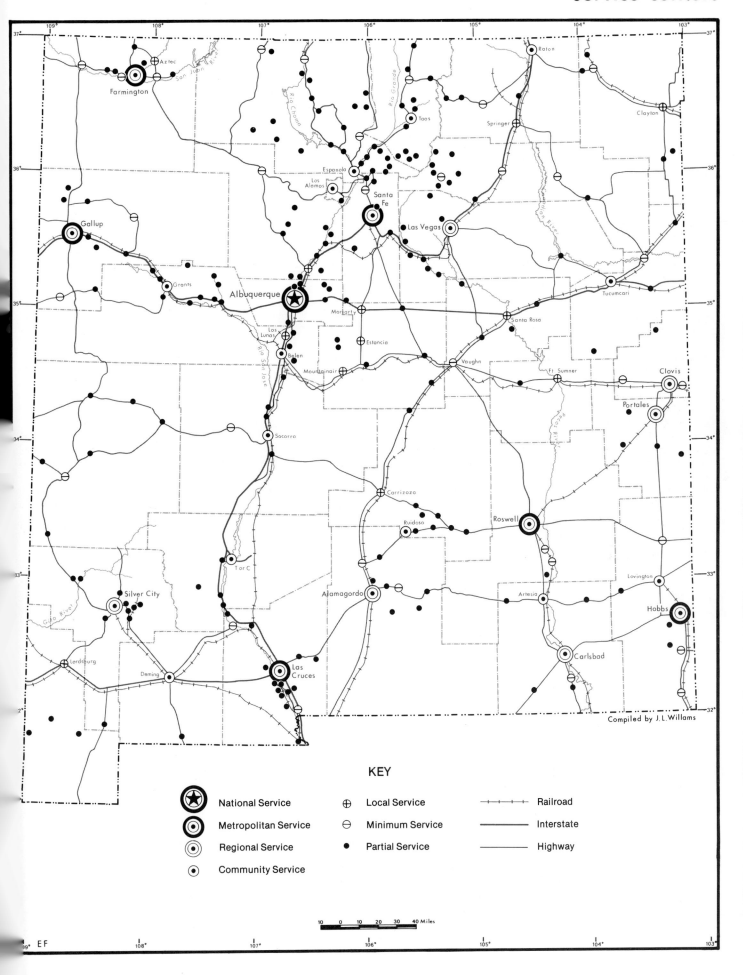

Compiled by J.L.Willams

KEY

Symbol	Service	Symbol	Service	Symbol	Type
★	National Service	⊕	Local Service	┼┼┼┼	Railroad
◉	Metropolitan Service	⊖	Minimum Service	━━━	Interstate
⊙	Regional Service	●	Partial Service	───	Highway
⊙	Community Service				

10 0   10   20   30   40 Miles

urban area: albuquerque

The original settlement of Albuquerque (San Felipe de Neri de Albuquerque) was settled in the early eighteenth century (1705–1710) on a depositional mound along the east bank of the Rio Grande. Surrounded by a broad, arable plain, the site (area A) was located near a good fording place in the river. By 1750 this village consisted of 300 non-Indians in 20 to 30 residential units, with their field patterns radiating outward.

The first Mexican census in 1823 reported a population in Albuquerque of about 2500, including 400 farmers. Fifteen merchants were established by 1830, focusing trade activity first with the freight wagons to Chihuahua, Mexico, and later with caravan travelers to the west coast. The Atlantic and Pacific Railroad reached Albuquerque in 1880 and selected a route along the eastern edge of the floodplain, approximately one and one-half miles from the San Felipe town plaza and the Bernalillo County courthouse. A new town 35 block-grid was platted west from the railroad line in the low lying former river channel (area B). The railroad constructed its largest on-line workshops south of the newly-surveyed town site, creating such an economic impetus that the city center shifted from the river site to the more flood prone location on the eastern edge of the floodplain. The county offices in Old Town and the railroad depots of New Town, separated by agricultural land, were joined in the 1880's by a mule-drawn street railway along Railroad Avenue (later named Central Avenue). Ribbons of commerce grew along the axes formed by the railroad and Central Avenue and land values near this junction skyrocketed. By 1898 the population of New Town was 6,000 with residential areas located south of the commercial center along Central and east of the railroad along the low terraces of the east mesa. The urban area of the mid-Rio Grande in 1900 contained a population of approximately 15,000.

By the time New Mexico attained statehood in 1912, Albuquerque had become a railroad boom-town and had expanded eastward onto the gently sloping mesa between the railroad line and the Sandia Mountains. A Coal Avenue viaduct had been constructed over the tracks and a streetcar system connected the valley centers to the University of New Mexico (built on an isolated edge of the east mesa). Between World War I and World War II Albuquerque began to fill the empty areas between the older residential locations, as well as along the major roads leading into the city. The focus of new expansion in the 1920's was the auto-oriented development along 4th Street and Central Avenue, designated as national highways 85 and 66 respectively.

The federal government contributed to the easterly orientation of growth when the WPA constructed the Central Avenue and Tijeras underpasses beneath the railroad in the 1930's. Also developed were new facilities such as an airport terminal south of the university and Indian and Veterans hospitals along Lomas and Gibson respectively. By 1940, the urban area (area C) had expanded to the edge of the new State Fairgrounds (which replaced the old Territorial Fairgrounds near Old Town) on the east mesa at Central and Louisiana, and northward to the area of the Indian School. Old Town remained a separate center until 1945 when it was annexed to the rapidly expanding commercial area of New Town.

After World War II, commercial ribbons along major streets and subdivision housing tracts began to grow north and south of Central Avenue. The first suburban shopping center appeared in the early 1950's at Nob Hill on Central Avenue (east of the university campus) representing the initial east mesa competition to downtown services. In the 1950's developers established a road system on the east mesa based on township and range survey sections (one mile square) with a grid of east-west arterials (Gibson, Lomas, Indian School, Candelaria, and Montgomery) joined by north-south feeder-routes (San Mateo, Louisiana, Wyoming, Eubank, Juan Tabo). This network stimulated the development of detached single family housing subdivisions over much of the east mesa. The population shift was shortly followed by commerce (Winrock-Coronado super-regional malls), high-rise office centers, and industrial parks. The former city center near the railroad was left without an identifiable focus save government services and banking facilities.

By the mid-1970's, the urbanized area (area D) of Albuquerque (with an estimated population of 350,000) had approached its eastern limit of expansion as constrained by the federal government in the forms of Cibola National Forest, Sandia Indian Reservation, and Sandia-Kirtland Military Reservation. Therefore the focus of growth shifted northward into Albuquerque Acres on the east mesa, and Los Ranchos de Albuquerque and Corrales in the valley. Although the south valley experienced much infill from small subdivisions, this area could be termed "slow-growth" relative to the eastward and northward expansion. The western terraces of the Rio Grande and the barren west mesa received very little development attention until the 1960's. One of the first nodes was the development on the northern portion of the west mesa, as were smaller subdivisions at Paradise Hills, Taylor Ranch, Volcano Cliffs, and Westgate Heights. These developments may eventually be joined in a continuous belt west of the Rio Grande.

Although Albuquerque appears to be nearing its limit of horizontal expansion, a 1977 survey indicated there are almost 23,000 acres of vacant land within the established urban area and more than 31,000 vacant acres in the peripheral areas (identified in the 1977 Comprehensive Plan as the east slope of the west mesa, North Albuquerque Acres, the north valley, and part of the south valley).

Future expansion of the urban area is limited by environmental constraints such as water supply and automobile emissions. Water for Albuquerque is supplied from a large mid-Rio Grande aquifer that has been estimated as a satisfactory supply for a population range as low as 200,000 and as much as 1,000,000. Yet questions have arisen about the pumping costs to supply water to the newer residential areas on distant and higher elevations and the possible salinity of the entire water supply as the water table lowers and sulfur-saline water is siphoned into the aquifer.

The urban area is auto-oriented: nearly two vehicles are registered to each adult in Bernalillo County, who drives an average of 33 miles daily. Carbon monoxide has contributed enormously to the smog of the mid-Rio Grande Valley. With development of the west mesa, the increase in auto emissions may be even more hazardous to the health of the population and serve as an unattractive element of Albuquerque to visitors or potential residents.

Jerry L. Williams

100

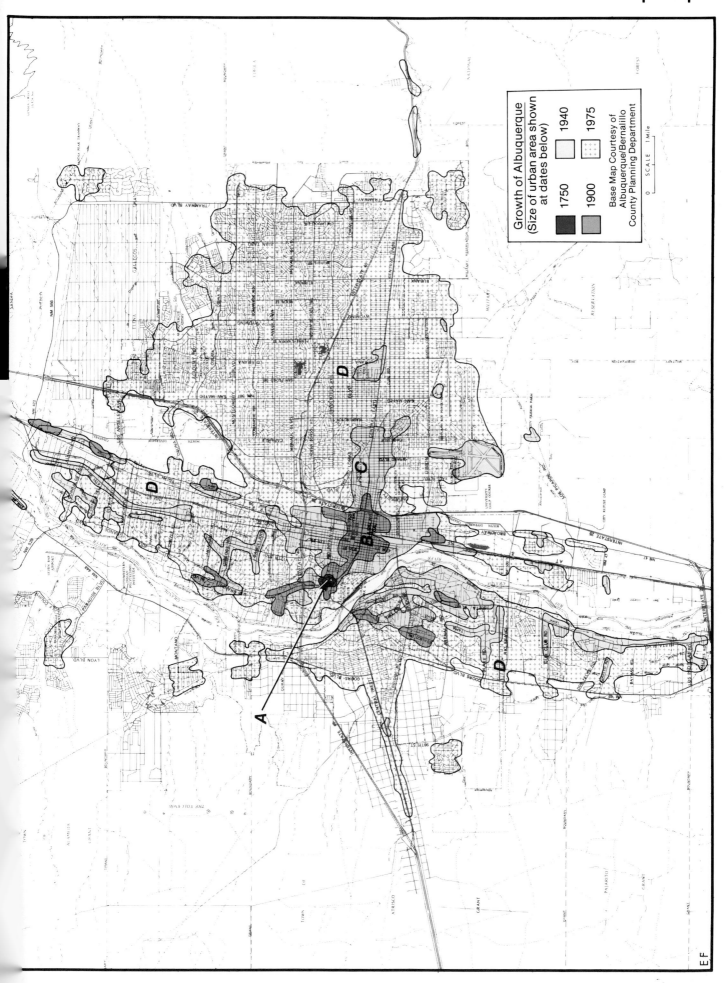

Growth of Albuquerque
(Size of urban area shown
at dates below)

1750   1940

1900   1975

Base Map Courtesy of
Albuquerque/Bernalillo
County Planning Department

0   SCALE   1 Mile

urban area: farmington

In 1876, William Hendrickson led a small party of pioneers from Animas City, Colorado to an area near the confluence of the Animas and San Juan rivers. The dispersed farmsteads of these early pioneers staked out along the floodplain east of the Animas River represented the first white settlement in the area of present-day San Juan County. The only evidence of the previous residents of the same area were the ruins of the kivas (ceremonial rooms) and structures of the Anasazi Indians (the old ones) which were still visible in the late 19th century. Indian settlement in the San Juan Basin dates back several thousand years. The region is thought to be the early hearth of the modern Pueblo Indian people who presently reside along the Rio Grande and San Jose river valleys in the center of the state. The earliest historical reference of the San Juan River was by Juan Maria de Rivera in 1765 when he was lured to the region from Santa Fe by rumor of rich mineral deposits. He did recognize the area to be a favorable 'wet' route connecting Santa Fe with the coastal settlement of San Gabriel, California.

Homesteading on 160-acre tracts began in the San Juan region in 1880, and as the population began to increase, a small commercial service center evolved on a river terrace north of the mouth of the Animas River. The center of this new cluster was near the present junction of Orchard Avenue and Main Street. The name Farmingtown (shortened at a later date) was an obvious selection during this time as the townsite was completely surrounded with irrigation ditches, farms, and an intensively cultivated flood plain. An 1881 map filed with the office of the surveyor general indicated there were fifteen structures in the town, aligned in an east–west direction. The prominent buildings of that time were a school built in 1877 and a fourteen-room house, both located along Main Street. The large house served as a rooming facility and in 1881 became the first unofficial postal station of Farmington. Mail arrived by wagon along the Togay Trail, a freight and mail route connecting Fort Wingate (first located near Grants and later near Gallup) and Fort Lewis, Colorado (Durango). In 1886, the first official post office was located in a new building along Main Street.

San Juan County was formed from Rio Arriba County in 1887, and there began immediate competition between Farmington, Junction City, Largo, and Mesa City for the location of the new courthouse. Farmington was expected to receive the honor. With several hundred residents it had grown to be the largest settlement in the San Juan Basin. A committee was sent from Santa Fe to select the site for the county seat. The group first visited Aztec and in response to the graciousness of their host (and probably some financial arrangements) the committee returned to Santa Fe without visiting any of the other sites. Aztec was selected for the courthouse and the competing towns immediately filed suit. The territorial court ordered an election to take place to decide the site and Junction City, a former town across the Animas River from Farmington, won the contest. The county seat was "officially" located across the river from Farmington for approximately one year. In 1892 the Supreme Court ordered the county records back to Aztec. During the year the county seat was in Junction City, the first San Juan County fair was held at a farm three miles east of Farmington. Although the economic value of being the center of county government was denied the largest town of the area, the county fair continued to be held in Farmington at a permanent site one-half mile south of Main Street along the Animas River.

By the turn of the century Farmington had more than 500 residents and expanded its services to include several saloons, a drug store, doctor, several mercantile companies, a butchery, a hotel, a public bath and barber shop, and a boarding house facing a plaza at the east end of Main Street. The school, relocated in a two-story brick building on a hill above Main Street, became a landmark of the town. A Navajo Indian mission school was established in 1891 by the Methodist Church along the San Juan River southwest of town. The flood of 1911 completely destroyed the mission and it was relocated at its present campus style site west of town in 1912.

During the first decade of the 20th century a railroad war was in progress as several railway companies expressed interest in connecting the mining districts of southwestern Colorado with the

agricultural belt of the lower San Juan. From 1902 to 1910, Farmington was crowded with railroad survey teams from the Denver and Rio Grande railroad, the El Paso and Southwestern Company (owned by the Southern Pacific Corporation), the Rock Island Company, and several smaller independents. The first survey, along the Animas River from Farmington to Durango, was completed by the Colorado and Arizona Railway in 1902 and the company received a franchise for a terminal at Farmington. The Denver and Rio Grande built their tracks over the route surveyed by the Colorado and Arizona before the latter company could begin construction. The first train ran from Durango to Farmington in 1905, and in 1909 the Denver and Rio Grande was subjected to a major legal suit over stolen right-of-way. The court decided in favor of the Colorado and Arizona Company and offered to turn over the full service between Durango and Farmington if the railway would continue the line, within ten years, from Farmington to a connection with the Santa Fe railroad line at Gallup. After four years of intensive surveying, the Southern Pacific (parent company of the Colorado and Arizona) lost interest in the long line through the unpopulated area and withdrew. Farmington was served by the narrow-gauge Denver and Rio Grande railroad from 1905 until 1965, when the unprofitable line was discontinued.

Growth of Farmington was very slow during the first half of the present century. By 1950 the population was less than four thousand and barely one-fifth of the county residents lived in the town. Several thousand acres along the San Juan and its tributaries had been opened for homesteading between 1900 and 1920 and the size of the county population increased more rapidly than the size of Farmington. Although less than 10 percent of San Juan County's population lived in the town as late as 1940, it was the dominant commercial and service center of northwestern New Mexico. The low proportion of population living in Farmington could also be attributed to the large number of Navajo and Ute Indians who lived on reservations in San Juan County. The Indian factor, along with the elements that have affected growth since 1950, are reflected in the low percentage of county population still found in Farmington.

The rapid expansion of the city occurred during the 1950's when oil and natural gas fields in the San Juan Basin were developed and the resources piped to refineries at a distant location. Farmington grew by 636 percent in this decade and changed overnight from a small rural farming community to an energy boom town. Unprepared for such an onslaught of people, the settlement expanded chaotically as ribbons of mobile home parks and commercial strips developed. Housing subdivisions covered much of the early agricultural land and reached the top edge of the mesa north of town. As the production level and area of the gasfields expanded Bloomfield (12 miles east of Farmington) and Aztec (14 miles north of Farmington) became places of minor population booms. The river valleys connecting these settlements with Farmington have been urban fringe infill areas since 1960. With acceleration of the population growth rate during the 1970's there appears little doubt that a continuous urban area will evolve from Bloomfield to Aztec with Farmington at the apex.

The discovery of extensive supplies of strippable low-sulfur coal west of Farmington and the construction of massive coal-powered electricity generating stations have made the lower San Juan are one of the largest power producing regions in the world. The employment opportunities created by the mines and power plants have been responsible for much of the present and westward oriented growth of Farmington. The city is expected to spread along the north bank of the San Juan River and eventually encompass the present communities of Kirtland, Fruitland, and Waterflow. Since 1970, the urbanization of the lower San Juan area has been at the expense of agriculture as the demand for housing has encouraged the extension of subdivisions along the floodplains. Farmington and San Juan County planners have not been able to provide services (schools, utilities, security) at a rate comparable with the immigration of people. Overcrowded facilities and chaotic growth appear to be the expected response until the population boom subsides.

Jerry L. William

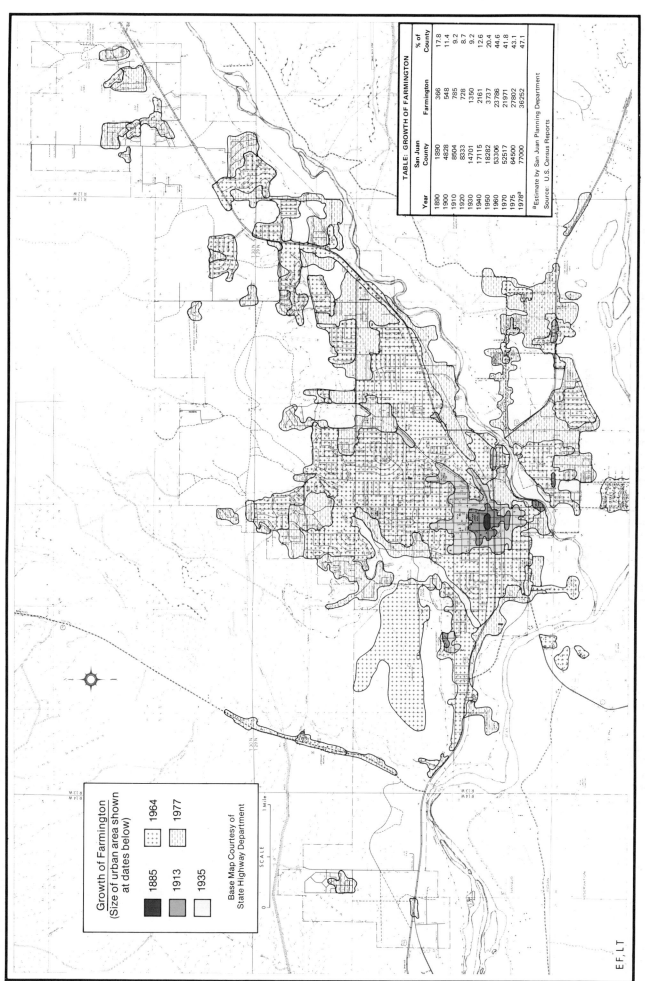

Growth of Farmington
(Size of urban area shown
at dates below)

1885	1964
1913	1977
1935	

Base Map Courtesy of
State Highway Department

SCALE
0   1 Mile

	TABLE: GROWTH OF FARMINGTON		
Year	San Juan County	Farmington	% of County
1890	1890	366	17.8
1900	4828	548	11.4
1910	8504	785	9.2
1920	8333	728	8.7
1930	14701	1350	9.2
1940	17115	2161	12.6
1950	18282	3737	20.4
1960	53306	23786	44.6
1970	52517	21971	41.8
1975	64500	27802	43.1
1978[a]	77000	36252	47.1

[a]Estimate by San Juan Planning Department
Source: U.S. Census Reports

E F, L T

103

urban area: santa fe

Santa Fe is the most familiar New Mexico place name to people of the United States, its name being associated with two famous 19th century transportation systems: the Santa Fe Trail and the Atchison, Topeka, and Santa Fe Railroad. But these two trails and the frontier era only encompass about one-fourth of the history of the settlement.

The original inhabitants on the flatland portion of the Santa Fe River were the Tewa Indians, indicated by artifacts uncovered in present-day excavations throughout Santa Fe. When the Spanish arrived in the 16th century, the Indians were no longer farming in the area and had abandoned their villages. The first Spanish settlement was an unimpressive temporary camp established around 1550. Although it is believed the explorer Juan de Oñate founded a small settlement along the Santa Fe River in 1608, the first official townsite of Santa Fe was constructed in 1610 by Pedro de Peralta, governor of the territory. The Spanish viceroy in Mexico who appointed Peralta as governor in 1609 commissioned him to select a site, build a new capitol, and shift the administrators from the San Gabriel site (near San Juan Pueblo) chosen by Oñate in 1598. The construction of Santa Fe as a capitol city began forty-five years after the founding of the first Spanish city in North America at Saint Augustine, Florida (the nation's oldest city) and ten years before the Pilgrims reached the coast of New England.

The name Santa Fe (holy faith), chosen by Peralta, was probably taken from the name of the famous siege town built by Spain's King Ferdinand and Queen Isabela during the conflict in the late 15th century over Granada. The rulers built a substantial fortified town, called Santa Fe de Granada, planned to resemble a modified grid of the Roman garrison design. The convenience of the plan was so obvious the royalty decreed its design should be duplicated in the construction of all new cities in the Spanish dominions.

The central focus of the city from its beginning on the north bank of the Santa Fe River was a large rectangular open space designated as the main plaza. The grid of streets facing the plaza, the base for a network of parallel streets away from the central square, was important in the early days for locating significant merchants and residents of high status. The prestige of a family was frequently measured by residential location relative to the governor's palace. The most important structure facing the plaza and occupying much of the northern side was the highly fortified office-residential complex called the *Casa Real* or Palace of the Governors. On the west and south sides of the plaza was a town hall and jail (with a gibbet and whipping post) and several important family residences that faced inward toward central courtyards. The first religious structure at Santa Fe was San Miguel mission, built on the south side of the river to serve the Christian Indian servants who lived in an impoverished cluster of small buildings in a settlement called Analco.

The Palace of Governors was the early administrative center for a vast portion of North America. At one time the sovereignty extended as far east as the Mississippi River and west and north to the Pacific Ocean, including San Francisco. An extensive network of trails radiated out of Santa Fe to various outposts in the territory, with the main passage and supply route (the Camino Real) following the Rio Grande southward to Mexico. The palace proved to be a significant fortress during the Pueblo Revolt of 1680 when the Indians reclaimed control of the north central area of New Mexico. The building was the final stronghold of resistance to the Indians and when the water supply was severed, the remaining Spanish people fled the city for refuge in the south at El Paso. Santa Fe became an Indian settlement again for twelve years (1680-1692). For three centuries over one hundred governors and captains-general occupied the seat of the government in the names of Spanish, Mexican, and Confederate or Union Americans.

The heart of Santa Fe was never as attractive as it is today. The plaza, which was the destination of all travellers, was described as one open space of mud and dirt during the Spanish and Mexican periods. The plaza was a congested market place, bazaar, and campground occupied by soldiers, citizens, vehicles, livestock of all kinds, teamsters, Indians, and roustabouts. Many of the occupants were seated around cooking fires that added to the general

haze and odor of the town center. Around 1850, General Kearney of the occupation Army of the West built a street across the plaza, designated walkways, planted trees and alfalfa, and restricted the types of use of the property. By the twentieth century a more permanent park was created in the square. The two-storied commercial structures surrounding the plaza were added around the mid-nineteenth century.

There were an estimated 2000 residents of Santa Fe in 1780 who mainly clustered around the palace, but were also dispersed for seven miles up and down both sides of the Santa Fe River. There were cornfields throughout the town with lanes and paths wandering toward the outlying residences. The streets, designed to handle wagons, were poorly maintained and overcrowded. Practically the entire town was one-story adobe construction until the mid-nineteenth century when the construction of a sawmill and introduction of fired brick changed the architectural style. The railroad lowered the cost of imported materials, and by the beginning of the twentieth century a wide variety of building styles appeared throughout the valley. It is a tribute to the people of Santa Fe that most of these buildings have been preserved until today within a large historic zone. In keeping with the historic flavor of the city, even the new construction throughout the urban area follows either the Spanish-Mexican or early Territorial styles.

Most Americans associate Santa Fe with the Santa Fe Trail (1820-1880) which opened the southwest initially as a trade link with the midwest and later as a destination of immigrants. In 1829 trading companies from Kansas had outposts in the town and trains of freight-laden oxen wagons were operating over the trail. The route entered Santa Fe from the southeast along what is presently highway 85. As commerce and settlers entered the city, so did the brothels, fandangos, and pleasure halls. For most of the Mexican Period (1825-1846) and the early American Territorial Period (1846-1880), Santa Fe was a hell-raising sin spot that attracted numerous outlaws along with the immigrants and prospectors. The only calming influence of the nineteenth century was the arrival of Bishop Lamy in 1850 and the influence he exerted in establishing a school system and constructing a cathedral.

Hotels multiplied in number as the Santa Fe Trail became a major link in a transcontinental stage route, with Santa Fe as a major terminal. The Harvey hotel called La Fonda ("Inn at the End of the Trail"), which has become a landmark of the city, occupies the former site of the Exchange Hotel. There was a classic Victorian-style hotel called The Palace, which offered the most exclusive accommodations of the city. The expansion of the town seemed imminent with the arrival of the railroad in the 1880's and much land speculation occurred in anticipation of the growth. Unfortunately, the steep grade on the south rim of the Santa Fe basin caused the main line of the railroad to detour to the south and the city was connected by an eighteen-mile spur. Without the mainline traffic the expected growth did not occur, with the exceptions of linear fingers of expansion along the roads toward Albuquerque (Camino Real) and San Miguel (Santa Fe Trail). The settlement remained compact until the mid-twentieth century, stretching east and west along the Santa Fe River.

With the post-war (WW II) population boom in Albuquerque which elevated it to the status of a metropolitan area, the expansion of Santa Fe followed a southwest direction along the route leading to this center. The location of the new airport, the industrial park, the college and multiple uses of a former military base, the state prison, and the by-pass of an interstate highway have all reinforced a continuance of this southern direction of growth. The only other outward growth has been in recent suburban residential expansion onto the hills north of town. State government employment has currently spread the employee residential area of Santa Fe into a one-hour commuter zone that stretches into Rio Arriba, Taos, and Santa Fe counties. Due to the large and expanding employment base, and the attraction of the town as an exclusive retirement area, the growth of Santa Fe should be expected by 1980 to surpass the 50,000 population figure necessary to achieve metropolitan status by the Bureau of Census.

Jerry L. Williams

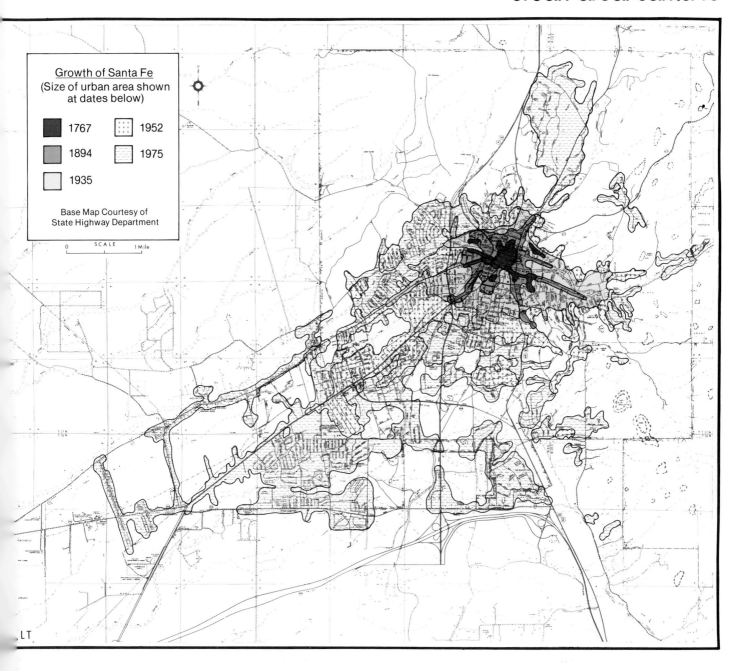

Growth of Santa Fe
(Size of urban area shown
at dates below)

- 1767
- 1894
- 1935
- 1952
- 1975

Base Map Courtesy of
State Highway Department

SCALE
0   1 Mile

TABLE: POPULATION OF SANTA FE			
YEAR	SANTA FE COUNTY	SANTA FE CITY	% OF COUNTY POPULATION
1850 a	—————	4539	—————
1860 a	8114	4635	57.1
1870 a	—————	4765	—————
1880 a	—————	6635	—————
1890 a	13582	6185	45.5
1900 a	14658	5603	38.2
1910	14770	5072	34.3
1920	15030	7236	48.1
1930	19567	11126	56.9
1940	30826	20325	65.9
1950	38153	27998	73.4
1960	44970	33394	74.3
1970	54774	41167	75.1
1975	62000	44937	72.5

[a]Not comparable with present statistics—county was not of same size and shape.

Source: U.S. Census Reports

urban area: roswell

Roswell is the largest trade center in the southeastern portion of New Mexico. Its vast commercial market reaches as far north as Vaughn and Clovis and south to Hobbs and Carlsbad. This wide range of influence is due to Roswell's sheltered location, separated from the dominance of either Albuquerque or El Paso by the rugged eastern front of the Rockies.

The town formed at the junction of the eastward flowing Hondo River, which drains the Capitan and Jicarilla mountains of present-day Lincoln County, and the broad north-south valley of the Pecos River. The Pecos is a natural access to the historical southwest center of Santa Fe. Its lower valley near Roswell was covered with gramma grass and made an excellent route for the northern transit of livestock from Texas to the military forts of Colorado.

Much of the Pecos and practically all of the Hondo permeates layers of limestone and contributes to the large artesian water supply of the lower Pecos Valley. Once discovered, this artesian supply attracted settlers and farmers to the area and the center expanded to serve them.

In the 1860's many Texas cattlemen (Goodnight, Loving, and Chisum) camped at the mouth of the Hondo. The high water table and abundant grass cover provided an excellent holding area before the cattle were driven to Ft. Sumner or places futher north. The first recorded structures on the present site of Roswell were a cattle pen, a house, and an old adobe unit that functioned as a cattlemen's primitive trail hotel during the late 1860's. In 1869 Van C. Smith of Omaha, Nebraska, arrived from Santa Fe with his partner, Aaron Wilburn, and purchased the old adobe hotel and trading post. They constructed two buildings in 1870 (at the present intersection of 4th Street and Main) that served as general store, post office, and guest house. The site was named Roswell after Van Smith's father, and the settlement was filed as a land claim in both the district (Lincoln) and territorial (Santa Fe) offices.

The post office, which opened in 1873, was on a Star mail route between Mesilla and Las Vegas, Roswell being a carrier stop midway between Lincoln and Ft. Sumner. Van Smith transformed the very wide Main Street (to accommodate cattle herds that were frequently driven through) into a half-mile seasonal racetrack between the store and the Hondo River. During the late 1870's the town became a known sport gambling center for transient cattlemen along the Pecos. During the same period, two cattle barons settled in the Roswell area. John Chisum, one of the largest cattle owners in the United States in the 19th Century, established his ranch headquarters at South Spring, six miles south of Roswell. The Chisum ranch became an important political and social center of southeastern New Mexico, attracting Roswell residents to nearly every important annual event. Joseph Lea located the center of his cattle empire northwest of Roswell. He is often referred to as the founder of the city as he purchased the holdings of Smith and Wilburn, purchased and established a 160-acre townsite, and began establishing the settlement as an important trading center.

In 1885 the original townsite was officially plotted between First Street and Eighth Street as a strip four blocks wide (two blocks east and west of Main Street) occupying 134 acres. Nearly four hundred lots were recorded (14 to a block) yet only a few at that time held the nine houses, mill, several stores, blacksmith shop, and hotel. It is doubtful that the population within the townsite exceeded one hundred persons during the 1880's, although several times that number resided within a five-mile radius. The area south and southeast of the townsite, along the Pecos River, had been settled by farmers in the 1870's. The population of the concentrated small-farm plots, called The Farms, was estimated to exceed three hundred persons. This area became the site of the first school in the Roswell area.

By the turn of the century the settlement had the appearance of a healthy frontier town. A courthouse had been constructed on a piece of land donated by Joseph Lea and the small town was the county seat for Chaves County, which was subdivided from Lincoln County in 1889. A military school had been constructed in 1891 on the northern fringes of the town after "Captain" Lea had persuaded the commandant of Fort Worth Military University to locate a prep school in the territory. In 1893 the school was named the New Mexico Military Institute. At this time the town had three doctors, four attorneys, two churches, a town school (three others in the nearby valley), the military school, a courthouse, thirty businesses and a population in excess of five hundred people.

The discovery of artesian free-flowing water in 1890 was necessary for the development and expansion of vast apple orchards throughout the lower Pecos Valley. Apples, cattle, lambs, and wool were the chief exports from Roswell when the Pecos Valley railroad arrived from Eddy (Carlsbad) in 1894. The rail service was extended to Amarillo (via Portales) in 1899 and Roswell became the rail center of southeast New Mexico. The abundance of water for agriculture and the economic stimulus of the railroad account for the 600% increase in the town population between 1890 and 1900. This growth, centered around an agricultural economy, continued at a much slower pace from 1900 until 1940.

In 1941, the War Department established an Army Flying School on land south of the site of Roswell. This small military operation was expanded in the 1950's by the construction of Walker Air Force Base, a permanent installation of the Strategic Air Command. As B-52 bombers became commonplace in the air space above Roswell, the land area was settled by some seven thousand Air Force employees and their families. In 1960 additional military personnel arrived to the rapidly expanding town to construct and operate a ring of Atlas intercontinental ballistic missiles. Roswell prospered as a short-lived military town.

The missile sites were closed in 1965 and Walker Air Base was deactivated in 1967. With the immediate vacation of approximately ten thousand people, the economy of Roswell appeared to be on the verge of collapse. Civic leaders wisely acquired the vacant military base and reorganized the existing infrastructure into an economic and cultural growth pole of the city. Renamed the Roswell Industrial Air Center, the former air base now houses a two-year branch college of Eastern New Mexico University, several industries including a major Greyhound bus assembly plant, numerous regional and state government offices, a rehabilitation center and hospital, and the city's airport facilities. The houses and schools constructed on the base provide low cost housing units and educational facilities for employees of the industrial park.

In 1975 Roswell had the necessary infrastructure to support a great increase in population within the present city limits with little capital expenditure needed to expand existing city services. City growth had leapfrogged during the military era so that an estimated twenty thousand people could now be accommodated in the existing vacant parcels within the corporate limits. The growth of Roswell will benefit both Chaves and Eddy counties as the labor force of the city is drawn from areas ranging for fifty miles. There is commuter traffic flow from Dexter and Hagerman, and from places as distant as Artesia. As Roswell increases its employment base by agglomerating more small industries and a skilled labor pool, the services and outreach of the growing city will continue to overlap the existing facilities of the southeastern towns. Roswell is expected to double its 1975 population as early as 1995. If so, most of the high plains area of New Mexico will be dependent on this urban center for some form of service.

Jerry L. William

TABLE: GROWTH OF ROSWELL

Year	Chaves County	Roswell	% of County	Year	Chaves County	Roswell	% of County
1890	no county	343[a]		1940	23,980	13,482	56.2
1900	4,773[b]	2,049	42.9	1950	40,605	25,738	63.4
1910	16,850[b]	6,172	56.2	1960	57,649	39,593	68.7
1920	12,070	7,033	58.3	1970	43,335	33,908	78.2
1930	19,549	11,173	57.2	1975	47,600	37,980	79.8

[a]population of the census district

[b]county not in present location and present boundary

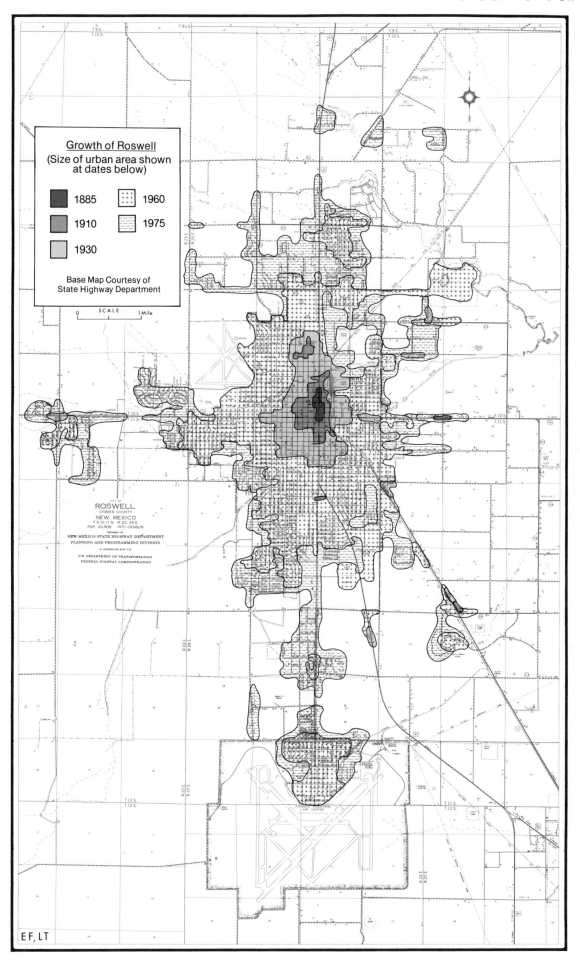

urban area: las cruces

The settlement pattern of the mid-Mesilla Valley follows the familiar old town–new town sequence that occurred at a number of places in the southwest (Las Vegas and Albuquerque in New Mexico and Tucson in Arizona). The unique development in this area was that the "old town" of La Mesilla and the "new town" of Las Cruces were both spawned from the same parent settlement of Doña Ana at about the same time. La Mesilla took on the appearance of a Spanish-Mexican village with an unplanned street pattern surrounding a central church plaza while Las Cruces became the typical Anglo (American) form of settlement designed on a rigid rectangular grid. La Mesilla was constructed on the flood-plain to provide residents access to fields and irrigation systems in the lower portion of the valley. Las Cruces was constructed on a river terrace at the edge of the flood-plain in an area more attractive for railroad development. La Mesilla grew as the dominant center of the Mesilla Valley for about forty years following the 1846 American military occupation of New Mexico. When the railroad arrived in 1881 commercial interest focused on Las Cruces and that town quickly became the dominant settlement of Doña Ana County.

The area near the site of Mesilla was named "Trenequel de la Mesilla" by the Spanish explorer Juan de Oñate in 1598. Although he gave the valley a name as he travelled north on the route to be later known as the Camino Real or Chihuahua Trail, an established settlement was not to occur until nearly 250 years later. The governor of New Mexico camped in the vicinity during his retreat from Santa Fe during the Pueblo Revolt of 1680, and there are records of temporary Indian settlements along the valley in the late eighteenth century. Hispanic settlers from northern New Mexico flocked to the Mesilla Valley in 1846 when the American Army of the West marched into the territory. A garrison of Mexican troops was stationed at the site to become known as La Mesilla and Spanish-speaking settlers, who distrusted the Americans, believed the area to be a final refuge and defense against United States occupation. The Treaty of Guadalupe Hidalgo in 1848, signed upon cessation of hostilities between the United States and Mexico, left in dispute the control of land between the Rio Grande and Colorado rivers and between the present Mexican border and the Gila River. Since La Mesilla was at that time on the western bank of the Rio Grande, it became part of the disputed territory and the Mexican government called for New Mexicans to move into the area to avoid becoming American citizens. Father Ortiz was named the first commissioner to the Mesilla Colony Land Grant in 1850. He established the San Albino church at the present plaza in La Mesilla and led a group of settlers from Doña Ana (which was believed to be part of the United States) to the new settlement on the floodplain.

Although 1850 is the date frequently given as the founding of La Mesilla, an American census of that same date indicated 3000 people already resided near the plaza. The census count may not be completely reliable as the United States government was trying to show cause for gaining control of the disputed area and may have inflated the figures. In 1854, the U.S. Congress ratified the Gadsden Purchase and the controversial 29,670 square miles of land, including Mesilla, were annexed to Doña Ana County. The town was no longer a refuge area for Spanish-speaking residents, but as a large population center it began to attract commercial interests and became the major trading town in southern New Mexico.

Mesilla prospered during the 1850's as the town grew into a service center for nearby Fort Fillmore, established by the American government in 1851. By the 1860's the settlement was a crossroads of two major regional stage coach lines, a transcontinental mail and passenger route, and the main line of a freight route to California. The 1860 territorial census indicated that Mesilla, with 2,420 residents, was the second largest town in New Mexico compared to Santa Fe which had 4,600 people. In 1861 it became the short-lived Confederate capitol of the Arizona Territory as a reward to the Southern-sympathizing residents of the small town. In 1862 the Confederate army was defeated near Santa Fe and as it retreated to Texas the political influence of Mesilla declined.

In 1863 the Rio Grande cut a secondary channel west of Mesilla and for twenty years the settlement rested on an island that was either surrounded with water in the season of high runoff or with a brackish back-water swamp during the drier periods. The river selected the western course as a single channel in 1885 and the former eastern course gradually filled with sediment, breaking the

isolation of the town. By this time the neighboring community of Las Cruces had been selected for the railroad line and the subsequent growth of the railway town would correspond to the decline and later slow growth of La Mesilla.

Las Cruces was founded in 1849 when the Prefect of the town of Doña Ana requested the army to survey a townsite near the end of a newly completed irrigation canal. A grid pattern of wide north-south streets with intersecting east-west routes assured uniform-sized square blocks. Residents of the town of Doña Ana were encouraged to move to the new site with the offer of a quarter of each grid block for any family that would resettle. The name Las Cruces (the crosses) originated from an 1830 Apache massacre of about forty travellers near the site and the resulting field of crosses which covered the area. Merchants and freighters established the first Las Cruces business community in the 1850's when Mesilla was claimed by the Mexicans and Fort Fillmore needed a new trading station. In 1852 Las Cruces became the county seat of the newly formed Doña Ana County which stretched from Texas to Arizona. An 1854 military census recorded a population of 600 in Las Cruces and the town was expanding as an outfitting center for the profitable mineral discoveries in the nearby Organ Mountains. In 1855 La Mesilla became part of Doña Ana County and the county seat was transferred from Las Cruces to its larger and more prosperous neighbor. The courthouse remained at Mesilla until 1882, the year after the railroad arrived in Las Cruces. Las Cruces has been the county seat of Doña Ana County since that time and Mesilla lost practically all of its political influence in the Mesilla Valley.

In 1880 a small institution called Las Cruces College was founded on land several miles south of the town. The college became the New Mexico College of Agriculture and Mechanical Arts in 1889 and grew during the twentieth century as New Mexico State University, the second largest university in the state. The prosperity of Las Cruces, closely related to the agricultural wealth of the Mesilla Valley, was enhanced during the twentieth century by the construction of Caballo and Elephant Butte dams sixty and seventy-five miles respectively upstream on the Rio Grande. The two reservoirs allowed for an expanded canal and drainage system throughout the entire lower valley and provided an efficient and orderly water distribution system throughout the long growing season. The Mesilla Valley quickly became one of the richest agricultural areas of the state (cotton, pecan nuts, and vegetables) and there was a rapid increase in the rural population between 1920 and 1940. The steady income from agricultural exports for the farmers and many farm laborers indirectly benefited the commercial shopping center of Las Cruces.

The population boom of the city in the late 1940's was the result of the federal government establishing the nearby White Sands Missile Range; Las Cruces serving as a convenient residential area for the federal employees. Mainly as a result of White Sands, the population of the city increased at the rate of nearly 14 percent a year during the 1950's (compared to the rate of 4½ percent per year from 1920 to 1950). In the 1960's the federal government again boosted employment opportunities by establishing the National Aeronautic and Space Administration (NASA) testing facility northeast of Las Cruces. Many of the employment centers, including the university, were not located in the town of Las Cruces and a large proportion of new residents since 1960 settled in the less expensive county areas along the Rio Grande. Even between 1970 and 1975, the corporate area still barely encompassed half of the county population.

In 1976, the five-mile extraterritorial area (five miles from the city limit) was estimated to contain more than twenty thousand persons and had a growth rate greater than that of Las Cruces. This urban area, created by combining Las Cruces with the extraterritorial population, accounted for approximately 80 percent of the population of Doña Ana County. The greater Las Cruces urbanized area is one of the fastest growing places in the southwest with about one-fourth of the immigrant population settling in the area on retirement incomes. The university has been a major factor during this growth era as it expanded from a small campus of 3,300 students in 1960 to an enrollment over 11,000 in 1975. Local employment opportunities, which have not kept pace with the population growth, have forced many residents of the Las Cruces urban area to join the flow of commuter traffic to the industrial center of El Paso, Texas, forty-five miles to the south.

Jerry L. Williams

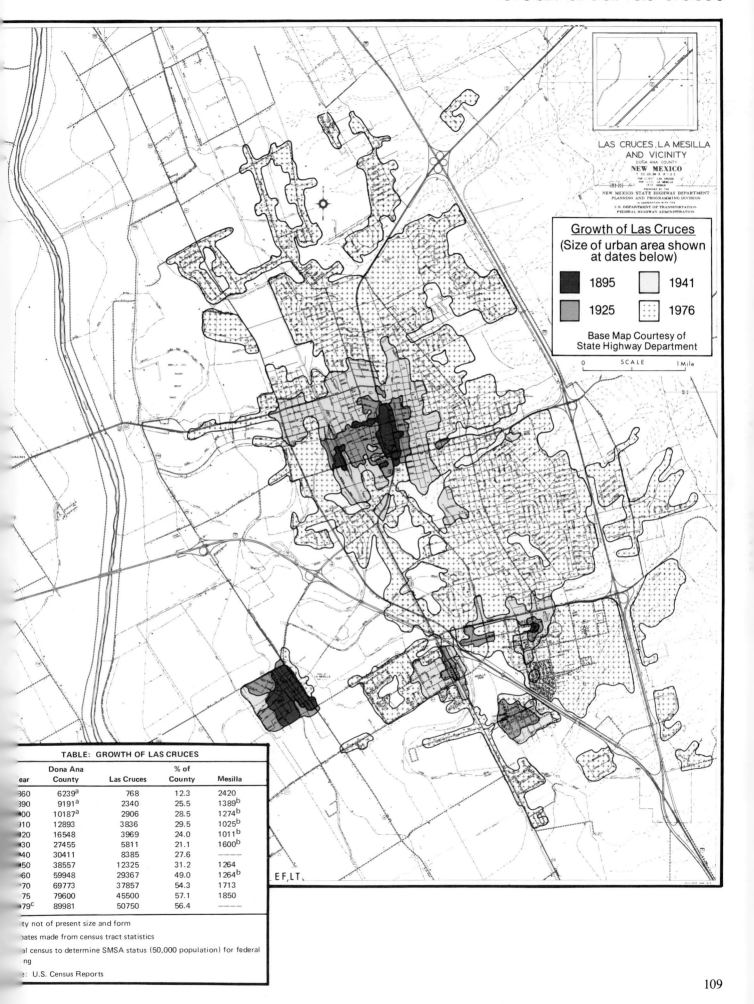

LAS CRUCES, LA MESILLA
AND VICINITY
DOÑA ANA COUNTY
NEW MEXICO
T. 22, 23, 24, S. R. 1, 2 E.
POP 1,097 LAS CRUCES
1970 CENSUS
POP 1,713 LA MESILLA
PREPARED BY THE
NEW MEXICO STATE HIGHWAY DEPARTMENT
PLANNING AND PROGRAMMING DIVISION
IN COOPERATION WITH THE
U.S. DEPARTMENT OF TRANSPORTATION
FEDERAL HIGHWAY ADMINISTRATION

Growth of Las Cruces
(Size of urban area shown
at dates below)

■	1895	▨	1941
▨	1925	⊞	1976

Base Map Courtesy of
State Highway Department

0   SCALE   1 Mile

TABLE: GROWTH OF LAS CRUCES			
	Dona Ana		% of	
Year	County	Las Cruces	County	Mesilla
1860	6239[a]	768	12.3	2420
1890	9191[a]	2340	25.5	1389[b]
1900	10187[a]	2906	28.5	1274[b]
1910	12893	3836	29.5	1025[b]
1920	16548	3969	24.0	1011[b]
1930	27455	5811	21.1	1600[b]
1940	30411	8385	27.6	----
1950	38557	12325	31.2	1264
1960	59948	29367	49.0	1264[b]
1970	69773	37857	54.3	1713
1975	79600	45500	57.1	1850
1979[c]	89981	50750	56.4	----

[city] not of present size and form

[estim]ates made from census tract statistics

[specia]l census to determine SMSA status (50,000 population) for federal

[fundi]ng

[Sourc]e: U.S. Census Reports

E F, LT.

109

ambient air quality

On August 7, 1977, President Carter signed into law the Clean Air Act Amendments which augmented the Clean Air Act of 1970. These amendments impose rather stringent requirements in areas where National Ambient Air Quality Standards (NAAQS) are being exceeded. The five criteria pollutants considered are carbon monoxide (CO), nitrogen dioxide (NO_2), sulfur dioxide (SO_2), photochemical oxidants (O_x) and total suspended particulates (TSP). The objective of the 1977 amendments is that all areas of the country attain and maintain the NAAQS's by 1982 with a possible extension to 1987. Where extensions are requested by the state, stringent requirements are imposed.

In the case of stationary air pollutant sources, provisions in the law preventing significant air quality deterioration and new source performance standards apply, which may result in prohibiting new stationary source construction by a company. An equivalent emission reduction would be required by one or more existing stationary sources under ownership of the same company before a new stationary source can be constructed. If an extension is requested in an area where non-attainment is caused by mobile sources (automobiles), a periodic motor vehicle inspection maintenance program is mandated by the Act.

Geographic areas of the state classified by the Environmental Protection Agency are depicted in pie-chart form on the map for four of the five criteria pollutants. The entire state has met the standards for nitrogen dioxide, which is the fifth pollutant. Bernalillo County does not meet standards for carbon monoxide, with automobiles the principle (over 90%) cause. Several discrete areas in Albuquerque also exceed the TSP standards while a portion of the County is classified as exceeding the O_x standard. Portions of Valencia and Sandoval, the Counties adjacent to Bernalillo (mid Rio Grande airshed), are suspected (because of lack of monitors) to exceed CO and O_x standards, as well as contributing to Bernalillo County's problem.

San Juan County coal burning power plants are the cause of that County's monitoring stations exceeding the limits for SO_2. Sulfur dioxide standards as well as the TSP standards are surpassed in the southwest corner of New Mexico in and around Hurley, the site of a large copper ore smelter.

The total suspended particulate standard is exceeded in a variety of locations within Eddy County. The primary source of these emissions is potash mining and processing by four large companies.

Congress provided sanctions and penalties for non-compliant states and municipalities in the form of withholding federal highway, sewage treatment and HUD funds where efforts are not directed to address the pollutant sources.

A number of areas around the state have been designated as unclassified on the basis that insufficient monitoring data exists in order to make a determination. Portions of Bernalillo, Lea, Valencia, Eddy and Sandoval are so classified for photochemical oxidants.

Limited and discrete areas of Santa Fe, Farmington and Las Cruces have been designated as exceeding the carbon monoxide standard.

Don Anderson

TABLE 1. NATIONAL AMBIENT AIR QUALITY STANDARDS (NAAQS)

Pollutant	Primary Standard*	Secondary Standard**
Carbon Monoxide (CO)	35 ppm hourly average, not to be exceeded more than once a year	same as primary
	9 ppm eight hour average, not to be exceeded more than once a year	
Nitrogen Dioxide (NO_2)	0.05 ppm annual average	same as primary
Non-methane Hydrocarbons[+]	0.24 ppm 6-9 a.m. average, not to be exceeded more than once a year	same as primary
Photochemical Oxidants	0.08 ppm hourly average measured as ozone, not to be exceeded more than once a year	same as primary
Total Suspended Particulate Matter	260 ug/m³ 24-hour average, not to be exceeded more than once a year	150 ug/m³ 24-hour average, not to be exceeded more than once a year
	75 ug/m³ annual geometric mean	60 ug/m³ annual geometric mean[+]
Sulfur Dioxide (SO_2)	365 ug/m³ (0.14 ppm) 24-hour average, not to be exceeded more than once a year	1,300 ug/m³ (0.5 ppm) three hour average, not to be exceeded more than once a year
	80 ug/m³ (0.03 ppm) annual average	

*Primary standards define levels of air quality which the U.S. Environmental Protection Agency's Administrator judges necessary to protect the public health with an adequate margin of safety.

**Secondary standards define levels of air quality which the EPA Administrator judges necessary to protect the public welfare from any known or anticipated adverse effects of a pollutant.

[+]These are for use as guides in achieving other standards. The non-methane hydrocarbon level relates to the oxidant standard; the 60 ug/m³ geometric mean relates to the 24-hour standard for particulates.

TABLE 2. CITIES IN NEW MEXICO WHICH HAVE EXCEEDED THE APPROPRIATE FEDERAL STANDARD ONE OR MORE TIMES IN PERIOD 1973-1976

24 hr. Particulate (260 ug/m³)			24 hr. Sulfur Dioxide (0.10 ppm)	1 hr. Carbon Monoxide (35 ppm)	1 hr. Ozone (80 ppb)*
Farmington	Artesia	T or C	Anapara	Albuquerque	Albuquerque
Shiprock	Monument	Tularosa	Bayard		LA Union
Gallup	Carlsbad	Ruidoso	Hurley		Leasburg
Churchrock	Roswell	Silver City	Bolton		
Albuquerque	Alamogordo	Harley			
Belen	Las Cruces	Deming			*This standard may be changed to 100 PPB which would eliminate Leasburg.
Taos	Anthony	Bolton			
Las Vegas	Anapara	Lordsburg			
Hobbs	Hatch	Paguate			
		Milan			

110

ambient air quality

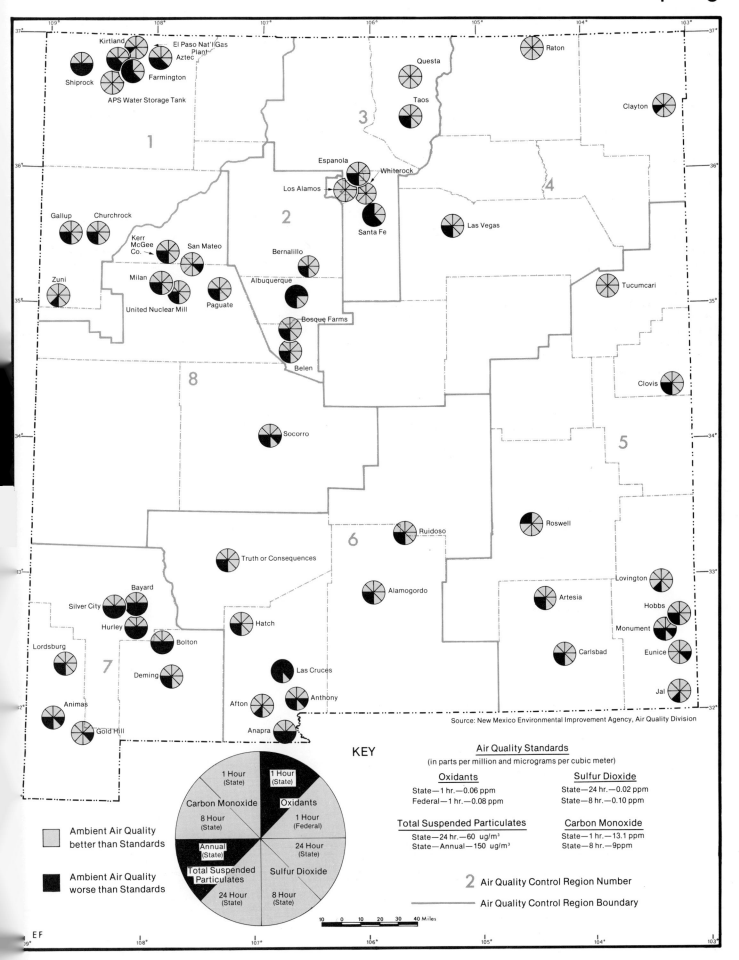

Source: New Mexico Environmental Improvement Agency, Air Quality Division

KEY

Ambient Air Quality better than Standards

Ambient Air Quality worse than Standards

Key pie chart segments:
- 1 Hour (State) — Carbon Monoxide
- 8 Hour (State) — Carbon Monoxide
- Annual (State) — Total Suspended Particulates
- 24 Hour (State) — Total Suspended Particulates
- 8 Hour (State) — Sulfur Dioxide
- 24 Hour (State) — Sulfur Dioxide
- 1 Hour (Federal) — Oxidants
- 1 Hour (State) — Oxidants

Air Quality Standards
(in parts per million and micrograms per cubic meter)

Oxidants
State—1 hr.—0.06 ppm
Federal—1 hr.—0.08 ppm

Sulfur Dioxide
State—24 hr.—0.02 ppm
State—8 hr.—0.10 ppm

Total Suspended Particulates
State—24 hr.—60 ug/m³
State—Annual—150 ug/m³

Carbon Monoxide
State—1 hr.—13.1 ppm
State—8 hr.—9ppm

2 Air Quality Control Region Number

Air Quality Control Region Boundary

10 0 10 20 30 40 Miles

111

economic characteristics

land use

There are six "area-extensive" uses of New Mexico's land. In this context the idea of land-use must be kept distinct from either that of land cover or land ownership. The dominant economic use of a given area is not necessarily reflected by its vegetation cover, nor in all cases will the use suggest who (private, federal, or state) is the legal owner. For example there are thousands of acres of piñon-juniper woodland in the state that are not shown as forestry areas because grazing, not wood products, is the major economic activity. Furthermore, grazing as an economic pursuit cuts across virtually all ownership boundaries. The vegetation and land ownership maps contained in this atlas should be referred to for a more accurate representation of those distributions.

The word "area-extensive" is used advisedly since New Mexico's extractive industries (mineral and energy production) are not shown. This is because such activity consists of wells, ponds, or relatively small spoil piles and mine excavations. The areas of greatest concentration are: oil and gas production in both the southeast and northwest; coal and uranium in the northwest; and copper in the southwest. Mineral and energy activities represent exceedingly important multiple uses for large parts of the state.

GRAZING

Grazing provides an economic back drop to the entire state. The history of New Mexico is essentially a story of how other economic pursuits have diffused into the region or been legislatively mandated. Cattle and sheep are the major herd animals, though horses, deer, elk, bighorn sheep, and a few buffalo are also locally important. In recent years grazing land in the southern portion of the state has been set aside for African imports of ibex and gazelle which have proven to be successful game animals.

AGRICULTURE

Agriculture during the early period of European settlement was concentrated in the Rio Grande Valley. With improved technology, additional large acreages were cleared for dryland production which have shifted from time to time depending upon crop types, climatic cycles and economic conditions. Aerial photos frequently show old field borders of dry land plots that have long since reverted to grazing. Much of our modern agriculture is done through large mechanized irrigation systems that permit increased productivity of extensive upland areas. The pattern shown here presents both dry land and irrigated agriculture as a single category. In the Deming, Roswell, and Portales areas both types

are important, while in the Estancia Valley most of the activity is still dry land. Virtually all of the agriculture along the Rio Grande and San Juan Rivers is ditch irrigated.

FORESTRY

Forestry in the context used here refers to areas used primarily for harvestable timber, though much of the total is also subject to grazing leases, and/or the impact of recreational use. The distribution is synonymous in large part with areas set aside as national or state forest and for the most part consists of spruce-fir and pine-fir types.

RECREATION

Recreation is a category of use reserved for national parks, national monuments, game preserves and refuges, wilderness areas, and state parks. This economic use transcends almost all of the biological zones found in the state from the gypsum sands near Alamogordo to the alpine meadows of the Pecos Wilderness Area. By law these areas cannot be mined, grazed, logged, developed or trespassed upon except in the pursuit of leisure, camping and nature appreciation.

MILITARY

Military reservations are set aside by legislative statute or presidential proclamation and are closed to all entry and development. The largest such reservation in New Mexico is White Sands Missile Range. It occupies the lion's share of the territory between Socorro, Las Cruces and Alamogordo. Smaller reservations are located near Albuquerque (Kirtland Air Force Base and Weapons Testing Facility), Gallup and Silver City.

URBAN

Urban land-use is unquestionably the most complex of all land uses because of the array of economic uses for land in metropolitan areas. The map shows only those cities in New Mexico with incorporated areas larger than the minimum mapping area.

NO DOMINANT USE

No dominant use includes all land having no dominant economic use. In essence this means totally barren land or land associated with broken lava flows where even grazing is uneconomic. A large portion of this land is located in the southwest quadrant between Socorro, Deming, and Lordsburg.

Stan Morain

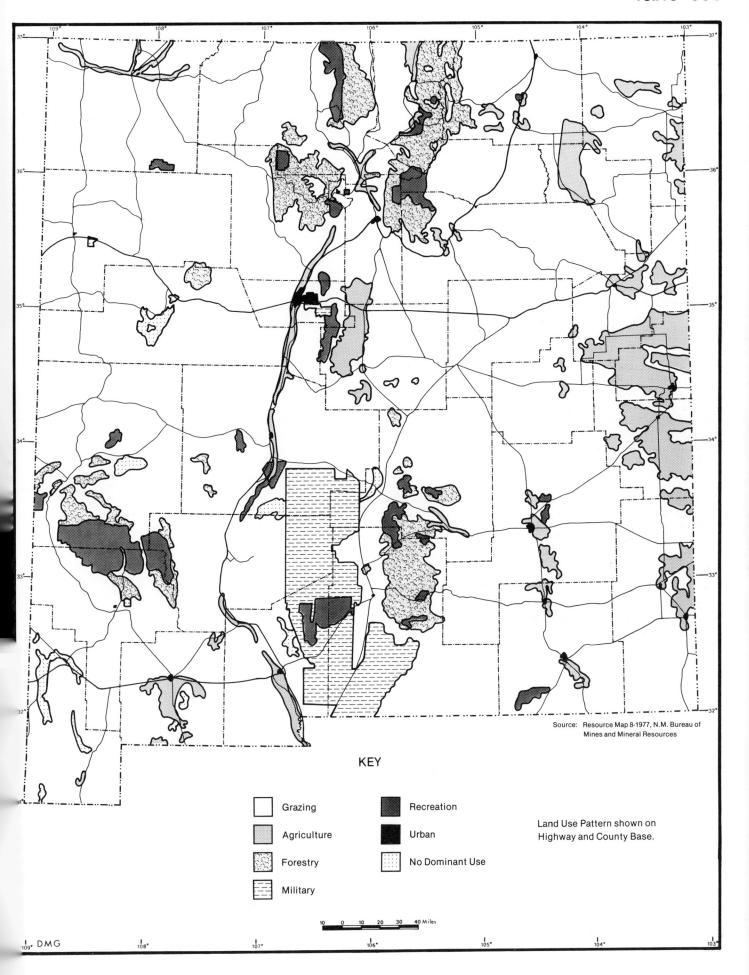

Source: Resource Map 8-1977, N.M. Bureau of
Mines and Mineral Resources

KEY

☐	Grazing	■	Recreation	
	Agriculture	■	Urban	
	Forestry		No Dominant Use	
	Military			

Land Use Pattern shown on
Highway and County Base.

10   0   10   20   30   40 Miles

DMG

land ownership

The map indicates that large areas in New Mexico are under a single type of ownership, but the scale has made it necessary to generalize greatly about the predominant types of land ownership. Many of the areas indicated as state or federal, contain small interspersed private holdings. The national forests contain some state and private holdings, and Indian lands outside reservation boundaries include federal, state, and private tracts. Only the federal military areas and Indian reservations are likely to be controlled by one entity.

Private holdings constitute the largest category of land ownership. In fifteen of the thirty-two counties, 50 percent or more of the land is privately owned. In these counties, located mainly in the northeast quadrant of the state, land grants, ranching, and homesteading have been the deciding forces in land acquisition.

Like several western states, much of New Mexico is in the public domain. The table indicates that slightly over one-third of the state's area is owned and administered by the federal government. In ten counties, federal land exceeds 50 percent of the total

acreage. Of these counties, those in the northern and southwestern parts of the state contain extensive sections of national forest, and those in the south contain Bureau of Land Management and military land.

State land occupies about 12 percent of New Mexico's area. Unlike federally owned sections, state government lands generally consist of smaller, broken tracts located primarily in the eastern and southern half of the state.

The smallest category of ownership is Indian land. Almost all of these holdings, except the Mescalero Apache Reservation in Otero County, are in the state's northwest quadrant. While many maps of the state show the location of Indian reservations and pueblos, this cartographic depiction provides a more realistic picture of the extent of Indian holdings. The greatest expansion of Indian land, beyond the traditional reservation boundaries, has occurred in McKinley County.

Paul McAllister

LAND OWNERSHIP BY COUNTY, 1972

	Total Acres	Federal		State		Indian		Private	
		Acres	%	Acres	%	Acres	%	Acres	%
Bernalillo	748,160	154,590	20.7	32,201	4.3	222,527	29.7	338,842	45.3
Catron	4,414,720	2,799,004	63.4	533,037	12.1	0		1,082,679	24.5
Chaves	3,900,800	1,265,500	32.4	703,706	18.0	0		1,931,594	49.5
Colfax	2,413,440	15,740	0.6	278,186	11.5	0		2,119,511	87.8
Curry	898,560	3,862	0.4	60,667	6.8	0		834,031	92.8
De Baca	1,514,240	90,848	6.0	243,570	16.1	0		1,179,822	77.9
Dona Ana	2,434,560	1,821,515	74.8	286,910	11.8	0		326,135	13.4
Eddy	2,675,200	1,648,563	61.6	477,730	17.9	0		548,907	20.5
Grant	2,540,800	1,294,877	51.0	367,685	14.5	0		878,238	34.6
Guadalupe	1,919,360	120,053	6.2	177,810	9.3	0		1,621,497	84.5
Harding	1,368,320	70,506	5.2	344,981	25.2	0		952,833	69.6
Hidalgo	2,206,080	893,679	40.5	354,431	16.1	0		957,970	43.4
Lea	2,812,160	466,952	16.6	873,748	31.1	0		1,471,460	52.3
Lincoln	3,109,760	1,103,482	35.5	300,841	9.7	0		1,705,437	54.8
Los Alamos	69,120	64,448	93.2	0		0		4,672	6.8
Luna	1,892,480	786,150	41.5	534,951	28.3	0		571,379	30.2
McKinley	3,495,040	564,580	16.2	183,974	5.3	2,158,410	61.8	588,076	16.8
Mora	1,244,160	107,642	8.6	81,638	6.6	0		1,054,880	84.8
Otero	4,248,320	2,886,626	68.0	449,908	10.6	460,255	10.8	451,531	10.6
Quay	1,845,120	14,535	0.8	237,714	12.9	0		1,592,871	86.3
Rio Arriba	3,765,120	1,953,173	51.9	108,530	2.9	646,932	17.2	1,056,485	28.1
Roosevelt	1,572,480	38,517	2.4	211,140	13.4	0		1,322,823	84.1
Sandoval	2,378,880	987,297	41.5	80,192	3.4	650,380	27.3	661,011	27.8
San Juan	3,530,240	1,039,281	29.4	168,416	4.8	2,110,692	59.8	211,851	6.0
San Miguel	3,050,880	394,215	12.9	173,808	5.7	0		2,482,857	81.4
Santa Fe	1,221,760	336,157	27.5	85,857	7.0	79,458	6.5	720,198	59.0
Sierra	2,700,160	1,830,310	67.8	361,195	13.4	0		508,655	18.8
Socorro	4,240,640	2,318,458	54.7	609,547	14.4	56,680	1.3	1,255,955	29.6
Taos	1,444,480	733,325	50.8	97,144	6.7	62,288	4.3	551,723	38.
Torrance	2,147,200	207,787	9.7	299,805	14.0	16,300	.8	1,623,308	75.
Union	2,442,880	58,725	2.4	441,946	18.1	0		1,942,209	79.
Valencia	3,621,120	700,034	19.3	251,746	7.0	849,551	23.5	1,819,789	50.
State Total*	77,866,240	26,735,431	34.3	9,413,017	12.1	7,348,563	9.4	34,369,229	44.

*May not total to 100% due to rounding error.

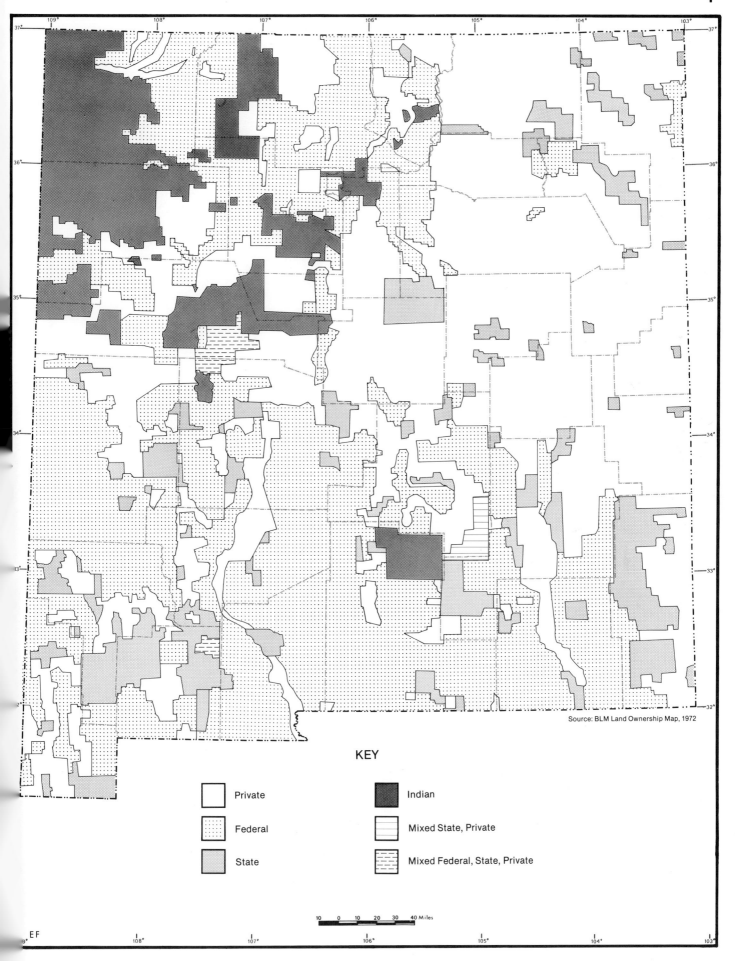

Source: BLM Land Ownership Map, 1972

KEY

Private	Indian
Federal	Mixed State, Private
State	Mixed Federal, State, Private

10 0 10 20 30 40 Miles

E F

labor force

Labor conditions in New Mexico have been unsettled during the 1970's. Table A shows a 36.8 percent increase in the size of the work force from 1971 to 1977 and a 37.4 percent increase in employment. However, the nationwide recession of the mid-1970's produced a negative impact on the state's economy, pushing unemployment to a high of ten percent in 1975. Since then, labor conditions have improved significantly; the preliminary estimates for 1978 suggest an unemployment rate of less than seven percent.

Based on employment totals, the leading economic sectors in New Mexico are trade and services, government, and development industries. Table B illustrates that overall, the percentage of the labor force employed in these various categories has remained relatively stable. However, two significant trends are evident: there has been a steady increase in the importance of the trade and service industries, and a steady decline in the governmental sector. These trends are bringing the state more in line with national employment proportions. However, New Mexico differs signif-

icantly from national averages with a higher percentage of the work force engaged in mining and government and a much smaller percentage in manufacturing.

Table C and the map present employment percentages for the individual counties. There is great diversity within each sector of the economy. Trade and services is probably the most uniform category although Catron, Los Alamos, Mora, Harding, and Guadalupe counties all have significantly smaller percentages of their labor force employed in these occupations. The high percentage employed in development industries in Hidalgo County results from the building of a massive smelter and associated company towns. Although the percentage of government employment is declining in the state, it remains the largest occupational category in thirteen counties and provides over 50 percent of total employment in six others, including a phenomenal 75 percent in Los Alamos County.

Paul McAllister

Table A
ESTIMATES OF EMPLOYMENT AND UNEMPLOYMENT 1971-1977

Year	Total[a] Work Force	Employment	Unemployment	Unemployment Rate (%)
1971	380,520	349,317	31,203	8.2
1972	397,265	367,470	29,795	7.5
1973	414,571	383,893	30,678	7.4
1974	430,814	395,487	35,327	8.2
1975	444,576	400,118	44,458	10.0
1976	482,599	438,200	44,399	9.2
1977	520,607	480,000	40,607	7.8

[a]Total wage and salary employment force, excludes proprietors.

Table B
LABOR FORCE EMPLOYMENT 1971-1975

Year	Percent[a] of Labor Force[b] in					
	Trade and Services	Development[c]	Manufacturing	Mining	Agriculture	Government
1971	38.4	15.7	6.4	4.8	2.3	32.6
1972	38.7	16.3	7.0	4.4	2.2	31.5
1973	39.0	16.6	7.2	4.3	2.1	30.8
1974	39.3	16.4	7.4	4.7	1.9	20.1
1975	40.3	16.1	7.1	5.1	2.0	29.4

[a]May not total to 100% due to rounding error.

[b]Wage and salary employment, excludes proprietors.

[c]Includes: construction, transportation, communications, utilities, finance, insurance, and real estate.

Table C
LABOR FORCE EMPLOYMENT 1975

County	Total Employed	Percent[a] of Labor Force[b] in					
		Trade and Services	Development[c]	Manufacturing	Mining	Agriculture	Government
Bernalillo	147,496	49.0	17.9	9.8	.1	.2	23.0
Catron	587	11.6	2.4	15.7	1.0	15.3	53.5
Chaves	15,455	41.5	15.3	13.0	2.4	7.3	20.4
Colfax	4,503	38.8	12.5	9.7	8.4	4.6	26.0
Curry	16,423	34.8	13.4	5.0	*	2.7	44.0
De Baca	577	32.6	11.4	1.6	0.0	14.9	39.5
Dona Ana	25,993	32.0	13.0	5.1	*	5.5	44.3
Eddy	15,234	38.0	15.4	5.5	23.8	3.4	13.9
Grant	7,748	24.8	10.2	5.6	32.4	1.9	25.1
Guadalupe	1,283	50.2	9.3	1.2	0.0	9.0	30.4
Harding	357	22.1	5.9	8.4	1.4	30.2	31.9
Hidalgo	2,637	29.1	47.6	.4	.7	6.8	15.4
Lea	20,466	34.7	20.0	4.8	27.4	1.8	11.2
Lincoln	2,800	46.0	20.0	1.8	1.1	7.2	23.9
Los Alamos	12,664	19.8	4.7	.2	0.0	0.0	75.3
Luna	3,622	40.1	15.3	9.8	.8	7.3	26.8
McKinley	15,978	34.8	12.9	7.9	16.2	.3	27.8
Mora	587	19.8	7.8	.3	0.0	13.0	59.1
Otero	17,886	27.4	9.4	6.7	*	.8	55.6
Quay	3,360	43.2	14.4	6.5	.4	6.6	29.0
Rio Arriba	5,896	44.5	9.6	6.0	.1	2.8	37.1
Roosevelt	4,138	31.4	12.6	4.8	1.0	9.6	40.6
Sandoval	3,780	34.6	18.2	15.3	1.8	1.4	28.6
San Juan	19,895	35.7	29.3	4.4	11.8	.5	18.2
San Miguel	5,248	29.3	9.8	2.5	*	2.8	55.5
Santa Fe	23,605	45.6	14.7	3.7	1.3	.5	34.2
Sierra	1,803	31.2	16.1	1.0	3.4	11.9	36.4
Socorro	2,578	29.4	10.8	2.7	*	5.5	51.4
Taos	5,263	45.7	9.7	6.4	14.2	.4	23.6
Torrance	1,336	35.5	8.8	1.9	0.0	10.5	43.3
Union	1,412	39.0	13.5	.9	3.3	12.4	31.0
Valencia	9,508	37.5	19.3	2.8	15.0	2.4	22.9
State Total	400,118	40.3	16.1	7.1	5.1	2.0	29.4

* Less than .1 percent

[a]May not total to 100% due to rounding error.

[b]Wage and salary employment, excludes proprietors.

[c]Includes: construction, transportation, communications, utilities, finance, insurance, and real estate.

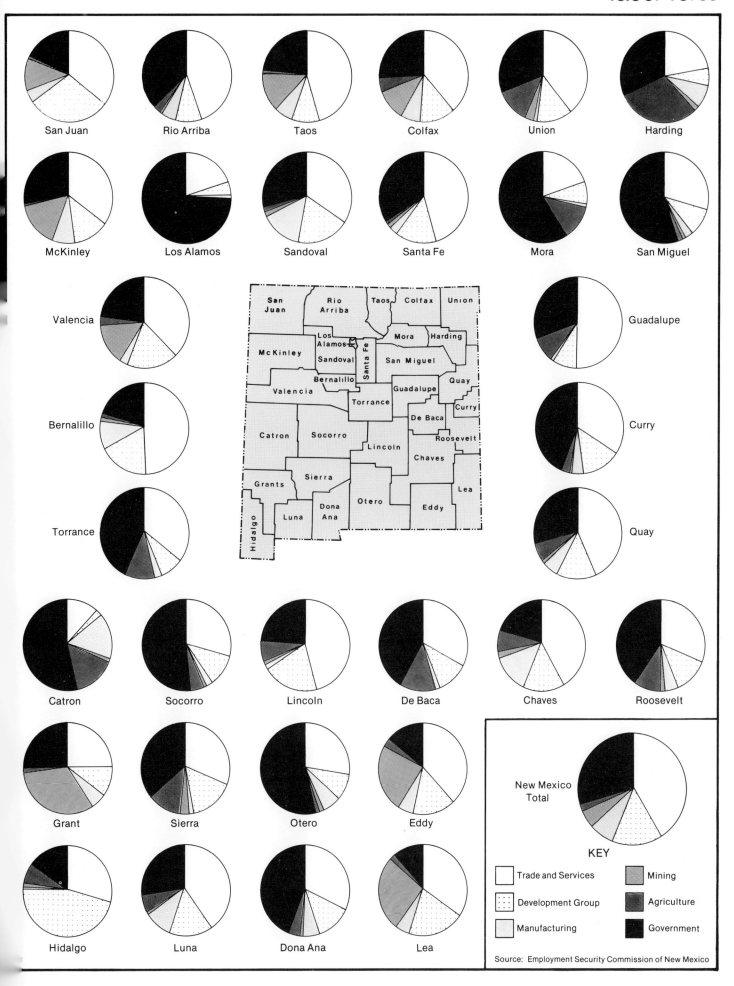

San Juan

Rio Arriba

Taos

Colfax

Union

Harding

McKinley

Los Alamos

Sandoval

Santa Fe

Mora

San Miguel

Valencia

Guadalupe

Bernalillo

Curry

Torrance

Quay

Catron

Socorro

Lincoln

De Baca

Chaves

Roosevelt

Grant

Sierra

Otero

Eddy

Hidalgo

Luna

Dona Ana

Lea

New Mexico Total

KEY

Trade and Services

Mining

Development Group

Agriculture

Manufacturing

Government

Source: Employment Security Commission of New Mexico

value of products

FARM

Climate and terrain render most of New Mexico unsuitable for farming. Even the use of irrigation has not been sufficient to make the state a major agricultural region.

The market value for all agricultural products (livestock and crops) in New Mexico has risen only gradually in the last decade. (This reflects a nationwide trend.) The value of products sold increased only 36.7 percent from 1964 and 45.4 percent from 1969 to 1974. Although all counties (except Grant and Guadalupe) have increased their farm product value in the last five years, only a few are significant agricultural producers. Twenty of the state's thirty-two counties produced less than $10,000,000 and as a group equal only 21.5 percent of total state production. The four counties having product values of $10-20,000,000 produced an additional 10.5 percent of the state total.

Slightly over two-thirds of New Mexico's agricultural production is contained in eight counties located on the eastern and southern plains and the lower Rio Grande Valley. Chaves County leads the state in value of farm products sold. The county derives most of its farm production from livestock ($58.8 million) and ranks as the 35th leading county in the nation in value of cattle and calves sold. However, Chaves ranked 23rd in that category nationally in 1969. The second most important agricultural county in the state is Curry. Again livestock is the major product with a value of $37,500,000 and a ranking 66th (up from 101st in 1969) in cattle and calves sales.

Doña Ana County in the lower Rio Grande Valley ranks third among the state's counties in agricultural value and is the nation's leading producer of pecans (10,568,826 lbs. in 1974). The county is also an important producer of cotton and chili. Other major agricultural products in the state include sheep, lambs, and wool in Chaves and Lincoln counties, and sorghum and peanuts in Roosevelt County.

MANUFACTURED

New Mexico is not a major manufacturing state. However, the value of manufacturing is important to the economy of several counties. As the table indicates, most counties experienced an increase in the value of manufactured products from 1967 to 1972. The greatest percentage increase (142.5%) among the leading manufacturing counties occurred in San Juan where energy related industries are important.

As might be expected, manufacturing activity in New Mexico is concentrated in the state's most populous county, Bernalillo, which produced nearly 35 percent of the state's total value of manufactured goods. The major manufacturing firms in the county make electrical and nonelectrical machinery, and apparel items. Curry County, situated in the eastern part of the state, is second in value of manufactured products, accounting for almost 13 percent of the state's output. As the table and map indicate, these are the only two counties producing more than one hundred million dollars in manufactured products. Only two other counties, Chaves and McKinley, exceed fifty million dollars in manufactured goods. The majority of New Mexico counties have manufactured product values of less than fifteen million dollars.

The data, however, present a slightly misleading picture of manufacturing in New Mexico. The 1972 values for 10 counties have been withheld to avoid disclosing figures for individual companies. The total value withheld is 158.3 million dollars or 17.2 percent of the state's total. It is certain that the undisclosed total is not evenly distributed among the ten counties. Grant and Hidalgo counties, with their mining associated industries, and Otero County, with a variety of firms including wood, machinery, food, and printing, probably account for a large percentage of the undisclosed output.

Leo Carbajal and Paul McAllister

VALUE OF AGRICULTURAL PRODUCTS

	Market Value of All Agricultural Products Sold ($1000)			% Increase Value Farm Products Sold, 1969-1974
	1964	1969	1974	
STATE	$227,127	$358,826	$521,694	45.4
Bernalillo	9,866	10,392	15,141	45.7
Catron	2,531	4,170	4,634	11.1
Chaves	33,554	63,144	84,146	33.3
Colfax	4,395	8,282	11,953	44.3
Curry	21,030	30,999	59,479	91.9
De Baca	3,083	5,087	6,562	29.0
Dona Ana	28,078	32,163	53,694	66.9
Eddy	16,467	19,153	27,737	44.8
Grant	3,152	4,314	3,600	−16.6
Guadalupe	2,353	9,067	8,760	−3.4
Harding	2,824	4,294	5,415	26.1
Hidalgo	5,841	6,341	8,645	36.3
Lea	14,214	13,152	24,710	87.9
Lincoln	4,168	6,226	6,931	11.3
Los Alamos	NA	NA	131	NA
Luna	7,599	9,807	17,810	81.6
McKinley	1,942	2,758	4,258	54.4
Mora	2,836	3,812	5,175	35.8
Otero	3,144	3,906	5,670	45.2
Quay	7,570	11,639	27,352	135.0
Rio Arriba	3,133	4,131	5,039	22.0
Roosevelt	16,445	29,074	38,344	31.9
Sandoval	986	2,822	3,421	21.2
San Juan	3,012	4,123	5,585	35.5
San Miguel	3,737	7,690	7,933	3.2
Santa Fe	2,070	5,580	6,183	10.8
Sierra	2,594	5,032	7,423	47.5
Socorro	3,296	5,726	7,623	33.1
Taos	882	844	1,514	79.4
Torrance	3,287	6,547	8,192	25.1
Union	7,714	30,799	38,580	25.3
Valencia	5,324	7,752	10,054	29.7

VALUE OF SHIPMENTS OF MANUFACTURED PRODUCTS (in millions)

	1967	1972
Bernalillo	166.9	320.1
Catron	D	D
Chaves	29.9	66.6
Colfax	5.2	7.5
Curry	59.7	119.0
De Baca	D	D
Dona Ana	16.3	32.1
Eddy	32.4	18.4
Grant	D	D
Guadalupe	D	D
Harding	D	D
Hidalgo	D	D
Lea	13.3	26.8
Lincoln*	.4	3.2
Los Alamos	D	.4
Luna	6.7	9.2
McKinley	35.7	54.1
Mora*	.1	D
Otero	6.6	D
Quay*	.6	7.5
Rio Arriba*	3.2	8.3
Roosevelt	4.9	5.9
Sandoval*	2.3	12.9
San Juan	14.6	35.4
San Miguel	5.0	3.8
Santa Fe	12.1	18.1
Sierra	D	.3
Socorro	1.8	1.8
Taos*	.9	3.6
Torrance*	.1	D
Union*	.4	D
Valencia	D	5.6
State Withheld	67.2	158.3
State Total	486.3	918.9

D Withheld to avoid disclosing figures for individual companies.
* For 1967 over 30 percent of the data for this line was estimat

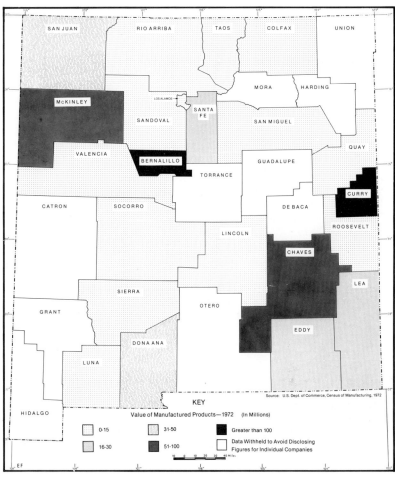

KEY

Value of Manufactured Products—1972 (In Millions)

0-15	31-50	Greater than 100
16-30	51-100	Data Withheld to Avoid Disclosing Figures for Individual Companies

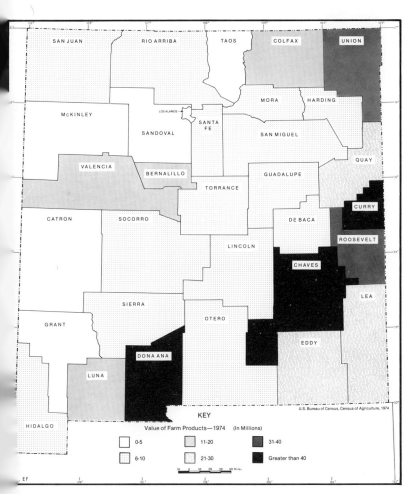

KEY

Value of Farm Products—1974 (In Millions)

0-5	11-20	31-40
6-10	21-30	Greater than 40

121

mineral mining

New Mexico contains vast mineral wealth which has been mined for at least 12,000 years. Most of the early mining efforts were limited and not until the 19th century did mining take on an important role within the state. As advances in technology and transportation occurred and the demand for minerals rose, mining began to play a significant role in providing employment (approximately 21,300 people in 1977), salaries (approximately $175 million in 1977), and revenue for New Mexico. Presently the state ranks 8th nationally in total value of mineral products amounting to $744 million annually.

A wide variety of minerals are produced including fuels, metals and nonmetals. Mines in the state produce more than 30 of the 91 minerals listed by the U.S. Bureau of Mines as essential mineral materials. In 1978 the state was the leading producer in the nation of perlite (87%), potassium salts (84%), and uranium (44%) as well as a major producer of copper, molybdenum, lead, zinc, gold and silver. Surface and subsurface mines are located throughout the state with concentrations in Grant, Eddy, Socorro, McKinley, Sierra, Valencia, Sandoval and Santa Fe counties.

Today's mining is a result of thousands of years of mineral resource utilization. The history of mining is a central theme in the physical and cultural development of the state. The earliest demand was for silica minerals which, when shaped, provided basic tools such as arrowheads and scrapers for early man. Although most prospecting was limited to surface finds, some sites such as Cerro Pedernal (flint hill) contains ancient mine workings. Clay for pottery and stone for building were extensively sought but it was the turquoise which was exploited most by early surface miners. Some of the oldest mines were found near Cerrillos on Mount Chalchihuitl (turquoise). Mining technology was limited and tools were composed primarily of stone or wood. Spaniards arriving at Mount Chalchihuitl reported one pit mine to be 200 ft. across at the top, 100 ft. across at the bottom and 130 ft. at the deepest point. Associated waste dumps covered several acres.

Early Spanish exploration was based on the chasing of legends rather than prospecting and not until the 18th century did mining for minerals take place. Again, near Cerrillos the La Mina del Tiro Mine produced lead and possibly silver from shafts within a lead vein. Later in the century the Santa Rita del Cobre Grant was obtained by Col. Manuel Carrasco and Don Francisco Manuel Elguea and extensive copper mining near Silver City began. At one point 6,000,000 pounds of copper were sent to Mexico City annually.

The first American influence was felt in the 1820's as optimistic prospectors examined the mineral regions which later led to major mining developments. Two gold rushes took place before 1840, spurring the interest and imagination of Mexican and American miners. Ralston, Shakespeare (Valarde), Georgetown, and Chloride Flat (Silver City) in Grant County became famous for silver production, as well as the Black Range communities of Cokes Peak, Lake Valley, Hillsboro, Kingston, and Chloride in western Socorro and Doña Ana counties. Gold strikes gave rise in the 1880's to the famous mining towns of White Oaks, Mogollon-Cooney, Golden, and Winston as the emphasis shifted from the exhausted districts in the Sangre de Cristo Mountains to the new resources in the central and southwestern portions of the territory.

During the last 40 years of the 19th century, New Mexico's population and transportation continued to grow. Burgeoning railroads were linking the eastern markets to the mineral wealth of the state. Spur lines were built to coal deposits of Madrid, the gold district of Cerrillos, to the lead deposits of Kelly, silver deposits of Lake Valley, copper deposits at Santa Rita and at Hanover. Not only did improved transportation provide an outlet for minerals but also a supply route for the new technology. Advanced machinery used in mining and smelting were shipped from eastern manufacturers to revolutionize the mining industry.

The national financial crisis and depression, which followed the collapse of silver prices in 1893, initiated a decline in mining. With the arrival of the twentieth century, a shift in interest from precious metals to minerals took place. The demand for industrial minerals such as copper, molybdenum and zinc outstripped all previous production and value of production. Large capital needs for massive development could only be dealt with by corporations. New Mexico's mining industry rapidly expanded to become one of the major mineral-producing states.

With the advent of nuclear power in the 1950's, a demand was established for uranium, previously a mineral used in coloring of glass and ceramic glazes and of little value. As the demand for uranium to supply the increasing number of nuclear generating plants rose, the uranium reserves of the state were developed. The Grants Uranium Region became an area of intense exploration and surface and subsurface mining.

Mining districts are established within areas of past or present mineral production. Of the mining districts in New Mexico, based on data reported to the U.S. Bureau of Mines, there are seven mining districts which have a cumulative production greater than $100 million (as of 1978).

The **Carlsbad** mining district produces potassium minerals from an Upper Permian salt formation approximately 2,450 ft. thick. All mine workings are underground with vertical shafts accessing the various ore zones.

The **Santa Rita** district is principally concerned with copper, although gold, silver and molybdenum are retrieved. The ore mined is found in Pennsylvanian limestones and shales, Cretaceous sandstones and shales, diorite sills and Tertiary porphyries. Mine operations are open pit although new leaching of waste dump materials for further recovery of minerals is being applied.

Copper is the major mineral mined in the **Big Burro** metallic mining district and lesser amounts of gold & silver result from the mining activity. The copper ore is extracted through surface mining of a Tertiary and Cretaceous porphyry.

The **Ambrosia Lake** mining district's principal minerals are uranium, molybdenum, and vanadium. Most ore is found in Jurassic formations and to a lesser extent in Cretaceous formations. Most of the uranium ore is associated with organic matter within the sandstone rocks and all of the ore is produced by deep mining.

Uranium and vanadium are the principal minerals mined in the **Laguna** mining district. As in the Ambrosia Lake district, the ore is found in a Jurassic sandstone of 100 to 200 feet thick. Mining is performed by both surface and underground mining techniques.

Fruitland and the York Canyon-Vermejo Park are two mining districts which produce coal. The Fruitland district coal is used principally in power generation and the York Canyon-Vermejo Park district produces high quality coking coal for use in the making of steel in southern California.

Michael Inglis

Mining Districts (Cumulative Production greater than $100 million)	Value of Production
Carlsbad (Potassium minerals) 1941-1977	$2,754,145,000
Ambrosia Lake (Uranium & vanadium) 1951-1975	$1,050,000,000
Big Burro (Copper only) 1904-1977	$ 853,511,000
Santa Rita (Copper only) 1930-1977	$ 629,987,921
Laguna (Uranium & vanadium) 1952-1975	$ 510,300,000
Fruitland (Coal) 1969-1977	$ 195,592,000
York Canyon-Vermejo Park (Coal) 1968-1977	$ 135,548,000

Mining Companies (By County)

BERNALILLO COUNTY
1—Ideal Basic Industries: Cement, Clay, Stone
2—Kinney Brick Company, Inc.: Clay
3—Rocky Mountain Stone: Stone

CATRON COUNTY
4—Challenge Mining Company: Gold
5—Pueblo Zuni Salt Corporation: Salt

DONA ANA COUNTY
6—El Paso Brick Company: Clay
7—Del Norte Masonry: Pumice
8—Morton Brothers: Pumice
9—Apache Springs Company: Stone
10—Burn Construction Company, Inc.: Stone
11—Guillen Construction: Stone

EDDY COUNTY
12—Max Chemical Corporation: Potash
13—Doval Corporation: Potash, Salt
14—International Minerals and Chemical Corporation: Potash
15—Kerr-McGee Corporation: Potash
16—Mississippi Chemical Company: Potash, Salt
17—Potash Company of America (Ideal Basic Ind.): Potash, Salt
18—Hereford Salt: Salt
19—United Salt Corporation: Salt

GRANT COUNTY
20—ASARCO, Inc.: Copper, Gold, Lead, Silver
21—Kennecott Copper Corporation: Copper, Gold, Lime, Silver
22—Phelps-Dodge: Copper, Gold, Silver
23—U. V. Industries: Copper, Gold, Iron Ore, Lead, Silver
24—Dresser Minerals (Division of Dresser Industries, Inc.: Gold, Silver
25—Summit Minerals, Inc.: Gold, Silver
26—Mathis & Mathis: Lime
27—Luck Mining: Manganiferous Ore

HARDING COUNTY
28—S.E.C. Corporation: CO₂

HIDALGO COUNTY
22—Phelps-Dodge: Stone

LEA COUNTY
29—National Potash: Potash
30—Williams Brine Service: Salt
31—Thomason Construction Company: Stone

LINCOLN COUNTY
32—H. N. LaRue and Sons: Iron Ore

LUNA COUNTY
26—Mathis & Mathis: Clay
33—W. H. Thomas Quarries: Stone

McKINLEY COUNTY
34—A. & D. Marinella: Stone
35—Mendosa Red Dog: Stone
36—Midwest Industries Company: Stone
37—Cobb Nuclear Corporation: Uranium
39—Gulf Mineral Resources, Uranium
40—M & M Mining Company: Uranium
41—Todilto Exploration & Development Company: Uranium

RIO ARRIBA COUNTY
42—American Exploration and Management, Inc.: Diatomaceous Earth
43—Colorado Aggregate Company, Inc.: Pumice
44—General Pumice Corporation: Pumice

SANDOVAL COUNTY
45—Farm Guard Products: Clay
46—Pomeroy, Inc.: Gypsum
47—Ernest Teeter Trucking: Gypsum
48—Alpha Organic Material: Peat
49—Humus Organic Products: Peat
50—Utility Block Company, Inc.: Pumice

SAN JUAN COUNTY
51—Garcia & Sons: Clay, Pumice
52—Western Helium: Helium

SAN MIGUEL COUNTY
53—Armstrong & Armstrong: Stone

SANTA FE COUNTY
54—CAC Mining: Copper, Gold
55—Western Mining Company: Gypsum
56—Colony Materials, Inc.: Pumice
57—Copar Pumice Company: Pumice
58—Crego Block Company: Pumice
70—Gold Field Mining: Gold

SOCORRO COUNTY
38—Farris Mines: Barite, Florite, Lead
59—L. M. & M., Inc.: Iron Ore
60—Grefco, Inc.: Perlite
3—Rocky Mountain Stone: Stone

TAOS COUNTY
61—Mineral Industries Commodities of America, Inc.: Mica
62—Molybdenum Corporation: Mica
63—Johns-Manville Perlite Corporation: Perlite
64—Silbrico Corporation: Perlite

UNION COUNTY
65—Twin Mountain Rock Company: Pumice

VALENCIA COUNTY
38—Farris Mines: Uranium
66—U.S. Gypsum Company: Perlite
67—Sohio Natural Resources Company: Uranium
68—Anaconda Company: Uranium

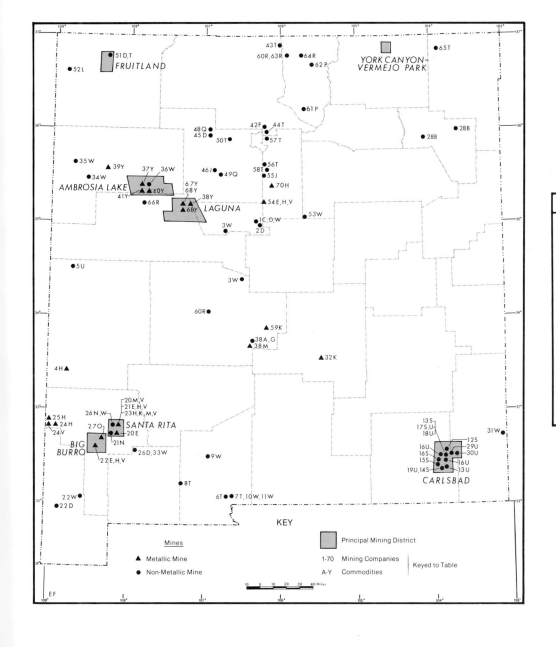

Commodities

A—Barite
B—Carbon Dioxide
C—Cement
D—Clay
E—Copper
F—Diatomaceous Earth
G—Fluorite
H—Gold
I—Gold/Silver
J—Gypsum
K—Iron Ore
L—Helium
M—Lead
N—Lime
O—Manganiferous Oxide
P—Mica
Q—Peat
R—Perlite
S—Potash
T—Pumice
U—Salt
V—Silver
W—Stone
X—Sulfur
Y—Uranium

KEY

Mines

▲ Metallic Mine
● Non-Metallic Mine

■ Principal Mining District

1-70 Mining Companies
A-Y Commodities

Keyed to Table

10 0 10 20 30 40 Miles

retail trade and service sectors

The contribution of the trade sector and the services sector to total income in New Mexico is substantial. The trade sector includes establishments primarily engaged in selling merchandise. The services sector includes establishments primarily engaged in providing services for individuals and organizations. Examples of types of businesses in the service sector are hotels, auto repair shops, movie theaters and educational institutions. When combined, trade and services contribute about a third of total income in the state while the government sector, the largest economic sector in the state, contributes about a quarter of total income in New Mexico. Trade and services also provided about 42.5 percent of total nonagricultural wage and salary employment in 1977 and the first half of 1978. Their shares of total employment have increased steadily since 1970.

The sector distribution of retail sales in New Mexico and the United States is compared in table A. As can be seen, the state and the nation have similar distributions. The largest differences in the shares of total retail sales contributed by each category in 1977 occurred in the automotive sector (21.7 percent for New Mexico and 19.7 percent for the U.S.), general merchandise (12.0 percent for New Mexico and 13.9 percent for the U.S.), and retail sales in the "other" category (29.6 percent and 27.4 percent).

In the eating and drinking places category, the general merchandise category and the drug category, the share of total sales since 1973 has decreased for the state and remained about the same for the nation. All other categories show significant increases in their shares of total retail sales in New Mexico between 1973 and 1977.

The table also illustrates the dollar amount of retail sales in New Mexico for 1973 and 1977. The categories of food; furniture, home furnishings, and appliances; and automotive realized the largest percentage gains between 1973 and 1977. Total retail sales

in New Mexico increased by 49 percent during this five-year period.

Businesses in Bernalillo County, the most populous county in the state, recorded 1.345 billion dollars in retail sales in 1977, contributing 36.6 percent of the 3.670 billion dollars in retail sales in New Mexico in 1977 (a 7 percent higher total figure for 1977 is obtained by using data from the State of New Mexico, Bureau of Revenue, Tax Research Division). By contrast, the combined retail sales in 21 of New Mexico's 32 counties account for only 16.3 percent of the state's total.

Counties with the largest increases in their levels of retail sales between 1973 and 1977 include Torrance with a 225.8 percent rise, Socorro with a 179.5 percent gain and Lincoln with a 177.9 percent increase. Only three counties in New Mexico experienced a drop in retail sales in the 1973 to 1977 period. Harding County had the largest drop (44.1 percent) followed by Catron County with an 18.5 percent decrease and Curry County with a 7.9 percent fall in retail sales.

Tourism is an important source of income to New Mexico and in particular to the trade and services sectors. The total number of visitors annually to New Mexico's national parks and monuments between 1973 and 1977 are:

Year	1973	1974	1975	1976	1977
(in thousands)	2016	1671	1948	2108	1984

Carlsbad Caverns, White Sands and Bandelier National Monument attracted 82 percent of all visitors to the state's national parks and monuments in 1977. A decline in visits to the state's parks and monuments in 1974 is most probably attributable to increased gasoline prices during that time with a subsequent decrease in auto travel.

Michael T. Byrnes

TABLE A

NEW MEXICO AND UNITED STATES RETAIL SALES SECTOR DISTRIBUTION	(N.M. $ millions)		% Change	(PERCENT OF TOTAL SALES)			
				1973		1977	
	1973	1977	1973-77	N.M.	U.S.	N.M.	U.S.
TOTAL	$2463	$3670	49.0	100.0	100.0	100.0	100.0
Food	521	802	53.9	21.2	22.1	21.9	22.0
Eating and Drinking Places	200	261	30.5	8.1	8.8	7.1	8.8
General Merchandise	335	442	31.9	13.6	14.2	12.0	13.9
Furniture, Home Furnishings, Appliances	108	181	67.6	4.4	4.7	4.9	5.0
Automotive	512	798	55.9	20.8	19.3	21.7	19.7
Drug	76	100	31.6	3.1	3.2	2.7	3.2
Other	711	1086	52.7	28.9	27.7	29.6	27.4

TABLE B

	Percent Change 1973-77	Amount ($ millions) 1977		Percent Change 1973-77	Amount ($ millions) 1977
Bernalillo	44.5	$1345	Mora	33.4	3
Catron	−18.5	3	Otero	89.5	108
Chavez	25.1	162	Quay	8.3	36
Colfax	53.8	39	Rio Arriba	104.3	52
Curry	−7.9	120	Roosevelt	16.1	36
De Baca	25.0	7	Sandoval	33.7	20
Dona Ana	23.7	217	San Juan	145.7	239
Eddy	58.3	150	San Miguel	73.5	50
Grant	5.5	62	Santa Fe	51.2	248
Guadalupe	49.5	20	Sierra	50.7	19
Harding	−44.1	2	Socorro	179.5	28
Hidalgo	45.8	18	Taos	25.8	46
Lea	47.5	174	Torrance	225.8	17
Lincoln	177.9	39	Union	23.8	14
Los Alamos	84.4	44	Valencia	61.4	125
Luna	60.9	44	STATE TOTAL	49.0	$3670
McKinley	102.4	184			

Article and tables compiled directly from bibliographic sources.

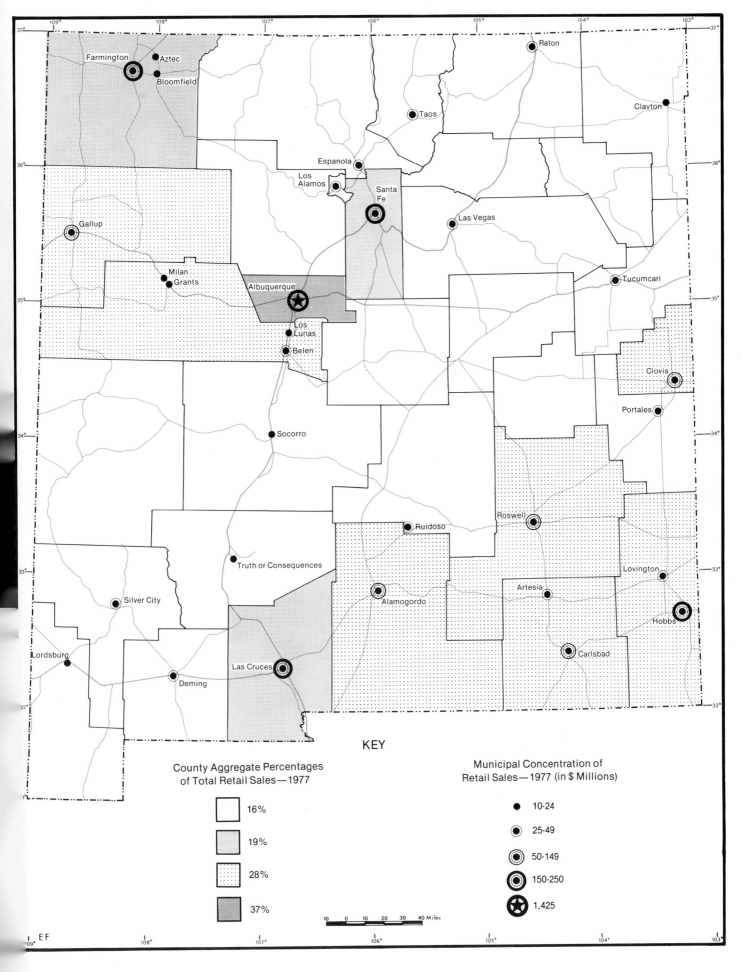

KEY

County Aggregate Percentages
of Total Retail Sales—1977

- 16%
- 19%
- 28%
- 37%

Municipal Concentration of
Retail Sales—1977 (in $ Millions)

- 10-24
- 25-49
- 50-149
- 150-250
- 1,425

10 0 10 20 30 40 Miles

E F

energy: oil and gas

In 1977, New Mexico rated fourth in the country in gas production and seventh in oil production. Oil and gas have an enormous impact on the state in terms of revenue derived for operation of the state government and the public schools and universities. The direct taxes collected from the industry in 1977 totaled $135 million, of which $40.3 million was listed as the "emergency school tax." The state received other revenues (lease rentals, royalties, and severance taxes from gas and oil production), increasing the 1977 contribution to more than $325 million.

The public school system is a major beneficiary of those revenues, receiving nearly $118 million or 35% of the total statewide school operating costs during the 1976-77 school year. Each of the eighty-eight school districts received operating funds although 95% of the gas and oil was produced in only four of the counties. The seven state universities and colleges and twelve other institutions of higher education received $15.8 million from assessments on the oil and gas industry.

The petroleum industry accounted for 69% of the 1977 value of mineral production in New Mexico. This industry provided jobs for more than 20,000 people of which over 9,000 were employed in the production of crude oil and natural gas. The remainder were involved with the refinement, transportation and distribution of production.

OIL

The first official report of oil was in 1882 when a prospecting party discovered a flowing oil well only a few miles from the Navajo Reservation in northwestern New Mexico. Commercial production started in San Juan County in 1922 when the Midwest Refining Company completed a gas well at the Dome Field and discovered the nearby Hogback oil pool. By 1924 the Artesia oil field in Eddy County was developed and the discovery of the famous Hobbs pool in 1929 quickly boosted the state as a major oil producer. By 1932 large oil pipelines extended into Lea County to transport New Mexico crude to the eastern markets. Crude oil was transported by pipeline from the Rattlesnake and Table Mesa fields of San Juan County to Gallup and subsequently shipped by a railway tank car to the Continental refinery in Albuquerque.

During the past fifty years, New Mexico has moved from 17th to 7th among the states in production of oil. One and two-tenths million barrels were produced in 1928, compared to 87 million barrels in 1977. Production peaked in 1969, with over 129 million barrels. Ninety-three percent of the 1977 production came from the Permian Basin in Lea County, Eddy County, Chaves County, and Roosevelt County. The southeastern dominance in production is expected to continue as 1,084 of the 1,255 known oil and gas pools are in the Permian Basin. The remaining production was from the San Juan Basin counties of San Juan and Rio Arriba.

Thirty-five percent of the oil produced in New Mexico in 1977 was processed at the eight refineries located in the state, operating at 75% of their capacity. The consumption of oil products in New Mexico during the same year exceeded refinery production by more than 13 million barrels. The plant at Monument was closed at the end of 1977, however, when a new refinery planned for construction in Las Cruces is completed, the loss of capacity at Monument shall be more than compensated for.

NATURAL GAS

By 1921 pockets of natural gas in the San Juan basin were producing fuel for lighting and heat in the town of Aztec. Other towns located near gas wells were able to use the fuel as a resource, but due to a lack of a nearby market, most of the gas discovered in oil drilling was either capped or the fumes flared into the atmosphere. The development of new pipeline technology enabled El Paso Natural Gas to operate a 16-inch line from the Lea County fields into Arizona and Mexico. By 1956 New Mexico's San Juan Basin had pipelines extending into California and the Pacific Northwest. Since 1935 the state has produced around 25 trillion cubic feet of gas, with the major increase in development occurring in the mid-1950's.

The northwest corner of New Mexico is primarily a gas-producing province, accounting for 47% of the 1977 natural gas production in the state, against only 7% of the recovered oil. The oil-rich Permian Basin of the southeast accounted for the remaining 53% of the natural gas production. Nearly all of the 1,184 billion cubic feet produced in 1977 came from the counties of Lea, San Juan, Eddy, and Rio Arriba.

Forty-one natural gas plants in New Mexico processed over a trillion cubic feet of gas in 1977. By-products of the field gas were 50.7 million barrels of butane, propane, natural gasoline, and composite liquids. Most of the processing plants are located in Lea, Eddy, and San Juan counties. Natural gas is second to coal as an energy fuel for electricity generation in New Mexico. In 1976 power plants along the Rio Grande and in the southeast consumed over 68 billion cubic feet of natural gas in generating 31% of the electricity produced in New Mexico.

If the current rate of oil production (100 million barrels per year) is sustained without significant new discoveries, New Mexico's oil resources could theoretically be depleted by 1980. As pools and pressures decline, however, production will decline and extend the deadline beyond 1980. General world shortages of oil and the spiralling price of crude oil may spur exploration into the deeper shales and sedimentary basins throughout the state and permit more expensive recovery processes to become economically feasible.

Natural gas reserves in the state declined sharply from the 23.5 trillion cubic feet in 1956 to 14 trillion cubic feet in 1962. The discovery of new gas fields in Eddy County have contributed to slight increases in reserves in the 1970's. However, the steady rise in production to over 1.2 trillion cubic feet of gas in 1975 implies a theoretical depletion of the resource by 1989, with a pressure decline curve stretching the date into the 1990's. Even at the present rate of discoveries, only two years can be added to the life expectancy of reserves.

Jerry L. Williams

OIL REFINERIES OF NEW MEXICO—1976

Name	Location	Capacity barrels/day
Navajo	Artesia	29,900
Southern Union	Monument	5,000
Southern Union	Lovington	37,000
Shell Oil	Ciniza	18,000
Plateau	Bloomfield	8,400
Caribou	Kirtland	2,500
Thriftway	Bloomfield	7,500
Giant	Bloomfield	6,200

OIL AND NATURAL GAS PRODUCTION IN NEW MEXICO

Year	Oil Production in Barrels (1,000's)	Value of Oil Production ($1,000's)	Gas Production in MCF* (1,000's)	Value of Gas Production ($1,000's)
1945	37,351	$ 37,610	124,480	$ 2,103
1950	47,351	115,100	225,212	7,858
1955	82,426	224,200	520,209	45,458
1960	107,388	307,131	792,541	87,180
1965	119,141	345,508	901,522	112,760
1970	128,184	410,187	1,131,630	164,443
1975	95,063	788,068	1,203,107	485,333

1 barrel = 42 gallons

*MCF = one thousand cubic feet

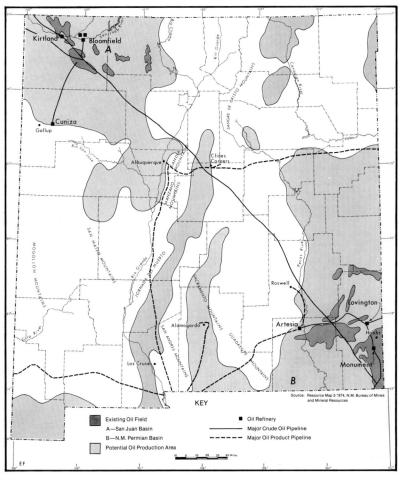

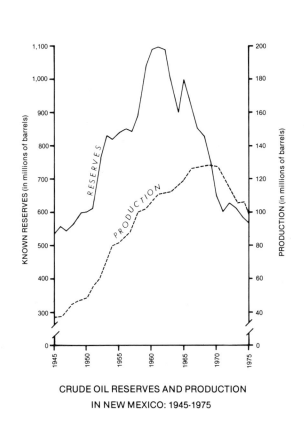

CRUDE OIL RESERVES AND PRODUCTION
IN NEW MEXICO: 1945-1975

KEY

Existing Oil Field

A—San Juan Basin

B—N.M. Permian Basin

Potential Oil Production Area

■ Oil Refinery

Major Crude Oil Pipeline

Major Oil Product Pipeline

Source: Resource Map 3-'1974, N.M. Bureau of Mines and Mineral Resources

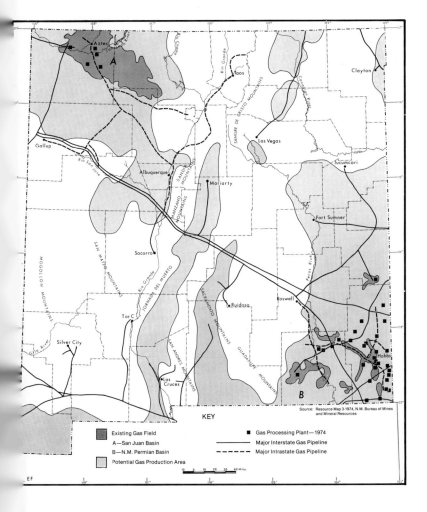

KEY

Existing Gas Field

A—San Juan Basin

B—N.M. Permian Basin

Potential Gas Production Area

■ Gas Processing Plant—1974

Major Interstate Gas Pipeline

Major Intrastate Gas Pipeline

Source: Resource Map 3-1974, N.M. Bureau of Mines and Mineral Resources

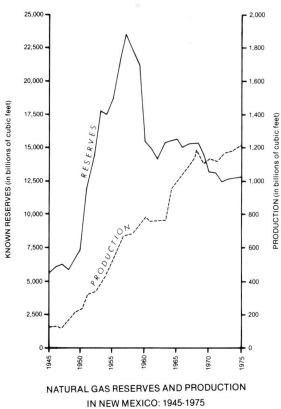

NATURAL GAS RESERVES AND PRODUCTION
IN NEW MEXICO: 1945-1975

127

energy: coal

Coal-bearing formations underlie approximately one-fifth of New Mexico and contain reserves that are estimated to exceed 282 billion short tons. The use of coal has a long history in the state as coal ash has been found in the excavations of 14th century pueblos and was recorded as a fuel resource for the Spanish in the 18th century. The Cerrillos Field was commercially mined as early as 1835, but it was the coming of the railroad and development of copper and lead smelters in the southwest in the late 19th century that provided sufficient demand to develop the coal fields of New Mexico. The first formal records in 1882 indicated that 164,000 short tons were produced at the Carthage, Cerrillos, and Raton fields.

The importance of the coal deposits in the late 19th century could be measured by their access to railway transport. Of the more than 200 underground coal mines that came into operation between 1880 and 1940, all but a few small isolated diggings were connected to the railroad. Coalara, in the Sierra Blanca Field, was the only producing mine location that required major railway construction to reach it. Coal production in the early 20th century steadily advanced and peaked in 1917-1918 with over 4 million tons produced. Coal demand dropped to less than 1.5 million tons during the Depression years with only a slight resurgence during World War II.

The attraction and use of the clean and inexpensive oil and natural gas fuels during the 1950's destroyed the coal economy. In 1958 only 117,000 tons were produced, the lowest total production value since 1890. In the late 1950's the only coal activity was in the Raton Field where Kaiser Steel reopened the underground York Canyon mine as a source of coking fuel for its mills in California.

Several factors contributed to the coal resurrection in New Mexico during the 1960's. Environmental controls forced industry to focus attention on the low sulphur content coal fields in the western states, and the large reserves accessible by inexpensive surface mining methods in the San Juan Basin drove production upward to 3 million tons per year by 1965.

In 1969 and 1970 the two major units of the Four Corners electricity generating plant near Farmington came on line and production soared to nearly 7½ million tons. The San Juan generating plant also opened on the coal field north of Farmington in 1972 and the McKinley Field north of Gallup began providing fuel for a generating facility in northern Arizona. By 1976 over 60% of the electricity generated in the state used coal fuel as a heat resource and a number of plants were in the process of converting from the more expensive oil and natural gas. By 1977 coal production had exceeded 11 million tons and the number of surface mines were expected to increase from four to ten by 1985. Proposed development of a rail spur from Prewitt into the San Juan Basin and additions to the generating stations in the area indicate that production will continue to rise. A major difficulty with surface mining in many of the new fields is the presence of invaluable vertebrate fossils overlying the coal. Thus the opening of a new area such as Star Lake-Bisti (50 miles north of Grants) requires several years of study prior to consideration for mining approval. Even so, the estimated 5.7 billion tons of strippable coal in the northwest and over 275 billion tons of deep coal throughout the state assure New Mexico of a long-term period of production.

Jerry L. Williams

NEW MEXICO COAL MINES—1978

Map Key		Mine	Average Production 1974-1976 (tons)	Employees 1976
6	Carbon Coal Company	Mentmore	—0—	
4	Utah International	Navajo	6,595,000	440
3	Western Coal Company	San Juan	1,186,000	71
5	Kaiser Steel Corp.	York Canyon	934,000	447
2	Pittsburgh and Midway	McKinley	607,000	71
1	Amcoal Company	Sundance	100,000*	22

*mine data unavailable in 1975 and 1976

COAL PRODUCTION IN NEW MEXICO

Year	Short tons* (1,000's)	Value in Dollars ($1,000)
1900	1,299	1,776
1920	3,683	13,568
1940	1,111	3,300
1950	727	3,918
1960	295	1,748
1965	3,212	10,710
1970	7,361	21,249
1975	8,785	60,030
1977	11,645	101,432

*Short ton = 2000 lbs.

Source: *Resource Map 10,* "Coal Fields and Mines of New Mexico," by David Tabet and Stephen Frost, New Mexico Bureau of Mines and Mineral Resources, 1978.

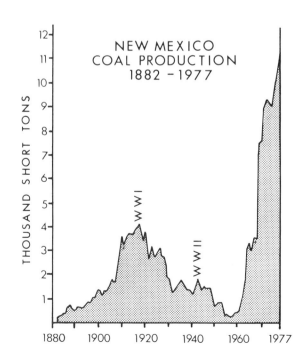

NEW MEXICO COAL PRODUCTION 1882 – 1977

THOUSAND SHORT TONS

W W I

W W II

1880 1900 1920 1940 1960 1977

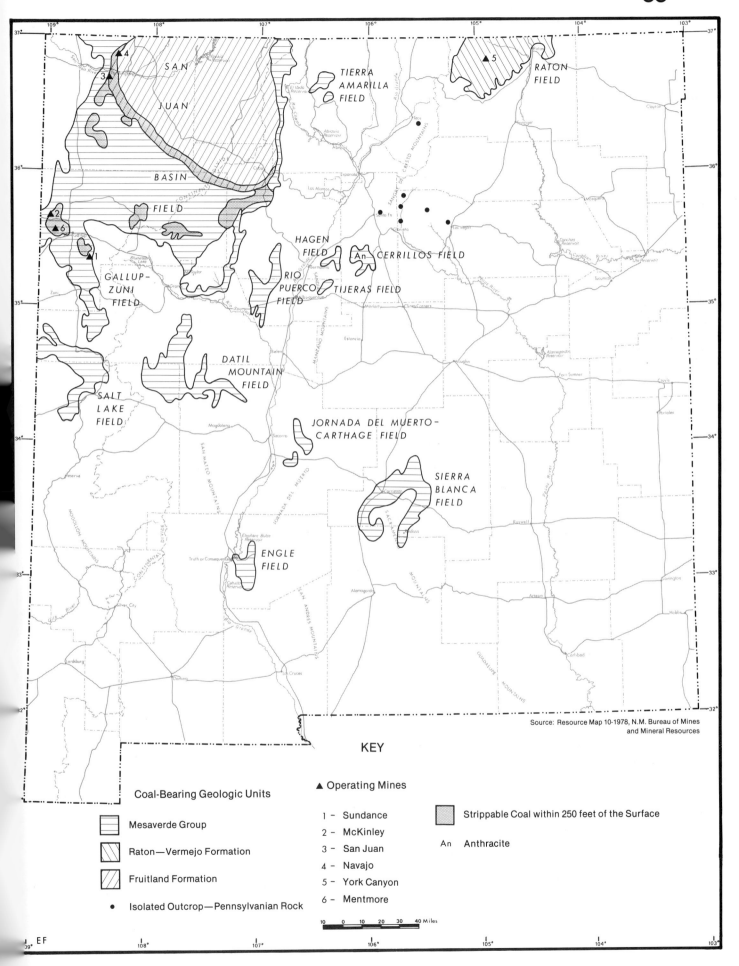

Source: Resource Map 10-1978, N.M. Bureau of Mines
and Mineral Resources

KEY

Coal-Bearing Geologic Units

▲ Operating Mines

	Mesaverde Group
	Raton—Vermejo Formation
	Fruitland Formation
•	Isolated Outcrop—Pennsylvanian Rock

1 – Sundance
2 – McKinley
3 – San Juan
4 – Navajo
5 – York Canyon
6 – Mentmore

Strippable Coal within 250 feet of the Surface

An   Anthracite

10 0 10 20 30 40 Miles

129

energy: uranium and electricity

URANIUM

In 1977 New Mexico produced more than 47% of the nation's supply of uranium and it was estimated that over half of the country's reserves were in the state. The present demand for uranium energy is based on more than 200 commercial reactors that shall be in operation by 1990. Government estimates indicate that New Mexico will have to increase production to around 42 million pounds of yellowcake by 1990 to meet the nation's demand. Yellowcake is a chemical concentrate that is milled from the natural uranium ore. The product is shipped to Illinois and Oklahoma for refining and to Kentucky or Tennessee for enrichment as a nuclear energy resource.

Uranium was discovered in Morrison formation outcrops 10 to 20 miles northwest of Grants in 1950. By 1952 the Atomic Energy Commission (AEC) had established a limestone treatment mill ten miles northwest of Grants near Bluewater. Exploration for uranium ore has now expanded the mining area. The Grants Uranium Belt consists of four conterminous mining districts: Gallup–Churchrock, Smith Lake–Crownpoint, Ambrosia Lake–San Mateo near Grants, and Jackpile–Poquate and Marquez mines on the Laguna Pueblo Reservation. The main consumer of uranium ore between 1955 and 1965 was the AEC for production of nuclear weapons and creation of strategic stockpiles. The peak purchase year was 1960 when over fifteen million pounds of yellowcake were exported at a value of more than 125 million dollars. The market and production declined rapidly in the 1960's when the federal government began phasing out purchases for nuclear weapons. The steady production since 1968 has been due to the rise in "peace time" use of nuclear energy as a power generating fuel.

ELECTRICITY GENERATION

Production and export of electricity is a major industry of New Mexico. The state consumes only about one-third of its present generating capacity. The bulk of its power production is exported from the huge generating plants near Farmington to Arizona, while the more distant southern and eastern portions of the state purchase a significant amount of power from generating plants in Texas.

The combined capacity of the coal-fired Four Corners (2085 MW) plant near Fruitland and the San Juan (685 MW) plant northwest of Farmington accounts for over two-thirds of the state's production and is presently one of the largest electricity-providing complexes in the nation. The present 2800 megawatt production is expected to be boosted to nearly 3600 MW by the year 1981 with the addition of two more generating units at the San Juan station. Coal production will also be increased by the proposed construction of four 500 MW coal fired generating units in the Bisti area of the northwest during the 1980's. As the oil and natural gas pools diminish, coal will increasingly be used as the electricity generating fuel for New Mexico. Hydroelectric production is presently confined to the small power station at Elephant Butte Dam. The unpredictable water regime of the state does not increase the likelihood of more power dams in the future.

Experimentation is now underway for the production of geothermal power in the Jemez Mountains west of Santa Fe and the use of solar power near Albuquerque. NASA has constructed an experimental wind generator on the high plains at Clayton. Utility companies have begun investing in water rights at basins in the eastern areas of the state, possibly for electricity production by nuclear or coal fueled generators to supply future demands of eastern New Mexico and western Texas. Most of these production units are in their infancy or only on drawing boards and may not bear fruit for several decades. Meanwhile coal provides the most economic production of electricity in the state and will likely continue as the main fuel source far into the future.

Jerry L. Williams

URANIUM PRODUCTION MILLS—1977

Map Key	Company	Location	Capacity tons/day
3	Anaconda	Bluewater	5,000
2	Kerr-McGee	Ambrosia Lake	7,000
5	Sohio-Reserve	Cebolleta	1,700
1	United	Churchrock	3,000
4	United-Homestake	Milan	3,500
		Total	20,200

URANIUM PRODUCTION IN NEW MEXICO

Year	Yellowcake (1000 lbs.)	Value in Dollars ($1,000)	% of U.S. Production
1970	11,542	66,713	44.7
1971	10,610	63,660	43.2
1972	10,928	65,022	42.4
1973	9,268	58,852	35.0
1974	9,902	67,631	43.0
1975	10,382	82,848	44.8
1976	12,118	151,960	47.5

Source: *Energytics New Mexico*, P.R. Grant, Jr., 1977.

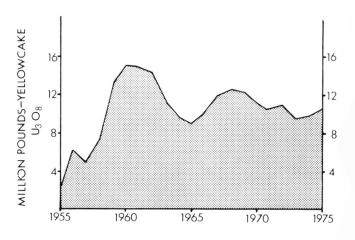

NEW MEXICO URANIUM PRODUCTION
1955–1975

energy: uranium and electricity

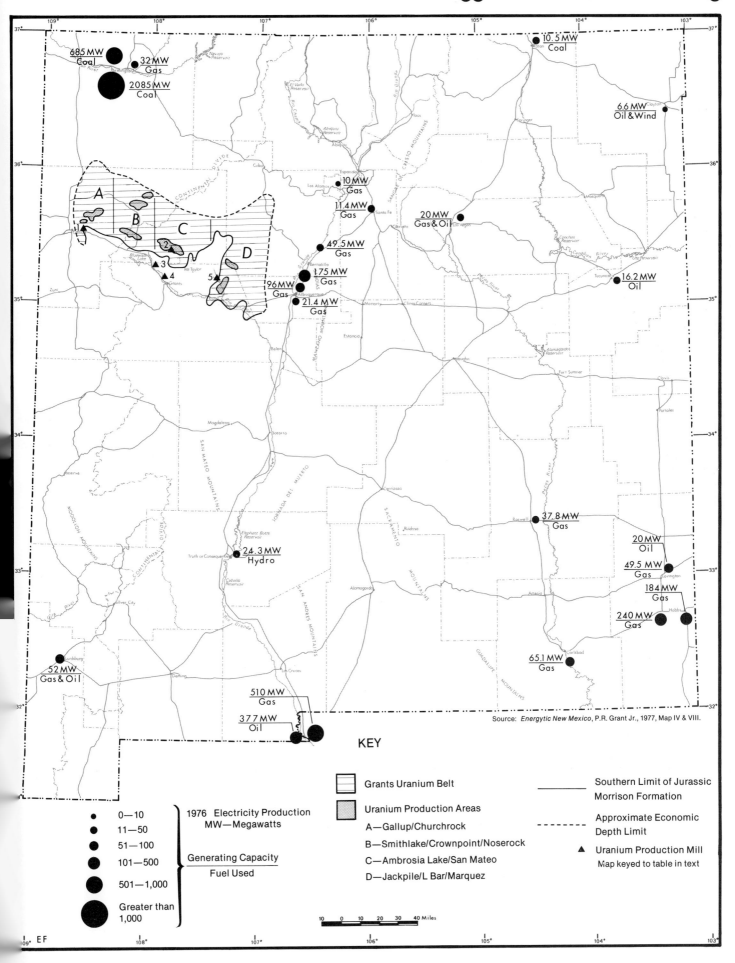

Source: *Energytic New Mexico*, P.R. Grant Jr., 1977, Map IV & VIII.

KEY

0—10
11—50
51—100
101—500
501—1,000
Greater than 1,000

1976 Electricity Production
MW—Megawatts

Generating Capacity
Fuel Used

Grants Uranium Belt

Uranium Production Areas
A—Gallup/Churchrock
B—Smithlake/Crownpoint/Noserock
C—Ambrosia Lake/San Mateo
D—Jackpile/L Bar/Marquez

Southern Limit of Jurassic
Morrison Formation

Approximate Economic
Depth Limit

▲ Uranium Production Mill
Map keyed to table in text

10 0 10 20 30 40 Miles

public transportation

New Mexico is served by three commercial carrier modes of passenger transportation: air carriers, rail service and intercity buses. These modes, which together account for less than ten percent of the intercity passenger-miles of travel within the state, are compared on the basis of their 1977 routes and ridership. It must be noted that routes and service are continually changing, especially in the air transport area.

Regularly scheduled air service is provided to thirteen New Mexico communities by eight airlines. These airlines include three domestic trunk lines (TWA, Continental and American), two local service airlines (Frontier and Texas International) and three commuter (third-level) airlines (Crown, Ross and Zia). The third-level airlines provide the only scheduled service to Las Cruces, Los Alamos, Santa Fe and Taos. Data on departing passengers at the nine airports served by the major air carriers are summarized in the table.

Albuquerque International, with over 976,000 departing passengers, is the state's principal airport, as well as the only FAA hub in New Mexico. All eight airlines serve Albuquerque, and they provide 93 departure flights per day. Approximately half of these departures are intrastate flights, while the remainder provide nonstop service to Chicago, Dallas, Denver, Kansas City, Los Angeles, Phoenix, San Francisco, St. Louis and other cities. Annual growth in air travel from Albuquerque, which has been 11%, continued through 1978, when there were 1,093,000 departing passengers.

Several airlines have begun service to New Mexico cities in response to recent Civil Aeronautics Board regulation changes which have facilitated both route abandonment and market entry.

The National Railroad Passenger Corporation operates two AMTRAK lines within New Mexico, with a trackage totaling approximately 600 miles. The Southwest Limited, which provides one passenger train (in each direction) daily between Los Angeles and Chicago, enters New Mexico near Gallup, goes through Albuquerque, and leaves near Raton. The Sunset Limited operates one train in each direction daily between Los Angeles and New

Orleans. This route, which enters the state near Lordsburg and leaves near El Paso, Texas, serves the southwestern part of New Mexico. The accompanying table presents AMTRAK's estimates of the number of passengers boarding the trains in 1977.

The statistics on the number of persons boarding AMTRAK at the seven New Mexico stations are less accurate than the departing passenger-values for air travel. AMTRAK maintains statistics on ticket sales, rather than boarding passengers, and therefore the numbers are estimates. The major portion of the travel on both AMTRAK lines is interstate, rather than intrastate, and most of the passengers on these trains have neither an origin nor a destination in New Mexico.

The two major intercity bus companies, Greyhound and Trailways, provide extensive service throughout New Mexico. Greyhound operates on 2100 miles of highway in New Mexico, and provides service to 35 communities. Trailways operates on 1350 miles of highway, providing service to 22 communities. The service is even more extensive than these numbers suggest, because the buses will discharge passengers at intermediate points.

The bus companies maintain statistics on ticket sales, rather than boarding passengers. Estimates of passengers boarding in Albuquerque in 1977 are 75,000 for Trailways and 125,000 for Greyhound. Albuquerque is clearly the principal New Mexico terminal for both companies. Trailways has 17 daily departures from Albuquerque, while Greyhound has 26. Other locations on New Mexico's Interstate Highway corridors receive somewhat lower frequencies of service, and some communities have between 2 and 4 departures per day.

Aside from city transit systems, the only other regularly scheduled personal transportation system in New Mexico is the 2.7 mile long Sandia Peak Aerial Tramway. This tramway, which is located northeast of Albuquerque, operates two 60 passenger vehicles at approximately 30 minute intervals. The annual ridership, consisting primarily of tourists and social/recreational users, amounts to 183,000.

Jerome Hall

1977 PUBLIC TRANSPORTATION STATISTICS

Airport	Airline				Station	Line
	Departing Passengers				**Railroad Passengers**	
	CO	FL	TI	TWA		
					Southwest Limited	
Alamogordo		10,200			Gallup	5,500
Albuquerque	341,100	158,100	155,500	321,500	Albuquerque	58,400
Carlsbad			8,400		Lamy	4,000
Clovis			9,100		Las Vegas	3,000
Farmington		58,100			Raton	2,600
Gallup		12,300				
Hobbs			7,900		Sunset Limited	
Roswell			27,600		Lordsburg	1,800
Silver City		6,100			Deming	2,100

CO — Continental   TI — Texas International
FL — Frontier   TWA — Trans World Airlines

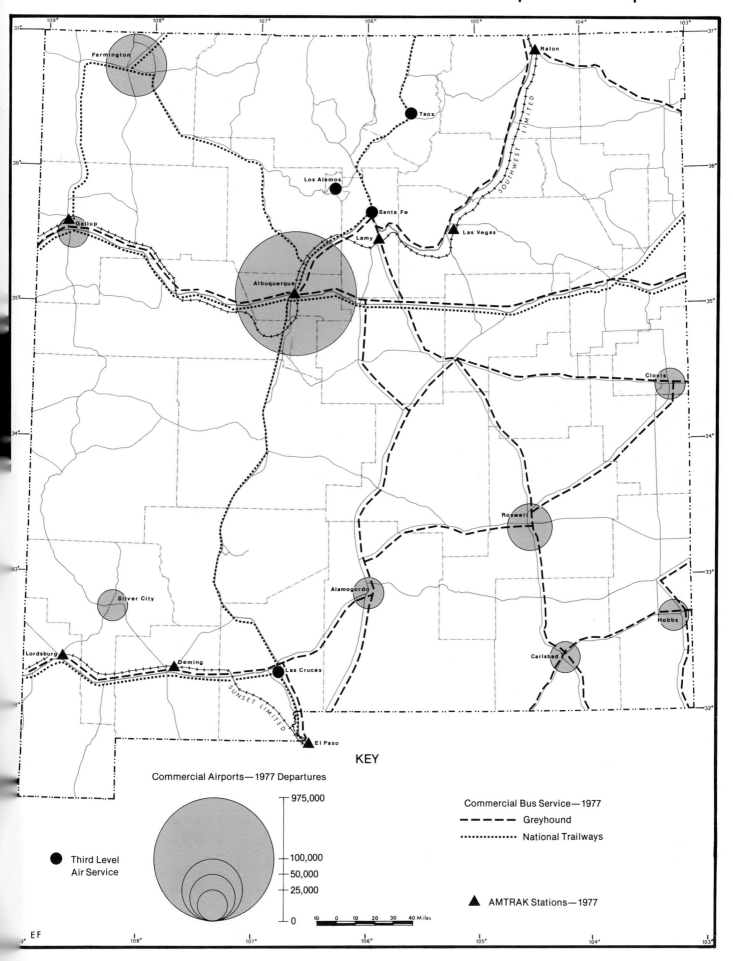

KEY

Commercial Airports—1977 Departures

975,000

100,000
50,000
25,000

0

● Third Level
Air Service

Commercial Bus Service—1977

— — — Greyhound

········· National Trailways

▲ AMTRAK Stations—1977

10 0   10   20   30   40 Miles

133

highway traffic

There were over 70,000 miles of streets and highways in New Mexico in 1975 and more than 80% of this network was classified as "locally maintained." The most extensive highway system is the county-maintained routes designed to provide access for rural residents to an arterial route leading to an urban center.

Five major categories of highway have been classified by the Highway Department for use in analyzing the flow of traffic. The interstate system is the primary carrier of high-volume traffic and crosses the state for more than 1000 miles in both east-west and north-south directions. The volume of interstate traffic on the east-west I-40 and I-10 has been more than double that of the north-south flow of I-25. I-25 is used primarily as an intrastate connector between Albuquerque and Las Cruces and as a commuter route between Albuquerque and Santa Fe. In fact, many state highways designed for a lower volume of traffic (Highway 44 between Bernalillo and Bloomfield and Highway 70 from Alamogordo to Roswell) carry significantly higher volumes than I-25 does outside the urban commuter field. As expected, commuter traffic, which is centered in the heavily populated north-central section of the state, accounts for the highest volume of vehicles on the highway system.

The major federally aided primary and secondary roads serve respectively as the major arterials and minor arterials of New Mexico, connecting urban places. Parts of this system have been supplemented by the construction of several state highways (Highway 18 between Clovis and Hobbs) that provide shorter access routes between remote places.

Most of the state and county roads are classified as major collectors and minor collectors and provide access between the arterial routes and an intricate system of local feeder routes. The collectors and feeder routes, although a significant base of the transportation system of New Mexico, are too numerous to be mapped on the scale used for this book. All routes, except the feeder roads, are sampled for an estimated average daily traffic (ADT) flow by automatic and manual control recording systems. These records are valuable in projecting future construction or modification needs to the existing network.

The passenger car accounts for nearly 70% of the vehicle-miles traveled in New Mexico in 1976 (Table A). This figure would rise to nearly 90% if the pick-up truck, which functions in New Mexico as a passenger car, did not fall into the cateogry of light trucks. The traffic volume of a county is correlated to the population figures for that county (Bernalillo County had 24% of the vehicle-miles of the state in 1976 and 25% of the population). Distortions of this relationship may occur if cross-state travel on the interstate highways raises the traffic volume of some rural counties and if commuter flows within far reaching urban fields effect the traffic of rural counties neighboring major urban areas. The impact of the 1973 fuel crises is barely distinguishable in the statistical annual increase of vehicle-miles of traffic in New Mexico from 1965 to 1976.

Jerry L. Williams

TABLE A

VEHICLE MILES TRAVELED BY VEHICLE TYPE
(in millions)

	1965	1968	1970	1972	1974	1976
Passenger Cars (New Mexico)	2861	3169	3636	4148	4561	5291
Passenger Cars (out-of-state)	1348	1386	1537	1807	1655	1855
Light Trucks	997	1234	1460	1881	2119	2168
Heavy Commercial	443	512	601	716	810	864
Miscellaneous	145	177	229	301	293	346
TOTAL	5794	6478	7463	8853	9438	0524

Source: "New Mexico Traffic Survey 1975 and 1976," NM Highway Department, Planning and Programming Division

TABLE B

NEW MEXICO TRAFFIC SURVEY
AVERAGE DAILY VEHICLE-MILES OF TRAVEL IN NEW MEXICO BY COUNTY AND ROAD SYSTEM, 1976

	I Interstate (a)	II Other Fed.-Aid Primary (a)	III Fed.-Aid Secondary (a)	IV Other State (a)	V County and Local (a)	VI Urban & Municipal (b)	VII Unassigned (c)	All Systems
Bernalillo	441,731	24,506	106,262	10,078	39,662	6,239,052	18,977	6,880,268
Catron	—	83,522	22,755	6,559	26,387	2,659	—	141,882
Chaves	—	357,681	72,817	28,328	75,648	422,566	—	957,040
Colfax	140,736	134,889	25,529	23,947	16,247	101,863	1,947	445,158
Curry	—	212,638	34,464	25,434	50,131	344,590	—	667,257
De Baca	—	100,556	9,140	6,041	35,220	13,948	—	164,905
Dona Ana	574,640	135,638	198,397	76,572	127,197	665,962	10,532	1,788,938
Eddy	—	379,838	55,721	18,654	49,994	352,716	—	856,923
Grant	139,754	190,567	46,251	15,425	124,873	177,810	134	694,814
Guadalupe	493,303	122,444	3,225	10,701	16,135	59,467	1,149	706,424
Harding	—	21,934	5,663	1,558	6,712	4,516	—	40,383
Hidalgo	204,716	47,194	21,387	26,905	4,500	62,490	2,597	369,789
Lea	—	472,946	112,471	38,140	70,278	472,777	—	1,166,612
Lincoln	—	251,943	21,635	7,871	25,867	115,414	—	422,730
Los Alamos	—	9,934	13,128	—	63,205	116,720	—	202,987
Luna	401,075	116,032	9,997	16,556	20,486	98,699	617	663,462
McKinley	541,509	283,024	162,638	38,224	183,090	312,833	48,589	1,569,907
Mora	86,564	38,505	12,460	10,255	12,766	2,676	999	164,525
Otero	—	522,985	11,727	13,638	33,180	332,618	—	914,148
Quay	364,913	116,557	20,541	9,545	22,902	162,861	362	697,681
Rio Arriba	—	360,638	88,866	35,090	56,708	88,631	—	629,933
Roosevelt	—	171,010	48,124	16,971	37,572	141,052	—	414,729
San Juan	—	771,134	51,280	22,184	82,555	547,474	—	1,474,627
San Miguel	196,681	87,496	42,189	11,732	36,328	128,954	6,002	509,382
Sandoval	360,878	289,139	113,348	7,139	38,781	47,562	58	856,905
Santa Fe	363,880	375,684	89,635	40,510	51,139	638,412	8,199	1,567,459
Sierra	144,430	14,676	27,229	9,267	15,396	59,099	501	270,598
Socorro	282,021	98,881	4,767	27,079	107,410	68,258	5,803	594,219
Taos	—	233,868	69,709	22,395	33,579	50,769	—	410,320
Torrance	373,027	137,161	22,277	4,821	29,896	50,802	2,317	620,301
Union	—	166,166	12,658	7,758	17,249	30,524	—	234,355
Valencia	715,878	98,334	187,508	117,142	211,463	318,843	6,473	1,655,641
Total Vehicle Miles	5,825,736	6,427,820	1,723,798	706,519	1,722,556	12,232,617	115,256	28,754,302
Percent of Total Vehicle Miles	20.3%	22.3%	6.0%	2.5%	6.0%	42.5%	.4%	100.0%
Total Road Mileage	892.8	4,000.6	3,166.3	3,699.0	53,687.7	5,411.7	578.9	71,437.0
Percent of Total Road Mileage	1.2%	5.6%	4.4%	5.2%	75.2%	7.6%	.8%	100.%

(a). Excludes travel in urban areas (incorporated places with population of more than 5,000 and their urban areas) and in other incorporated places.
(b). Includes travel in all incorporated places and their urban areas.
(c). Includes frontage roads and other sections of bypassed mileage for which system status has not been clarified.

Source: *New Mexico Traffic Survey—1976*

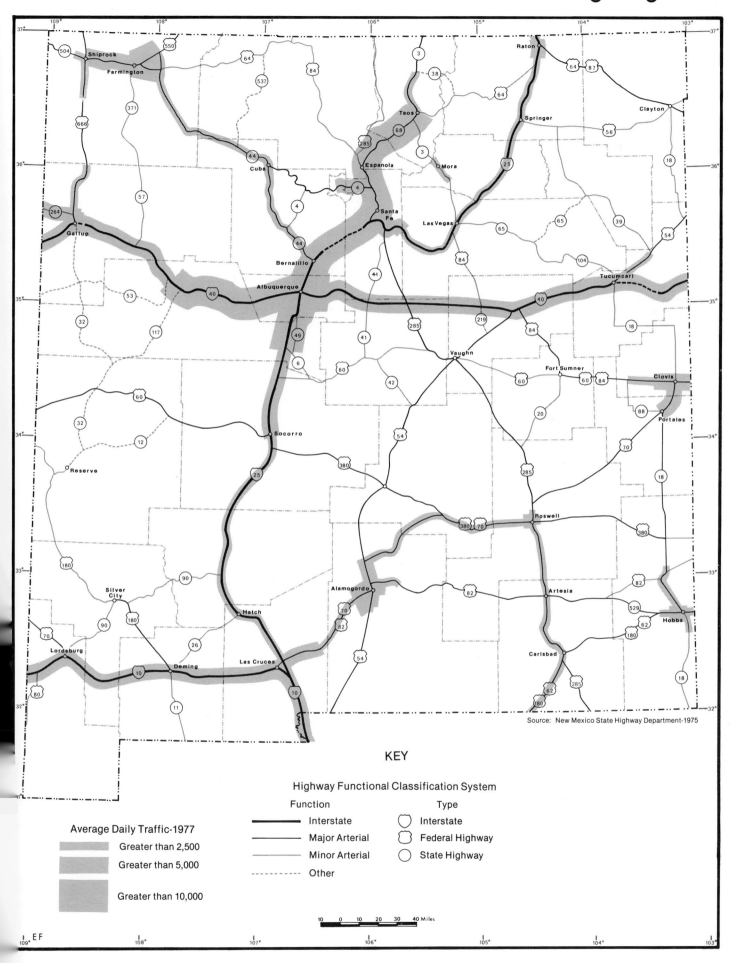

Source: New Mexico State Highway Department-1975

KEY

Highway Functional Classification System

Function		Type	
▬▬▬	Interstate	⬭	Interstate
————	Major Arterial	⬡	Federal Highway
————	Minor Arterial	◯	State Highway
- - - -	Other		

Average Daily Traffic-1977

Greater than 2,500

Greater than 5,000

Greater than 10,000

10 0 10 20 30 40 Miles

EF

135

communications: newspapers

The two largest New Mexican dailies, the *Albuquerque Journal* and *Albuquerque Tribune,* are distributed to more than 47% of the households that receive newspapers in the state. Bernalillo County alone, with a *Journal* and *Tribune* circulation exceeding 87,000 papers, accounts for over 36% of the total statewide newspaper distribution. The two Albuquerque daily newspapers also dominate the printed news in 39% of the households in Guadalupe County, 42% in Los Alamos County, 35% in Sandoval County, 36% in Socorro County, and 39% of the households in Valencia County. More than 5% of the households in every urban center of the northern two-thirds of the state, including Lincoln and Sierra Counties, subscribe to the Albuquerque daily newspapers.

The major competition of the *Journal* and *Tribune* for the primary market of New Mexico is the *Santa Fe New Mexican* which controls the distribution in the central portion of the northern sector of the state, and the *El Paso Herald-Post* and *El Paso Times* (New Mexico circulation of 12,500) which have broad distributions throughout the southern section of the state. The El Paso publications are increasing their circulation area with the recent introduction of a New Mexico section in their daily newspapers and the initiation of rural home deliveries. The eastern plains region is dominated by local dailies with a wide distribution of the Roswell and Clovis newspapers in the southeastern market area and the Amarillo newspapers (2500 circulation in New Mexico) circulating well in the northeast. In addition, every county except Catron, Mora, and Harding has at least one daily or weekly newspaper, allowing most New Mexico residents the choice of two or more written news sources.

The weekly and twice weekly papers are of great significance, in areas served by a local urban daily or in those areas under the influence of the metropolitan dailies. Most weekly papers are located in county seats and carry official notices of the county government. The weeklies also concentrate on news of interest to the local social, agricultural, and business communities. The weekly *Albuquerque News* has the largest circulation of any newspaper in New Mexico (although three-quarters of the press run is distributed free to the residents of Albuquerque). The *Albuquerque News* provides very little national or international coverage, instead focusing on local social and political issues.

A unique situation exists in Deming where the *Head-Light* and the *Graphic,* both weeklies distributed on different days, have the same editor and publisher. Although the two papers differ slightly, Deming can be characterized more as a center with a twice-weekly paper than one with two separate weeklies.

A large number of households in the state also subscribe to a few monthly news magazines published in New Mexico. The *New Mexico Magazine,* a statewide travel and historical publication produced in Santa Fe, has a monthly circulation in excess of 72,000 households. The *New Mexico Stockman* from Albuquerque (10,800 circulation) and the *New Mexico Farm and Ranch* from Las Cruces (13,600 circulation) are widely distributed in the agricultural communities throughout the state.

Jerry L. Williams

DAILIES	Date Estab.	Daily (1978) Circulation*		Sunday (1978) Circulation*
Alamogordo News	1898	(M-F)	8,719	9,538
Albuquerque Journal	1880	(M-S)[a]	76,662	114,161
Albuquerque Tribune	1922	(M-S)	37,345	
Artesia Press	1954	(M-F)	3,100	3,100
Carlsbad Current-Argus	1886	(M-F)	7,800	7,950
Clovis News-Journal	1929	(M-F)	10,125	10,767
Farmington Times	1897	(M-F)	13,222	13,918
Gallup Independent	1889	(M-S)	9,519	
Grants Beacon	1940	(M-F)	3,890	
Hobbs News-Sun	1927	(M-F)	9,624	11,042
Las Cruces Sun-News	1882	(M-F)	13,313	14,503
Las Vegas Optic	1879	(M-F)	3,475	
Los Alamos Monitor	1963	(T-F)	4,402	4,402
Lovington Leader	1909	(M-F)[b]	2,900	2,900
Portales News-Tribune	1901	(M-F)	3,938	4,198
Raton Range	1881	(M-F)	3,150	
Roswell Record	1888	(M-F)	12,754	13,541
Santa Fe New Mexican	1849	(M-F)	18,878	21,940
Silver City Press and Indpt.	1892	(M-S)	6,575	
Tucumcari News	1901	(M-F)	2,200	

*1978 Ayer Director of Publications (Philadelphia, PA)

[a]morning delivery

[b]morning delivery on Monday only

M—Monday   F—Friday
T—Tuesday   S—Saturday

TWICE-WEEKLY	Date Estab.	Days	Circulation* (1978)
25. Belen: Express	---	Mon/Thurs	4,200
26. Clovis: Curry County Times	1932	Wed/Sat	2,200
27. Los Alamos: Hill Bulletin	1973	Tues/Thurs	
28. Los Lunas: Valencia County News Bulletin	1910	Mon/Thurs	5,517
29. Ruidoso: News	1946	Mon/Thurs	4,232
30. Socorro: Defensor-Chieftan	1866	Tues/Thurs	2,569

WEEKLY	Date Estab.	Day	Circulation (1978)*
1. Albuquerque: El Hispano	1966	Friday	5,000
2. Albuquerque: El Independiente	1898	Friday	6,000
3. Albuquerque: News	1963	Thursday	98,000
4. Albuquerque: Health City Sun-News Chieftan	1873	Friday	1,000
5. Aztec: Independent-Review	1888	Thursday	2,115
6. Bernalillo: Sandoval County Times-Independent	1933	Friday	2,000
7. Carrizozo: Lincoln County News	1905	Thursday	1,300
8. Clayton: Union County Leader	1929	Wednesday	2,350
9. Corrales: The Observer	1973	Wednesday	11,000
10. Deming: Graphic	1902	Monday	5,460
11. Deming: Headlight	1881	Thursday	5,515
12. Espanola: Rio Grande Sun	1956	Thursday	5,832
13. Estancia: Torrance County Citizen	1960	Thursday	1,300
14. Eunice: Star	---	Thursday	1,200
15. Fort Sumner: De Baca County News	1901	Thursday	1,200
16. Hagerman: Star-Tribune	1957	Thursday	1,217
17. Hobbs: Flare	1948	Thursday	4,100
18. Jal: Record	1950	Thursday	1,225
19. Lordsburg: Liberal	1887	Friday	2,700
20. Santa Fe: Reporter	1974	Thursday	16,700
21. Santa Rosa: News	1924	Thursday	2,000
22. Silver City: Enterprise	1882	Thursday	1,850
23. Taos: News	1949	Thursday	5,432
24. T or C: Herald	1929	Thursday	2,788

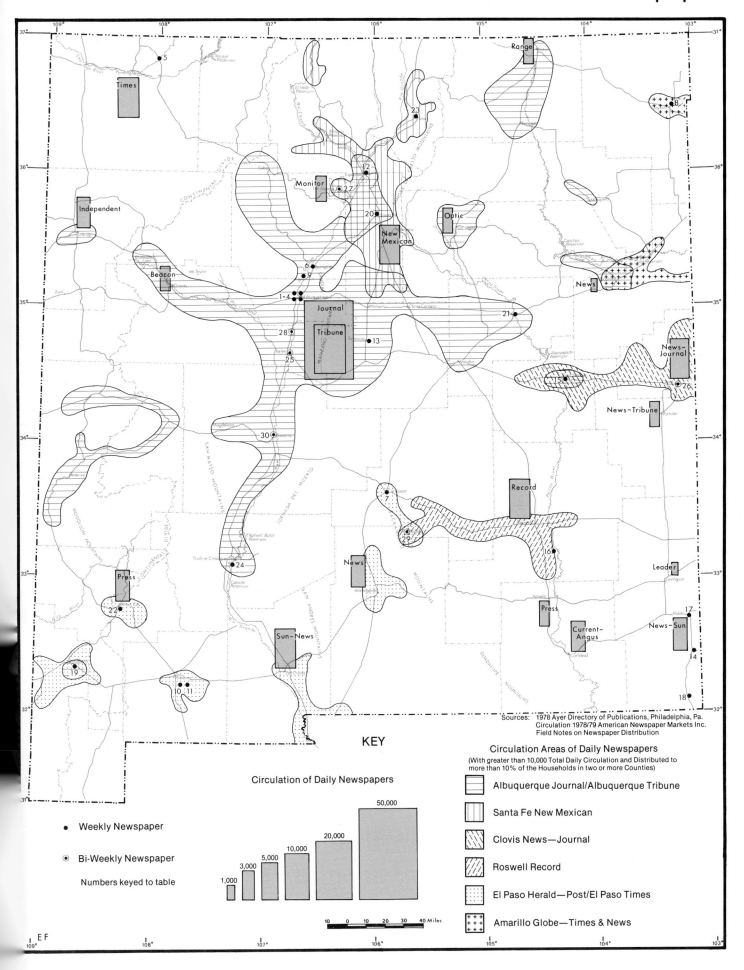

Sources: 1978 Ayer Directory of Publications, Philadelphia, Pa.
Circulation 1978/79 American Newspaper Markets Inc.
Field Notes on Newspaper Distribution

KEY

Circulation Areas of Daily Newspapers
(With greater than 10,000 Total Daily Circulation and Distributed to
more than 10% of the Households in two or more Counties)

Circulation of Daily Newspapers

• Weekly Newspaper

◉ Bi-Weekly Newspaper

Numbers keyed to table

50,000

20,000

10,000

5,000

3,000

1,000

10 0 10 20 30 40 Miles

Albuquerque Journal/Albuquerque Tribune

Santa Fe New Mexican

Clovis News—Journal

Roswell Record

El Paso Herald—Post/El Paso Times

Amarillo Globe—Times & News

137

communications: radio

There are 98 radio stations in New Mexico—56 of which broadcast on the AM frequency. The distribution of stations is related to the population distribution and the commercial market of the state. Counties with light population densities and without a dominant retail center (Mora, Harding, De Baca, Torrance, Catron, and Hidalgo) do not have local radio stations.

The largest AM stations, with transmitting capacities greater than 10,000 watts, are located in Albuquerque and Roswell. Some of the stations in the sparsely populated areas have an output of 5000 watts, but most of them have a transmitting capacity of only 1000 watts. Thus, many areas where customer distance from the station is greatest have the weakest local signal. The Federal Communications Commission (FCC) often compensates for this problem by allowing the rural stations to broadcast on a lower frequency, which increases the range of the radio signal.

News is one of the mainstays of present day radio. Network-affiliated stations carry network news and the independents have reports of local, regional, and international events conveniently available through the Associated Press and United Press wire services. A number of stations are affiliated with the news services of Inter-Mountain News and Audio News. ABC (American Broadcasting Corporation) has the most widespread network news in the state, followed by MBS (Mutual Broadcasting System) and APR (American Public Radio). NBC (National Broadcasting Corporation) and CBS (Columbia Broadcasting System) are barely represented, the sole NBC station broadcasts day and night from the 50,000 watt KOB transmitter located atop Sandia Crest near Albuquerque. This unobstructed signal assures NBC of a wide market range in the central portion of the state. The greatest area coverage within the state is by the forty-six stations that remain independent of network affiliation, allowing the stations more time to report local news and to become involved in programming community events. Coverage of this type is especially valuable to small towns and rural areas that do not have the service of a local daily newspaper.

Jerry L. Williams

RADIO STATIONS IN NEW MEXICO

Location	Call Letters	Date Estab.	Network Affiliation	Transmit Power Day/Night (Watts)	Frequency
Alamogordo	KALG-AM	1950	MBS	1000/——250	1230 khz
	KINN-AM	1957	ABC	1000/————	1270 khz
Albuquerque	KABQ-AM	1947	Independent	5000/——500	1350 khz
	KAMX-AM	1971	Independent	1000/————	1520 khz
	KDAZ-AM	1959	Independent	1000/————	730 khz
	KKIM-AM	1972	Independent	10000/————	1000 khz
	KOB -AM	1922	NBC	50000/50000	770 khz
	KPAR-AM	1969	Independent	1000/————	1190 khz
	KQEO-AM	1947	APR	1000/——500	920 khz
	KRKE-AM	1928	CBS/MBS/AN	5000/—5000	610 khz
	KRZY-AM	1956	CBS	1000/——250	1450 khz
	KUFF-AM	1953	ABC	5000/——500	1150 khz
	KZIA-AM	1956	ABC/MBS	1000/————	1580 khz
	KFMG-FM	1976	Independent	5000	107.5 mhz
	KANW-FM	1950	ABC	7500	89.1 mhz
	KHFM-FM	1954	Independent	3300–Stereo	96.3 mhz
	KIPC-FM	1976	NPR	8300–Stereo	91.5 mhz
	KLYT-FM	1977	Independent	3400–Stereo	88.3 mhz
	KMYR-FM	1963	ABC	22500–Stereo	99.5 mhz
	KOB -FM	1967	Independent	21500–Stereo	93.3 mhz
	KPAR-FM	1974	Independent	9000–Stereo	100.3 mhz
	KRKE-FM	1961	Independent	3500	94.1 mhz
	KRST-FM	1965	Independent	22000–Stereo	92.3 mhz
	KUNM-FM	1966	AN	8700–Stereo	90.1 mhz
	KZZX-FM	1978	Independent	20000–Stereo	99.5 mhz
Artesia	KSVP-AM	1946	MBS	1000/——250	990 khz
	KSVP-FM	1969	Independent	50000–Stereo	92.9 mhz
Aztec	KHAP-AM	1959	Independent	1000/——250	1340 khz
	KWYK-FM	———	Independent	30000	94.9 mhz
Bayard	KNFT-AM	1968	AN/APR	5000/————	950 khz
	KLCJ-FM	1978	Independent	3000	92.7 mhz
Belen	KARS-AM	1961	ABC	250/————	860 khz
Carlsbad	KBAD-AM	1950	ABC/APR/AN	1000/————	740 khz
	KCCC-AM	1966	MBS	1000/————	930 khz
	KBAD-FM	1966	ABC	3000	92.1 mhz
Clayton	KLMX-AM	1949	Independent	1000/——250	1450 khz
Clovis	KCLV-AM	1953	ABC/AN	1000/——250	1240 khz
	KICA-AM	1933	Independent	1000/—1000	980 khz
	KWKA-AM	1971	CBS	500/——500	680 khz
	KMTY-FM	1970	MB	100000–Stereo	99.1 mhz
	KTQM-FM	1963	Independent	50000	99.9 mhz
Deming	KOTS-AM	1954	ABC	1000/——250	1230 khz
	KDEM-FM	1977	Independent	3000–Stereo	94.3 mhz
Espanola	KDCE-AM	———	Independent	1000/————	970 khz
	KBSO-FM	1975	Independent	1100	102.3 mhz
Farmington	KENN-AM	1951	ABC/IMN	5000/—1000	1390 khz
	KRZE-AM	1958	APR/AN	5000/————	1280 khz
	KWYK-AM	1957	Independent	1000/————	960 khz
	KRWN-FM	1974	Independent	30000–Stereo	92.9 mhz
	KRAZ-FM	1969	Independent	30000	96.9 mhz
Gallup	KGAK-AM	1945	MBS	5000/—1000	1330 khz
	KYVA-AM	1959	ABC/IMN	1000/——250	1230 khz
	KQNM-FM	1975	Independent	30000	93.7 mhz
	KGLP-FM	1974	Independent	25000	94.5 mhz
Grants	KMIN-AM	1956	IMN	1000/————	980 khz
Hobbs	KHOB-AM	1954	APR/IMN/AN	5000/————	1390 khz
	KWEW-AM	1938	MBS	5000/—1000	1480 khz
	KSCR-FM	1965	Independent	36000–Stereo	95.7 mhz
Humble City	KCIA-AM	1971	ABC	1000/————	1110 khz
	KPOE-FM	1975	Independent	100000–Stereo	94.1 mhz
Las Cruces	KGRT-AM	1955	ABC	5000/————	570 khz
	KOBE-AM	1947	APR/AN	1000/——250	1450 khz
	KASK-FM	1974	ABC	780–Stereo	103.1 mhz
	KGRD-FM	1966	Independent	2700–Stereo	103.9 mhz
	KRWG-FM	1964	ABC/NPR	100000–Stereo	90.7 mhz
Las Vegas	KFUN-AM	1941	ABC	1000/——250	1230 khz
	KEDP-FM	1967	Independent	72	91.1 mhz
	KFUN-FM	1973	Independent	3000	100.9 mhz
Los Alamos	KRSN-AM	1949	ABC	1000/——250	1490 khz
	KRSN-FM	1956	ABC	15000–Stereo	98.5 mhz
Lovington	KLEA-AM	1952	APR/AN	500/————	630 khz
	KLEA-FM	1965	AN	3000–Stereo	101.7 mhz
Mesilla Park	KOPE-FM	1965	AN	3000–Stereo	104.9 mhz
Portales	KENM-AM	1950	Independent	1000/——250	1450 khz
Ramah	KTDB-FM	1972	NPR	2600	89.9 mhz
Raton	KRTN-AM	1948	Independent	1000/——250	1490 khz
Roswell	KBCQ-AM	1965	APR/AN	50000/50000	1020 khz
	KBIM-AM	1953	ABC	5000/——500	910 khz
	KKAT-AM	1927	CBS	5000/—1000	1430 khz
	KRDD-AM	1963	Independent	1000/————	1320 khz
	KRSY-AM	1947	Independent	1000/——250	1230 khz
	KBIM-FM	1959	Independent	100000–Stereo	94.9 mhz
	KRSY-FM	1977	Independent	30000–Stereo	97.1 mhz
Ruidoso	KRRR-AM	1959	APR/AN	5000/————	1360 khz
Santa Fe	KAFE-AM	1966	Independent	5000/————	810 khz
	KTRC-AM	1947	ABC	1000/——250	1400 khz
	KVSF-AM	1935	MBS	1000/—1000	1260 khz
	KAFE-FM	1969	Independent	28000	97.3 mhz
	KSNM-FM	1965	Independent	29500–Stereo	95.5 mhz
Santa Rosa	KSYX-AM	1960	Keystone	1000/————	1420 khz
Silver City	KSIL-AM	1946	ABC	1000/——250	1340 khz
Socorro	KSRC-AM	1958	Independent	1000/————	1290 khz
Taos	KKIT-AM	1961	ABC/IMN	1000/——250	1340 khz
	KTAS-FM	1977	Independent	3000	101.7 mhz
T or C	KCHS-AM	1944	Independent	250/——250	1400 khz
Tucumcari	KTNM-AM	1941	Independent	1000/——250	1400 khz
	KTNM-FM	1968	Independent	3000	92.7 mhz
Zuni	KSHI-FM	1977	APR/AN	10–Stereo	90.9 mhz

ABC—American Broadcasting Company
MBS—Mutual Broadcasting System
NBC—National Broadcasting Corporation
CBS—Columbia Broadcasting System
APR—American Public Radio

NPR—National Public Radio
IMN—InterMountain News
AN—Audio News
MB—Mutual Black

Source: *Broadcasting Yearbook*, 1978.

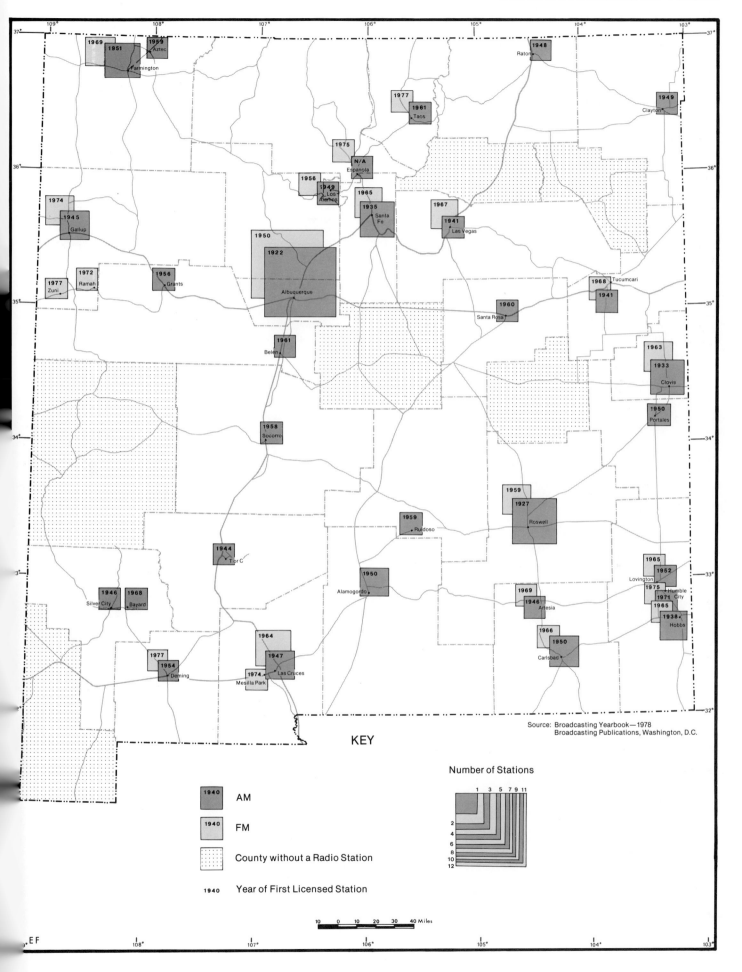

1969 1951 1959
                Aztec
            Farmington

1948
Raton

1977
      1961
      Taos   1949
                                              Clayton

1975

N/A
Espanola

1956
      1949
      Los
      Alamos
            1965
      1935 Santa
            Fe   1967
                      1941
1974   Las Vegas
1945
Gallup

1950
1922
Albuquerque   1968 Tucumcari
                                              1941
1977 1972   1956
Zuni Ramah   Grants

                  1961   1960
                  Belen   Santa Rosa

                                                   1963
                                                   1933
                                                   Clovis

                                                   1950
                                                   Portales
            1958
            Socorro

                                    1959
                                    1927
                                    Roswell

                        1959
                        Ruidoso   1965
                                                       1952
            1944   Lovington Humble
            T or C   1975   City
                                                             1971
                  1950   1969   1965
                  Alamogordo   1946   1938
                                                  Artesia   Hobbs
1946 1968
Silver City Bayard
                                                  1966
                        1964   1950
            1977   Carlsbad
            1954
            Deming
                  1974 Las Cruces
                  Mesilla Park

KEY

Source: Broadcasting Yearbook—1978
        Broadcasting Publications, Washington, D.C.

Number of Stations

1
3
5 7 9 11
2
4
6
8
10
12

1940 AM

1940 FM

      County without a Radio Station

1940 Year of First Licensed Station

10 0 10 20 30 40 Miles

E F
                108°   107°   106°   105°   104°   103°

communications: television

Three major television market areas in New Mexico are covered by direct transmission from towers located at the broadcasting stations. The mid-Rio Grande axis from Socorro to Espanola, an area containing nearly one-half (40-45%) of the state's population, is within the broadcast range of the stations of Albuquerque, four of which have agglomerated their antennas on the Sandia Crest (elevation 10,600 ft) northeast of the city. Although the Federal Communications Commission (FCC) limits the signal power of the station according to the elevation of the antenna, the non-restricted distance a beam travels from this mountain crest offers a distinct coverage advantage to these stations. KOB-TV, one of the stations with transmitters on the crest, began broadcasting as early as 1948 to approximately a dozen receivers in the city of Albuquerque.

The other two populated markets, the southern Rio Grande Valley and the southeast Plains, also receive direct coverage from the major television networks. Las Cruces, which offers single transmission from the local educational station, is well within the broadcast range of the seven stations in Juarez, Mexico and El Paso, Texas. The market area of the southeast is likewise served by a chain of five stations broadcasting from the Mescalero Ridge in Chaves and Eddy counties, and from locations east of Portales. Hobbs is the only major market of the southeast without its own station. Direct coverage surrounding the city is strong as this area lies in a broadcast overlap zone of the Carlsbad–Roswell stations to the west and the Monahans–Odessa–Midlands stations in Texas to the east.

The small but growing market of the San Juan Basin is served by two stations: a local broadcast medium from Farmington and a transmission from Durango, Colorado that can be received in portions of San Juan and Rio Arriba counties. In addition to the 12 broadcasting facilities in operation in 1978, there are two applications pending with the FCC for broadcasting licenses. Gallup is proposed as a satellite station of KGGM-TV in Albuquerque, and investors intend to resurrect the Santa Fe channel formerly occupied by station KFUR-TV.

Four types of television stations serve New Mexico: network, public, independent, and foreign. The three major networks, American Broadcasting Corporation (ABC), Columbia Broadcasting System (CBS), and National Broadcasting Corporation (NBC), concentrate on the three market areas of Albuquerque-Santa Fe, Roswell-Carlsbad, and El Paso-Las Cruces. NBC has the largest direct broadcasting coverage and ABC the smallest. The educational television stations (PBS) are operated by the largest universities in the state: University of New Mexico in Albuquerque (KNME), New Mexico State University in Las Cruces (KRWG), and Eastern New Mexico University in Portales (KENW). Las Cruces also receives the signal from the educational station at the University of Texas in El Paso (KCOS). The independent broadcasting coverage in the state is very small: a Spanish- language UHF station in Albuquerque (KMXN), and KREZ in Durango, Colorado which covers a small portion of northern New Mexico. Two stations in Juarez, Mexico broadcast into Luna and Doña Ana counties.

Although the transmitter coverage zones are mapped as semi-circular areas modified by topography, not all residents within a zone necessarily have access to that particular signal. Local topographic and atmospheric conditions create broadcast shadows that block transmission to some locations. Conversely, these conditions may also enable people outside the circular ranges to receive a direct signal. The importance of cable systems and translators in New Mexico is evident. A cable system brings programming from several stations into a concentrated population area for a fee. In many cases local news and weather reports, FM music, and programs from areas such as Los Angeles, Phoenix, Juarez, and southern Colorado are provided by the cable company to the community. A translator is a small station which receives the broadcast signal from another station and rebroadcasts it in a local area. Translators have a small range and tend to be important to the scattered rural population and to small settlements in isolated areas.

Most of populated New Mexico has television reception. Only small pocket valleys of the north-central and southwestern portions of the state are without this communication medium. Yet even there, long wires often stretch to antennas on nearby mesas and hilltops in efforts to catch unpredictable signals from distant transmitters or translators.

Jerry L. Williams

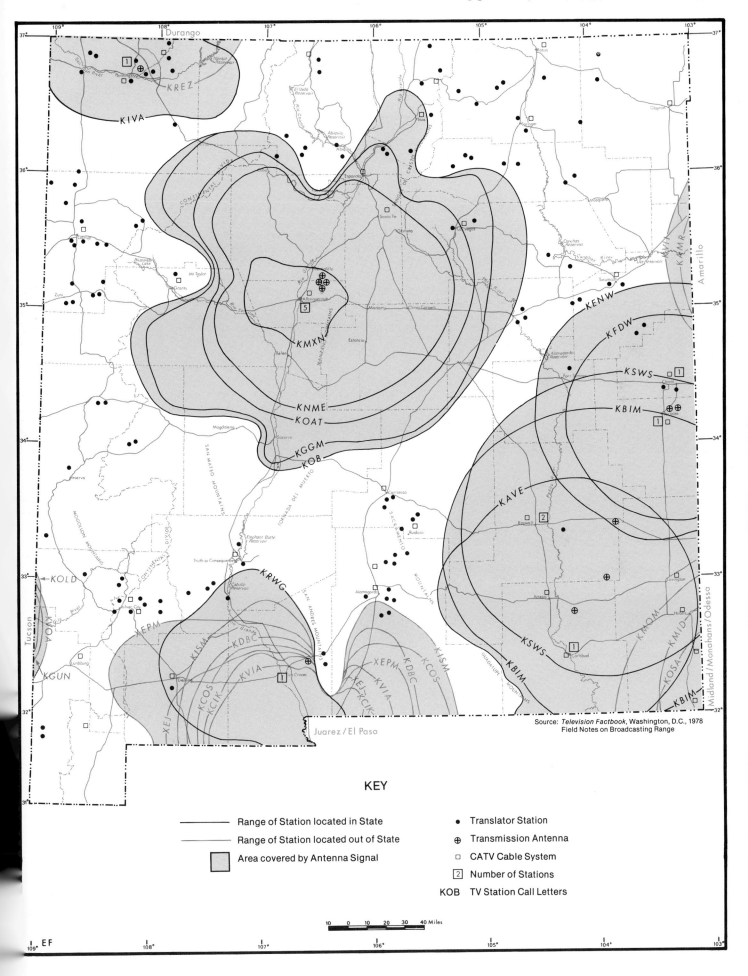

Source: *Television Factbook,* Washington, D.C., 1978
Field Notes on Broadcasting Range

KEY

Range of Station located in State

Range of Station located out of State

Area covered by Antenna Signal

●   Translator Station

⊕   Transmission Antenna

□   CATV Cable System

2   Number of Stations

KOB   TV Station Call Letters

10   0   10   20   30   40 Miles

communications: telephone

Since its invention in 1876, the telephone has evolved from a curiosity into a necessity. The first phones were often ridiculed by newspapers. The heavy use of telephone lines, the proliferation of many small telephone companies, and the rapid geographic expansion of telephone service forecasted the potential of this segment of the communications industry.

The first telephone exchange in New Mexico was established at Las Vegas in 1881. Several small companies were formed over the next few decades, but the number of phones increased slowly due to the rural nature of the state and also to the constantly changing technology within the industry. By 1902 there were 2,510 phones in the territory, and on the eve of statehood in 1912 the number had increased to only 10,349 or approximately 29 phones for every 1000 residents.

Rapid expansion began when several small companies merged to form Mountain States Telephone in 1911, later to be the Mountain Bell System in the 70's. World War II produced material shortages but stimulated research and development within the electronics and communications industries. These improvements lowered the consumer cost of the service and there has since been a steadily increasing demand for phone services in New Mexico.

This demand is being met not only by Mountain Bell, the state's largest phone company, but also by a surprising number of smaller companies. Government regulation has prevented Mountain Bell from expanding its area of business. Large areas of the state are served either by a second nationwide company, such as General Telephone, or by small local companies.

The map shows the geographic area in which each of the state's seventeen telephone companies is authorized to provide services. Although the entire state is included within the various company jurisdictions, many areas are without phone service because of the sparse population and the great cost of running lines.

The table shows the approximate number of phones (extensions are not included) serviced by each company. Mountain Bell clearly dominates the telephone industry in New Mexico. Although the company has actually decreased its area of operations (by selling small territories to some local companies) it has increased its percentage of the state total in both residential and business phones. In 1978 Mountain Bell serviced approximately 90 percent of all residential phones and 95 percent of all business phones in the state.

The demand for telephone service in New Mexico is great, and many of the companies (including Mountain Bell) are finding it difficult to quickly fill all requests. Several of the local companies are experiencing severe problems as they attempt to provide service to relatively large geographic areas with sparse populations. Public dissatisfaction with the service offered by such companies has not been great enough to change present government regulations which discourage consolidation or acquisition of existing enterprises.

Paul McAllister

TELEPHONE COMPANIES IN NEW MEXICO

Company	Phones 1975				Phones 1978				% Change 75-78
	Residence	Business	% Res.	Total	Residence	Business	% Res.	Total	
Continental Telephone Co.	12,998	3,329	79.6	16,327	15,000	3,083	83.0	18,083	10.8
Corona Telephone Co.	128	28	82.0	156	123	23	84.2	146	−6.4
Dell Telephone Cooperative, Inc.	NA	NA	NA	NA	NA	NA	NA	NA	NA
Eastern New Mexico Rural Telephone Cooperative	855	49	94.6	904	1,289	75	94.5	1,364	50.9
General Telephone Co. of the Southwest	22,670	5,183	81.4	27,853	25,606	5,274	82.9	30,880	10.9
La Jicarita Rural Telephone Cooperative, Inc.	713	83	89.6	796	841	102	89.2	943	18.5
Laughlin Telephone Co.	41	6	87.2	47	65	11	85.5	76	61.7
Leaco Rural Telephone Cooperative, Inc.	514	133	79.4	647	559	145	79.4	704	8.8
Maxwell Telephone Co.	138	10	93.2	148	157	6	96.3	163	10.1
Mountain Bell Telephone Co.	401,873	171,052	70.1	572,925	470,609	193,798	70.8	664,407	16.0
Navajo Communications Co., Inc.	1,420	622	69.5	2,042	1,912	620	75.5	2,532	24.0
Panhandle Telephone Cooperative	NA	NA	NA	NA	NA	NA	NA	NA	NA
Penasco Valley Telephone Cooperative, Inc.	723	161	81.8	884	869	138	86.3	1,007	13.9
Roosevelt County Rural Telephone Cooperative	966	81	92.3	1,047	937	82	92.0	1,019	−2.7
Universal Telephone Co. of the Southwest	1,029	297	77.6	1,326	1,412	322	81.4	1,734	30.8
Valley Telephone Cooperative, Inc.	369	66	84.8	435	510	99	83.7	609	40.0
Western New Mexico Telephone Co.	555	121	82.1	676	621	127	83.0	748	10.6
Total	444,992	181,221	71.1	626,213	520,510	203,905	71.8	724,415	15.7

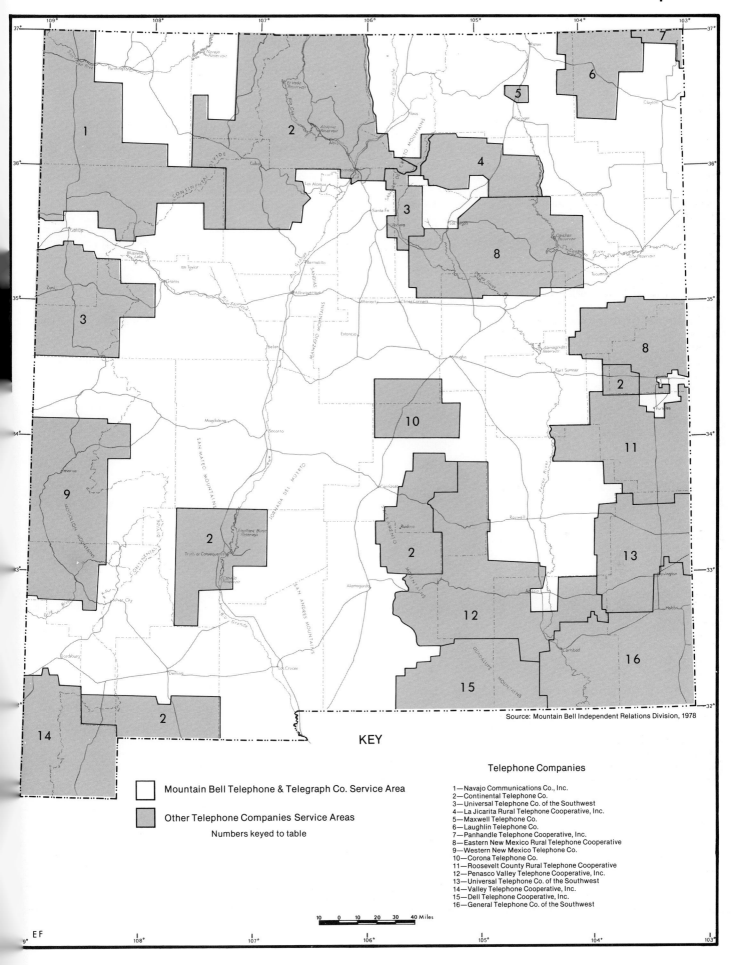

Source: Mountain Bell Independent Relations Division, 1978

KEY

Mountain Bell Telephone & Telegraph Co. Service Area

Other Telephone Companies Service Areas

Numbers keyed to table

Telephone Companies

1—Navajo Communications Co., Inc.
2—Continental Telephone Co.
3—Universal Telephone Co. of the Southwest
4—La Jicarita Rural Telephone Cooperative, Inc.
5—Maxwell Telephone Co.
6—Laughlin Telephone Co.
7—Panhandle Telephone Cooperative, Inc.
8—Eastern New Mexico Rural Telephone Cooperative
9—Western New Mexico Telephone Co.
10—Corona Telephone Co.
11—Roosevelt County Rural Telephone Cooperative
12—Penasco Valley Telephone Cooperative, Inc.
13—Universal Telephone Co. of the Southwest
14—Valley Telephone Cooperative, Inc.
15—Dell Telephone Cooperative, Inc.
16—General Telephone Co. of the Southwest

10 0 10 20 30 40 Miles

movies made in new mexico

Motion pictures have been filmed in New Mexico essentially since the beginning of the industry. Thomas Edison experimented with the process in the 19th century at the old mining camp of Delores near Cerrillos. Mary Pickford, Romaine Fielding, and Tom Mix were also attracted to the "natural light" of the state in the early filming era. Las Vegas was the first motion picture center of New Mexico, where an entire house and sidelot were converted to sets for the silent screen stars. In the 1940's and early 1950's many western films were filmed in the Gallup area and attractive accommodations influenced the large studios to locate there.

In 1968 the governor of New Mexico recognized the income potential in turning the state into a natural "backlot" for Hollywood and other documentary and commercial film units. Over 100 productions have been filmed since then, with an estimated $70 million in revenue realized for the state. In 1975 the Motion Picture Commission became an agency of the Department of Development and has engaged in active competition with other states in attracting the film industry to New Mexico.

Facilities in New Mexico attractive to motion picture industries include the scenic backdrops of north-central New Mexico in the Chama-Abiquiu-Taos-Santa Fe region, with accommodations at nearby major cities for the extended housing of cast, crew, and equipment. Outdoor facilities have been established in several 19th century sets on the Eaves Ranch south of Santa Fe; and an Albuquerque television station has donated its sound stage for interior scenes. The northern concentration of motion picture production has primarily been attributed to lack of accommodation and access in the south. As these problems are alleviated much of the scenic beauty in the outlying areas of the southern counties may become potential sets for films in New Mexico.

Jerry L. Williams

FEATURE FILMS MADE IN NEW MEXICO

Date	Film Title	Star(s)	Company	Location(s)
1898	Indian Day School	Experimental	Edison	Isleta Pueblo
1912A	The Johnson-Flynn Championship Fight			Las Vegas
1912B	Pueblo Legend	Mary Pickford	Biograph	Isleta Pueblo
1912C	The Tourists	Mable Norman	Biograph	Albuquerque
1912D	The Old Actor	Mary Pickford	Biograph	Albuquerque
1913A	The Clod	Romaine Fielding	Lubin	Silver City
1913B	The Rattlesnake	Romaine Fielding	Lubin	Las Vegas
1914A	Toll of Fear	Romaine Fielding	Lubin	Las Vegas
1914B	Hiawanda's Cross	Romaine Fielding	Lubin	Las Vegas
1914C	The Rancher's Daughter	Tom Mix	Selig	Las Vegas
1914D	The Country Drugstore	Tom Mix	Selig	Las Vegas
1915A	Local Color	Tom Mix	Selig	Las Vegas
1915B	The Hazards of Helen	Helen Holmes	(100 Episodes)	west of Las Vegas
1928	Redskin	Richard Dix Gladys Belmont	Paramount	90 mi. NW of Gallup
1940	The Bad Man	Wallace Berry Ronald Reagan	MGM	north of Gallup
1941	Sundown	Gene Tierney Bruce Cabot	Wanger	Gallup
1942A	The Desert Song	Dennis Morgan	Warner Bros.	Gallup
1942B	Flying Tigers	———	———	Santa Fe
1944	Song of the Nile	Maria Montez Jon Hall	Universal	Gallup
1946	Pursued	Robert Mitchum	Warner Bros.	Gallup
1947	Four Faces West	Joel McCrea	Enterprise	Gallup
1948A	Colorado Territory	Joel McCrea Virginia Mayo Dorothy Malone	Pine-Thomas	Gallup
1948B	Streets of Laredo	William Holden William Bendix	Paramount	Gallup
1948C	Albuquerque	Randolph Scott	———	Albuquerque
1950A	Rocky Mountain	Errol Flynn	Warner Bros.	Gallup
1950B	Big Carnival	Kirk Douglas	Paramount	Gallup
1950C	Only the Valiant	Gregory Peck	Cagney	Gallup
1950D	Quantrelle Raiders	Alan Ladd	Paramount	Gallup
1951A	Raton Pass	Dennis Morgan	Warner Bros.	Gallup
1951B	New Mexico	Lew Ayres Marilyn Maxwell	Irving Pred	Gallup
1951C	Fort Defiance	Dane Clark	Ventura	Gallup
1955	Strange Lady in Town	Greer Garson Dana Andrews	Warner Bros.	Santa Fe
1957	Fort Massacre	Joel McCrea Forrest Tucker	United Artist	west of Gallup
1958A	The Left Handed Gun	Paul Newman	Warner Bros.	Santa Fe
1958B	The Nine Lives of Elfego Baca	———	Walt Disney	Cerrillos
1963	A Distant Trumpet	Troy Donahue Suzanne Pleshette	Warner Bros.	Gallup
1964	Hallelujah Trail	Burt Lancaster Lee Remick	M. Kappa	Gallup
1966A	A Covenant With Death	George Maharis	Warner Bros.	Santa Fe
1966B	And Now Miguel	Pat Cardi Guy Stockwell	Universal	Ghost Ranch area
1968A	The Good Guys and the Bad Guys	Robert Mitchum George Kennedy	Warner Bros.	near Chama
1968B	Hang Your Hat on the Wind	———	Walt Disney	near Santa Fe
1968C	Pancho	———	Walt Disney	Cerrillos/Santa Fe
1968D	Dead Heat	———	United	Ruidoso
1968E	Butch Cassidy and the Sundance Kid	Paul Newman Robert Redford	20th Century	Taos and Chama
1968F	The Young Thieves	Diane McBain	Commonwealth	near Santa Fe
1968G	The Money Gun	Jim Brown	Columbia	Acoma Pueblo
1968H	When I've Got the Moon	Helen Hayes	———	Santa Fe/Las Vegas
1968I	Easy Rider	Peter Fonda Dennis Hopper	Pando	Taos/Santa Fe
1968J	Heaven With a Gun	Glenn Ford Carolyn Jones	MGM	Santa Fe
1968K	Cats	Eva Dahlbeck	Italian	Santa Fe
1969A	Flap	Anthony Quinn	Warner Bros.	Santa Clara Pueblo/ Madrid/Albuquerque
1969B	Chisum	John Wayne	Warner Bros.	Eaves Ranch
1969C	There Was a Crooked Man	Henry Fonda	Warner Bros.	near La Joya
1969D	King Gun	Phil Harris Pat Wayne	Paramount	Eaves Ranch/near Ghost Ranch
1969E	The McMasters	Burl Ives Jack Palance	Goldwyn	near Santa Fe/Madrid
1969F	Cheynne Social Club	James Stewart Henry Fonda	National General	Eaves Ranch
1969G	Pieces of Dreams	Robert Foster Lauren Harper	United Artists	State Fairground/Ruidoso
1970A	A Gunfight	Kirk Douglas Johnny Cash	Columbia	Santa Fe
1970B	Two Lane Blacktop	James Taylor	Laughlin	Santa Fe/Tucumcari
1970C	The Hired Hand	Peter Fonda	Pando	Albuquerque
1970D	Billy Jack	Tom Laughlin	National Student	Santa Clara/Eaves Ranch/ Bandelier
1970E	Bunny O'Hare	Bette Davis	American	Belen/Los Lunas
1970F	Making It	Kris Tabori	Paramount	Albuquerque
1970G	Red Sky At Morning	Desi Arnez, Jr.	Universal	Eaves Ranch/Taos
1970H	Up in The Cellar	———	American	Las Cruces
1970I	Shootout	Gregory Peck	Universal	Chama/Los Alamos
1970J	Scandalous John	Brian Keith	Disney	Alamogordo
1970K	Deadhead Miles	———	———	Santa Fe
1970L	Julio and Stein	Dean Stockwell	Fourleaf	Albuquerque
1971A	The Cowboys	John Wayne	Warner Bros.	Chama/Eaves Ranch
1971B	Cactus	Vera Miles	Malibu	Santa Fe/Alamogordo
1971C	The Honkers	Slim Pickens	Gardner-Levy	Carlsbad
1971D	Wheels	Max Evans	Max Evans	Alamogordo
1971E	Pocket Money	Paul Newman Lee Marvin	Coleytown	Santa Fe/Truchas
1971F	Legend of Nigger Charlie	Fred Williamson	Spangler	Eaves Ranch
1971G	Greaser's Palace	———	Pyxiduim	Santa Fe
1971H	Man and The City	Anthony Quinn	Universal	Albuquerque
1971I	Five Days Home	Jessie Vint Alan Vint	20th Century	Carlsbad/Hope
1971J	Ripped Off	Robert Blake Ernest Borgnine	Spanish	Albuquerque
1971K	Man With the Icy Eyes	Victor Buono	Spanish	Albuquerque
1971L	El Salvaje	———	Garcia	Santa Fe/Ghost Ranch
1971M	When Legends Die	Richard Widmark	Millar	Farmington
1971N	Culpepper Cattle Company	Bo Hopkins	———	Santa Fe
1971O	My Little Sparrow	———	Matofsky	Albuquerque/Cuba
1971P	Squares Won't Fit	Andrew Prine	Plateau	Santa Fe/Albuquerque
1971Q	Resurrection of S-C-W	Leslie Nielsen	Madison	Albuquerque
1972A	Groove Tube	———	KS Prodns.	Ghost Ranch area
1972B	Gargoyles	Cornell Wilde	Tomorrow	Carlsbad
1972C	Mustang	———	Calgary	Los Lunas/Santa Fe
1972D	Ginger in the Morning	Martin Miller Sissy Spacek	Kyma Circle	Santa Fe/Albuquerque
1972E	Showdown	Dean Martin Rock Hudson	Universal	Chama/Abiquiu
1972F	Don't Play Us Cheap	———	Yeah	Santa Fe
1972G	Running Wild	———	Golden Circle	Ghost Ranch
1972H	Santee	Glenn Ford	Vagabond	Eaves Ranch
1972I	Track of the Moon Beast	———	Lizard	Albuquerque
1972J	Catch My Soul	Richie Havens	Metromedia	Santa Fe/Espanola
1973A	Truck Stop Woman	Jim Mitchum Claudia Jennings	Traynor	Las Cruces/near T. or C.
1973B	Consigliori	Martin Balsom	Italian	Albuquerque/Santa Fe
1973C	Devil and Leroy Bassett	———	Pearson	Santa Fe/Pecos
1973D	Audrey Papers	———	Wolper	Albuquerque/Carlsbad
1973E	All Hell Broke Loose	———	Colorado	Albuquerque
1973F	Joint Crossing	———	Spanish	Las Cruces
1973G	My Name is Nobody	Henry Fonda Terrence Hill	Italian	Acoma/Mogollon/ Alamogordo/Albuquerque
1973H	Jonathon L. Seagull	———	Hal Bartlett	Carlsbad
1973I	Thomasine and Bushrod	Max Julien Vonetta McGee	Columbia	Eaves Ranch
1974A	Bite the Bullet	James Colburn Gene Hackman Candice Bergen	Columbia	Chama/Taos/south of Alamogordo
1974B	Las Cruces	Jim Mitchum	C&M	Radium Springs
1974C	Boss Nigger	Fred Williamson	Western	Eaves Ranch/Santa Fe
1974D	Born Innocent	Linda Blair	Tomorrow	Albuquerque
1974E	Search for the Gods	Ralph Bellamy	Warner Bros.	Taos
1974F	Love is Forever	———	Luna	Taos
1975A	The Man Who Fell to Earth	David Bowie	EMI	White Sands Park
1975B	Bobbi Jo and The Outlaw Man	Marjoe Gortner Lynda Carter	American	Albuquerque
1975C	Adios Amigo	Fred Williamson Richard Pryor	Po'Boy	Eaves Ranch
1975D	Sweet Hostage	Linda Blair Martin Sheen	Brut	Taos area
1976A	The White Buffalo	Charles Bronson	———	Chama
1976B	Casey's Shadow	Walter Mathau Alexis Smith	Columbia	Ruidoso
1976C	Southern Doublecross	Anne Jeffries	———	Eaves Ranch
1976D	Santa Fe–1836	Margot Kidder Geoffrey Lewis	———	Santa Fe area
1976E	The Sorcerer	Roy Scheider	———	Farmington
1976F	Sidewinder One	Marjoe Gortner	———	Albuquerque/Taos
1977A	Convoy	Kris Kristofferson Ernest Borgnine Ali MacGraw	EMI	Albuquerque area
1977B	Peter Lundy and the Medicine Hat Stallion	———	NBC TV	San Ildefondo Pueblo/ Valle Grande
1977C	Hatter Fox	Ronnie Cox	EMI	Santa Fe/Albuquerque
1977D	Cry Demon	Richard Crenna Victor Buono	Rangoon	Las Vegas/Montezuma Hotel
1977E	The Long Escape	George Peppard	Powder Horn	Albuquerque/Santa Fe/ Espanola
1977F	Chance	Christopher Clark	Appaloosa	Chama
1977G	Special Olympics	Charles Darning	EMI	Albuquerque
1978A	Superman	Marlon Brando Valerie Perrine	Warner Bros.	Gallup (Amtrak) Galisteo area
1978B	Butch and Sundance: The Early Days	William Katt Tom Berringer Jeff Corey	20th Century	Santa Fe/Eaves Ranch/ Jemez Springs
1978C	Nightwing	David Warner	Columbia	Laguna Pueblo/ Albuquerque area
1978D	Every Which Way But Loose	Clint Eastwood	Warner Bros.	Albuquerque/Taos/ Santa Fe
1978E	When Are You Coming Back Red Ryder?	Lee Grant Marjoe Gortner Hal Linden	Gortner	Las Cruces area
1978F	Hide in Plain Sight	James Caan	MGM	Albuquerque
1978G	Fleisch	———	German	Las Cruces
1978H	Monster	———	Academy	Espanola
1978I	Hamster of Happiness	Robert Black	———	Orogrande

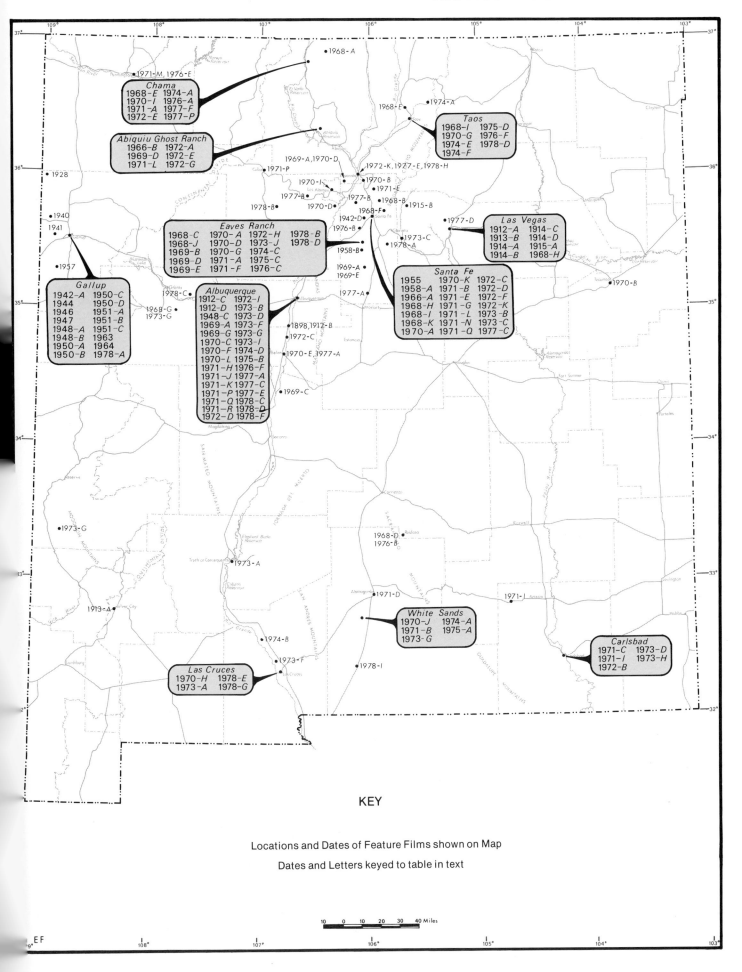

•1968-A

•1971-M,1976-E

Chama
1968-E	1974-A
1970-I	1976-A
1971-A	1977-F
1972-E	1977-P

•1968-E   •1974-A

Taos
1968-I	1975-D
1970-G	1976-F
1974-E	1978-D
1974-F	

Abiquiu Ghost Ranch
1966-B	1972-A
1969-D	1972-E
1971-L	1972-G

•1928

1969-A,1970-D
1971-P

1970-B
1970-I
1971-E
1977-B   1968-B•   •1915-B
1977-B•
1970-D•   1968-F•
1942-D•

1972-K,1977-E,1978-H

•1977-D

Las Vegas
1912-A	1914-C
1913-B	1914-D
1914-A	1915-A
1914-B	1968-H

•1940
•1941

1978-B•

•1957

1976-B•
1958-B•

1973-C•
•1978-A

Eaves Ranch
1968-C	1972-H	1978-B
1968-J	1970-D	1973-J	1978-D
1969-B	1970-G	1974-C	
1969-D	1971-A	1975-C	
1969-E	1971-F	1976-C	

Santa Fe
1955	1970-K	1972-C
1958-A	1971-B	1972-D
1966-A	1971-E	1972-F
1968-H	1971-G	1972-K
1968-I	1971-L	1973-B
1968-K	1971-N	1973-C
1970-A	1971-Q	1977-C

1969-A•
1969-E•

Gallup
1942-A	1950-C
1944	1950-D
1946	1951-A
1947	1951-B
1948-A	1951-C
1948-B	1963
1950-A	1964
1950-B	1978-A

1978-C•
1968-G•
1973-G•

•1970-B

1977-A•

Albuquerque
1912-C	1972-I
1912-D	1973-B
1948-C	1973-D
1969-A	1973-F
1969-G	1973-G
1970-C	1973-I
1970-F	1974-D
1970-L	1975-B
1971-H	1976-F
1971-J	1977-A
1971-K	1977-C
1971-P	1977-E
1971-Q	1978-C
1971-R	1978-D
1972-D	1978-F

•1898,1912-B

•1972-C

1970-E•,1977-A

•1969-C

•1973-G

1968-D•
1976-B•

•1973-A

1913-A•

•1971-D

1971-I•

White Sands
1970-J	1974-A
1971-B	1975-A
1973-G	

•1974-B

•1973-F

•1978-I

Carlsbad
1971-C	1973-D
1971-I	1973-H
1972-B	

Las Cruces
1970-H	1978-E
1973-A	1978-G

EF

KEY

Locations and Dates of Feature Films shown on Map

Dates and Letters keyed to table in text

10 0 10 20 30 40 Miles

recreation and government

recreation and tourism I—federal and state facilities

New Mexico forest and woodlands total over 21 million acres or about one-fourth of the land area of the state. The National Forest Service controls approximately one-half of all forest resources, containing about four million acres of high elevation commercial timber land and over six million acres of low elevation noncommercial woodland. Both forest and woodlands are valued for recreational, wildlife, grazing, and watershed control benefits to the state. Residents also find them an important resource for local needs of lumber, posts and poles, fuel wood, and Christmas trees.

Within the National Forest are more than one million acres of wilderness and primitive areas. These lands remain open for recreational use, but restrict the use of mechanized equipment, logging, or the addition of man-made improvements. The first wilderness area in the United States was established in 1924 in the Gila National Forest of southwestern New Mexico. By the mid-1930's virtually all of the nearly 15 million acres of wilderness and undeveloped lands in the nation had been delineated by the Forest Service. Three-hundred and thirty-six thousand acres of primitive area await congressional designation to wilderness in New Mexico and an additional 400,000 acres are under study for possible addition to the National Wilderness Preservation System. Fifty-three miles of the Rio Grande River Gorge were included in the National Wild and Scenic River System which classifies the waterbody as wild if it is unpolluted, undammed, and accessible only by trails. Fifty-two miles of the Rio Grande were so designated with a remaining mile set aside for accessible recreational space.

The state offers both resident and out-of-state visitor an in-teresting selection of natural and man-made scenic areas. Most of the attractions have been preserved and made accessible to the public by both the federal and state governments. Nearly sixty parks and monuments throughout New Mexico are primarily located in places where there are old Indian or Spanish structures, where unique areas of natural features are found, and along portions of the lakes and reservoirs that offer additional attraction to people in the arid and semiarid environment. Several parks and monument areas surround frontier features such as forts and pioneer homes and in one instance a frontier town (Lincoln) was designated as a monument. The facilities that are available vary widely at each of the state and federal locations with most places providing shelters and hiking trails in addition to the accommodations indicated on Table 2.

A number of significant features, not part of the park and monument network, are listed as additional attractions worth visiting. Many of these points of scenic interest have been established for public use by the U.S. Forest Service, but a number of places are on private land and a visit may require special permission. Whether the scenery that one seeks is located in the National Forests, the Indian Reservations, the parks and monuments, or on private property, the recreational and touring possibilities of New Mexico are extremely varied. This wide range of opportunities has contributed greatly to the state's claim to being the Land of Enchantment.

Jerry L. Williams

TABLE 1: NATIONAL FORESTS AND GRASSLANDS*

National Forest	Map Key	Wilderness or Primitive Area	Date Estab.	1978 Acreage in New Mexico	Unit Headquarters
Apache NF				650 219	Springerville, Ariz.
	A	Blue Range Primitive	1933	36 598	
Carson NF				1 491 423	Taos
	B	Wheeler Peak	1960	6 029	
	C	Rio Grande Wild River	1970	16,880	
	D	Chama River Canyon**	1978	2 900	
	E	Pecos Wilderness**	1933	24 735	
Cibola NF				2 108 882	Albuquerque
	F	Manzano Wilderness	1978	37 000	
	G	Sandia Wilderness	1978	30 930	
Coronado NF				71 541	Tucson, Arizona
Gila NF				2 797 617	Silver City
	H	Gila Wilderness	1924	429 738	
	I	Gila Primitive	1933	130 637	
	J	Black Range Primitive	1933	169 356	
Lincoln NF				1 272 069	Alamogordo
	K	White Mountain Wilderness	1933	31 283	
Santa Fe NF				1 734 536	Santa Fe
	D	Chama River Canyon**	1978	47 400	
	E	Pecos Wilderness**	1933	143 597	
	L	San Pedro Parks	1931	41 132	
Kiowa National Grassland				143 492	Clayton

*Albuquerque Regional Headquarters
**Located in more than one National Forest

TOTAL:
National Forest   10 125 287 acres
Primitive and
  Wilderness   1 148 215 acres

Source: U.S. Forest Service, Southwest Region.

TABLE 2: NATIONAL AND STATE PARKS AND MONUMENTS

Type	Place	Facilities		Type	Place	Facilities
NATIONAL PARKS				**STATE PARKS**		
1.	Carlsbad Caverns	a,c,d		29.	Living Desert	a,c,d
				30.	Manzano Mountains	a,b,c,d
NATIONAL MONUMENTS				31.	Morphy Lake	a,b,c,g,h
2.	Aztec Ruins	a,c,d		32.	Navajo Lake	a,b,c,d,e,g,h,j
3.	Bandelier Ruins	a,b,c,d		33.	Sims Mesa	a,b,c,d,g,h,j
4.	Capulin Mountain	a,c,d		34.	Oasis	a,b,c,d,e,f,h,j
5.	Chaco Canyon Ruins	a,b,c,d		35.	Pancho Villa	a,b,c,d,j
6.	El Morro (Inscription Rock)	a,b,c,d		36.	Percha Dam	a,b,c,d,f,h,j
7.	Fort Union	a,c,d		37.	Red Rock	a,b,c,d,e,f,j
8.	Gila Cliff Dwellings	a,b,c,d		38.	Rio Grande Gorge	a,b,c,d,h,j
9.	Gran Quivira Ruins	a,c,d		39.	Rock Hound	a,b,c,d,e,f,j
10.	Pecos Ruins	a,c,d		40.	San Gabriel	a,b,c,d,j
11.	White Sands	a,c,d		41.	Santa Fe River	a,d
				42.	Smokey Bear	a,c,d
STATE PARKS				43.	Storrie Lake	a,b,c,d,f,g,h,i,j
12.	Belen Valley	a,c,d		44.	Sumner Lake	a,b,c,d,e,f,g,h,j
13.	Bluewater Lake	(ALL)		45.	Ute Lake	a,b,c,d,f,g,h,i
14.	Bottomless Lakes	(ALL)		46.	Valley of Fires	a,b,c,d,j
15.	Caballo Lake	(ALL)		47.	Villanueva	a,b,c,d,f,h,j
16.	Chicosa Lake	a,b,c,d,j		48.	Lea County	a,c,d,h,j
17.	City of Rocks	a,b,c,d,j				
18.	Clayton Lake	a,b,c,d,f,g,h,j		**STATE MONUMENTS**		
19.	Conchas Lake	(ALL)		49.	Abo Mission	none
20.	Coronado Ruins	a,b,c,d,f,j		50.	Coronado Pueblo	a,c,d
21.	Coyote Creek	a,b,c,d,h,j		51.	Dorsey Mansion	none
22.	Elephant Butte	(ALL)		52.	Fort Selden	c,d
23.	El Vado Lake	a,b,c,d,g,h,i,j		53.	Fort Sumner	a,c,d
24.	Heron Lake	a,b,c,d,g,h		54.	Jemez Mission	c,d
25.	Hyde Park	a,b,c,d,j		55.	La Mesilla Plaza	a,d,j
26.	Indian Petroglyph	a,c,d		56.	Lincoln Town	c,d
27.	Kit Carson Memorial	a,c,d,j		57.	Palace of the Governors	c,d
28.	Leasburg	a,b,c,d,f,g,h,j		58.	Quarai Mission	a,c,d

a—picnicking   f—showers
b—camping   g—boating
c—toilets   h—fishing
d—drinking water   i—swimming
e—electricity   j—playgrounds

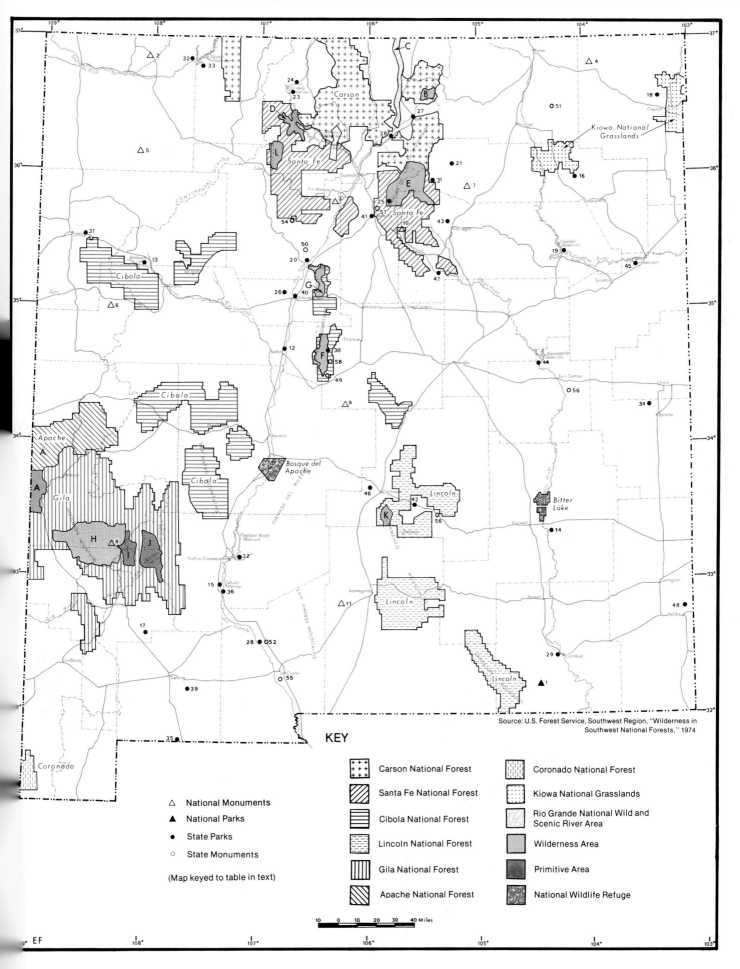

Source: U.S. Forest Service, Southwest Region, "Wilderness in Southwest National Forests," 1974

KEY

△ National Monuments

▲ National Parks

● State Parks

○ State Monuments

(Map keyed to table in text)

Carson National Forest	Coronado National Forest
Santa Fe National Forest	Kiowa National Grasslands
Cibola National Forest	Rio Grande National Wild and Scenic River Area
Lincoln National Forest	Wilderness Area
Gila National Forest	Primitive Area
Apache National Forest	National Wildlife Refuge

10 0 10 20 30 40 Miles

149

recreation and tourism II—fish and wildlife

New Mexico fishing provides something for everyone as the geography of the state offers ample opportunity to fly-cast in cool high country streams, spin-cast on the reservoirs and large rivers, or for the casual line-lunker attracted to the small lakes, ponds, and riverside drains. Fishermen directly finance the maintenance of fish supply by management and hatchery programs through the purchase of state license fees. Revenue is also indirectly received for fisheries research and management through the Federal Aid in Sport Fish Restoration Act which levies a 10 percent excise tax on the manufacture of fishing equipment. The federally funded programs in the state are supervised by the U.S. Fish and Wildlife Service. Fishing lakes have been constructed, lands have been purchased and leased, and most of the fishing areas in New Mexico have benefited from federal revenue.

The State Department of Game and Fish maintain over 5600 water surface-acres of fishing areas, stocked from six hatcheries. Most of the stocking is done in fairly small bodies of water (Ute Lake is the only water body over 500 acres) by a formula based on current fish density, water availability, and number of anglers using the location. The more popular the fishing area, the greater the number of new plantings. All of the state hatcheries specialize in trout rearing, with the Rock Lake station the sole warm water hatchery, specializing in walleye and bass. All hatcheries underwent remodeling in 1973 and 1974 to increase productivity. Red River hatchery alone provides nearly 200,000 pounds of stocker rainbow trout per year. Parkview hatches between 7 million and 9 million rainbow and brown trout annually with many of the fingerlings transferred to the other hatcheries. The mapbook *New Mexico Fishing Waters* is available from the Department of Game and Fish. It provides detailed descriptions of all areas of the state currently stocked and the period of stocking.

The fifty-eight wildlife management areas of New Mexico are operated directly from license fees paid by hunters and indirectly from excise fees on the purchase of hunting equipment collected under the Federal Aid in Wildlife Restoration Act. Four of the management units (1, 3, 11, and 35) are Indian reservations that impose special game restrictions on non-Indian hunters and permits are available only from each specific tribe. The remaining management units cut across national forests, state lands, private lands, and game department properties. Special use permits are also available for hunting in wilderness and primitive areas. Within the management units are pockets that are closed to all hunting of big game and turkey. These are national and state parks and monuments and the federal and state wildlife and waterfowl refuges.

The state controls over 140,000 acres of wildlife conservation areas (60% of it leased) and more than 11,000 acres preserved for waterfowl. The northern areas of the state provide good habitat and hunting facilities for deer, elk, bear, lion, barbary or bighorn sheep, and turkey. The southern half of the state includes waterfowl, game birds, ibex, gemsbok, javelina, and antelope in addition to bear, deer, and sheep. Along with desert bighorn sheep, imported ibex, gemsbok, kudu, and gazelle are reared at the Red Rock Wildlife area north of Lordsburg. Ibex and gemsbok breed successfully in the New Mexico environment and have been released for controlled hunting in the Tularosa Basin (unit 19) and Florida Mountains (unit 25).

The largest hunting areas of New Mexico are privately-owned preserves in the north. Vermejo Park Ranch is a massive 360,000 acre fishing and wildlife estate covering the northwest quarter of Colfax County in Unit 55. The National Rifle Association recently purchased the surface rights of the former Koehler coal mining claim, adjacent to Vermejo Park, for the purpose of establishing another large private hunting resort.

Jerry L. Williams

TABLE 1: FISH, WILDLIFE, AND WATERFOWL AREAS—1975

State Fish Hatcheries	Map Key	Date Estab.		Map Key	State Wildlife & Waterfowl Areas	Date Estab.	Size (acres)
Seven Springs	A	1933		G	Jackson Lake Waterfowl	1948	840
Glenwood	B	1938		H	Navajo Dam Wildlife	———	3785
Parkview	C	1932		I	Miller Mesa Waterfowl	1963	3060
Lisboa Springs	D	1921		J	Roque Wildlife	1966	9131
Red River	E	1941		K	Rio de Los Pinos Wildlife & Fishing	1953	850
Rock Lake	F	1964		L	Rio Chama Wildlife and Fishing	1953	13000
				M	Marquez Wildlife	1968	15000

Map Key	State Controlled Fishing Areas	Date Estab.	Size		Map Key	State Wildlife & Waterfowl Areas	Date Estab.	Size (acres)
1	San Juan Easement	1966	6 mi.		N	Water Canyon Wildlife	1953	2840
2	Chama Easement	1970	4.3 mi.		O	Rio Costilla Wildlife	1965	89000*
3	Hopewell Lake	1951	19 ac.		P	Uracca Wildlife	1966	13870
4	San Gregorio Reservoir	———	75 ac.		Q	Tres Piedras Wildlife	1940	3260
5	Fenton Lake Fish and Waterfowl	1952	256 ac.		R	Cimarron Canyon Wildlife	1950	33116
6	McGaffey Lake	1954	14 ac.		S	Elliott Barker Wildlife	1966	5415
7	Springer Lake	1960	400 ac.		T	Bert Clancey Wildlife and Fishing	———	2166
8	Charette Lakes Fish and Wildlife	1949	410 ac.		U1	McAllister Lake Fish and Wildlife	1944	623
9	Morphey Lake	1965	50 ac.		U2	Wagon Mound Lake Fish and Wildlife	1930	735
10	Monastery Lake	1965	12 ac.		V1	Belen Waterfowl	1959	230
11	Ute Lake	1962	4100 ac.		V2	Bernado Waterfowl	1961	1573
12	Quemado Lake	1972	130 ac.		W	La Joya Waterfowl	1928	3550
13	Snow Lake	1967	75 ac.		X	Heart Bar Wildlife	1951	797
14	Wall Lake	1948	15 ac.		Y	Red Rock Wildlife	1960	20000
15	Bill Evans Lake	1972	62 ac.		Z	Prairie Chicken Wildlife	1940	21000
16	Lake Roberts	1962	71 ac.		AA	Artesia Waterfowl	1962	640
17	Bear Canyon Reservoir	1949	25 ac.					
18	Sacramento Lake	1965	5 ac.					
19	Green Meadow Lake	1967	12 ac.					
20	Clayton Lake Fish and Waterfowl	1954	150 ac.					

*leased land

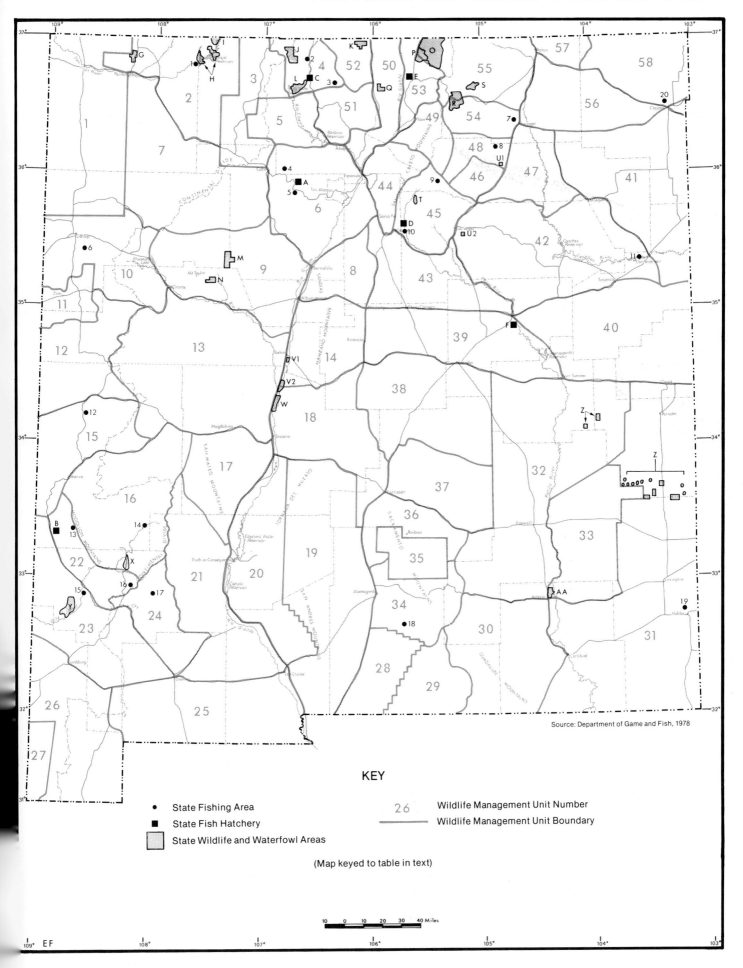

Source: Department of Game and Fish, 1978

KEY

- ● State Fishing Area
- ■ State Fish Hatchery
- ▨ State Wildlife and Waterfowl Areas

26 Wildlife Management Unit Number
── Wildlife Management Unit Boundary

(Map keyed to table in text)

10 0 10 20 30 40 Miles

recreation and tourism III—tourist facilities

New Mexico contains a variety of recreation and tourist facilities that provide year-round pleasures for both resident and visitor. Most of the facilities that are listed as winter sports areas also operate as summer resorts, and the Indian activities, although concentrated in the summer, occur on a limited basis throughout the year.

The eleven ski resorts operate on slopes that offer miles of trails for all levels of skiers. Most of the ski areas are in the north central portion of the state on the high north-facing slopes of the Sangre de Cristo Mountains. The largest resorts with advanced trails such as Red River, Taos Valley, and Angel Fire, are clustered with the smaller family-oriented slopes of Powder Puff, Val Verde and Sipapu, and provide one of the best concentrations of natural snow ski areas in the United States. Santa Fe Basin and Sandia Peak, which are south of the northern cluster, draw skiers primarily from the large nearby metropolitan populations of Santa Fe and Albuquerque. Skiing in the Sacramento Mountains of the south is largely peopled by tourists from Texas. The general ski season in New Mexico runs from December through March. The resorts at Red River, Taos, Angel Fire, Sierra Blanca, and Cloudcroft continue operating as summer resorts, offering extensive facilities in warm-weather activities such as horseback riding, swimming, golf, hiking, and grass skiing.

Lodges and guest ranches are mostly located in the high country areas throughout the state. The list provided in Table 2 is not comprehensive and many smaller facilities can be located by contacting the Tourist Division of the Department of Development. Many of the guest ranches are operating ranches that have added accommodations for the tourist. Others located along large waterbodies may have originated as fishing camps and expanded their functions to become more complete family resorts. Most of the ranches and resorts operate on a warm season schedule, although several advertise heated cabins and rooms with fireplaces for winter service.

Horse-racing operates on a short summer season and all tracks have facilities for pari-mutuel betting. A fifth racetrack is found in Albuquerque at the State Fairgrounds, but it only operates on a two-week season in conjunction with the State Fair in September. One of the richest racing purses in the world is claimed each year at Ruidoso Downs in the New Mexico Futurity for quarter horses. More than fifty golf courses throughout the state operate on a much longer season than the racetracks. In some areas of the state, where snow is a rare occurrence, the golf links are available all year. The main season, with tournament play, usually does not begin until May and lasts until the end of October.

Indian reservation lands are private and special permission from the governor of each area must be granted before visiting places outside of the main settlement sites. Likewise, the visitor must be familiar with the audio-visual regulations (camera, tape-recording) that are imposed by the tribal councils of each reservation. A booklet written by Bertha Dutton entitled *Indians of New Mexico* provides a summary of the general visitor restrictions to each tribal area. More current information can be obtained at the Indian Cultural Center in Albuquerque, or by going directly to the administrative buildings on the reservation you wish to visit. Failure to abide by the regulations can result in arrest and heavy fine.

Indian ceremonies and festivals on reservations mainly occur from late spring until early fall in conjunction with the planting and harvest cycles of the growing season. As most reservations have been under the mission influence for several centuries, a number of special ceremonies are held during Christmas and Easter. Visitors are invited to most of the Indian programs providing they abide by the conditions dictated by the tribe. There are two places off of the reservations where people can view traditional Indian dancing and crafts. The Indian Cultural Center in Albuquerque offers a summer schedule of inter-tribal dances and displays of Native American wares. At Red Rocks State Park near Gallup, the annual Intertribal Indian Ceremonial each August provides visitors with entertainment by tribes from a number of western states.

Jerry L. Williams

TABLE 1: WINTER SPORTS FACILITIES

	Base Elevation (ft)	Vertical Rise (ft)
1. Taos	9207	2612
2. Powder Puff	8700	150
3. Red River	8750	1530
4. Val Verde	8300	350
5. Angel Fire	8500	2180
6. Sugarite	8000	1000
7. Sipapu	8200	800
8. Santa Fe	10400	1600
9. Sandia Peak	8700	1660
10. Sierra Blanca	9700	1700
11. Cloudcroft	8350	450
*12. Ruidoso Ski Basin	7400	500

*night skiing

Cross County Skiing
concentrated in U.S. forest areas of the Sangre de Cristo, San Juan, Jemez, Manzano and Sandia Mountains.

TABLE 2: GUEST RANCHES AND RESORTS

New Mexico Guest Ranches and Resorts	Nearest Town	1978 Capacity	New Mexico Guest Ranches and Resorts	Nearest Town	1978 Capacity
12 Angel Fire Resort	Eagle Nest	300	25 High Country Lodge	Alto	132
13 Aspen Park Ranch	Red River	80	26 Inn of the Mountain		
14 Bar X Bar Ranch	Pecos	18	Gods	Ruidoso	140
15 Bear Mountain Ranch	Silver City	25	27 La Junta Ranch	Alto	70
16 Bishop's Lodge	Santa Fe	130	28 Lobo Lodge	Chama	30
17 Bitter Lake Ranch	Red River	36	29 Los Olmos Resort	Glenwood	35
18 Cerro Pelon Ranch	Sapello	8	30 Los Pinos Ranch	Pecos	16
19 Brazos Lodge	Tierra		31 Pendaries Village Inn	Sapello	20
	Amarilla	22	32 Tall Pines Resort	Red River	120
20 Cloudcroft Lodge	Cloudcroft	50	33 Taos Ski Valley		
21 Conchas Lake Lodge	Conchas	136	Resorts	Taos	820
22 Elephant Butte Inn	T. or C.	190	34 Tres Lagunas Ranch	Pecos	24
23 El Vado Ranch	Tierra		35 Vermejo Park Resorts	Raton	70
	Amarilla	50	36 Youngs Ranch	Red River	154
24 Gascon Ranch	Rociada	22	37 Ghost Ranch	Abiquiu	350

Source: New Mexico Department of Development, Tourist Division. "New Mexico Guest Ranches and Resorts" (1978).

TABLE 3: GOLF COURSES AND COUNTRY CLUBS—1978
—Public and Semi-public
—Private

ALBUQUERQUE

Albuquerque Country Club
Arroyo Del Oso Golf Course
Four Hills Country Club
Los Altos Golf Course
Paradise Hills Country Club
Rio Rancho Golf and Country Club
Tanoan Country Club
Tijeras Arroyo Golf Course
University of New Mexico

NORTHWESTERN NEW MEXICO

San Juan Country Club (Farmington)
Hidden Valley Country Club (Aztec)
Gallup Municipal Golf Course
Grants-Milan Municipal Golf Course
Horizon Country Club (Belen)
Los Alamos Golf Coub
Santa Fe Country Club

NORTHEASTERN NEW MEXICO

Angel Fire Country Club (nr. Eagle Nest)
Pendaries Golf and Country Club (Mora County)
Raton Golf Course
Conchas Lake State Park Golf Course
Tucumcari Municipal Golf Course
Santa Rosa Golf Course

SOUTHWESTERN NEW MEXICO

New Mexico Tech Golf Course (Socorro)
T or C Golf Course
Elephant Butte Golf and Country Club (T or C)
Scott Park Golf Course (Silver City)
Lordsburg Golf Club
Rio Mimbres Country Club (Deming)
Las Cruces Country Club
New Mexico State University Golf Course (Las Cruces)
Anthony Country Club
Dos Lagos Golf Course (Anthony)
Santa Teresa Country Club (Sunland Park)

SOUTHEASTERN NEW MEXICO

Artesia Country Club
Lovington Country Club
Hobbs Country Club
Ocotillo Golf Course (Hobbs)
Lake Carlsbad Golf Course
Riverside Country Club (Carlsbad)
Eunice Municipal Golf Course
Jal Country Club
Carrizozo Municipal Golf Course
Alto Lakes Golf and Country Club (Ruidoso)
Cree Meadows Country Club (Ruidoso)
Inn of the Mountain Gods (Mescalero Apache)
Cloud Country Lodge Golf Course (Cloudcroft)
Timberon (SE of Cloudcroft)
Alamogordo Country Club
Apache Mesa Golf Club (Holloman Air Force Base)
White Sands Golf Course
Clovis Municipal Golf Course
Colonial Park Country Club (Clovis)
Portales Country Club
Cahoon Park Golf Course (Roswell)
Roswell Country Club
New Mexico Military Institute Golf Course (Roswell)

Source: *1977 Listings—Sun County Section of the PGA.*

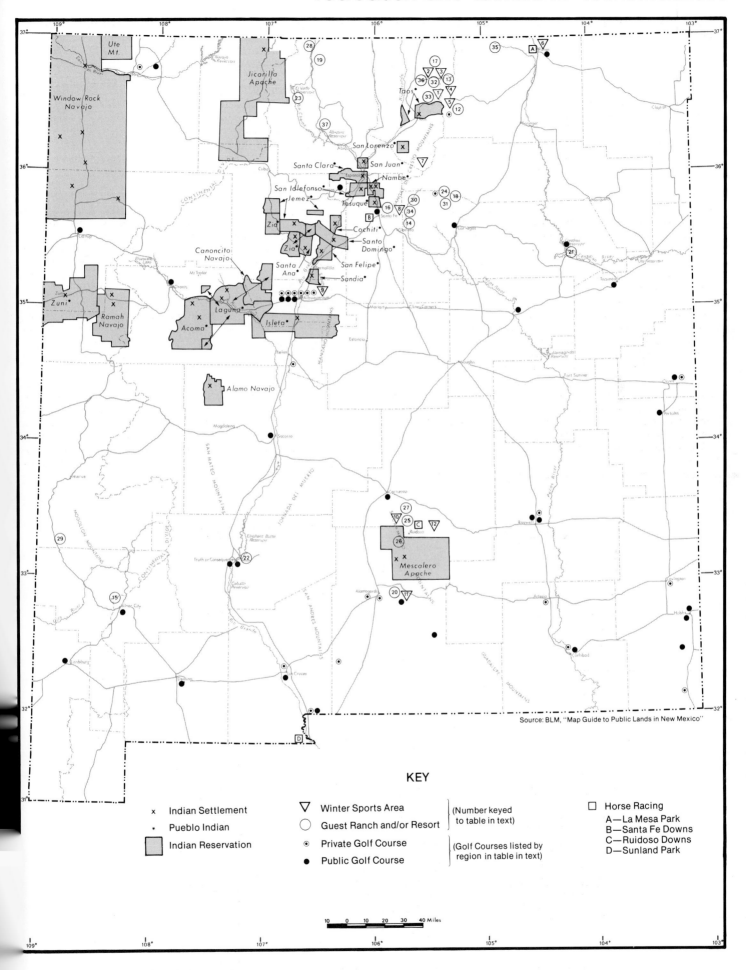

Source: BLM, "Map Guide to Public Lands in New Mexico"

KEY

x	Indian Settlement	▽	Winter Sports Area	(Number keyed to table in text)
*	Pueblo Indian	◯	Guest Ranch and/or Resort	
▨	Indian Reservation	⊙	Private Golf Course	(Golf Courses listed by region in table in text)
		●	Public Golf Course	

☐ Horse Racing
A—La Mesa Park
B—Santa Fe Downs
C—Ruidoso Downs
D—Sunland Park

10 0   10   20   30   40 Miles

153

museums

New Mexico has many museums throughout the state, most of which are open to the public free of charge. While many of these museums feature the history and arts and crafts of the Southwest, several emphasize the important role New Mexico has played in scientific and technological development. The list is keyed to numbers appearing on the map. Most of the state and national monuments have small museums that are not included in this section.

Paul McAllister

County	Map No.	Location	Museum Name and Control	Type
Bernalillo	1	Albuquerque	A. K. Mitchell Collection of Western Art, Lovelace Foundation	N* Western Art
	2	Albuquerque	Indian Pueblo Cultural Center	I Arts and Crafts
	3	Albuquerque	Jonson Gallery, University of New Mexico	U Art
	4	Albuquerque	Fine Arts Museum, University of New Mexico	U Art
	5	Albuquerque	State Fair Fine Arts Collection	S Art
	6	Albuquerque	National Atomic Museum	F Military Science
	7	Albuquerque	Sandia Labs Exhibit Center	N Science and Technology
	8	Albuquerque	Telephone Pioneer Museum	P Science and Technology
	9	Albuquerque	Biology Museum, University of New Mexico	U Southwest Biology
	10	Albuquerque	Geology Museum, University of New Mexico	U Geology
	11	Albuquerque	Rio Grande Zoological Park	L Wildlife
	12	Albuquerque	Maxwell Museum of Anthropology, University of New Mexico	U Anthropology
	13	Albuquerque	Museum of Albuquerque	L Regional History
	14	Albuquerque	Ernie Pyle Memorial Library	L House
Catron	15	Mogollon	Mogollon Ghost Town Museum	P History
Chaves	16	Roswell	Chaves County Historical Museum	N History
	17	Roswell	Roswell Museum and Art Center	L Art
Colfax	18	Raton	Raton Museum	N Art and History
	19	Springer	Santa Fe Trail Museum	L History
	20	Cimarron	E. T. Seton Memorial Library and Museum	N History
	21	Cimarron	Old Mill Museum	N History
	22	Cimarron	Kit Carson Museum	P General
De Baca	23	Fort Sumner	Grave of Billy the Kid and Old Fort Sumner	P History
Dona Ana	24	Mesilla	American Desert Museum	N Nature
	25	Mesilla	Gadsden Museum	P General
	26	Las Cruces	New Mexico State University Museum	U General
	27	Las Cruces	Museum of Old Dolls and Toys	P General
Eddy	28	Carlsbad	Carlsbad Municipal Museum	L Natural History
	29	Carlsbad	Million Dollar Museum	P General
	30	Artesia	Artesia Historical Museum and Art Center	L History and Art
Grant	31	Silver City	Silver City Museum	L History
	32	Silver City	Western New Mexico University Museum	U History
	33	Pinos Altos	Pinos Altos Historical Museum	P History
Hidalgo	34	Lordsburg	Shakespeare Ghost Town Museum	N History
Lea	35	Lovington	Lea County Museum	N General
	36	Hobbs	Confederate Air Force Museum	P Aeronautics
Lincoln	37	Lincoln	La Paloma Museum	P History
	38	Lincoln	Old Lincoln County Courthouse Museum	N History
	39	Capitan	Smokey Bear Museum	L Natural History
	40	Ancho	My House of Old Things	P General
Los Alamos	41	Los Alamos	Bradbury Science Hall and Museum	F Science and Technology
	42	Los Alamos	Los Alamos Historical Museum	N General
Luna	43	Deming	Chamber of Commerce Museum	N General
	44	Deming	Luna County Museum	N Art and History
	45	Columbus	Pancho Villa Museum	P Military
McKinley	46	Gallup	Museum of Indian Arts and Crafts	N Crafts
Otero	47	Alamogordo	International Space Hall of Fame	N Space
	48	Alamogordo	Otero County Historical Museum	L History
	49	Cloudcroft	Cloudcroft Museum	L General
	50	Tularosa	Tularosa Historical Museum	N History
Quay	51	Tucumcari	Tucumcari Historical Museum	L History
	52	San Jon	San Jon Pioneer Museum	L History
	53	Montoya	Richardson General Store	P General
Rio Arriba	54	Abiquiu	Ghost Ranch Museum	F Natural History
	55	Chama	Chama and Toltec Scenic Railroad	S Technology
Roosevelt	56	Portales	Blackwater Draw Museum	U Archeology
	57	Portales	Miles Museum	U Geology
	58	Portales	Paleo-Indian Institute and Museum	U Anthropology
	59	Portales	Roosevelt County Museum	U General
San Juan	60	Farmington	Farmington Historical Museum	U General
	61	Farmington	San Juan County Archeological Center	L Archeology
	62	Aztec	Chamber of Commerce Museum	L History
San Miguel	63	Las Vegas	Rough Riders Memorial and City Museum	L History
Santa Fe	64	Galisteo	Galisteo Museum	P History
	65	Madrid	Old Coal Mine Museum	P Technology
	66	La Cienega	El Rancho do Las Golondrinas Museum	N Cultural
	67	San Ildefonso	San Ildefonso Pueblo Museum	I Anthropology
	68	Santa Fe	Fine Arts Museum	S Art
	69	Santa Fe	Institute of American Indian Arts	F Art
	70	Santa Fe	Museum of International Folk Art	S Arts and Crafts
	71	Santa Fe	International Institute of Iberian Colonial Art	N Art
	72	Santa Fe	Laboratory of Anthropology	S Anthropology
	73	Santa Fe	The Wheelwright Museum	N Anthropology
	74	Santa Fe	Palace of the Governors	S History
	75	Santa Fe	Chapel of San Miguel	N History
	76	Santa Fe	Wings of Yesterday	P Aeronautics
Sierra	77	Truth or Consequences	Geronimo Springs Museum	N History
	78	Hillsboro	Black Range Museum	P General
	79	Kingston	Percha Valley Museum	P General
Socorro	80	Socorro	Mineral Museum, Bureau of Mines	S Minerals
Taos	81	Penasco	Picuris Pueblo Museum	I Historical Site
	82	Taos	Governor Bent Museum	P History
	83	Taos	Harwood Foundation	U Art
	84	Taos	Kit Carson Home and Museum	N Site
	85	Taos	Leon Gaspard House Museum	P General
	86	Taos	Millicent A. Rogers Memorial Museum	N Arts and Crafts
Torrance	87	Moriarty	Chamber of Commerce Museum	N General
Union	88	Folsom	Folsom Museum	P General
Valencia	89	Tome	Tome Parish Museum	N Religious
	90	Grants	Chamber of Commerce Museum	N Anthropology

*F—Federal Government
 I—Indian Government
 S—State Government
 L—Local Government

N—Non Profit Organization
P—Private
U—University

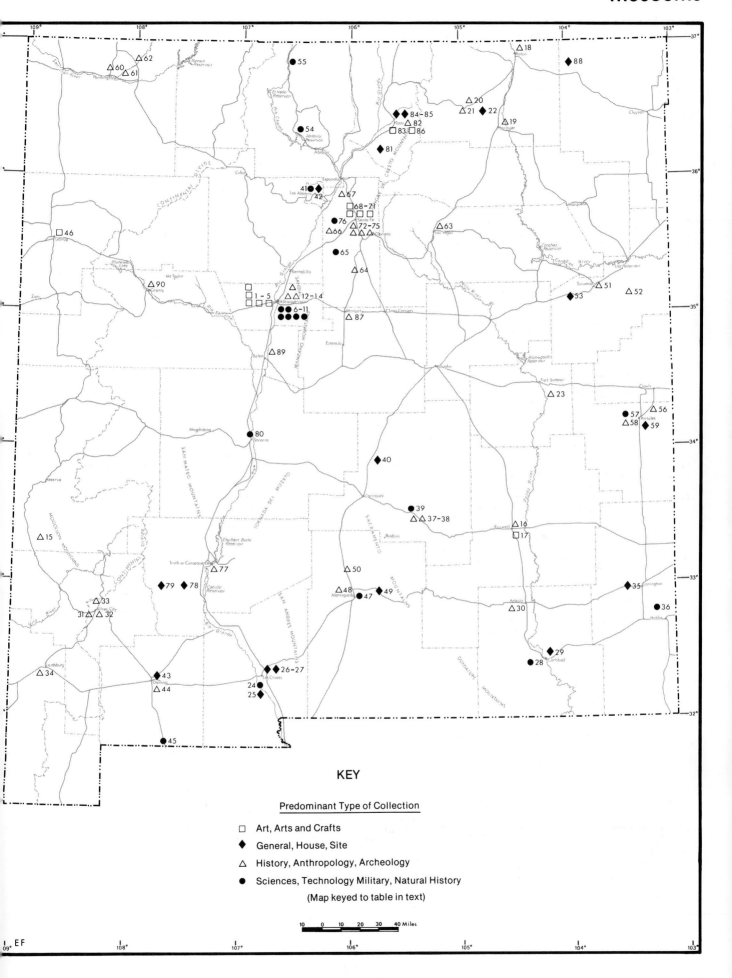

KEY

Predominant Type of Collection

□ Art, Arts and Crafts

◆ General, House, Site

△ History, Anthropology, Archeology

● Sciences, Technology Military, Natural History

(Map keyed to table in text)

10 0 10 20 30 40 Miles

historic sites

The United States has an official program for preserving, restoring, and maintaining the nation's historic and cultural environment. A major part of that program is the National Register of Historic Places, an official list authorized by federal statute, designating cultural resources worthy of preservation. Nominations to the National Register are made by the states and various federal agencies. Each entry must meet rigid criteria to guarantee that the site has historical, architectural, archeological, or cultural significance.

New Mexico's efforts at historic preservation long preceded those of the federal government. Through private and state efforts, several historically significant structures, such as the Palace of the Governors in Santa Fe and Gran Quivira in Socorro County, were saved prior to the passage of federal legislation. Nonetheless, when the federal government enacted the National Historic Preservation Act in 1966, New Mexico still lacked the basic legislation, staff, and comprehensive planning necessary for an adequate historic preservation program. Efforts to remedy this condition began immediately. In 1968 Governor David F. Cargo appointed an historic site review committee, and basic histori preservation legislation was introduced in January 1969 by Stat Senator Tibo J. Chavez.

As of January 1978, New Mexico had 138 listings on the Na tional Register. These entries, which reflect the multicultura heritage of the state, are shown on the table. The numbers on th table correspond to the map and give the name of the site and it approximate location. Inclusion on the National Register does no signify that a particular site is owned by the government nor that i is open to the public.

Many sites are in private ownership and permission must be obtained before attempting to visit them. Even some of the government owned sites (primarily archeological) are closed to the public and are listed with only vague locations to protect them from vandalism. Fortunately, most National Register sites in New Mexic are open to the public or may be viewed from public thoroughfares.

Paul McAlliste

NEW MEXICO PROPERTIES ON THE NATIONAL REGISTER OF HISTORIC PLACES

County	Vicinity	Historic Site	Address or Location
1. Bernalillo	Albuquerque	Armijo, Salvador, House	618 Rio Grande Blvd. NW
2. Bernalillo	Albuquerque	First Methodist Episcopal Church	3rd St. & Lead Ave.
3. Bernalillo	Albuquerque	Hodgin Hall	University of New Mexico
4. Bernalillo	Albuquerque	Kimo Theater	421 Central Ave.
5. Bernalillo	Albuquerque	Occidental Insurance Co. Bldg.	3rd St. & Gold Ave.
6. Bernalillo	Albuquerque	Rancho de Carnue Site	Off U.S. 66
7. Bernalillo	Albuquerque	San Felipe de Neri Church	Old Town Plaza
8. Bernalillo	Albuquerque	Spitz, Berthold, House	323 N 10th St.
9. Bernalillo	Albuquerque	Superintendent's House, Atlantic and Pacific Railroad	1023 2nd SW
10. Bernalillo	Isleta	Isleta Pueblo	U.S. 85
11. Catron	Datil	Ake Site	SE of Datil
12. Catron	Horse Springs	Bate Cave	S of Horse Springs
13. Catron	Silver City	Gila Cliff Dwellings National Monument	N of Silver City on NM 15
14. Colfax	Abbott	Dorsey Mansion	12 mi NE Abbott off U.S. 56
15. Colfax	Cimmaron	Cimmaron Historic District	S edge of city along NM 21
16. Colfax	Folsom	Folsom Man Site	8 mi W of Folsom
17. Colfax	Raton	Raton Downtown Historic District	Rio Grande-Clark & 1st-3rd Sts.
18. Colfax	Raton	Raton Pass	U.S. 85-87, CO/NM border
19. Colfax	Springer	Melvin W. Mills House	509 1st St.
20. De Baca	Fort Sumner	Fort Sumner Ruins State Monument	SE Fort Sumner off NM 212
21. Doña Ana	El Paso	International Boundary Marker No. 1	W of El Paso off I 10
22. Doña Ana	Las Cruces	Armijo, Nesor, House	Lohman Ave. & Church St.
23. Doña Ana	Las Cruces	Fort Fillmore	SE Las Cruces off U.S. 85
24. Dona Ana	Las Cruces	Fort Selden	18 mi N of Las Cruces
25. Doña Ana	Las Cruces	Mesilla Plaza	2 mi S Las Cruces on NM 28
26. Eddy	Carlsbad	First National Bank of Eddy	303 West Fox St.
27. Eddy	Carlsbad	Carlsbad Reclamation Project	N of Carlsbad
28. Eddy	Carlsbad	Painted Grotto	SW Carlsbad in Carlsbad Caverns National Park
29. Grant	Cliff	Woodrow Ruin	5 mi NE of Cliff
30. Grant	Silver City	Ailman, H. B., House	314 W Broadway
31. Grant	Tyrone	Burro Springs Site	In Gila National Forest
32. Hidalgo	Lordsburg	Shakespeare Ghost Town	S of Lordsburg
33. Lincoln	Capitan	Fort Stanton	7 mi. SE of Capitan
34. Lincoln	Lincoln	Lincoln Historic District	U.S. 380
35. Lincoln	Lincoln	Feather Cave	Lincoln vicinity
36. Lincoln	White Oaks	White Oaks Historic District	12 NE Carrizozo on NM 349
37. Los Alamos	Los Alamos	Los Alamos Scientific Laboratory	Central Ave.
38. Luna	Columbus	Village of Columbus & Camp Furlong	NM 11
39. Luna	Deming	Luna County Courthouse & Park	700 S. Silver Ave.
40. McKinley	Manuelito	Manuelito Complex	S of Manuelito
41. McKinley	Zuni	Halona Pueblo (Zuni Pueblo)	On NM 53
42. Mora	Mora	St. Vrain's Mill	On NM 38
43. Mora	Mora	La Cueva Historic District	6 mi. SE of Mora at jct. NM 3 & 2
44. Mora	Wagon Mound	Wagon Mound	E of Wagon Mound on U.S. 85
45. Mora	Watrous	Watrous (La Junta)	U.S. 85
46. Mora	Watrous	Fort Union National Monument	9 mi. N Watrous on NM 477
47. Rio Arriba	Blanco	Frances Canyon Ruin	17 mi. NE of Blanco
48. Rio Arriba	Canones	Tsiping Ruin	7 mi. W of Abiquiu
49. Rio Arriba	Chama	Cumbres and Toltec Scenic Railroad	Chama, runs into Colorado
50. Rio Arriba	Espanola	Puye Ruins	14 mi. W of Espanola
51. Rio Arriba	Espanola	San Gabriel De Yungue-Ouinge	4 mi. N of Espanola
52. Rio Arriba	Espanola	Pueblo of San Juan	N of Espanola
53. Rio Arriba	Espanola	Pueblo of Santa Clara	S of Espanola off NM 30
54. Rio Arriba	Farmington	Crow Canyon Archeological Site	E of Farmington
55. Roosevelt	Clovis	Anderson Basin (Blackwater Draw)	12 mi. S of Clovis
56. San Juan	Aztec	Aztec Ruins National Monument	1 mi. N of Aztec
57. San Juan	Farmington	Gallegos Wash Archeological District	SE of Farmington
58. San Juan	Farmington	Salmon Ruin	9 mi. E of Farmington off NM 17
59. San Miguel	Bell Ranch	Bell Ranch Headquarters	N & E of Conchas Reservoir
60. San Miguel	Las Vegas	Las Vegas Plaza	Valencia, Gonzales, & Moreno Sts. and Hot Springs Blvd.
61. San Miguel	Las Vegas	Our Lady of Sorrows Church	W. National Ave.
62. San Miguel	Las Vegas	St. Paul's Memorial Episcopal Church and Guild Hall	714-716 National Ave.
63. San Miguel	Las Vegas	Montezuma Hotel Complex	6 mi. NW Las Vegas on NM 65
64. San Miguel	Pecos	Pecos National Monument	S of Pecos on NM 63
65. San Miguel	San Jose	San Miguel Del Vado Historic District	SE of San Jose on NM 3
66. Sandoval	Bernalillo	Our Lady of Sorrows Church	U.S. 85
67. Sandoval	Bernalillo	Jemez Pueblo	28 mi. N of Bernalillo on NM 4
68. Sandoval	Bernalillo	Kuaua Ruin (Coronado State Monument)	N of Bernalillo off NM 44
69. Sandoval	Bernalillo	Sandia Cave	11 mi. E of Bernalillo
70. Sandoval	Bernalillo	Pueblo of Santo Domingto (Kiua)	18 mi. N of Bernalillo off I 25
71. Sandoval	Bernalillo	Tamaya (Santa Ana Pueblo)	N of Bernalillo off NM 44
72. Sandoval	Bernalillo	Zia Pueblo	18 mi. W of Bernalillo on NM 4
73. Sandoval	Casa Salazar	Big Bead Mesa	W of Casa Salazar
74. Sandoval	Jemez Springs	San Juan Mesa Ruin	4 mi. E of Jemez Springs
75. Sandoval	Jemez Springs	Jemez State Monument (Giusewq)	NM 4
76. Sandoval	Los Alamos	Bandelier National Monument	NM 4 12 mi. S of Los Alamos
77. Sandoval	Santa Fe	Cochiti Pueblo	27 mi. S of Santa Fe off I 25
78. Santa Fe	Chimayo	Plaza del Cerro	SW of jct. Rtes. 76 & 4
79. Santa Fe	Espanola	San Ildefonso Pueblo	SW Espanola off NM 4
80. Santa Fe	Madrid	Madrid Historic District	SW Santa Fe off NM 14
81. Santa Fe	Santa Cruz	La Iglesia y la Plaza de Santa Cruz de la Canada	Santa Cruz
82. Santa Fe	Santa Fe	Barrio de Analco Historic District	Bounded by E. De Vargas and College Sts. & Santa Fe River
83. Santa Fe	Santa Fe	Bergere, Alfred M., House	135 Grant Avenue
84. Santa Fe	Santa Fe	Crespin, Gregorio, House	132 E. De Vargas St.
85. Santa Fe	Santa Fe	Davey, Randall, House	Upper Canyon Rd.
86. Santa Fe	Santa Fe	Federal Building	Cathedral Pl. at Palace St.
87. Santa Fe	Santa Fe	Fort Marcy Officer's Residence	116 Lincoln Ave.
88. Santa Fe	Santa Fe	Fort Marcy Ruins	Off NM 475
89. Santa Fe	Santa Fe	Hayt-Wientge House	620 Paseo de la Cuma
90. Santa Fe	Santa Fe	National Park Service Southwest Regional Office	Old Santa Fe Trail
91. Santa Fe	Santa Fe	Palace of the Governors	The Plaza
92. Santa Fe	Santa Fe	Reredos of Our Lady of Light	Christo Rey Church, Canyon R
93. Santa Fe	Santa Fe	Santa Fe Historic District	
94. Santa Fe	Santa Fe	Santa Fe Plaza	
95. Santa Fe	Santa Fe	Shonnard, Eugenie, House	226 Hickox St.
96. Santa Fe	Santa Fe	Spiegelberg House (Spitz House)	237 E. Palace St.
97. Santa Fe	Santa Fe	Tully, Pinckney R., House	138 Grant Ave.
98. Santa Fe	Santa Fe	U.S. Courthouse	Federal Pl.
99. Santa Fe	Santa Fe	Vigil, Donaciano, House	518 Alto St.
100. Santa Fe	Santa Fe	Glorieta Pass Battlefield	10 mi. SE off I 25
101. Santa Fe	Santa Fe	Otowi Historic District	25 mi. N on NM 4
102. Santa Fe	Santa Fe	Pueblo of Nambe	about 16 mi. off NM 4
103. Santa Fe	Santa Fe	Pueblo of San Lazaro	25 mi. S of Santa Fe
104. Santa Fe	Santa Fe	Pueblo of Tesuque	8 mi. N on W bank Tesuque Riv
105. Santa Fe	Santa Fe	Seton Village (Castle)	6 mi. S off US 84/85
106. Santa Fe	Truchas	El Santuario de Chimayo	S of Truchas in Chimayo
107. Socorro	Bingham	Trinity Site	25 mi. S of US 380
108. Socorro	Gran Quivira	Gran Quivira National Monument	1 mi. E of Gran Quivira on NM
109. Socorro	Magdalena	Gallinas Springs Ruin	N in Cibola National Forest
110. Socorro	Socorro	Bursum House	326 Church St.
111. Socorro	Socorro	Garcia Opera House	Terry Ave. & California St.
112. Socorro	Socorro	Illinois Brewery	Neal Ave. & 6th St.
113. Socorro	Socorro	Val Verde Hotel	203 Manzanares St.
114. Socorro	Socorro	Fort Craig	37 mi. S of Socorro
115. Taos	Las Trampas	Las Trampas Historic District	On NM 76
116. Taos	Las Trampas	San Jose de Gracia Church	N side of Plaza
117. Taos	Ojo Caliente	Chapel of Santa Cruz	S side of Plaza off US 285
118. Taos	Ranchos de Taos	San Francisco de Assisi Mission Church	The Plaza
119. Taos	Taos	Blumenschein, Ernest L., House	Ledoux St.
120. Taos	Taos	Carson, Kit, House	Kit Carson Ave.
121. Taos	Taos	Harwood Foundation (Smith H. Simpson House)	Ledoux St.
122. Taos	Taos	Martinez, Severino, House	Lower Ranchitos Rd.
123. Taos	Taos	La Morada de Nuestra Senora de Guadalupe	E of Taos off US 64
124. Taos	Taos	Picuris Pueblo	S of Taos
125. Taos	Taos	Taos Pueblo	3 mi. N
126. Taos	Vadito	Laureano Cordova Mill	Off NM 75
127. Torrance	Abo	Abo State Monument	3 mi. W of Abo on U.S. 60
128. Torrance	Punta	Quarai State Monument	1 mi. S of Punta
129. Union	Clayton	Rabbit Ears (Clayton Complex)	NW of Clayton
130. Valencia	Acoma	Acoma Pueblo	13 mi. S of I40 on NM 23
131. Valencia	Acoma	San Estevan de Acoma Mission Church	Acoma
132. Valencia	El Morro	El Morro National Monument	2 mi. W El Morro on NM 53
133. Valencia	Grants	Dittert Site	S of Grants
134. Valencia	Laguna	Laguna Pueblo	On I 40
135. Valencia	Laguna	San Jose de la Laguna Mission and Convento	Laguna Pueblo
136. Valencia	Los Lunas	Tranquilino Luna House	Jct of US 85 & NM 6
137. Valencia	Tome	Tome Jail	Tome Plaza
138. Valencia	Zuni	Hawikuh	12 mi. SW of Zuni

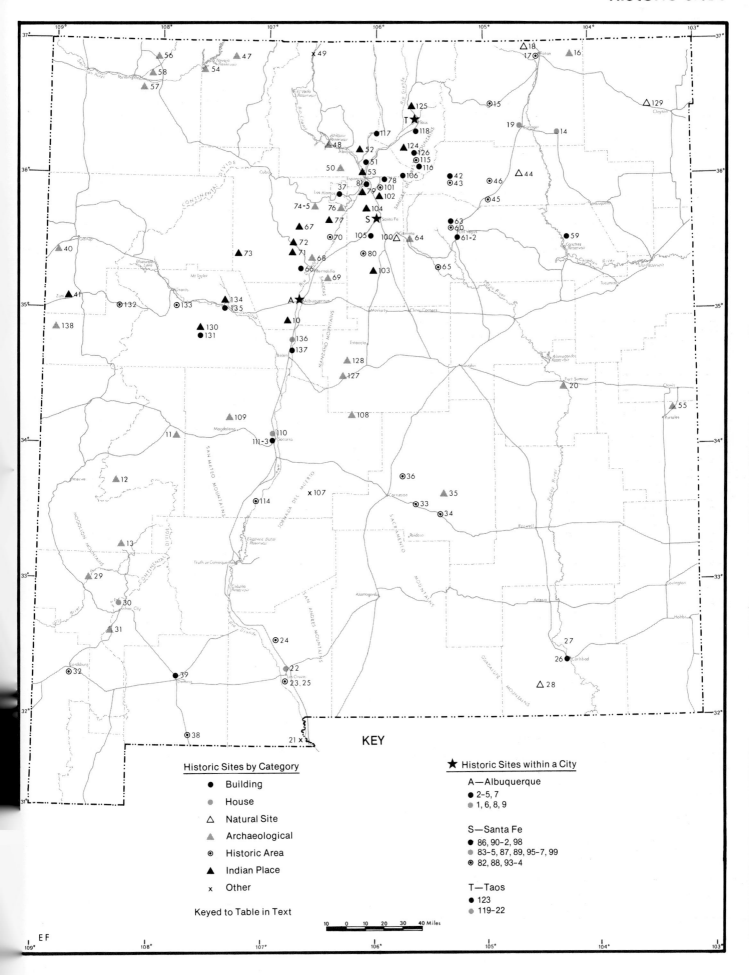

KEY

Historic Sites by Category

- ● Building
- ● House
- △ Natural Site
- ▲ Archaeological
- ◉ Historic Area
- ▲ Indian Place
- × Other

Keyed to Table in Text

10 0 10 20 30 40 Miles

★ Historic Sites within a City

A—Albuquerque
- ● 2-5, 7
- ● 1, 6, 8, 9

S—Santa Fe
- ● 86, 90-2, 98
- ● 83-5, 87, 89, 95-7, 99
- ◉ 82, 88, 93-4

T—Taos
- ● 123
- ● 119-22

E F

state governmental districts

State government has divided New Mexico into varying districts according to administrative needs. Districts for four basic governmental responsibilities are shown here.

There are fourteen State Police Districts which follow county lines except where terrain and accessibility indicate more suitable boundaries (Map 1). The districts vary considerably in area, population, and number of uniformed officers (Table 1). District 5 (the largest in population) has only one uniformed officer for every 13,181 inhabitants, while District 14 with a population of only 18,200 has an officer-inhabitant ratio of 1:1,400. These two districts are the extremes; other districts average one officer per 4000 residents.

The thirteen State Judicial Districts are also organized on a county basis (Map 2). Theoretically the goal is to create districts which provide easy public access to the seats of justice and equal caseloads for law officials. However, as Table 2 indicates, these goals are not easily met. Although additional judges significantly reduced the 1977 caseload in Districts 6, 7, 9, 11, and 12, the disparity between districts remains large with some judges presiding at almost three times as many cases as others.

The five State Highway Districts (Map 3), are responsible for maintenance of all federal and state roads within their boundaries. Counties, municipalities, and local districts are responsible for non-state owned roads. Table 3 illustrates that miles maintained as well as total vehicle miles and vehicle registration vary significantly by district.

The State Board of Education determines public school and vocational education policies and has control over the management of all public schools. The Board is composed of ten members elected for six year terms. They represent districts based on county, rather than local school district boundaries (Map 4). Bernalillo County elects three members representing specific areas of the county although it has only one school district. The exact number of pupils in each board district is difficult to determine but generally each board member represents approximately ten percent of the state school population.

Paul McAllister

TABLE 1: STATE POLICE DISTRICTS

District	1977 Estimated Population	Uniformed Officers	Ratio Uniformed Officers/Pop.	District	1977 Estimated Population	Uniformed Officers	Ratio Uniformed Officers/Pop.
1	90,000	19	1:4,737	8	54,200	20	1:2,710
2	34,300	15	1:2,287	9	77,800	21	1:3,705
3	94,400	16	1:5,900	10	75,275	17	1:4,428
4	128,900	23	1:5,604	11	68,000	19	1:3,579
5	408,600	31	1:13,181	12	54,100	10	1:5,410
6	101,300	22	1:4,605	13	19,900	8	1:2,488
7	29,800	13	1:2,292	14	18,200	13	1:1,400

TABLE 2: STATE JUDICIAL DISTRICTS

District	Number of Judges 1977	Caseload: 1973	Cases Filed 1975	Per Judge 1977	% Total Cases Filed In State, 1977	% State Population 1975
1	4	1,150	1,186	937	8.5	9.3
2	12	1,333	1,352	1,498	41.0	31.7
3	2	878	1,065	1,061	4.8	7.0
4	1	843	1,051	1,334	3.0	2.9
5	5	1,015	1,161	1,019	11.6	12.4
6	2	1,314	1,327	752	3.4	3.9
7	2	1,084	1,102	592	2.7	2.4
8	1	931	1,034	1,379	3.1	3.2
9	2	1,628	2,073	925	4.2	5.2
10	1	579	682	573	1.3	1.3
11	3	1,230	1,464	931	6.4	10.1
12	2	1,668	1,949	1,051	4.8	4.6
13	2	1,730	952	1,105	5.0	6.0
State Total	39	1,201	1,269	1,125	99.8*	100.0

*Error due to rounding

TABLE 3: HIGHWAY DISTRICTS

1975 Data	State Totals*	District 1 Deming	2 Roswell	3 Albuquerque	4 Las Vegas	5 Santa Fe
Miles of Highway Maintained by State	13,864	2,991	3,477	2,108	2,952	2,336
Percent of Miles Maintained by State	100.0	21.6	25.1	15.2	21.3	16.8
Total Motor Vehicle Registration (MVR)	915,852	115,771	213,921	374,296	45,421	152,555
Percent of State Total MVR	98.6*	12.6	23.4	40.9	5.0	16.7
Total Average Daily Vehicle Miles (ADVM)	27,179,811	4,330,679	5,385,922	10,227,493	2,678,726	4,556,991
Percent of State ADVM	100.0	15.9	19.8	37.6	9.9	16.8
Percent of State ADVM on County and Local Roads	100.0	25.5	22.3	26.3	7.7	18.2
Percent of State ADVM on Urban and Municipal Roads	100.0	8.9	18.3	57.0	4.1	11.7
Percent of State ADVM on Interstate Highways	100.0	30.9	0.0	34.7	22.1	12.3

*13,888 vehicles with foreign registration not listed by district

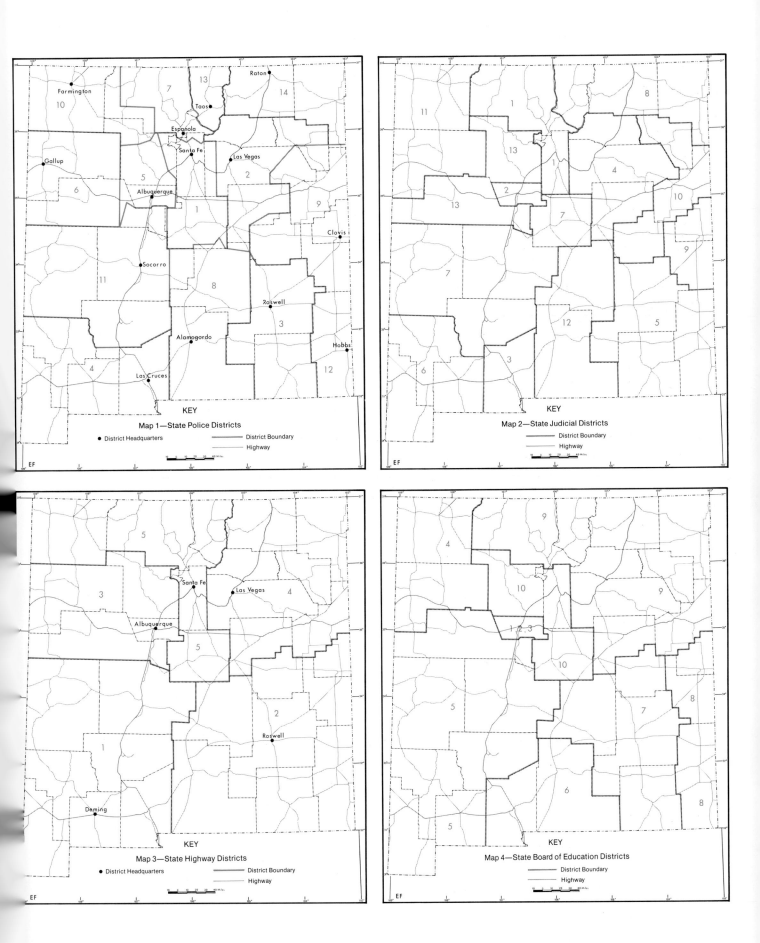

KEY

Map 1—State Police Districts

- District Headquarters
- District Boundary
- Highway

KEY

Map 2—State Judicial Districts

- District Boundary
- Highway

KEY

Map 3—State Highway Districts

- District Headquarters
- District Boundary
- Highway

KEY

Map 4—State Board of Education Districts

- District Boundary
- Highway

state legislative districts

New Mexico has a bicameral legislature similar to that found in most states. Members of both houses are chosen in even-numbered years from single-member districts. The House of Representatives has 70 members serving two-year terms. There are 42 Senators serving four-year terms on a staggered basis; 34 are elected in presidential election years, the other eight in off-year elections.

All legislators must be citizens of the United States and reside in the district from which they are elected. Federal, state, and county officials and employees are ineligible for election. The minimum age requirement is 21 for House members and 25 for Senators. Legislators are not salaried but receive a per diem for expenses during the 60 day regular session (odd-numbered years), the 30 day short session (even-numbered years), and for interim committee meetings. The lack of a sufficient salary is often cited as a major factor in the traditionally high rate of turnover among legislators.

In 1962, however, the U.S. Supreme Court ruled in a series of decisions (none directly involving New Mexico) that both houses of state legislatures must be apportioned on the basis of population. The New Mexico legislature attempted to prevent the creation of equal population districts, and it was only under direct court order that equitable districts were finally created. These 1972 legislative districts were drawn on the basis of the estimated populations of election precincts, and as far as the estimated populations are correct, produced districts with less than a five percent variance from equality.

Since the present legislative districts are based on the 1970 population figures, it seems likely that another substantial revision will be necessary once the 1980 census is completed.

New Mexico entered the Union in 1912 with a reasonably apportioned legislature. Unfortunately, the state constitution did not require reapportionment as the state's population distribution changed, and legislators were unwilling to make any changes in legislative districts although it became quite evident that the sparsely settled counties were drastically over-represented. Instead of striving for equity in representation, the legislature, in 1942, submitted to the voters a constitutional amendment which would legitimize the inequality. The amendment was defeated, but in 1949 an amendment was accepted which gave each county one senator and apportioned the House by population, although equal population districts were never created. Another amendment (1955) guaranteed every county at least one representative. By 1960 the New Mexico legislature was seriously malapportioned. It was possible for only 14 percent of the state's population to elect a majority in the Senate and for only 27 percent to elect a House majority. Since 1933, the Democrats have controlled both chambers with the exception of the House in 1953.

Paul McAllister

TABLE 1: POPULATION OF SENATE DISTRICTS, 1972 TO PRESENT

District	Estimated Population	Percent Deviation*
1	23,200	−4.09
2	24,517	1.35
3	24,130	−.24
4	23,878	−1.29
5	23,260	−3.84
6	23,553	−2.63
7	23,278	−3.77
8	23,268	−3.81
9	23,371	−3.38
10	24,706	2.13
11	25,330	4.71
12	23,687	−2.07
13	23,651	−2.22
14	23,714	−1.96
15	25,016	3.41
16	25,080	3.67
17	23,402	−3.25
18	23,284	−3.74
19	23,430	−3.14
20	24,001	−.78
21	23,106	−4.48
22	23,398	−3.27
23	24,885	2.87
24	24,398	.85
25	24,961	3.18
26	25,078	3.67
27	25,342	4.76
28	24,228	.15
29	25,057	3.58
30	25,245	4.36
31	25,124	3.86
32	25,079	3.67
33	25,374	4.85
34	25,356	4.82
35	23,629	−2.31
36	23,128	−4.39
37	23,140	−4.34
38	23,505	−2.83
39	23,812	−1.56
40	24,845	2.70
41	24,598	1.68
42	24,956	3.16

*Equitable population per district = 24,215

TABLE 2: POPULATION OF HOUSE DISTRICTS, 1972 TO PRESENT

District	Estimated Population	Percent Deviation*
1	14,975	3.17
2	14,994	3.30
3	14,915	2.76
4	14,734	1.51
5	14,945	2.96
6	14,979	3.20
7	15,112	4.12
8	14,898	2.64
9	14,616	.70
10	14,534	.13
11	14,736	1.52
12	14,219	−2.03
13	13,962	−3.80
14	14,812	2.05
15	14,180	−2.30
16	14,524	+.06
17	14,162	−2.42
18	14,859	2.37
19	14,391	−.84
20	14,865	2.41
21	14,374	−.96
22	14,832	2.19
23	15,030	3.55
24	14,134	−2.61
25	14,916	2.76
26	14,346	−1.15
27	13,923	−4.07
28	14,534	.13
29	13,885	−4.33
30	13,899	−4.23
31	14,753	1.64
32	14,883	2.54
33	14,825	2.14
34	14,099	−2.85
35	13,847	−4.59
36	13,795	−4.95
37	14,764	1.72
38	14,692	1.22
39	14,527	.08
40	14,374	−.96
41	14,004	−3.51
42	14,308	−1.41
43	15,198	4.71
44	14,989	3.27
45	13,949	−3.89
46	14,077	−3.01
47	13,967	−3.76
48	14,266	−1.70
49	14,105	−2.81
50	14,585	.48
51	13,985	−3.64
52	13,901	−4.22
53	14,961	3.07
54	14,614	.68
55	14,547	.22
56	14,119	−2.72
57	13,843	−4.62
58	14,698	1.26
59	14,520	.04
60	15,126	4.21
61	15,113	4.12
62	15,075	3.86
63	15,162	4.46
64	15,084	3.92
65	15,229	4.92
66	14,761	1.70
67	14,106	−2.81
68	13,892	−4.28
69	13,956	−3.84
70	14,016	−3.43

*Equitable population per district = 14,515

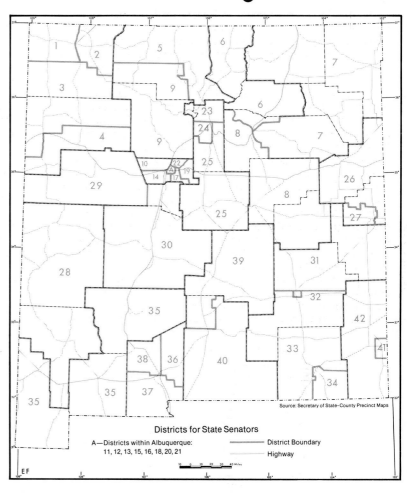

Districts for State Senators

A—Districts within Albuquerque:
11, 12, 13, 15, 16, 18, 20, 21

District Boundary

Highway

Source: Secretary of State-County Precinct Maps

10 0 20 30 40 Miles

E F
109°

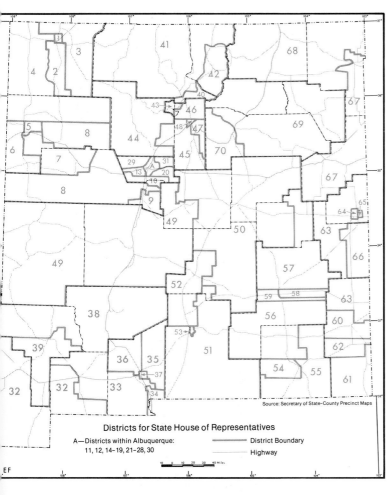

Districts for State House of Representatives

A—Districts within Albuquerque:
11, 12, 14-19, 21-28, 30

District Boundary

Highway

Source: Secretary of State-County Precinct Maps

10 0 20 30 40 Miles

E F
108°

gubernatorial elections

Thirty-one gubernatorial elections have been held between 1911 and 1974, twenty-one of which were won by democratic candidates (Tables 1 and 2). Election results for years with important nation-wide political changes are illustrated on the maps. The Republican resurgence of the 1950's was represented in New Mexico by Republican Governor Mechem's 1952 re-election in which he lost only six of the thirty-two counties (Map 1). His vote was only slightly less than Eisenhower's presidential total in the state. However, his re-election for a fourth term in 1960 was far less impressive (Map 2). It was in the 1960 elections that New Mexico supported different political parties in the gubernatorial and presidential races.

The re-election of Republican Governor Cargo in 1968 was also unimpressive (Map 3). Cargo, running in a two-party race, received a smaller percentage of the total vote than did Richard Nixon, the Republican candidate in the three-party presidential contest.

Beginning with the 1970 election, the term of office for New Mexico governors was increased from two to four years. The Democrats have won both elections since then. Democratic Governor Apodaca's victory was both an interesting and close contest (Map 4). The Republicans carried nineteen counties, but Apodaca received large majorities in some of the predominantly Spanish counties in the north-central part of the state, off-setting heavy Democratic losses in some of the predominantly Anglo counties in the east. Many counties are inconsistent in their support for either party.

Paul McAllister

TABLE 1: REPUBLICAN PERCENTAGE OF MAJOR-PARTY VOTE FOR GOVERNOR, 1911-1978

Year	Governor-Elect	Party	Republican Percentage	Year	Governor-Elect	Party	Republican Percentage
1911*	W. C. McDonald	D	49.0	1952	E. L. Mechem	R	53.8
1916	E. C. de Baca	D	49.1	1954	J. F. Simms	D	43.0
1918	O. A. Larrazolo	R	51.4	1956	E. L. Mechem	R	52.2
1920	M. C. Mechem	R	51.7	1958	J. Burroughs	D	49.5
1922	J. F. Hinkle	D	44.5	1960	E. L. Mechem	R	50.3
1924	A. T. Hannett	D	49.9	1962	J. M. Campbell	D	47.0
1926	R. C. Dillon	R	51.9	1964	J. M. Campbell	D	39.8
1928	R. C. Dillon	R	55.7	1966	D. F. Cargo	R	51.7
1930	A. Seligman	D	46.7	1968	D. F. Cargo	R	50.5
1932	A. Seligman	D	44.6	1970	B. King	D	47.5
1934	C. Tingley	D	47.8	1974	J. Apodaca	D	49.4
1936	C. Tingley	D	42.5	1978	B. King	D	49.5
1938	J. Miles	D	47.7				
1940	J. Miles	D	44.4				
1942	J. J. Dempsey	D	45.5				
1944	J. J. Dempsey	D	48.2				
1946	T. J. Mabry	D	47.2				
1948	T. J. Mabry	D	45.3				
1950	E. L. Mechem	R	53.7				

*The State Constitution provided a five year term for the first governor.

TABLE 2: REPUBLICAN PERCENTAGE OF THE MAJOR-PARTY VOTE FOR GOVERNOR, 1952-1974

	1952	1954	1956	1958	1960	1962	1964	1966	1968	1970	1974		1952	1954	1956	1958	1960	1962	1964	1966	1968	1970	1974
Bernalillo	55.0	45.8	59.0	60.6	55.5	49.1	44.4	63.1	50.6	54.9	53.5	McKinley	52.4	35.4	56.0	51.0	46.2	43.2	33.0	47.6	48.4	45.7	37.6
Catron	62.4	51.4	56.2	52.9	59.3	59.6	47.1	53.6	58.1	37.5	58.8	Mora	56.8	54.5	58.6	57.2	53.9	54.7	46.6	51.1	53.0	44.0	37.3
Chaves	60.6	47.1	52.2	49.3	57.1	59.0	46.8	53.3	60.0	58.3	65.8	Otero	54.8	41.0	48.6	46.7	50.0	49.5	36.3	43.6	48.4	45.4	51.8
Colfax	54.1	48.6	54.4	50.9	42.5	41.4	30.0	40.5	46.2	43.5	52.7	Quay	53.7	35.6	48.6	33.8	53.9	47.6	39.3	43.8	55.0	38.3	57.5
Curry	58.5	39.6	52.4	48.1	50.2	52.5	39.2	47.2	54.7	43.8	63.9	Rio Arriba	48.6	46.7	53.4	53.8	45.0	37.1	32.8	39.9	43.5	36.0	21.5
De Baca	54.6	38.4	50.2	50.1	56.2	50.1	38.9	38.6	47.8	30.9	57.9	Roosevelt	54.4	27.9	46.6	30.8	47.1	54.1	41.5	48.7	52.8	45.0	63.3
Dona Ana	60.6	41.6	54.5	44.2	52.8	49.8	38.7	48.5	47.3	45.9	43.9	Sandoval	51.5	47.7	53.7	49.0	40.8	35.0	26.8	40.0	35.0	33.4	37.8
Eddy	43.7	30.3	37.1	35.1	40.7	38.2	34.6	39.3	52.3	41.8	47.6	San Juan	68.4	51.4	53.8	52.1	60.2	46.8	43.7	53.8	59.9	52.1	58.9
Grant	41.1	29.3	38.3	29.9	43.1	41.7	24.5	32.5	47.4	36.9	45.2	San Miguel	52.2	45.8	54.5	48.6	48.6	43.1	38.8	53.3	50.4	43.2	30.0
Guadalupe	52.1	45.4	53.1	50.8	44.7	43.3	38.2	46.2	46.9	41.2	28.1	Santa Fe	53.5	46.6	51.6	53.3	51.2	44.8	33.2	48.7	45.7	37.9	35.3
Harding	65.4	50.1	57.8	55.1	57.0	56.3	50.6	52.2	56.7	52.2	58.6	Sierra	59.8	47.7	58.3	53.3	49.8	49.3	46.8	54.9	55.7	46.3	62.1
Hidalgo	46.3	29.7	37.9	37.8	43.9	42.8	29.4	29.3	46.0	28.6	52.2	Socorro	54.7	44.7	56.0	46.6	43.5	45.7	42.5	51.5	44.8	50.0	41.1
Lea	49.9	30.2	37.9	25.5	36.0	43.5	39.2	39.2	50.9	41.9	60.3	Taos	52.0	41.4	54.2	52.8	46.6	46.2	33.8	47.0	47.2	42.7	26.1
Lincoln	65.9	50.7	59.6	55.7	57.1	55.1	52.7	56.6	54.3	52.7	63.7	Torrance	52.0	47.1	53.0	49.7	48.2	49.3	44.6	52.0	52.5	32.0	55.1
Los Alamos	47.0	40.9	36.7	46.5	56.5	44.7	38.9	54.8	54.2	60.8	59.8	Union	63.7	48.3	50.4	46.6	53.9	49.3	44.0	44.5	55.1	39.0	60.6
Luna	55.3	37.1	38.5	35.5	43.1	46.1	36.4	38.8	56.3	42.6	56.3	Valencia	54.6	45.5	58.0	51.4	42.7	43.7	35.9	51.6	45.9	42.4	41.2
												State Total	53.8	43.0	52.2	49.5	50.3	47.0	39.8	51.7	50.5	47.5	49.4

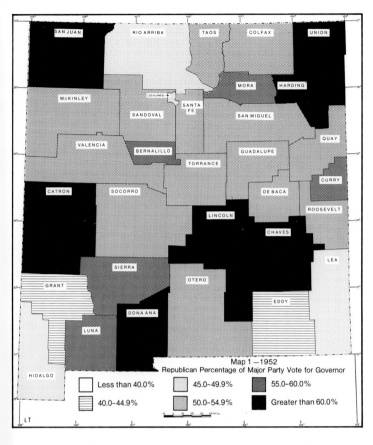

Map 1 — 1952
Republican Percentage of Major Party Vote for Governor

Less than 40.0%   45.0-49.9%   55.0-60.0%
40.0-44.9%   50.0-54.9%   Greater than 60.0%

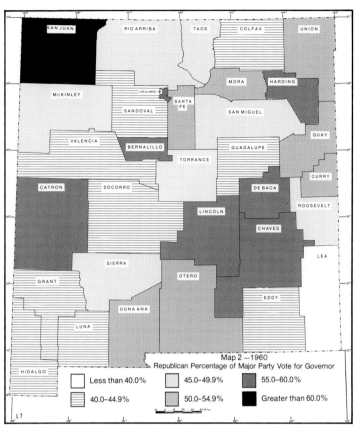

Map 2 — 1960
Republican Percentage of Major Party Vote for Governor

Less than 40.0%   45.0-49.9%   55.0-60.0%
40.0-44.9%   50.0-54.9%   Greater than 60.0%

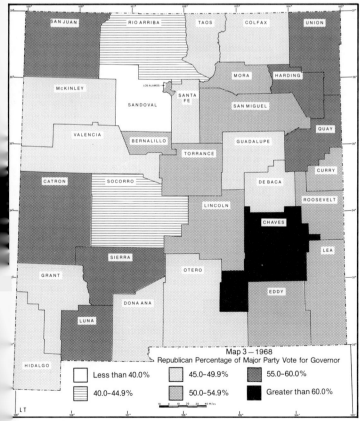

Map 3 — 1968
Republican Percentage of Major Party Vote for Governor

Less than 40.0%   45.0-49.9%   55.0-60.0%
40.0-44.9%   50.0-54.9%   Greater than 60.0%

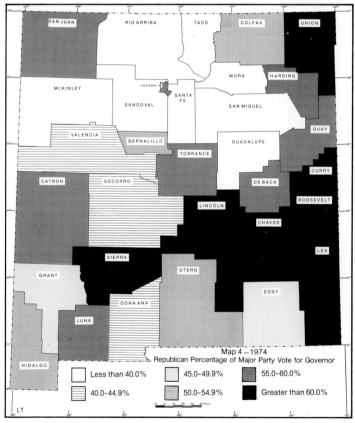

Map 4 — 1974
Republican Percentage of Major Party Vote for Governor

Less than 40.0%   45.0-49.9%   55.0-60.0%
40.0-44.9%   50.0-54.9%   Greater than 60.0%

163

united states congressional elections

New Mexico's congressional delegation is composed of one Republican and one Democratic Representative and two Republican Senators. Since 1968, the Representatives have been chosen by district (Table 1). Republican Manuel Lujan Jr. has dominated District 1 from his first election in 1968 (Maps 1 and 3). District 2 went to the Republicans in 1968 but has been dominated by Democrat Harold Runnels since 1970 (Maps 2 and 3). The Senate seats were dominated by the Democrats until 1972 when Pete Domenici received a solid 54 percent of the vote. Harrison Schmitt completed the Republican sweep of the Senate seats in 1976 with large victory margins in most counties (Map 4).

Paul McAllister

TABLE 1: REPUBLICAN PERCENTAGE OF MAJOR-PARTY VOTE FOR CONGRESSMAN, 1968-1976: DISTRICT 1 AND 2

	DISTRICT 1						DISTRICT 2				
County	1968	1970	1972	1974	1976	County	1968	1970	1972	1974	1976
Bernalillo	54.8	62.0	57.7	64.9	76.0	Catron	68.6	60.2	33.6	37.3	29.5
Colfax	44.4	55.7	57.9	62.7	70.3	Chaves	60.9	57.4	29.1	37.1	37.8
Guadalupe	53.2	56.8	50.5	46.4	62.1	Curry	53.1	51.2	34.1	38.8	32.5
Harding	59.9	64.3	67.8	69.4	72.0	De Baca	54.9	46.2	26.9	23.5	22.5
Los Alamos	39.3	64.6	56.7	80.9	88.4	Dona Ana	43.8	47.5	29.4	37.1	30.5
Mora	56.0	50.8	52.4	43.4	49.2	Eddy	48.8	46.0	21.3	24.9	27.3
Quay	37.8	54.5	65.9	63.3	67.5	Grant	36.2	40.0	19.1	34.8	31.2
Rio Arriba	48.9	46.1	44.5	35.9	52.8	Hidalgo	44.3	38.0	25.6	20.0	24.1
Sandoval	43.4	45.0	53.0	48.8	63.7	Lea	53.0	36.7	17.6	24.4	25.1
San Miguel	53.5	53.0	51.0	42.2	58.0	Lincoln	60.0	59.0	37.0	34.6	34.9
Santa Fe	57.7	55.1	50.1	52.9	71.5	Luna	52.8	51.8	32.3	31.0	31.0
Taos	57.3	50.9	50.4	43.6	60.1	McKinley	47.9	45.9	23.7	22.7	18.5
Torrance	51.1	59.5	60.8	62.4	69.9	Otero	45.3	44.2	31.2	25.2	29.3
Union	46.3	59.7	60.6	67.0	72.1	Roosevelt	56.5	58.3	26.8	45.9	39.1
						San Juan	60.6	61.5	35.7	42.2	31.7
District Total	53.1	58.5	55.7	59.6	72.5	Sierra	53.5	56.0	35.7	31.4	27.9
						Socorro	49.6	52.1	33.3	29.5	26.7
						Valencia	44.7	44.0	28.1	25.7	25.9
						District Total	50.7	48.6	27.8	32.3	29.7

TABLE 2: REPUBLICAN PERCENTAGE OF MAJOR-PARTY VOTE FOR SENATOR, 1946-1976

County	1946	1948	1952	1954	1958	1960	1966	1964	1970	1972	1976	County	1946	1948	1952	1954	1958	1960	1966	1964	1970	1972	1976
Bernalillo	53.0	45.4	53.1	43.8	44.0	39.4	49.0	50.5	50.1	57.0	61.2	Mora	36.3	55.6	46.3	52.5	38.2	51.0	38.7	50.1	37.6	50.9	36.3
Catron	46.6	48.0	52.2	54.0	32.8	46.1	54.3	62.1	54.5	60.5	59.7	Otero	52.5	37.6	41.7	42.2	23.8	30.7	42.4	39.1	43.4	57.2	57.4
Chaves	58.8	36.8	61.6	49.5	45.2	38.1	53.8	60.1	58.5	58.0	69.0	Quay	44.4	31.4	44.5	36.6	31.8	33.7	52.0	47.1	47.9	57.2	57.8
Colfax	53.5	40.1	47.9	42.8	46.6	33.6	41.4	39.0	41.2	53.6	55.4	Rio Arriba	38.7	49.2	37.6	45.1	29.0	33.8	32.4	36.1	31.3	45.8	31.8
Curry	51.7	26.0	45.6	42.6	31.7	40.4	48.8	46.4	53.8	57.8	59.9	Roosevelt	52.0	23.0	54.1	34.3	32.4	34.4	52.3	52.6	55.0	57.1	66.0
De Baca	45.9	41.4	43.3	42.8	33.7	38.9	48.0	58.6	47.6	54.4	55.9	Sandoval	41.8	49.7	45.7	43.5	29.4	31.5	25.8	33.7	30.1	48.9	47.6
Dona Ana	52.9	42.5	52.5	47.0	35.7	35.1	48.1	42.2	45.4	54.8	57.6	San Juan	62.4	57.3	67.8	53.0	43.7	43.0	53.2	53.7	62.0	58.9	63.8
Eddy	46.0	20.9	41.9	29.5	31.0	29.9	42.7	43.8	48.5	51.8	54.7	San Miguel	41.3	48.5	45.1	43.8	35.7	38.6	34.5	44.6	39.1	51.5	37.7
Grant	50.4	36.2	38.2	29.2	26.2	24.7	36.2	36.3	40.4	43.7	55.0	Santa Fe	49.8	55.2	51.6	46.1	39.5	38.2	37.7	42.7	34.2	51.6	48.6
Guadalupe	46.2	50.2	43.1	44.8	36.6	38.7	36.4	44.9	41.8	48.7	33.0	Sierra	55.4	46.4	53.1	50.7	45.4	44.1	50.2	53.9	51.2	59.9	58.8
Harding	48.7	50.1	56.8	51.7	47.5	48.5	55.5	53.3	55.8	63.1	60.0	Socorro	48.8	56.1	44.9	45.9	30.0	36.1	42.1	49.5	44.8	55.1	49.2
Hidalgo	46.1	25.1	43.6	32.0	31.1	24.3	43.8	33.3	40.4	43.1	55.3	Taos	35.1	50.1	36.8	42.1	28.6	37.2	33.7	41.0	34.0	50.5	39.3
Lea	42.7	19.4	42.1	35.3	28.6	30.5	49.5	48.7	57.6	36.5	57.9	Torrance	49.6	49.4	49.6	47.0	41.0	45.3	47.2	50.1	45.4	51.6	56.5
Lincoln	56.0	53.4	55.1	55.8	35.3	45.4	53.7	59.2	52.7	62.6	66.1	Union	52.3	42.6	57.2	47.7	47.9	41.6	52.7	49.2	51.3	53.8	63.6
Los Alamos	Not a county		47.9	27.5	44.4	26.5	46.6	33.4	50.2	61.5	52.7	Valencia	42.1	53.3	44.1	44.1	30.4	32.1	35.9	41.8	38.7	50.7	50.9
Luna	53.1	36.8	50.1	36.1	35.2	35.4	47.2	45.1	52.6	57.5	56.6	State Total	48.5	42.6	48.9	42.7	37.3	36.6	45.3	46.9	47.1	54.0	57.1
McKinley	44.9	41.0	45.9	36.9	37.9	34.5	34.9	43.3	43.8	47.3	42.7												

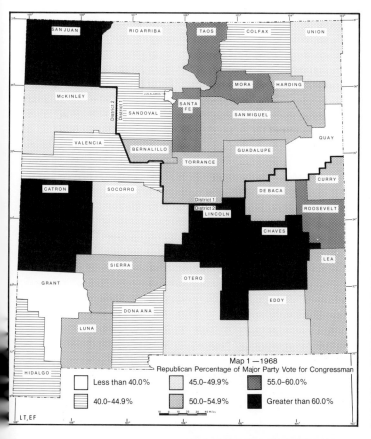

Map 1 —1968
Republican Percentage of Major Party Vote for Congressman

Less than 40.0% 45.0-49.9% 55.0-60.0%

40.0-44.9% 50.0-54.9% Greater than 60.0%

LT, EF

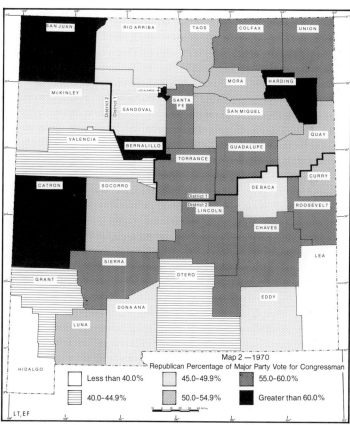

Map 2 —1970
Republican Percentage of Major Party Vote for Congressman

Less than 40.0% 45.0-49.9% 55.0-60.0%

40.0-44.9% 50.0-54.9% Greater than 60.0%

LT, EF

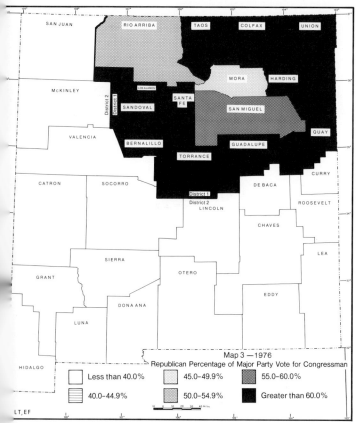

Map 3 —1976
Republican Percentage of Major Party Vote for Congressman

Less than 40.0% 45.0-49.9% 55.0-60.0%

40.0-44.9% 50.0-54.9% Greater than 60.0%

LT, EF

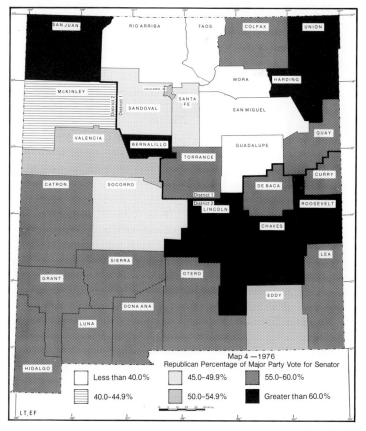

Map 4 —1976
Republican Percentage of Major Party Vote for Senator

Less than 40.0% 45.0-49.9% 55.0-60.0%

40.0-44.9% 50.0-54.9% Greater than 60.0%

LT, EF

165

presidential elections

New Mexico, since statehood in 1912, has supported the victorious presidential candidate in every election except that of 1976. The maps show the results of four important post-World War II elections. These elections were chosen for illustration because they are the ones in which control of the executive branch changed from one party to the other.

The Republicans regained the White House in 1952 after 20 years of Democratic control. After receiving only 42.9 percent of the vote in 1948, the Republicans used a popular candidate, General Eisenhower, and an unpopular Korean War to capture 55.6 percent of the 1952 vote. The Democrats retained their superiority in only 7 counties (Map 1 and Table). The Republicans received over 60 percent of the major-party vote in 7 counties; this high percentage indicates a lack of significant party competition and the likelihood of extended one-part dominance. Indeed, three of these counties (Harding, Lincoln, and Union) have remained Republican for the entire period, 1952-1976, while the other four (Catron, Chaves, San Juan, and Sierra) deviated from the Republican fold only in the Johnson–Goldwater contest of 1964. Even then these four counties far exceeded the Republican percentage of the total state vote.

The Democrats ended eight years of Republican rule with the very closely contested Kennedy–Nixon election of 1960. Although capturing 49.6 percent of the state total, the Republicans carried only 13 of the 32 counties. Map 2 shows the emergence of a Democratic stronghold in the north-central part of the state. In the 1964 Goldwater–Johnson campaign the Republicans could carry only three counties and 40.6 percent of the statewide vote. Many people were predicting the demise of the Republican Party.

The Democrats lost their advantage, however, in 1968 when another unpopular war, complicated by racial issues, led to deep divisions within the electorate. Although not regaining their 1950's strength, the Republicans and Richard Nixon made a dramatic comeback as they increased their percentage of the vote in every county. Votes for Democrat Hubert Humphrey declined sharply as the American-Independent Party drew 7.9 percent of the vote. Although 1972 was a two-party race, the Democratic percentage declined as Nixon led the Republicans to the greatest victory margin in the state since the Depression.

The 1976 election is the only one in which the state did not give a majority to Jimmy Carter, the president-elect. While increasing their percentage in every county and gaining the majority vote in 17 counties, the Democrats could not quite overcome Republican strength. Map 4 shows that in only five counties did one party receive more than 60 percent of the vote. New Mexico was an evenly divided and closely contested state.

Paul McAllister

PRESIDENTIAL ELECTIONS, 1952-1976

	Republican Percentage of Major party Vote (Republican-Democratic Total)														
County	1952	1956	1960	1964	1968*	1972	1976	County	1952	1956	1960	1964	1968*	1972	1976
Bernalillo	59.5	64.6	52.3	43.6	55.0	62.1	54.5	Mora	56.7	58.5	48.1	40.2	51.0	50.7	38.6
Catron	61.5	59.8	53.9	48.3	62.3	75.4	53.8	Otero	53.2	60.5	47.8	36.7	43.7	70.2	52.6
Chaves	64.4	63.8	59.4	49.3	63.6	72.8	59.8	Quay	53.3	53.8	56.4	48.1	51.4	73.5	49.6
Colfax	51.6	54.7	42.1	32.7	44.4	58.9	45.4	Rio Arriba	48.7	51.6	37.3	30.0	43.2	43.5	31.1
Curry	59.5	57.7	64.3	49.5	54.0	77.6	55.5	Roosevelt	56.9	54.7	69.6	48.7	58.1	74.6	51.2
De Baca	57.0	59.6	54.2	45.3	57.7	73.6	48.2	Sandoval	52.1	55.7	35.1	24.4	41.4	51.6	44.8
Dona Ana	56.4	58.8	46.7	40.4	54.1	60.7	53.6	San Juan	70.0	68.2	58.3	49.7	54.0	71.5	55.7
Eddy	44.6	46.1	47.8	37.6	47.7	66.3	45.9	San Miguel	54.6	55.9	41.9	32.0	48.1	48.7	37.8
Grant	44.2	43.9	36.1	28.0	38.5	52.1	44.2	Santa Fe	57.0	57.2	41.6	31.6	48.1	53.2	45.0
Guadalupe	53.9	56.2	43.9	39.1	51.4	51.9	43.2	Sierra	63.7	65.4	60.8	47.9	57.1	68.9	51.6
Harding	63.5	62.0	60.9	52.3	57.7	70.4	57.6	Socorro	55.6	61.6	43.6	42.5	52.1	57.1	46.5
Hidalgo	50.8	50.6	45.8	38.7	39.2	65.2	48.7	Taos	49.0	53.1	41.9	32.3	49.9	51.0	40.6
Lea	47.7	48.0	49.2	44.2	48.2	78.4	57.3	Torrance	55.1	56.6	54.3	45.0	52.9	65.9	48.9
Lincoln	64.7	64.9	58.3	52.9	64.5	78.4	62.1	Union	63.5	60.8	61.2	51.5	55.4	75.7	54.0
Los Alamos	49.4	52.1	48.9	33.5	54.8	67.4	65.1	Valencia	53.5	56.8	41.2	33.7	47.5	57.4	47.8
Luna	56.5	50.3	48.1	42.1	50.1	65.5	50.8	State Total	55.6	58.0	49.6	40.6	51.8	62.5	51.2
McKinley	49.9	57.2	43.2	30.0	45.7	51.2	40.2								

*1968 is percentage of Republican-Democratic-American Independent total.

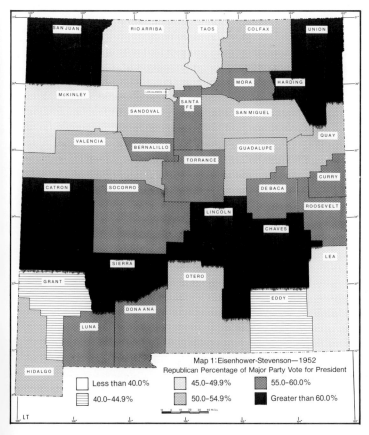

Map 1: Eisenhower-Stevenson—1952
Republican Percentage of Major Party Vote for President

Less than 40.0%   45.0–49.9%   55.0–60.0%
40.0–44.9%   50.0–54.9%   Greater than 60.0%

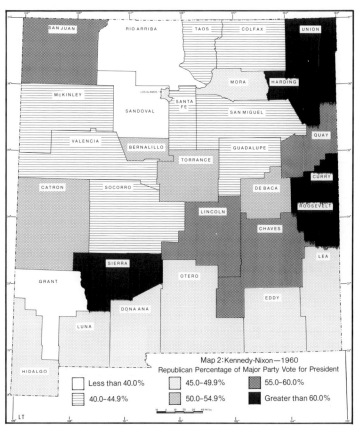

Map 2: Kennedy-Nixon—1960
Republican Percentage of Major Party Vote for President

Less than 40.0%   45.0–49.9%   55.0–60.0%
40.0–44.9%   50.0–54.9%   Greater than 60.0%

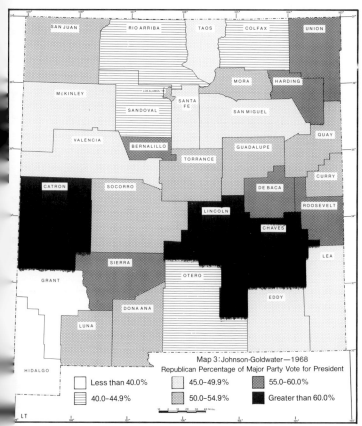

Map 3: Johnson-Goldwater—1968
Republican Percentage of Major Party Vote for President

Less than 40.0%   45.0–49.9%   55.0–60.0%
40.0–44.9%   50.0–54.9%   Greater than 60.0%

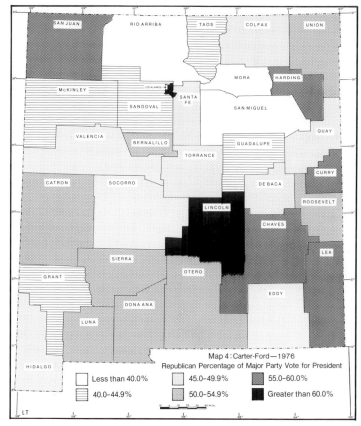

Map 4: Carter-Ford—1976
Republican Percentage of Major Party Vote for President

Less than 40.0%   45.0–49.9%   55.0–60.0%
40.0–44.9%   50.0–54.9%   Greater than 60.0%

167

selected references

NATURAL ENVIRONMENTAL

Geologic Structure

Christiansen, Paige W. and Frank E. Kottlowski. *Mosaic of New Mexico Scenery, Rocks and History.* New Mexico Bureau of Mines, 1972.

Dan, G. H. and G. O. Backman. Geologic Map of New Mexico. U.S. Geological Survey, 1965.

Young Faults and Geothermal Areas

Hawley, J. W., compiler. *Guidebook to Rio Grande Rift in New Mexico and Colorado.* Circular 163. New Mexico Bureau of Mines and Mineral Resources, 1978.

Woodward, L. A., J. F. Callender and R. E. Cilinski. *Tectonic Maps of Rio Grande Rift.* Geological Sciences of America, Map and Chart Services, MC-11.

Landforms

Kelley, V. C. *Albuquerque—Its Mountains, Valley, Water and Volcanoes.* Scenic Trips to the Geologic Past, No. 9. New Mexico Bureau of Mines and Mineral Resources, 1969.

U. S. Geological Survey. *Physical Divisions of the United States: Western United States.* Vol. II, 1962.

Temperature

Houghton, Frank E. *Climate of New Mexico.* U.S. Department of Commerce. Climates of the States Series. Washington, D.C., Revised 1972.

Yi-Fu Tuan, et al. *The Climate of New Mexico.* New Mexico State Planning Office, Revised 1973.

Precipitation

Houghton, Frank E. *Climate of New Mexico.* U.S. Department of Commerce. Climates of the States Series. Washington, D.C., Revised 1972.

Yi-Fu Tuan, et al. *The Climate of New Mexico.* New Mexico State Planning Office, Revised 1973.

Frost Conditions

Yi-Fu Tuan, et al. *The Climate of New Mexico.* New Mexico State Planning Office, Revised 1973.

Hydrology

U.S. Geological Survey. *Mineral and Water Resources of New Mexico.* Bulletin 87, 1965.

Aquifers

Hale, W. E., L. J. Reiland and J. P. Beverage, *Characteristics of the Water Supply in New Mexico.* U.S. Geological Survey, Technical Report No. 31, 1965.

U.S. Department of the Interior in Cooperation with the State of New Mexico. *New Mexico Water Resources Assessment for Planning Purposes.* Vol. I, 1976.

Soils

Agricultural Experiment Station. *Soils of New Mexico.* Research Report 285, 1974.

Soil Survey Staff. *Soil Taxonomy.* U.S. Department of Agriculture, Handbook No. 436, 1975.

Vegetation Cover Types

Morain, Stanley A., et al. *Vegetation and Land Use in New Mexico.* New Mexico Bureau of Mines and Mineral Resources, Resource Map 8, 1977.

HISTORICAL LANDSCAPES

Vertebrate Fossil and PaleoIndian Sites

Hester, James. *Blackwater Locality No. 1.* Taos, Fort Burgwin Research Center, 1972.

Irwin, Henry T. "Developments in Early Man Studies in Western North America, 1960–1970," *Arctic Anthropology,* 8(2): 42–67 (1971).

Irwin, Henry T. and H. M. Wormington. "PaleoIndian Tool Sites in the Great Plains," *American Antiquity,* 35(1), 24–34 (1970).

Judge, Williams James. *The PaleoIndian Occupation of the Central Rio Grande Valley.* Albuquerque: University of New Mexico Press, 1973.

Northrop, Stuart A. *New Mexico's Fossil Record.* Albuquerque: University of New Mexico Press, 1962.

Ratkevich, Ron and Near La Fon. *Field Guide to New Mexico Fossils.* Albuquerque: Dinograph Southwest, 1978.

Wormington, H. M. *Prehistoric Indians of the Southwest.* Denver: Denver Museum of Natural History, 1947

Wormington, H. M. *Ancient Man in North America.* Denver: Denver Museum of Natural History, 1957.

Native American Settlements

Beck, Warren A. and Ynez D. Haase. *Historical Atlas of New Mexico.* Norman: University of Oklahoma Press, 1969.

Department of the Interior, Bureau of Indian Affairs. *Indians of New Mexico Today.* Washington, D.C., 1966.

Dozier, Edward P. *Pueblo Indians of North America.* New York: Holt, Rinehart and Winston, 1970.

Smith, Anne, M. *New Mexico Indians.* Santa Fe, 1974.

Stubbs, Stanley A. *Birds-Eye View of the Pueblos.* Norman: University of Oklahoma Press, 1950.

Spanish Exploration

Forbes, Jack D. *Apache, Navajo and Spaniard.* The Civilization of American Indian Series. Norman: University of Oklahoma Press, 1960.

Hammond, George Peter, and Agapito Rey (editors and translators), from the Journal of Pérez De Luxán. *Expedition into New Mexico Made by Antonio De Espejo, 1582–1583.* Los Angeles: The Quivira Society, 1929.

Jenkins, Myra Ellen and Albert H. Schroeder. *A Brief History of New Mexico.* Albuquerque: University of New Mexico Press: 1974.

Powell, Phillip Wayne. *Soldiers, Indians, and Silver: The Northward Advance of New Spain, 1550–1600.* Berkeley: University of California Press, 1952.

Schroeder, Albert H. and Dan S. Matson (translators). *A Colony on the Move: Gasper Costanso de Sosa's Journal, 1590–1591.* Santa Fe: School of American Research, 1965.

Wellman, Paul I. *Glory, God and Gold: A Narrative History.* Garden City, New York: Doubleday, 1954.

Spanish Colonization 1598–1821

Beck, Warren A. *New Mexico: A History of Four Centuries.* Norman: University of Oklahoma Press, 1962.

Forbes, Jack D. *Apache, Navajo and Spaniard.* The Civilization of American Indian Series. Norman: University of Oklahoma Press, 1960.

Moorhead, Max. *New Mexico's Royal Road: Trade and Travel on the Chihuahua Trail.* Norman: University of Oklahoma Press, 1958.

Scholes, Frances. *Troublous Times in New Mexico, 1659–1670.* Publications in History. Albuquerque: University of New Mexico Press, 1942.

Simmons, Marc. *New Mexico: A Bicentennial History.* New York: Norton, 1977.

Simmons, Marc. *Spanish Government in New Mexico.* Albuquerque: University of New Mexico Press, 1968.

Spicer, Edward. *Cycles of Conquest: The Impact of Spain, Mexico, and the United States on the Indians of the Southwest, 1533–1960.* Tucson: University of Arizona Press, 1962.

Thomas, Alfred Barnaby (editor). *After Coronado: Spanish Explorations Northeast of New Mexico, 1696–1727.* Norman: University of Oklahoma Press, 1935.

Mexican Control 1821-1846

Field, Matthew C. *Matt Field on the Santa Fe Trail.* Edited, by John E. Sunder. Norman: University of Oklahoma Press, 1960.

Gregg, Josiah. *The Commerce of the Prairies.* Edited by Milo Milton Quaife. Lincoln: University of Nebraska Press, 1967.

Kendall, George Wilkins, *Narrative of the Texan-Santa Fe Expedition.* Chicago: Donnelley and Sons, 1929.

Twitchell, Ralph E. *The Leading Facts of New Mexico History.* Five Volumes. Cedar Rapids, Iowa: Torch Press, 1912-1917.

Weber, David J. *The Taos Trappers: The Fur Trade in the Far Southwest, 1540-1846.* Norman: University of Oklahoma Press, 1971.

Land Grants

Bradfute, Richard Wells. *The Court of Private Land Claims: The Abjudication of Spanish and Mexican Land Grant Titles, 1891-1904.* Albuquerque: University of New Mexico Press, 1975.

Brayer, Herbert O. *William Blackmore: The Spanish and Mexican Land Grants of New Mexico, 1863-1878.* Denver: Bradford Robinson, 1949.

Dunham, Harold. "New Mexico Land Grants," *New Mexico Historical Review,* No. 30: 1-22 (1955).

Keleher, William A. "Land Grant Law of New Mexico," *New Mexico Historical Review,* Vol. 4 (1929).

Leonard. Olen E. *The Role of the Land Grant in the Social Organization and Social Process of a Spanish American Village in New Mexico.* Baton Rouge: Louisiana State University Press, 1943.

Morrow, W. W. *Spanish and Mexican Land Grants.* San Francisco: Bancroft, Whitney & Co., 1923.

Perrigo, Lynn I. *The American Southwest.* Albuquerque: University of New Mexico Press, 1975.

Twitchell, Ralph E. *The Leading Facts of New Mexico History.* Five volumes. Cedar Rapids, Iowa: Torch Press, 1912-1917.

Territorial Period Conflicts

Bender, Averam B. "Government Explorations in the Territory of New Mexico, 1846-1859," *New Mexico Historical Review,* Vol. 9: 1-32 (1934).

Bender, Averam B. "Frontier Defense in the Territory of New Mexico, 1846-1853," *New Mexico Historical Review,* Vol. 9, 249-272 and 345-373 (1934).

Bender, Averam B. "Military Transportation in the Southwest: 1848-1860," *New Mexico Historical Review,* Vol. 32: 123-150 (1957).

Colton, Ray C. *The Civil War in the Western Territories.* Norman: University of Oklahoma Press, 1959.

Ganaway, Loomis Morton. *New Mexico and the Sectional Controversy.* Albuquerque: University of New Mexico Press, 1944.

Keleher, William A. *Turmoil in New Mexico: 1846-1868.* Santa Fe: 1952.

Kerby, Robert L. *The Confederate Invasion of New Mexico, 1861-1862.* Los Angeles, 1958.

Writer's Program. *New Mexico, A Guide to the Colorful State.* Miller and Alsberg (eds). Albuquerque: University of New Mexico Press, 1945.

The Frontier Period 1846-1912

Christiansen, Paige W. *The Story of Mining in New Mexico.* Scenic Trips to the Geologic Past Series No. 12. New Mexico Bureau of Mines and Mineral Resources. Socorro: 1974.

Dike, Sheldon H. "Territorial Post Offices of New Mexico," *New Mexico Historical Review,* Vol. 33: 322-327, Vol. 34: 54-69, 144-152, 1958 & 1959.

Jones, Billy M. *Health-Seekers in the Southwest: 1817-1900.* Norman: University of Oklahoma Press, 1967.

Keleher, William A. *The Fabulous Frontier: Twelve New Mexico Items.* Albuquerque: University of New Mexico Press, 1962.

Love, Clara M. "History of the Cattle Industry in the Southwest," *Southwestern Historical Quarterly,* Vol. 19: 370-399 (1916).

Parish, William. "The German Jew and the Commercial Revolution in Territorial New Mexico: 1850-1900," *New Mexico Historical Review,* Vol. 35: 1-29 (1960).

Rasch, Philip J. "The Rustlers War," *New Mexico Historical Review,* Vol. 39: 257-273 (1964).

Territory of New Mexico, Department of Immigration. "Guide to New Mexico for the Homeseeker" (Santa Fe, 1908).

Van Arsdale, Perry C. *Map of Pioneer New Mexico.* Cedar Grove, New Mexico, 1971.

Wallace, William S. "Short-Line Staging in New Mexico," *New Mexico Historical Review,* Vol. 26: 89-100 (1951).

Wallace, William S. "Stagecoaching in Territorial New Mexico," *New Mexico Historical Review,* Vol. 32: 204-210 (1957).

Wallis, George A. *Cattle Kings of the Staked Plains.* Denver: Sage Books, 1964.

Westphall, Victor. "The Public Domain in New Mexico: 1854-1891," *New Mexico Historical Review,* Vol. 33: 24-52 (1958).

Winther, Oscar Osburn. "The Southern Overland Mail and Stagecoach Line: 1857-1861," *New Mexico Historical Review,* Vol. 32: 81-106 (1957).

Railroad Development

Boatright, C. C. *Transportation and Communications in New Mexico.* State Planning Office. Santa Fe, 1966.

Greever, William S. "Railroad Development in the Southwest," *New Mexico Historical Review,* Vol. 32: 151-203 (1957).

Interstate Commerce Commission Reports (various years), "Transportation—Railroads" (Washington D.C.).

Meinig, D. W. *Southwest: Three Peoples in Geographical Change, 1600-1970.* New York: Oxford University Press, 1971.

Myrick, David F. *New Mexico Railroads.* Golden: Colorado Railroad Museum, 1970.

New Mexico 1912

Curry, George. *An Autobiography.* Edited by H. B. Hening. Albuquerque: University of New Mexico Press, 1958.

Gibson, A. M. *The Life and Death of Colonel Albert Jennings Fountain.* Norman: University of Oklahoma Press, 1965.

Holmes, Jack E. *Politics in New Mexico.* Albuquerque: University of New Mexico Press, 1967.

Lamar, Howard R. *The Far Southwest, 1846-1912. A Territorial History.* New Haven: Yale University Press, 1966.

Larson, Robert W. *New Mexico's Quest for Statehood, 1846-1912.* Albuquerque: University of New Mexico Press, 1968.

New Mexico 1940

Edgel, Ralph L. "New Mexico Population: Its Size and Its Changing Distribution," *New Mexico Business,* Vol. 12 (1958).

United States Department of Commerce. "Census of Business and Retail Trade: 1939," *Sixteenth Census of the United States: 1940* (1941).

United States Department of Commerce. "Mineral Industries-State and County Statistics," *Sixteenth Census of the United States: 1940* (1944).

United States Department of Commerce. "Characteristics of the Population," *Sixteenth Census of the United States: 1940* (1943).

United States Department of Commerce. "Housing," *Sixteenth Census of the United States: 1940* (1943).

County Boundaries

Coan, Charles F. "The County Boundaries of New Mexico," *Southwestern Political Science Quarterly,* Vol. 3: 252-286 (1922).

Distribution of Place Names

Pearce, T. M. (ed.). *New Mexico Place Names: A Geographical Dictionary.* Albuquerque: University of New Mexico Press 1965.

U.S. Postal Service. *Directory of Post Offices: 1977.* Washington D.C.

Abandoned Places

File, Lucien A. *Ghost Town Map of New Mexico.* New Mexico Bureau of Mines and Mineral Resources. Albuquerque: University of New Mexico Press, 1968.

Florin, Lambert. *New Mexico and Texas Ghost Towns.* Seattle: Superior Publishing, 1971.

Jenkinson, Michael. *Ghost Towns of New Mexico, Playthings of the Wind.* Albuquerque: University of New Mexico Press, 1967.

Jones, Fayette Alexander. *Old Mines and Ghost Camps of New Mexico.* New Mexico Mines and Minerals—1905. Fort Davis, Texas: Frontier Book, 1968.

Kinsey, Mary Ann. ''Schools and the Ghost Towns of New Mexico,'' unpublished MA thesis. University of New Mexico, 1963.

Looney, Ralph. *Haunted Highways, The Ghost Towns of New Mexico.* New York: Hastings House, 1968.

Pearce, T.M. (ed.). *New Mexico Place Names: A Geographical Dictionary.* Albuquerque: University of New Mexico Press, 1965.

Sherman, James E. and Barbara H. *Ghost Towns and Mining Camps of New Mexico.* Norman: University of Oklahoma Press, 1975.

Woods, Dora Elizabeth. *Ghost Towns and How to Get to Them.* Santa Fe: Press of the Territorian, 1964.

POPULATION CHARACTERISTICS

Population Change 1930–1970

United States Bureau of the Census. *U.S. Census of Population: 1930; 1940; 1950; 1960; and 1970.* Washington, D.C.

Population Growth 1970–1977

Bureau of Business and Economic Research (BBER). *New Mexico Statistical Abstract: 1978.*

United States Bureau of the Census. *Current Population Reports, Annual Population Estimates.* Washington, D.C.

Population Origins 1970

United States Bureau of the Census. *Census of Population, General Population Characteristics: 1970.* Washington, D.C.

Population Density 1975

New Mexico Highway Department. *Quadrangle Maps of the State of New Mexico* (Santa Fe).

United States Bureau of the Census. *Census of Population, General Population Characteristics: 1970.* Washington, D.C.

United States Bureau of the Census. *Current Population Reports: 1975.*

Ethnic Distribution 1970

United States Bureau of the Census. *Census of Population, General Population Characteristics: 1970.* Washington, D.C.

Sex-Age Characteristics 1970

United States Bureau of the Census. *Census of Population, General Population Characteristics: 1970.* Washington, D.C.

Family Income Characteristics 1970

United States Bureau of the Census. *Census of Population, General Social and Economic Characteristics: 1970.* Washington, D.C.

Housing Characteristics 1950–1970

United States Bureau of the Census, *Census of Housing, Detailed Housing Characteristics: 1970.*

Medical Facilities

Motor Transportation Department, State of New Mexico. *Ambulance Inspection Report: 1978* (Santa Fe).

New Mexico Health and Social Services Department. *Annual Hospital Report: 1977* (Santa Fe).

University of New Mexico Health Services Center. *Health Resources Registry: 1977 and 1978.* New Mexico Statistical Summary.

Natality and Mortality

Bureau of Business and Economic Research. *New Mexico Statistical Abstract: 1977,* Vital Statistics.

New Mexico Health and Social Services Department. *Annual Summary of Vital Statistics:* 1970 through 1975.

New Mexico Tumor Registry. *State Population Estimates, 1971–1974.*

U.S. Department of Commerce, Bureau of Census. *1970 Census of Population.* Vol. 1, part 33.

Suicide in New Mexico

Yates, Leo and Byron B. King. *Suicides in New Mexico by County.* Cooperative Extension Services. New Mexico State University. Las Cruces: May, 1978.

Traffic Accidents

Foraker-Thompson, Jane. *Review of the Problem of Traffic Fatalities Correlated with Drinking Drivers on New Mexico Highways.* New Mexico State Police, 1977.

New Mexico State Highway Department, Planning Division in cooperation with the United States Department of Transportation, Federal Highway Administration. *State of New Mexico Motor Vehicle Accidents: Deaths and Ratings, 1978.*

Crime Rate

New Mexico Governors Council on Criminal Justice Planning. *New Mexico: 1971–1975, Criminal Offense Statistics.* Santa Fe: April, 1976.

United States Department of Justice. *Crime in the United States: Uniform Crime Reports.* 1973 and 1976.

Major Religious Denominations

Johnson, Douglas W., Paul R. Picard, and Bernard Quinn. *Churches and Church Membership in the United States.* An Enumeration by Region, State, and County: 1971. Washington, D.C.: Glenmary Research Center, 1974.

Reeve, Frank D. *Church in Territorial New Mexico.* Albuquerque: 1964.

Marriages and Dissolutions

Yates, Leo. *Marriage and Divorce Rates in New Mexico: 1974–1977.* Cooperative Extension Service. Las Cruces: New Mexico State University, 1978.

Public School Characteristics

Department of Finance and Administration. *Statistics—Public School Finance: 1975–1976.* Santa Fe: December, 1976.

Pogrow, Stanley. ''School Finance Reform in New Mexico,'' *Division of Government Research Review,* University of New Mexico: June, 1975.

State Department of Education. *New Mexico School District Profiles:* 1972–1973; 1973–1974; 1974–1975; 1975–1976; and 1976–1977 (Santa Fe).

Higher Education

National Center of Educational Statistics. *Education Directory, Colleges and Universities: 1977–1978.*

United States Bureau of the Census. *Census of Population, General Social and Economic Characteristics: 1970.* Washington, D.C.

Urbanization

United States Bureau of the Census. *Census of Population, General Population Characteristics: 1880–1970.* Washington, D.C.

United States Bureau of the Census. *Current Population Reports: 1975.* Washington, D.C.

Urban Area: Albuquerque

Albuquerque—Bernalillo Planning Department. *Albuquerque Central Area Study*. December 1965.

Albuquerque—Bernalillo Planning Department. *Land Use Plan: 1985*. February, 1964.

Albuquerque—Bernalillo Planning Department. *Albuquerque—Bernalillo County Comprehensive Plan*. April, 1975.

Crane, David A. and Associates. *Quality in Environment, Urban Design for the City of Albuquerque*. February, 1970.

Fergusson, Erna. *Albuquerque*. Albuquerque: M. Armitage, 1947.

Kelley, V. C. *Albuquerque—Its Mountains, Valley, Water and Volcanoes*. Scenic Trips to the Geologic Past, No. 9. New Mexico Bureau of Mines and Mineral Resources, Revised 1974.

Oppenheimer, Allan J. *The Historical Background of Albuquerque, New Mexico*. Albuquerque: 1962.

Urban Area: Farmington

Farmington Chamber of Commerce. "General Information About Farmington, New Mexico" (August, 1978).

McDonald, Eleanor Davenport, and John Brown Arrington. *The San Juan Basin*. Denver: Green Mountain Press, 1970.

McGinn, Elinor M. "Sixty Years on the Durango—Aztec—Farmingtron Branch (of the Denver and Rio Grande Railroad): 1905-1965," *New Mexico Historical Review*, Vol. 42, pp. 63-74 (1967).

San Juan County Planning Department. *San Juan County Energy Impact Strategy Program*. September 1977.

San Juan County Planning Department. *San Juan County—The Next Decade*. Preliminary Draft of the 1978-1990 Land Use Plan.

Urban Area: Santa Fe

Baldwin, Brewster, and Frank E. Kottlowski. *Santa Fe*. Scenic Trips to the Geologic Past, No. 1. New Mexico Bureau of Mines and Mineral Resources, 1968.

Nusbaum, Rosemary. *The City Different and The Palace*. Santa Fe: The Sunstone Press, 1978.

Simmons, Marc. *Yesterday in Santa Fe, Episodes in a Turbulent History*. Santa Fe: San Marcos Press, 1969.

Urban Area: Roswell

Roswell Chamber of Development and Commerce. "Roswell, New Mexico, Yesterday and Today."

Roswell Chamber of Development and Commerce. "Statistical Summary—Roswell, New Mexico," 1977.

Shinkle, James D. *Fifty Years of Roswell History: 1867-1917*. Roswell: Hall-Poorbaugh Press, 1964.

Shinkle, James D. *Reminiscences of Roswell Pioneers*. Roswell: Hall-Poorbaugh Press, 1966.

Southeastern New Mexico Economic Development District. "Roswell Growth Center," *Overall Economic Development Program* (December, 1976).

Urban Area: Las Cruces

City of Las Cruces, Department of Planning and Environmental Concerns. "Las Cruces Tomorrow" (July, 1977).

City of Mesilla. "Historical Background," *Historical Plan for Mesilla*.

Las Cruces Chamber of Commerce. "Location and History of Las Cruces, New Mexico."

Ambient Air Quality

Office of the Federal Register, *Code of Federal Regulations*. Washington, D.C.: July, 1975.

State of New Mexico. *Ambient Air Quality Data Summaries: 1973-1976*. Environmental Improvement Agency, Air Quality Division. Santa Fe.

ECONOMIC CHARACTERISTICS

Land Use

Morain, Stanley A., Thomas K. Budge, and Mike E. White,

Vegetation and Land Use in New Mexico. Resource Map 8, New Mexico Bureau of Mines and Mineral Resources, Socorro: 1977.

Land Ownership

United States Bureau of Reclamation and New Mexico Interstate Stream Commission. Preliminary Draft, Situation Assessment Report. Washington, D.C.

United States Department of the Interior, Bureau of Land Management. *Areas of Responsibility and Land Status Map, 1972*. Washington, D.C.: 1972.

Labor Force

Employment Security Commission of New Mexico. *Annual Reports*. Albuquerque: selected years.

United States Department of Commerce, Bureau of Economic Analysis. Employment Data by State of New Mexico. Washington, D.C.: selected years.

Value of Products

New Mexico Department of Agriculture. *New Mexico Agricultural Statistics*. New Mexico State University. Las Cruces: selected years.

United States Bureau of Census. *Census of Agriculture, 1969 and 1974*. Washington, D.C.: selected years.

United States Department of Agriculture. "Farm Income, State Estimates," *Farm Income Situation*, Washington, D.C.: selected years.

United States Department of Commerce. *1972 Census of Manufacturers*. Washington, D.C.: 1972.

Mineral Mining

Christiansen, Paige W. *The Story of Mining in New Mexico*. Scenic Trips to the Geologic Past Series, Number 12. New Mexico Bureau of Mines and Mineral Resources. Socorro: 1974.

Mardirosian, Charles A. "Principal Mining Districts of New Mexico," *New Mexico Geology*, August 1979.

New Mexico Mining Association. *Mining . . . Who Needs It?*. 1977.

Northrup, Stuart A. *Minerals of New Mexico*. Albuquerque: University of New Mexico Press, 1959.

Sheffer, Herman W. "The Mineral Industry of New Mexico," *Minerals Yearbook*, United States Department of the Interior, Bureau of Mines, Vol. II, Domestic. Washington, D.C.: 1975.

Service Centers

Berry, B. J. L. *Geography of Market Centers and Retail Distribution*. Englewood Cliffs, N.J.: Prentice-Hall, 1967.

Borchert, John R. and Russell B. Adams. *Trade Centers and Trade Areas of the Upper Midwest*. Upper Midwest Economic Study, University of Minnesota, 1963.

Marshall, John U. *The Location of Service Towns*. Department of Geography, University of Toronto. Toronto: 1969.

Preston, R. E. "The Structure of Central Place Systems," *Economic Geography*, 1970.

Retail Trade and Service Sectors

Gross Receipts from Retail Trade—County/Municipal. State of New Mexico, Bureau of Revenue, Tax Research Division.

Resta, Mark C., and Lee B. Zink. *The New Mexico Economy, Change in the 1970's*. Governors Council of Economic Advisors, Institute for Applied Research Services, University of New Mexico, 1978.

Energy: Oil and Gas

Foster, R. W. and P. R. Grant. *Gas and Oil in New Mexico*. Resource Map Number 3, New Mexico Bureau of Mines and Mineral Resources. Socorro: 1974.

Grant, P. R. *Energytic New Mexico . . . the Power State*. 2nd ed. Albuquerque Industrial Development Service, Inc. and Industrial Foundation of Albuquerque, Inc. Albuquerque: November 1977.

New Mexico Oil and Gas Association. "Oil and Gas in New Mex

ico," supplement to the *Albuquerque Journal* and *Albuquerque Tribune* (October, 1978).

Energy: Coal

Grant, P. R. *Energytic New Mexico . . . the Power State.* 2nd ed. Albuquerque Industrial Development Service, Inc. and Industrial Foundation of Albuquerque, Inc. Albuquerque: November 1977.

Tabet, David and Stephen Frost. *Coal Fields and Mines of New Mexico.* Resource Map Number 10, New Mexico Bureau of Mines and Mineral Resources. Socorro: 1978.

Energy: Uranium and Electricity

Bierberman, Robert A. and Robert H. Weber. *New Mexico Energy Resources Map.* Resource Map Number 2, New Mexico Bureau of Mines and Mineral Resources. Socorro: 1969.

Grant, P. R. *Energytic New Mexico . . . the Power State.* 2nd ed. Albuquerque Industrial Development Service, Inc. and Industrial Foundation of Albuquerque, Inc. Albuquerque: November 1977.

Highway Traffic

New Mexico Highway Department, Planning and Programming Division. "New Mexico Traffic Survey 1975, 1976 and 1977."

Communications: Newspapers

Grove, Pearce S., Becky J. Barnett, and Sandra J. Hansen (eds.). *New Mexico Newspapers.* Albuquerque: University of New Mexico Press, 1975.

Communications: Radio

Broadcasting Yearbook, 1978. Washington, D.C.: Broadcasting Publications, 1978.

New Mexico Blue Book, 1976–1977. Directory of Radio and TV Stations in New Mexico. Santa Fe: 1978.

Communications: Television

Broadcasting Yearbook, 1978. Washington, D.C.: Broadcasting Publications, 1978.

Television Factbook, 1978, Services Volume and Stations Volume, Washington, D.C.: Television Digest Inc., 1978.

Communications: Telephone

Milestones in Communications: A brief History of Mountain Bell. Albuquerque.

Mountain Bell, Independent Relations Division. *Annual Report.* January, 1978.

Movies Made in New Mexico

File Memos. "Motion Picture Productions Shot in New Mexico, 1975-1978." Department of Development, New Mexico Motion Picture Industry Commission. Santa Fe, 1978.

"Film Bibliography of New Mexico." Chuck Mittlestadt, Public Relations Director of the New Mexico State Fairground. 1978.

Museum of New Mexico, Film Library. "Index to Motion Pictures Filmed in New Mexico," 1978.

U.S. Copyright Office: *Motion Pictures and Title Guide to the Talkies* (selected years).

RECREATION AND GOVERNMENT

Recreation and Tourism I—Federal and State Facilities

Forest Service Grasslands of the Southwest. *Kiowa, Rita Blanca, McClellan Creek, and Black Kettle National Grasslands.* 1975.

New Mexico State Park and Recreation Commission and Tourism Division of the New Mexico Department of Development. *State Parks and Monuments of New Mexico.* Santa Fe: 1978.

Stewart, Ronald L. *Monuments of New Mexico.* Boulder, Colorado: Pruett Publication, 1974.

United States Department of Agriculture, Forest Service. *National Forest Areas Report.* Land Administered by the Forest Service. September, 1978.

Wildernesses in Southwestern National Forests. National Forest Wildernesses and Primitive Areas in Arizona and New Mexico. June, 1974.

Recreation and Tourism II—Fish and Wildlife

New Mexico Department of Game and Fish. *New Mexico Wildlife.* Special Department Lands Issue. Vol. 19, No. 4. (1974).

New Mexico Department of Game and Fish. *New Mexico Fishing Waters,* Maps of Streams and Lakes. (No date).

United States Department of Interior, Bureau of Land Management. *A Guide to Public Lands in New Mexico,* maps of major fish and game areas. (No date).

Recreation and Tourism III—Tourist Facilities

Bureau of Land Management. *A Guide to Public Lands in New Mexico.*

New Mexico Department of Development, Tourist Division. *Ski New Mexico.* Santa Fe, 1978.

New Mexico Department of Development, Tourist Division. *Guest Ranches and Resorts.* Santa Fe, 1978.

New Mexico Department of Development, Tourist Division. *Indians of New Mexico.* Research by Bertha Dutton, Museum of New Mexico. Santa Fe.

Sun Country Section of the Professional Golf Association of America. *1977 Listing of Golf Courses and Country Clubs.* Albuquerque: 1977.

Museums

Chaves, Tom. "Museums and Similar Institutions," Education Division, Museum of New Mexico, 1978.

New Mexico Association of Museums. *A Directory of Museums in New Mexico.* 2nd ed. Albuquerque: Museum of Albuquerque, 1972.

New Mexico State Planning Office. "Lincoln, New Mexico: A Plan For Preservation and Growth," Santa Fe, 1974.

Historical Sites

Motto, Sytha. *Old Houses of New Mexico and The People Who Built Them.* Albuquerque: Calvin Horn, 1973.

"National Register of Historic Places: Annual Listing of Historic Properties," *Federal Register,* Vol. 43, No. 26. Washington, D.C.: February, 1978.

New Mexico State Planning Office. "Historic Preservation Program for New Mexico," Santa Fe, 1973.

Thomas W. Merlan. State Historic Preservation Officer, State of New Mexico (1978).

State Governmental Districts

Coughenour, Larry D. *1977 Annual Report, Administrative Office of the Courts.* Santa Fe, 1977.

Garcia, F. Chris, Paul L. Hain, and Harold Rhodes. *State and Local Government in New Mexico.* Albuquerque: University of New Mexico Press, 1979.

State of New Mexico. "State Police Reports—1977," Santa Fe, 1977.

State of New Mexico. "Department of Motor Vehicles Summary—1978," Santa Fe.

State of New Mexico. "State Highway Department, Planning and Programming Division—1978."

State Legislative Districts

Garcia, F. Chris and Paul L. Hain (eds.). *New Mexico Government.* Albuquerque: University of New Mexico Press, 1976.

Holmes, Jack Ellsworth. *Party, Legislature and Governor in the Politics of New Mexico, 1911-1963.* Chicago: University of Chicago Press, 1964.

Holmes, Jack Ellsworth. *Politics in New Mexico.* Albuquerque: University of New Mexico Press, 1967.

New Mexico Legislative Council Service. "Legislative Areas of New Mexico," Santa Fe, 1978.

New Mexico Office of the Secretary of State. "Map of State Legislative Districts," Santa Fe, 1978.

Gubernatorial Elections

Garcia and Hain (eds.). *New Mexico Government* (1976).

Hammond, George P. and Thomas C. Donnelly. *Story of New Mexico, Its History and Government.* Albuquerque: University of New Mexico Press, 1936.

Holmes, Jack Ellsworth. *Patterns of Voting in New Mexico Gubernatorial Elections, 1911–1955.* Relation to Population and Minor Offices. Santa Fe, 1958.

Holmes, Jack Ellsworth. *Party, Legislature and Governor in the Politics of New Mexico, 1911–1963.*

Office of the Secretary of State. "State of New Mexico Official Election Returns" (selected years).

U.S. Congressional Elections

Garcia and Hain (eds.). *New Mexico Government* (1976).

Office of the Secretary of State. "State of New Mexico Official Election Returns" (selected years).

Presidential Elections

Office of the Secretary of State. "State of New Mexico Official Election Returns" (selected years).

Phillip T. Wolf. Department of Government, University of New Mexico.

"The 1964 Elections in New Mexico." Paper presented at the Southwest Political Science Association Convention. Dallas, 1965.

"The 1968 Election from the Perspective of a Nixon State." Paper presented at the Southwest Social Science meeting. Houston, 1969.

"The 1972 Presidential Election in New Mexico." Paper presented at the Southwest Social Science meeting. Dallas, 1973.

index